THE NEW YORK FOUR
Published by DC Comics, 1700 Broadway, New York, NY 10019.

The stories, characters and incidents mentioned in this book
are entirely fictional.

Printed in Canada.
DC Comics, a Warner Bros.
Entertainment Company.

ISBN: 978-1-4012-1154-7

COVER BY RYAN KELLY

The New York Four

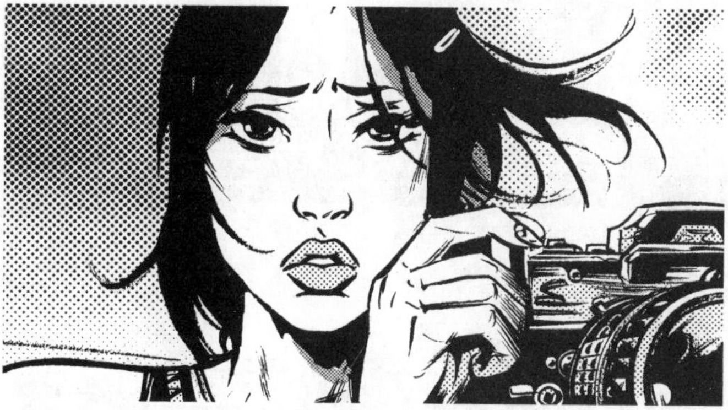

Written by Brian Wood
Illustrated by Ryan Kelly

Lettering by Jared K. Fletcher

minx

Chapter 1
Itchyhead

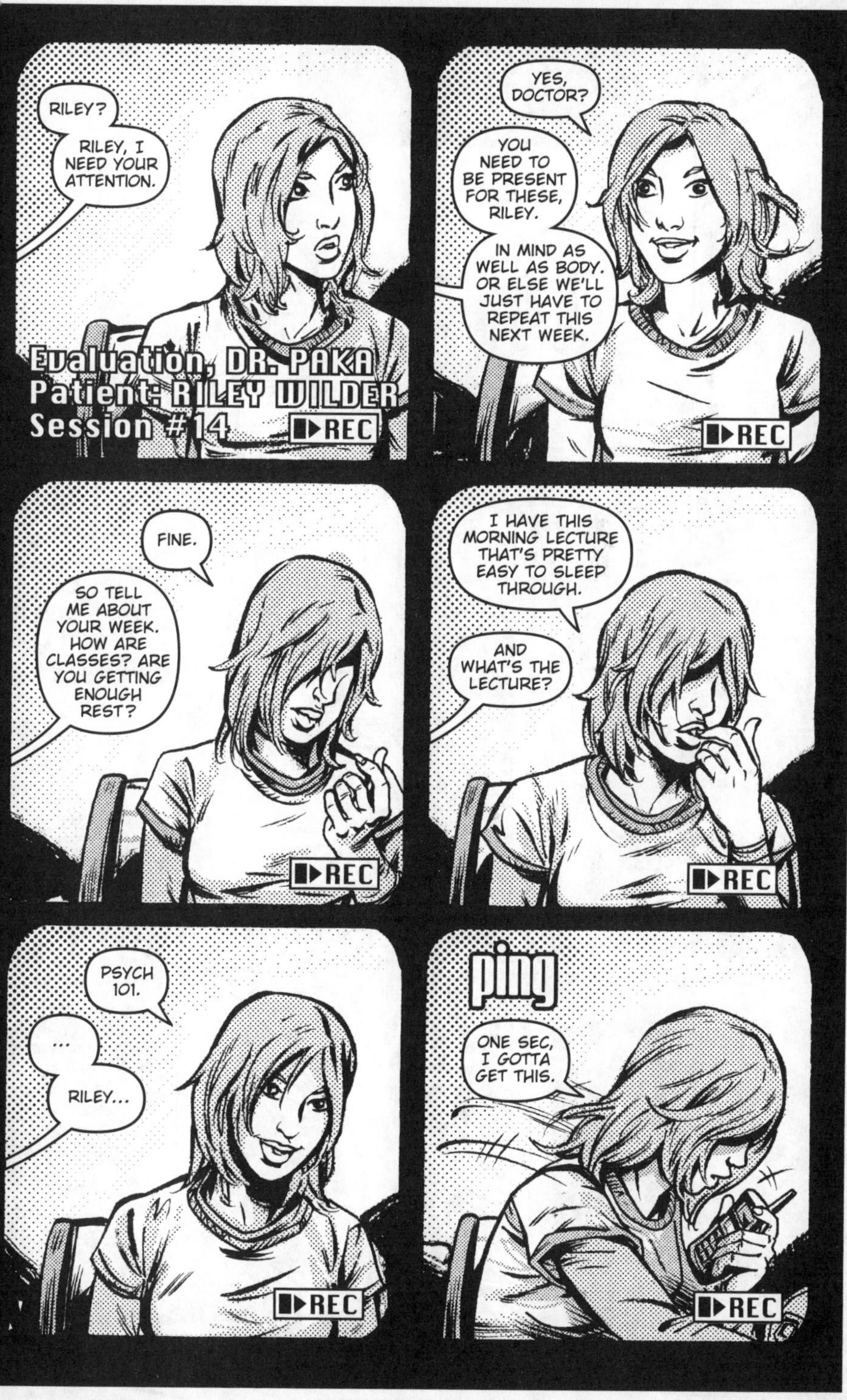
RILEY?
RILEY, I NEED YOUR ATTENTION.
Evaluation, DR. PAKA
Patient: RILEY WILDER
Session #14
REC
YES, DOCTOR?
YOU NEED TO BE PRESENT FOR THESE, RILEY.
IN MIND AS WELL AS BODY. OR ELSE WE'LL JUST HAVE TO REPEAT THIS NEXT WEEK.
REC
FINE.
SO TELL ME ABOUT YOUR WEEK. HOW ARE CLASSES? ARE YOU GETTING ENOUGH REST?
REC
I HAVE THIS MORNING LECTURE THAT'S PRETTY EASY TO SLEEP THROUGH.
AND WHAT'S THE LECTURE?
REC
PSYCH 101.
...
RILEY...
REC
ping
ONE SEC, I GOTTA GET THIS.
REC

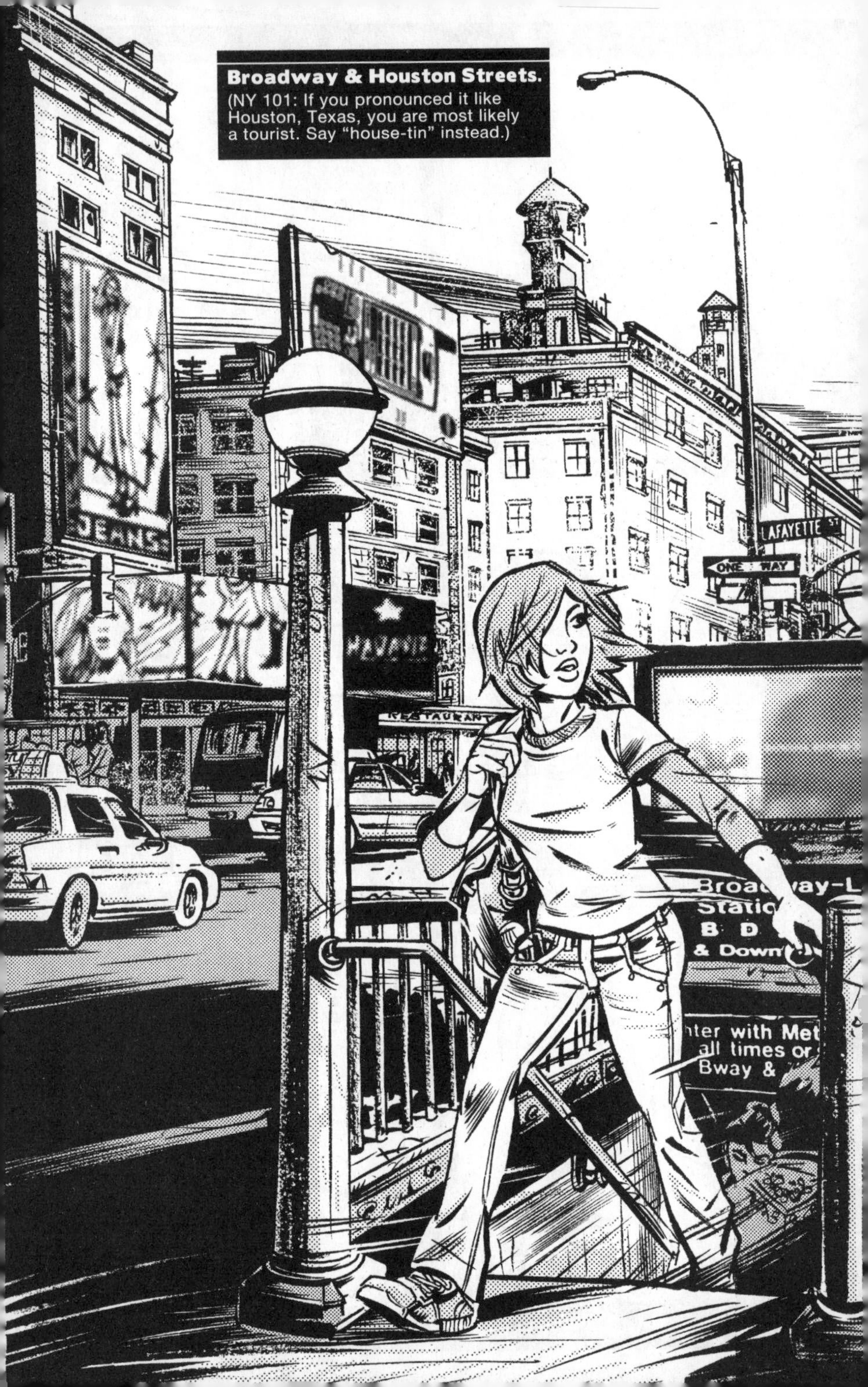
Broadway & Houston Streets.
(NY 101: If you pronounced it like Houston, Texas, you are most likely a tourist. Say "house-tin" instead.)
JEANS
RESTAURANT
LAFAYETTE ST
ONE WAY
Broadway-L
Statio
B D
& Down
nter with Met
all times or
Bway &

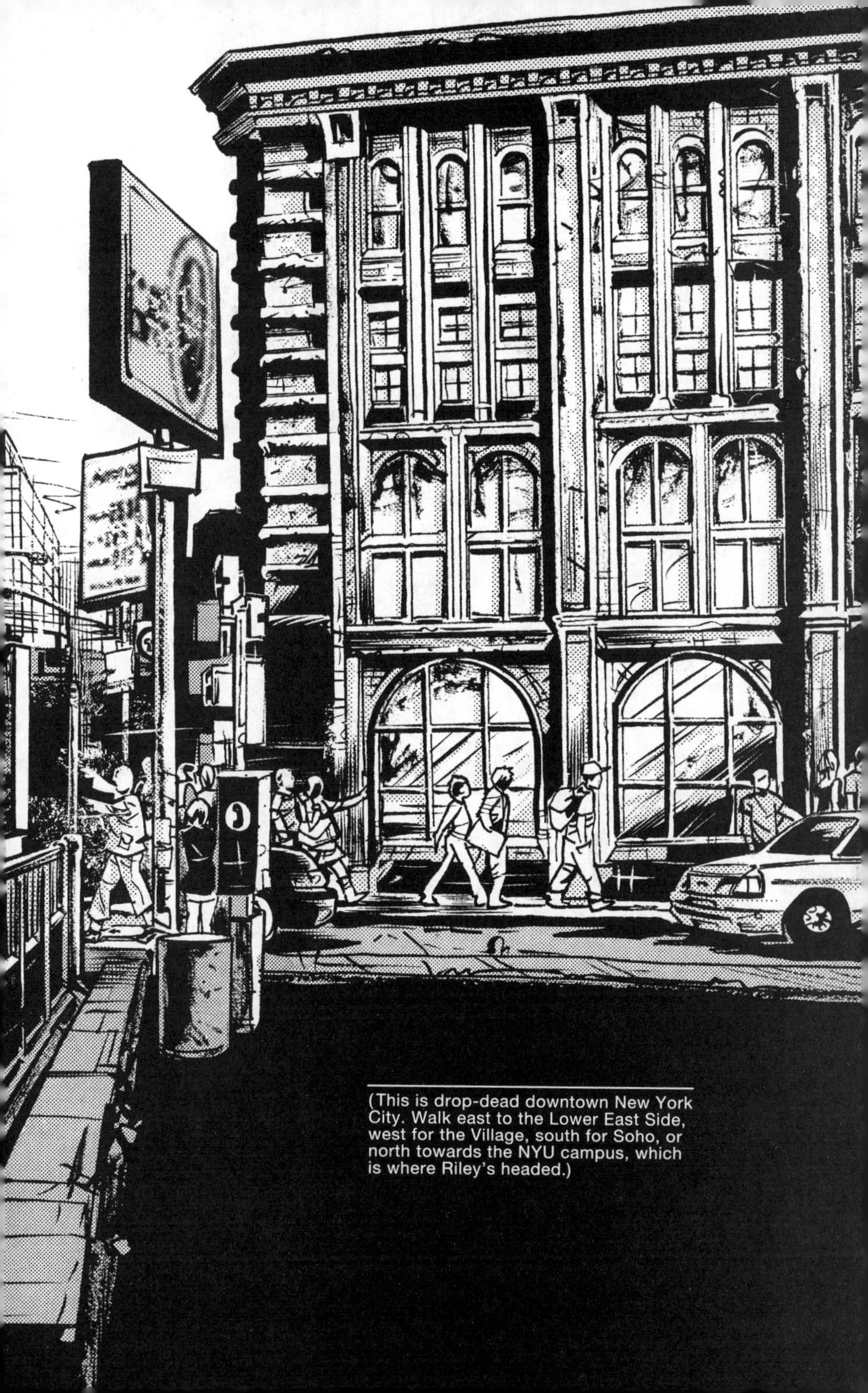
(This is drop-dead downtown New York City. Walk east to the Lower East Side, west for the Village, south for Soho, or north towards the NYU campus, which is where Riley's headed.)

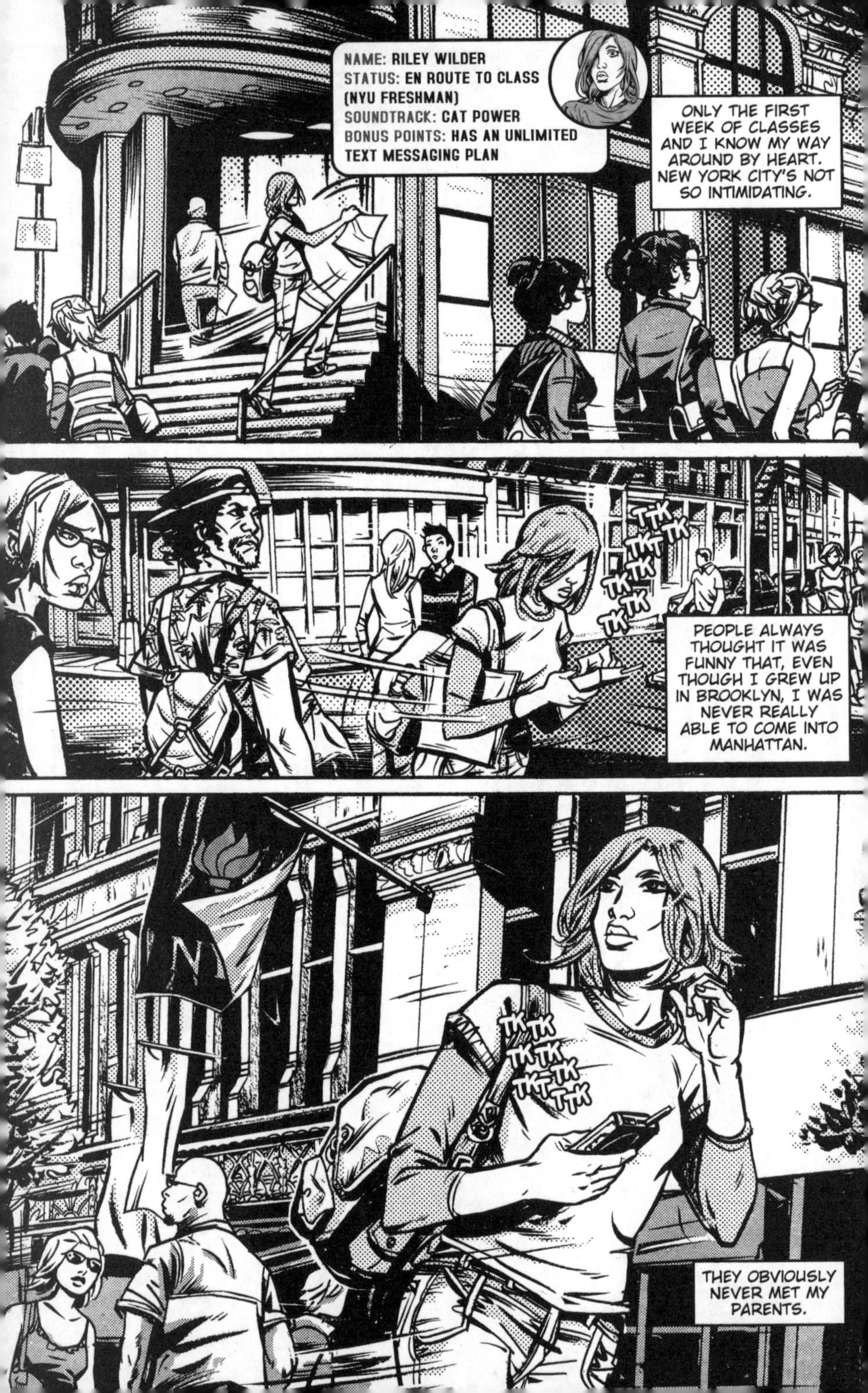
NAME: RILEY WILDER
STATUS: EN ROUTE TO CLASS (NYU FRESHMAN)
SOUNDTRACK: CAT POWER
BONUS POINTS: HAS AN UNLIMITED TEXT MESSAGING PLAN
ONLY THE FIRST WEEK OF CLASSES AND I KNOW MY WAY AROUND BY HEART. NEW YORK CITY'S NOT SO INTIMIDATING.
TK TK TK TK TK TK TK TK TK
PEOPLE ALWAYS THOUGHT IT WAS FUNNY THAT, EVEN THOUGH I GREW UP IN BROOKLYN, I WAS NEVER REALLY ABLE TO COME INTO MANHATTAN.
TK TK TK TK TK TK TK TK TK
THEY OBVIOUSLY NEVER MET MY PARENTS.

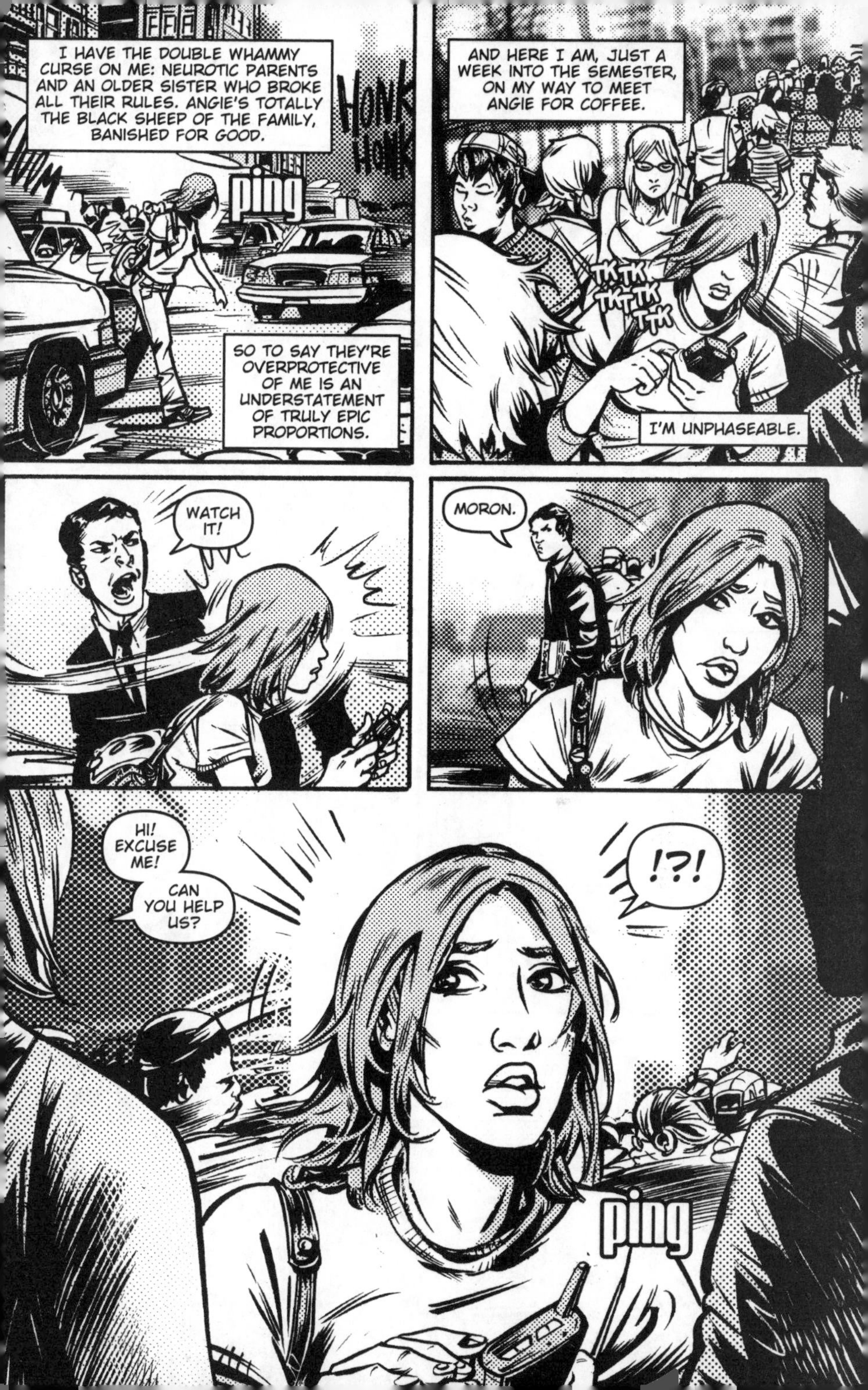
I HAVE THE DOUBLE WHAMMY CURSE ON ME: NEUROTIC PARENTS AND AN OLDER SISTER WHO BROKE ALL THEIR RULES. ANGIE'S TOTALLY THE BLACK SHEEP OF THE FAMILY, BANISHED FOR GOOD.
HONK HONK
ping
SO TO SAY THEY'RE OVERPROTECTIVE OF ME IS AN UNDERSTATEMENT OF TRULY EPIC PROPORTIONS.
AND HERE I AM, JUST A WEEK INTO THE SEMESTER, ON MY WAY TO MEET ANGIE FOR COFFEE.
TK TK TK TK TK TK
I'M UNPHASEABLE.
WATCH IT!
MORON.
HI! EXCUSE ME!
CAN YOU HELP US?
!?!
ping

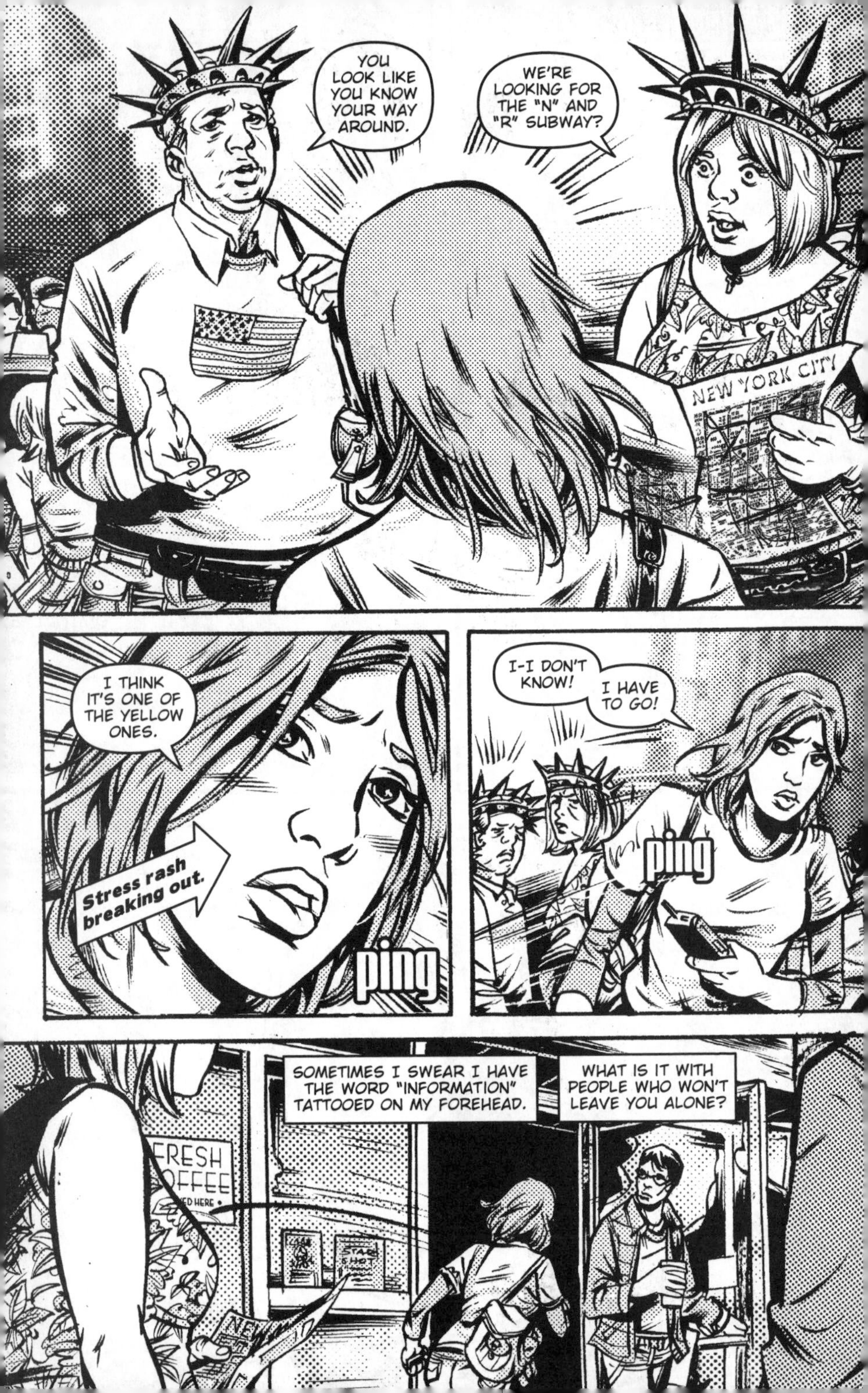
YOU LOOK LIKE YOU KNOW YOUR WAY AROUND.
WE'RE LOOKING FOR THE "N" AND "R" SUBWAY?
NEW YORK CITY
I THINK IT'S ONE OF THE YELLOW ONES.
Stress rash breaking out.
ping
I-I DON'T KNOW!
I HAVE TO GO!
ping
SOMETIMES I SWEAR I HAVE THE WORD "INFORMATION" TATTOOED ON MY FOREHEAD.
WHAT IS IT WITH PEOPLE WHO WON'T LEAVE YOU ALONE?
FRESH
OFFEE

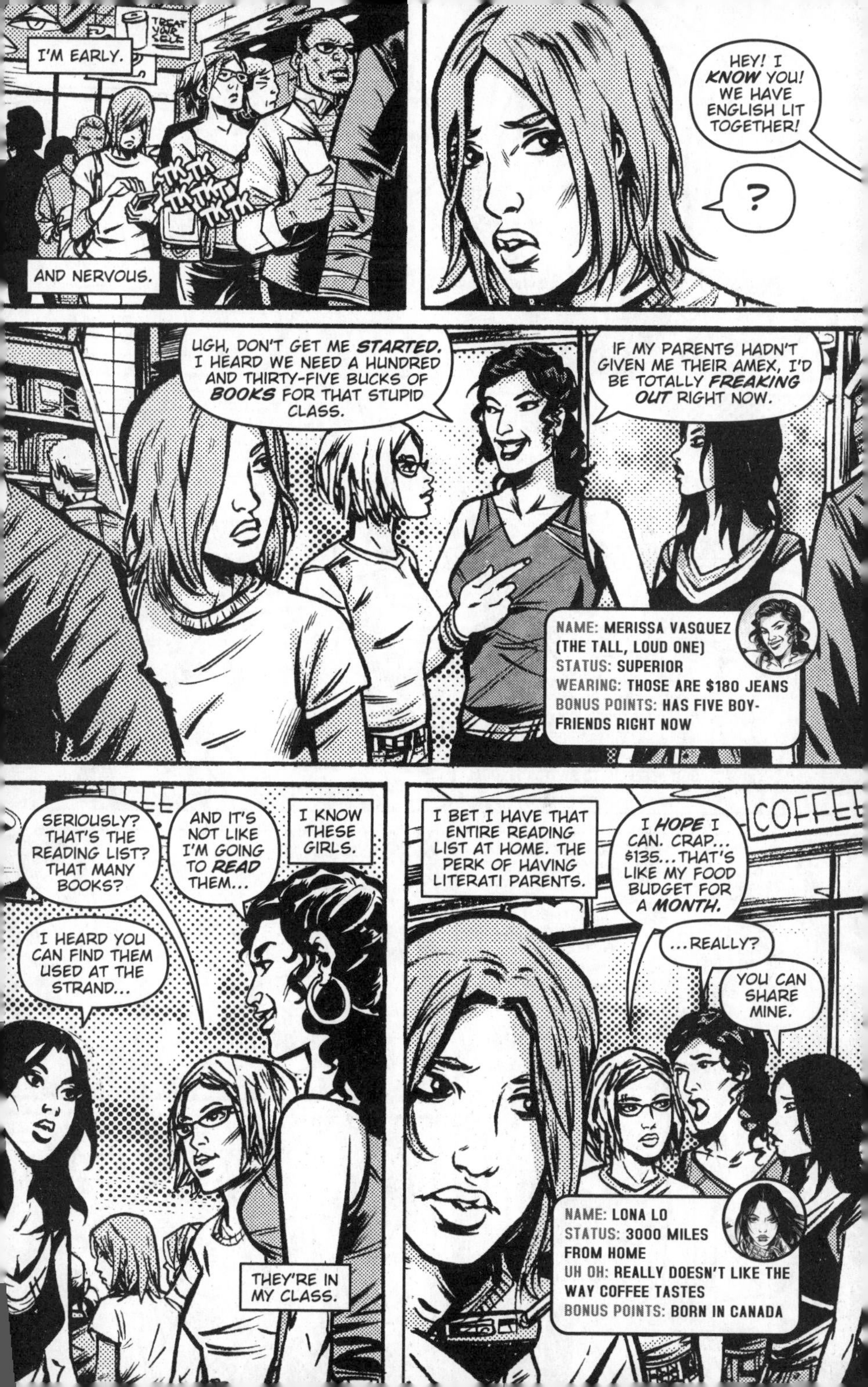
TREAT YOUR SELF
I'M EARLY.
TK TK TK TK TK TK TK
AND NERVOUS.
HEY! I KNOW YOU! WE HAVE ENGLISH LIT TOGETHER!
?
UGH, DON'T GET ME STARTED. I HEARD WE NEED A HUNDRED AND THIRTY-FIVE BUCKS OF BOOKS FOR THAT STUPID CLASS.
IF MY PARENTS HADN'T GIVEN ME THEIR AMEX, I'D BE TOTALLY FREAKING OUT RIGHT NOW.
NAME: MERISSA VASQUEZ (THE TALL, LOUD ONE)
STATUS: SUPERIOR
WEARING: THOSE ARE $180 JEANS
BONUS POINTS: HAS FIVE BOY-FRIENDS RIGHT NOW
SERIOUSLY? THAT'S THE READING LIST? THAT MANY BOOKS?
AND IT'S NOT LIKE I'M GOING TO READ THEM...
I KNOW THESE GIRLS.
I HEARD YOU CAN FIND THEM USED AT THE STRAND...
THEY'RE IN MY CLASS.
I BET I HAVE THAT ENTIRE READING LIST AT HOME. THE PERK OF HAVING LITERATI PARENTS.
I HOPE I CAN. CRAP... $135...THAT'S LIKE MY FOOD BUDGET FOR A MONTH.
COFFEE
...REALLY?
YOU CAN SHARE MINE.
NAME: LONA LO
STATUS: 3000 MILES FROM HOME
UH OH: REALLY DOESN'T LIKE THE WAY COFFEE TASTES
BONUS POINTS: BORN IN CANADA

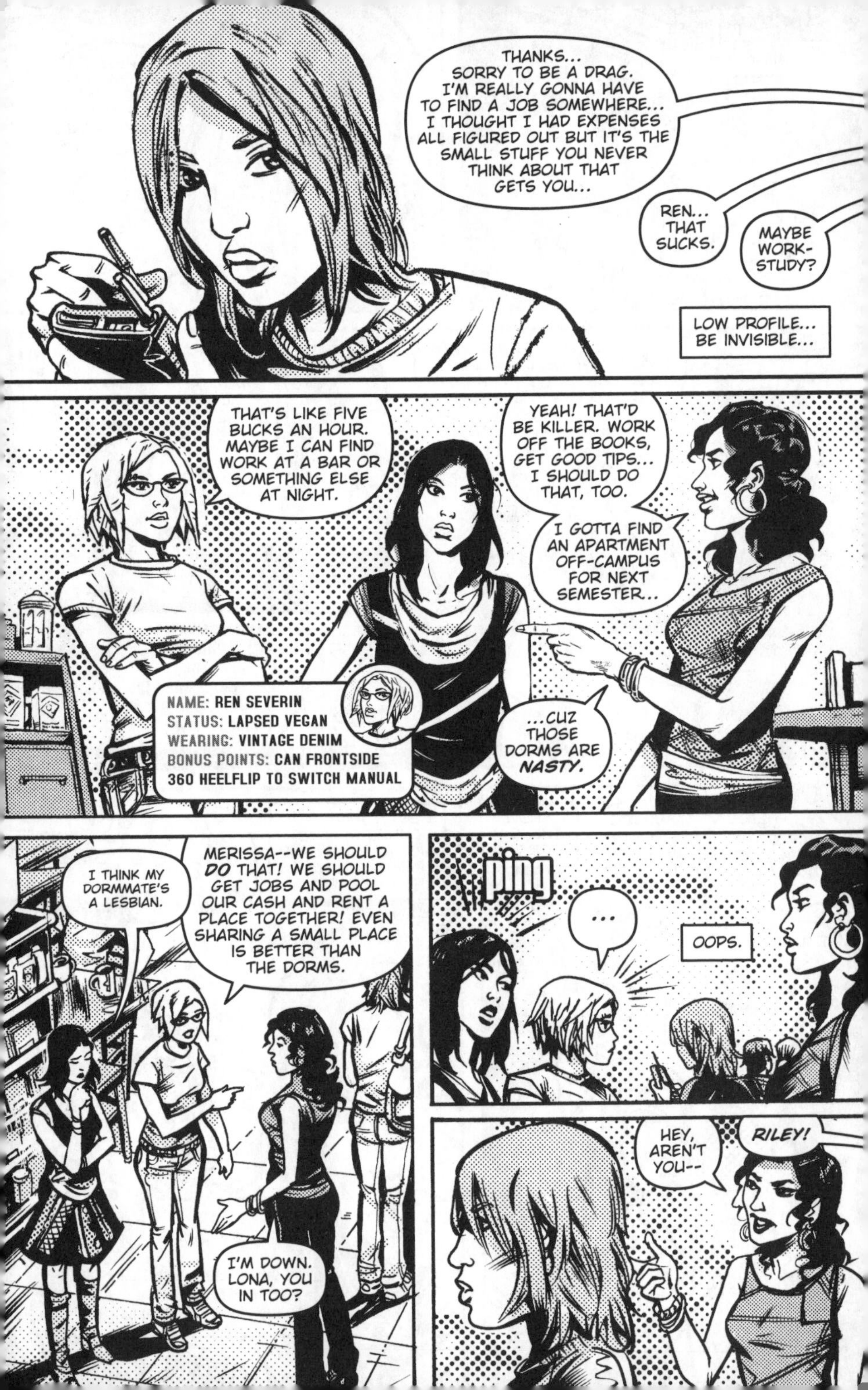
THANKS... SORRY TO BE A DRAG. I'M REALLY GONNA HAVE TO FIND A JOB SOMEWHERE... I THOUGHT I HAD EXPENSES ALL FIGURED OUT BUT IT'S THE SMALL STUFF YOU NEVER THINK ABOUT THAT GETS YOU...
REN... THAT SUCKS.
MAYBE WORK-STUDY?
LOW PROFILE... BE INVISIBLE...
THAT'S LIKE FIVE BUCKS AN HOUR. MAYBE I CAN FIND WORK AT A BAR OR SOMETHING ELSE AT NIGHT.
YEAH! THAT'D BE KILLER. WORK OFF THE BOOKS, GET GOOD TIPS... I SHOULD DO THAT, TOO.
I GOTTA FIND AN APARTMENT OFF-CAMPUS FOR NEXT SEMESTER...
NAME: REN SEVERIN
STATUS: LAPSED VEGAN
WEARING: VINTAGE DENIM
BONUS POINTS: CAN FRONTSIDE 360 HEELFLIP TO SWITCH MANUAL
...CUZ THOSE DORMS ARE NASTY.
I THINK MY DORMMATE'S A LESBIAN.
MERISSA--WE SHOULD DO THAT! WE SHOULD GET JOBS AND POOL OUR CASH AND RENT A PLACE TOGETHER! EVEN SHARING A SMALL PLACE IS BETTER THAN THE DORMS.
I'M DOWN. LONA, YOU IN TOO?
ping
...
OOPS.
HEY, AREN'T YOU--
RILEY!

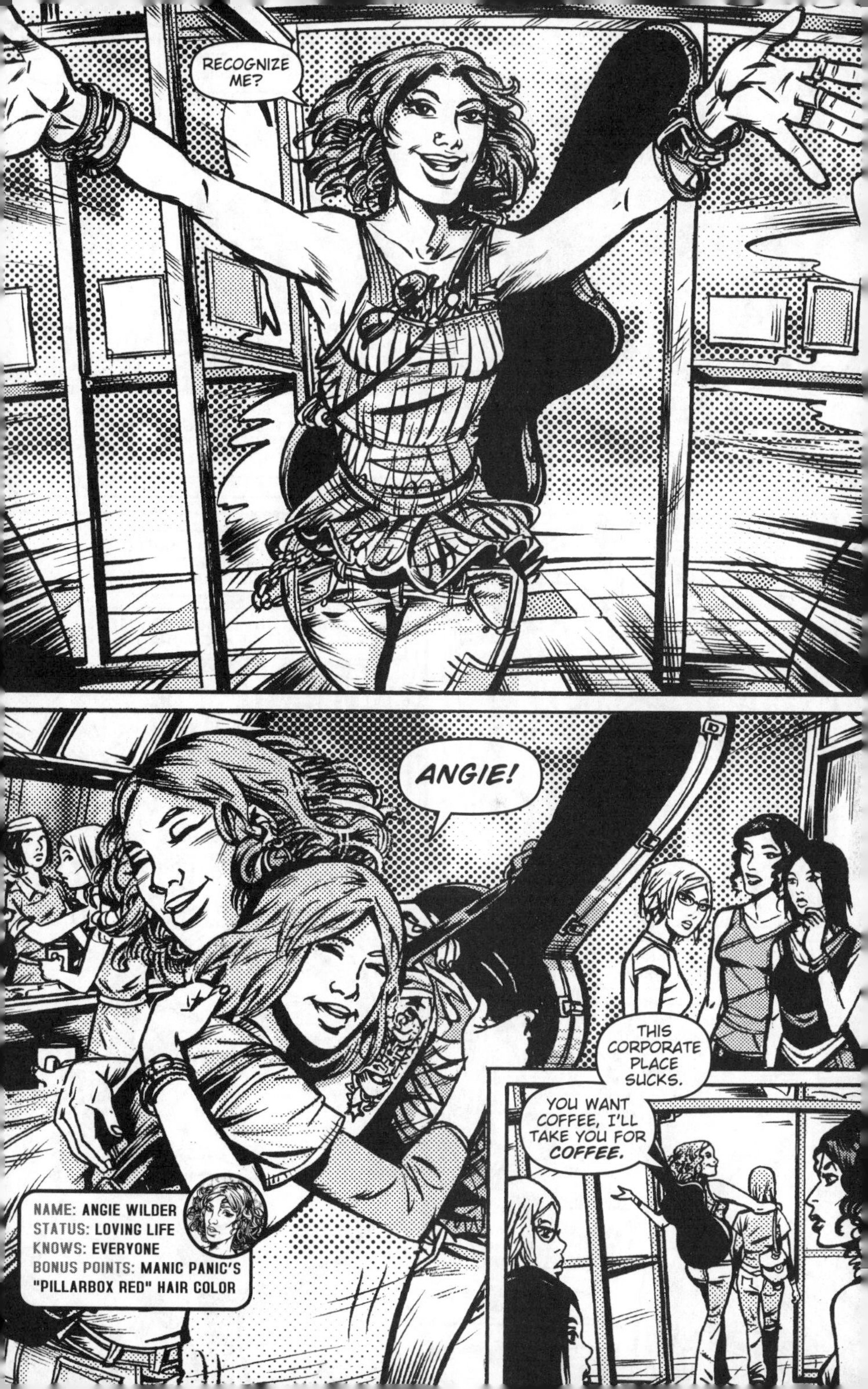
RECOGNIZE ME?
ANGIE!
NAME: ANGIE WILDER
STATUS: LOVING LIFE
KNOWS: EVERYONE
BONUS POINTS: MANIC PANIC'S "PILLARBOX RED" HAIR COLOR
THIS CORPORATE PLACE SUCKS.
YOU WANT COFFEE, I'LL TAKE YOU FOR COFFEE.

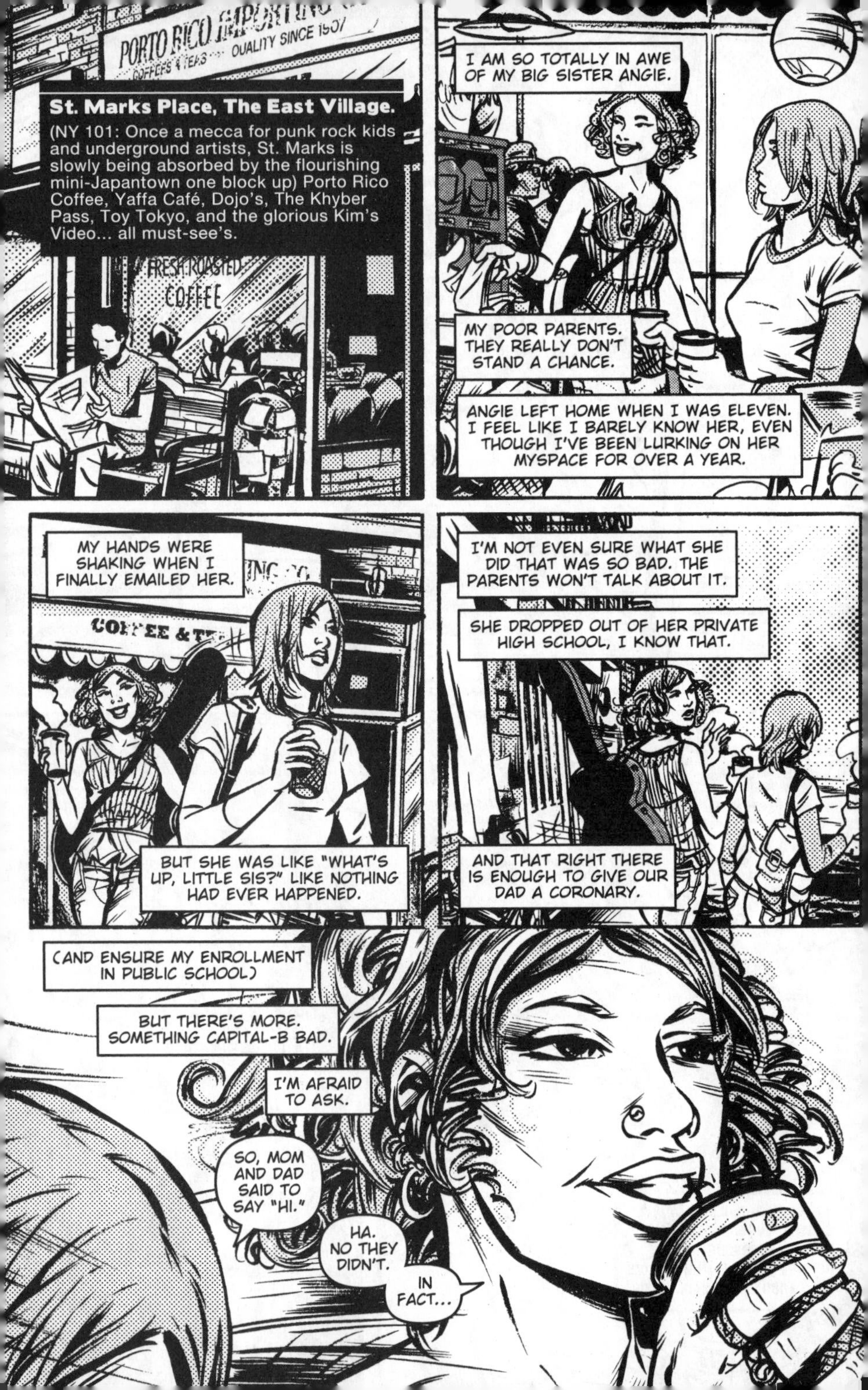
PORTO RICO IMPORTING
COFFEES & TEAS QUALITY SINCE 1907
St. Marks Place, The East Village.
(NY 101: Once a mecca for punk rock kids and underground artists, St. Marks is slowly being absorbed by the flourishing mini-Japantown one block up) Porto Rico Coffee, Yaffa Café, Dojo's, The Khyber Pass, Toy Tokyo, and the glorious Kim's Video... all must-see's.
FRESH ROASTED COFFEE
I AM SO TOTALLY IN AWE OF MY BIG SISTER ANGIE.
MY POOR PARENTS. THEY REALLY DON'T STAND A CHANCE.
ANGIE LEFT HOME WHEN I WAS ELEVEN. I FEEL LIKE I BARELY KNOW HER, EVEN THOUGH I'VE BEEN LURKING ON HER MYSPACE FOR OVER A YEAR.
MY HANDS WERE SHAKING WHEN I FINALLY EMAILED HER.
BUT SHE WAS LIKE "WHAT'S UP, LITTLE SIS?" LIKE NOTHING HAD EVER HAPPENED.
I'M NOT EVEN SURE WHAT SHE DID THAT WAS SO BAD. THE PARENTS WON'T TALK ABOUT IT.
SHE DROPPED OUT OF HER PRIVATE HIGH SCHOOL, I KNOW THAT.
AND THAT RIGHT THERE IS ENOUGH TO GIVE OUR DAD A CORONARY.
(AND ENSURE MY ENROLLMENT IN PUBLIC SCHOOL)
BUT THERE'S MORE. SOMETHING CAPITAL-B BAD.
I'M AFRAID TO ASK.
SO, MOM AND DAD SAID TO SAY "HI."
HA. NO THEY DIDN'T.
IN FACT...

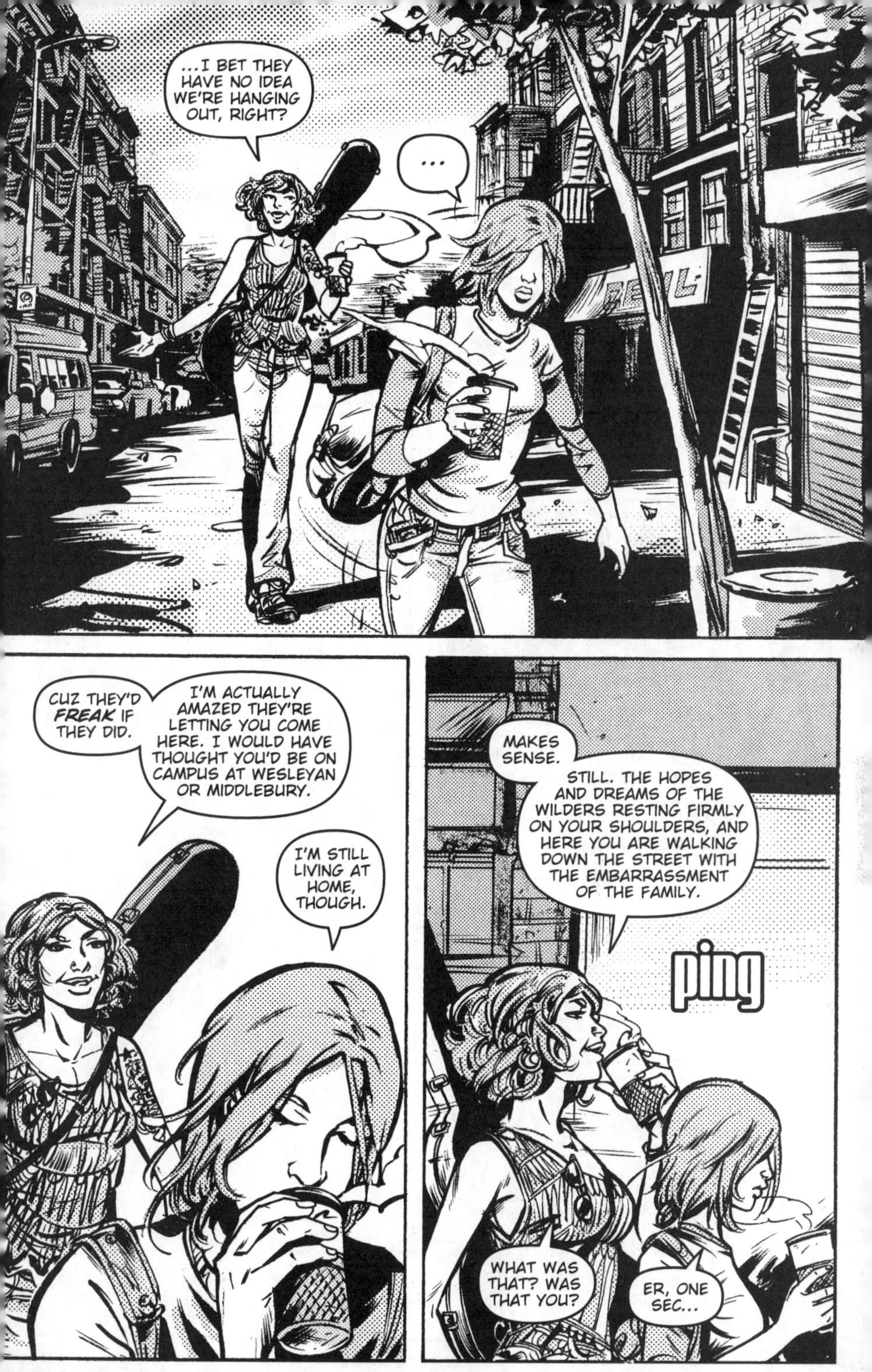
...I BET THEY HAVE NO IDEA WE'RE HANGING OUT, RIGHT?
...
CUZ THEY'D *FREAK* IF THEY DID.
I'M ACTUALLY AMAZED THEY'RE LETTING YOU COME HERE. I WOULD HAVE THOUGHT YOU'D BE ON CAMPUS AT WESLEYAN OR MIDDLEBURY.
I'M STILL LIVING AT HOME, THOUGH.
MAKES SENSE.
STILL. THE HOPES AND DREAMS OF THE WILDERS RESTING FIRMLY ON YOUR SHOULDERS, AND HERE YOU ARE WALKING DOWN THE STREET WITH THE EMBARRASSMENT OF THE FAMILY.
ping
WHAT WAS THAT? WAS THAT YOU?
ER, ONE SEC...

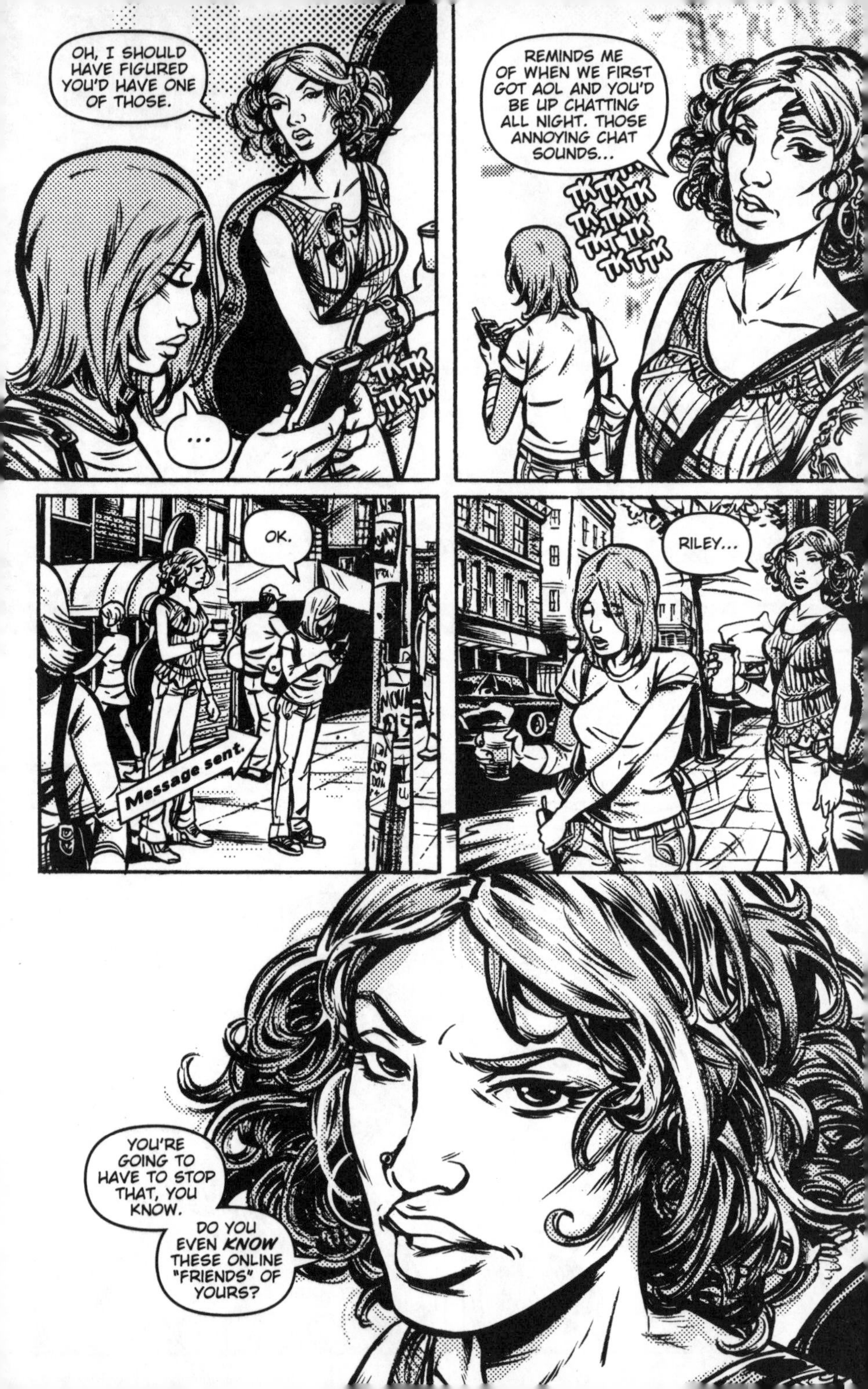

OH, I SHOULD HAVE FIGURED YOU'D HAVE ONE OF THOSE.
TK TK TK TK
...
REMINDS ME OF WHEN WE FIRST GOT AOL AND YOU'D BE UP CHATTING ALL NIGHT. THOSE ANNOYING CHAT SOUNDS...
TK TK TK TK TK TK TK TK TK TK TK
OK.
Message sent.
RILEY...
YOU'RE GOING TO HAVE TO STOP THAT, YOU KNOW.
DO YOU EVEN ***KNOW*** THESE ONLINE "FRIENDS" OF YOURS?

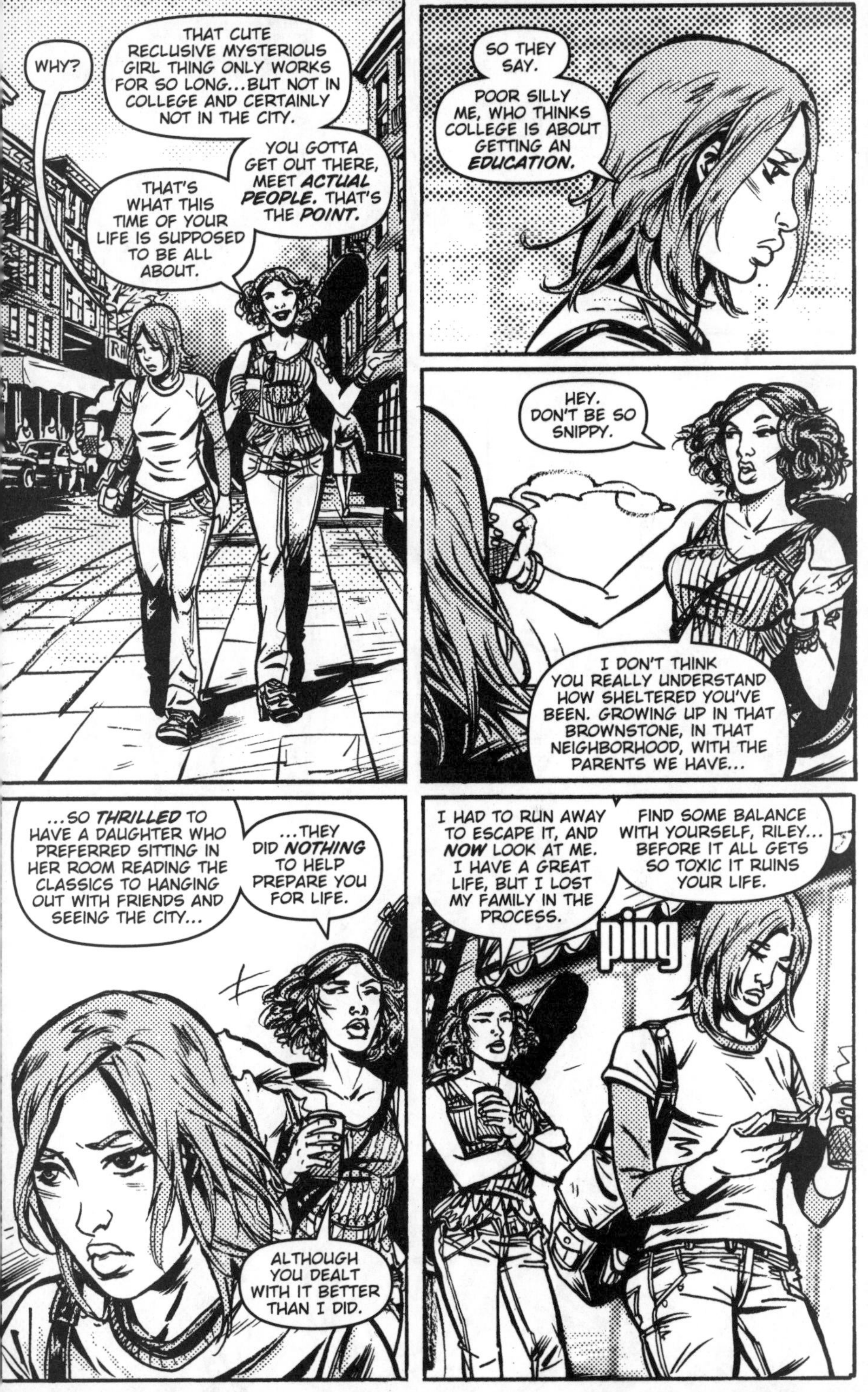

WHY?
THAT CUTE RECLUSIVE MYSTERIOUS GIRL THING ONLY WORKS FOR SO LONG... BUT NOT IN COLLEGE AND CERTAINLY NOT IN THE CITY.
THAT'S WHAT THIS TIME OF YOUR LIFE IS SUPPOSED TO BE ALL ABOUT.
YOU GOTTA GET OUT THERE, MEET ACTUAL PEOPLE. THAT'S THE POINT.
SO THEY SAY.
POOR SILLY ME, WHO THINKS COLLEGE IS ABOUT GETTING AN EDUCATION.
HEY. DON'T BE SO SNIPPY.
I DON'T THINK YOU REALLY UNDERSTAND HOW SHELTERED YOU'VE BEEN. GROWING UP IN THAT BROWNSTONE, IN THAT NEIGHBORHOOD, WITH THE PARENTS WE HAVE...
...SO THRILLED TO HAVE A DAUGHTER WHO PREFERRED SITTING IN HER ROOM READING THE CLASSICS TO HANGING OUT WITH FRIENDS AND SEEING THE CITY...
...THEY DID NOTHING TO HELP PREPARE YOU FOR LIFE.
ALTHOUGH YOU DEALT WITH IT BETTER THAN I DID.
I HAD TO RUN AWAY TO ESCAPE IT, AND NOW LOOK AT ME. I HAVE A GREAT LIFE, BUT I LOST MY FAMILY IN THE PROCESS.
FIND SOME BALANCE WITH YOURSELF, RILEY... BEFORE IT ALL GETS SO TOXIC IT RUINS YOUR LIFE.
ping

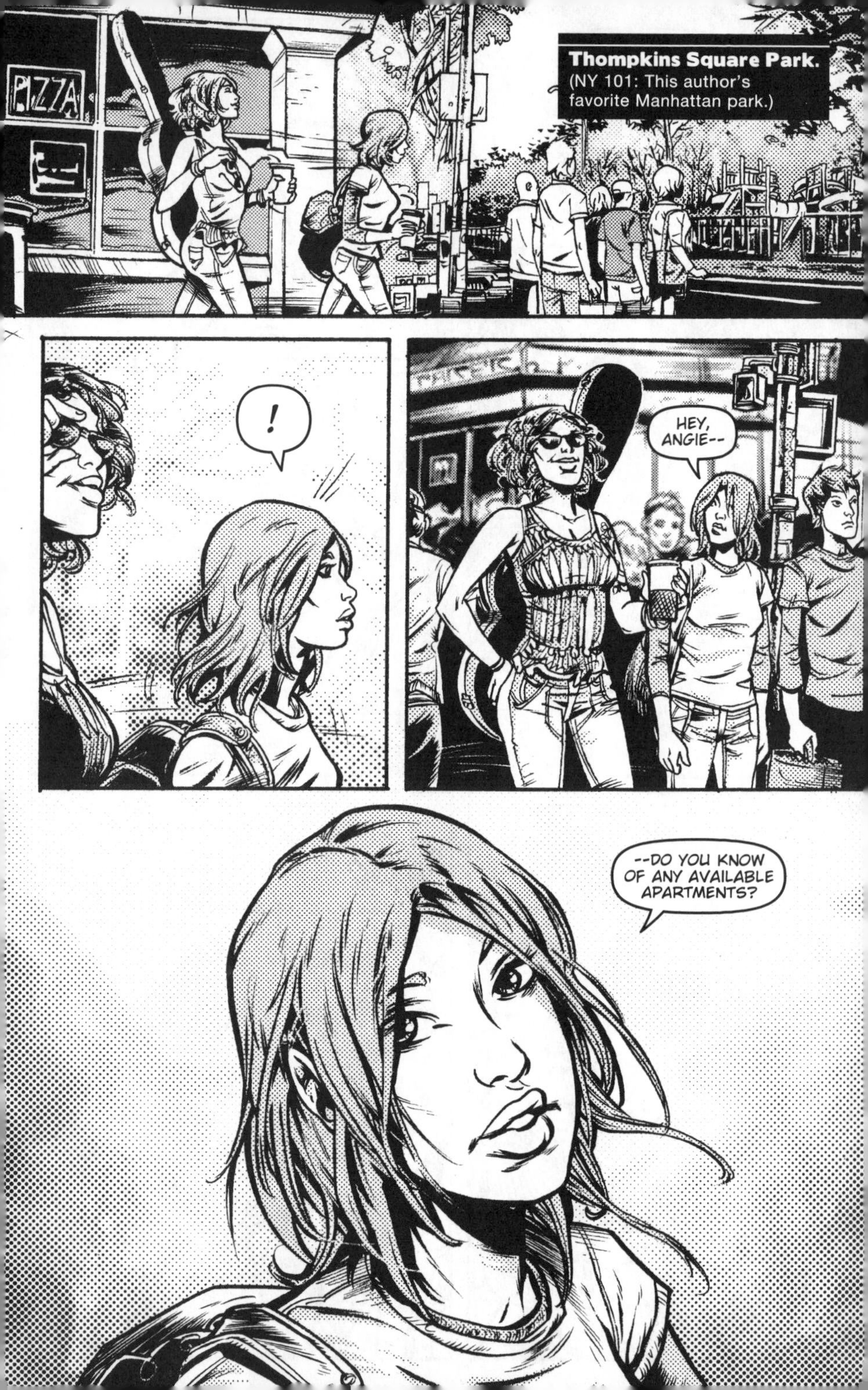
Thompkins Square Park.
(NY 101: This author's favorite Manhattan park.)
PIZZA
!
HEY, ANGIE--
--DO YOU KNOW OF ANY AVAILABLE APARTMENTS?

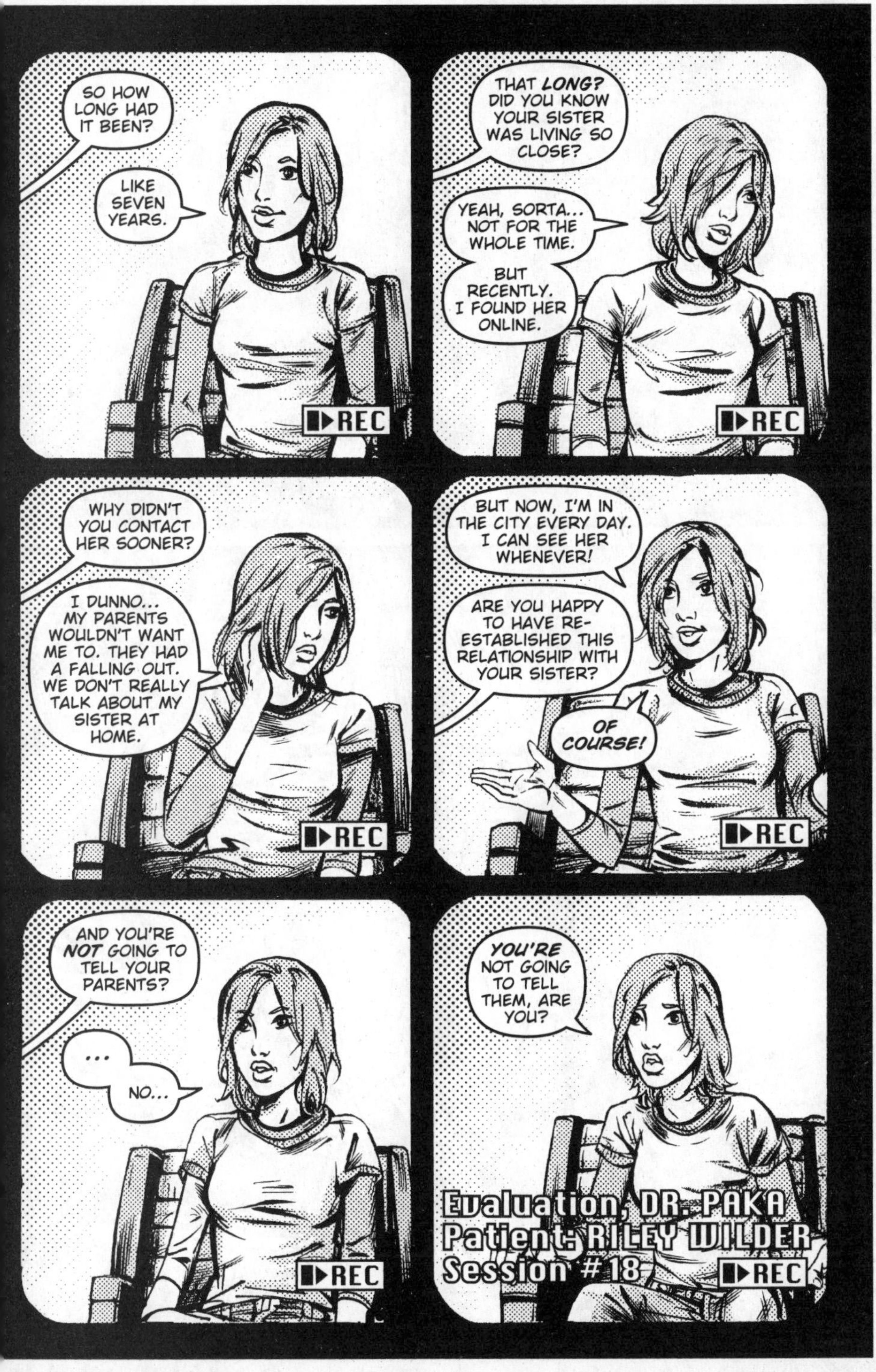
SO HOW LONG HAD IT BEEN?
LIKE SEVEN YEARS.
REC
THAT LONG? DID YOU KNOW YOUR SISTER WAS LIVING SO CLOSE?
YEAH, SORTA... NOT FOR THE WHOLE TIME.
BUT RECENTLY. I FOUND HER ONLINE.
REC
WHY DIDN'T YOU CONTACT HER SOONER?
I DUNNO... MY PARENTS WOULDN'T WANT ME TO. THEY HAD A FALLING OUT. WE DON'T REALLY TALK ABOUT MY SISTER AT HOME.
REC
BUT NOW, I'M IN THE CITY EVERY DAY. I CAN SEE HER WHENEVER!
ARE YOU HAPPY TO HAVE RE-ESTABLISHED THIS RELATIONSHIP WITH YOUR SISTER?
OF COURSE!
REC
AND YOU'RE NOT GOING TO TELL YOUR PARENTS?
...
NO...
REC
YOU'RE NOT GOING TO TELL THEM, ARE YOU?
Evaluation, DR. PAKA
Patient: RILEY WILDER
Session #18
REC

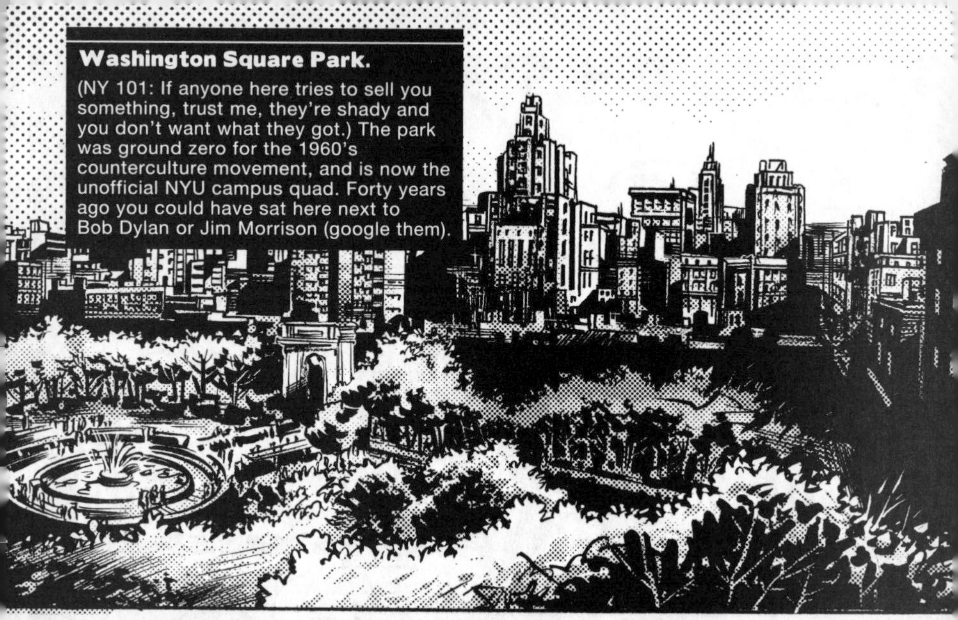
Washington Square Park.
(NY 101: If anyone here tries to sell you something, trust me, they're shady and you don't want what they got.) The park was ground zero for the 1960's counterculture movement, and is now the unofficial NYU campus quad. Forty years ago you could have sat here next to Bob Dylan or Jim Morrison (google them).

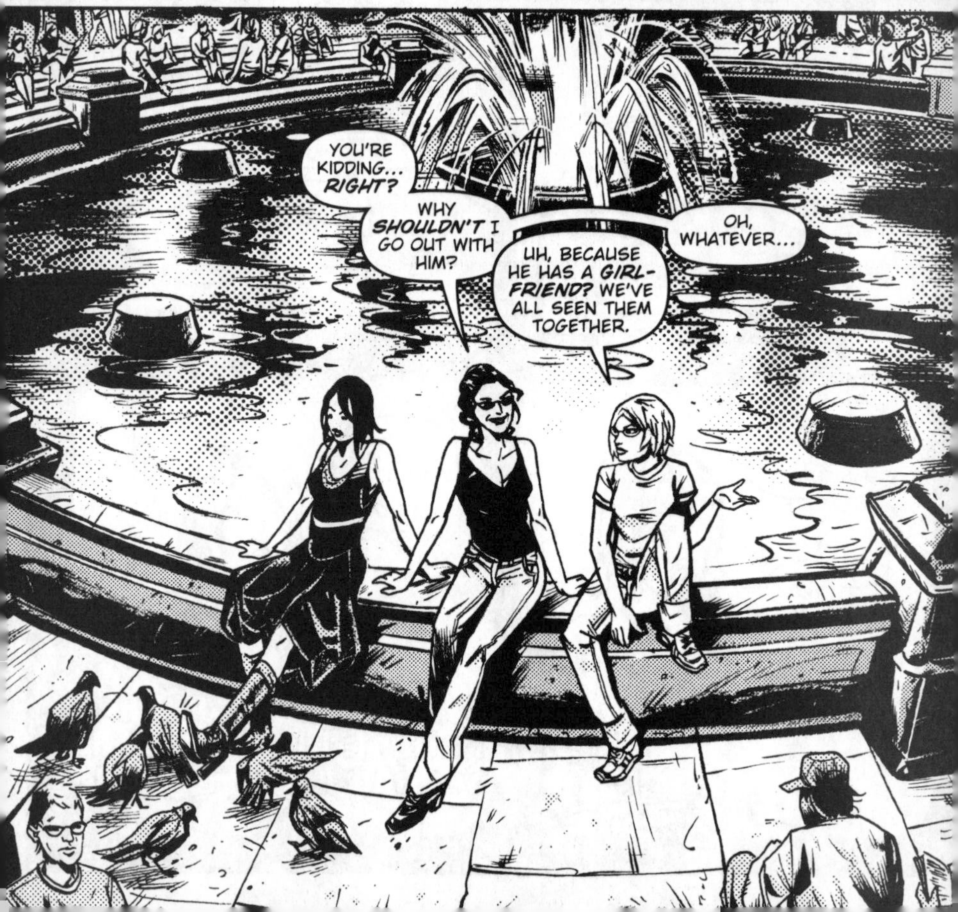
YOU'RE KIDDING... RIGHT?
WHY SHOULDN'T I GO OUT WITH HIM?
UH, BECAUSE HE HAS A GIRL-FRIEND? WE'VE ALL SEEN THEM TOGETHER.
OH, WHATEVER...

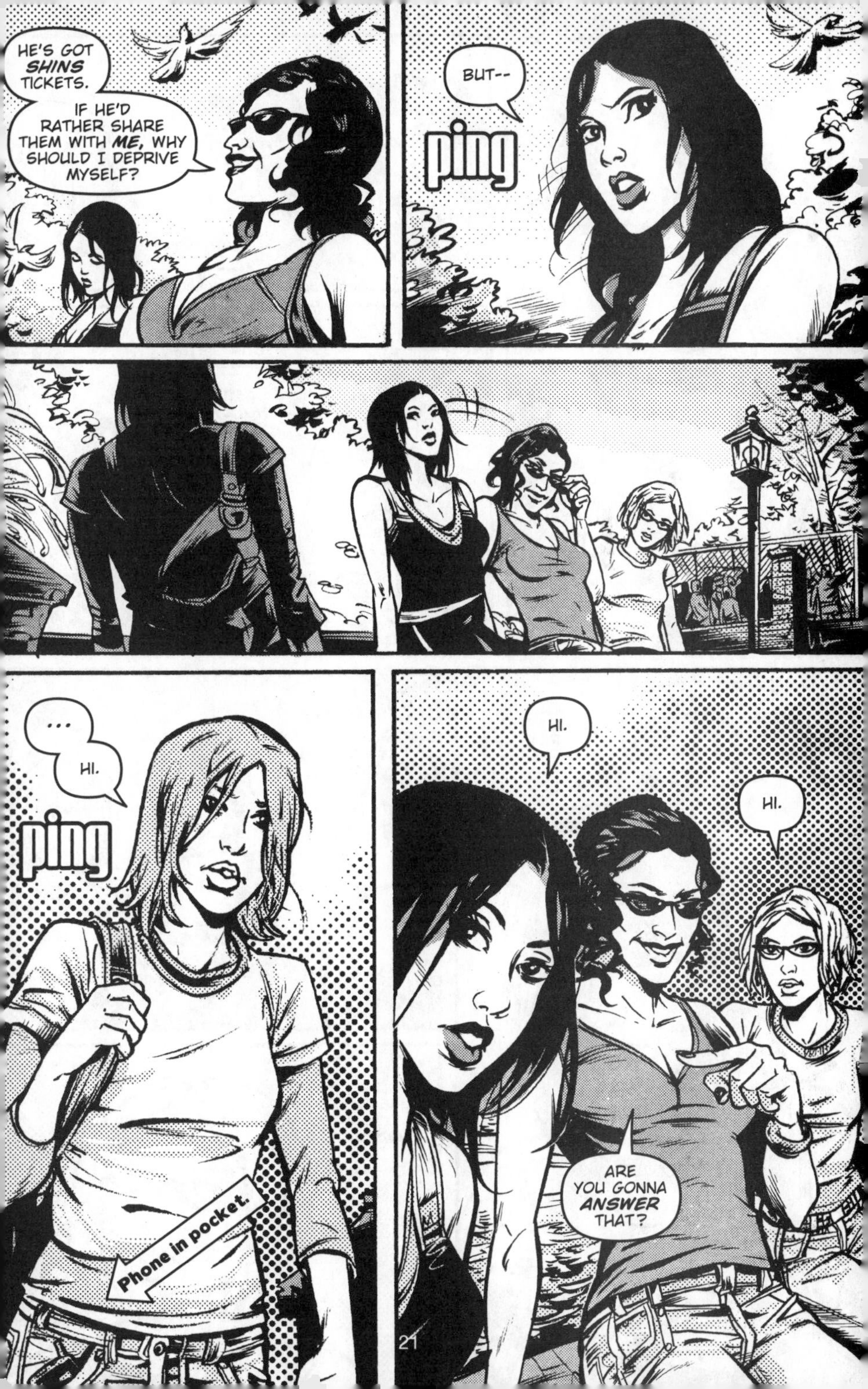
HE'S GOT *SHINS* TICKETS.
IF HE'D RATHER SHARE THEM WITH *ME,* WHY SHOULD I DEPRIVE MYSELF?
BUT--
ping
...
HI.
ping
Phone in pocket.
HI.
HI.
ARE YOU GONNA *ANSWER* THAT?

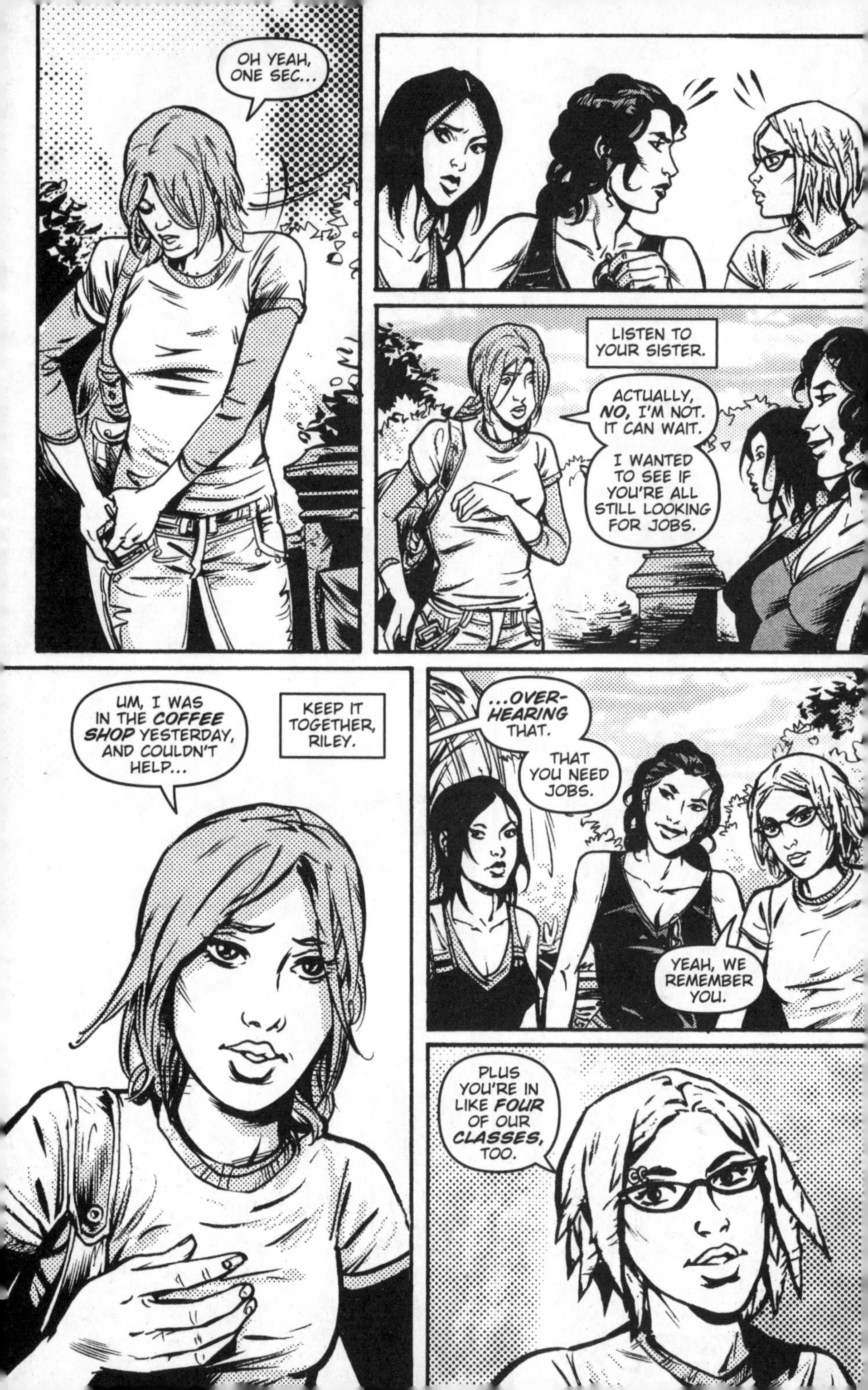
OH YEAH, ONE SEC...
LISTEN TO YOUR SISTER.
ACTUALLY, NO, I'M NOT. IT CAN WAIT.
I WANTED TO SEE IF YOU'RE ALL STILL LOOKING FOR JOBS.
UM, I WAS IN THE COFFEE SHOP YESTERDAY, AND COULDN'T HELP...
KEEP IT TOGETHER, RILEY.
...OVER-HEARING THAT.
THAT YOU NEED JOBS.
YEAH, WE REMEMBER YOU.
PLUS YOU'RE IN LIKE FOUR OF OUR CLASSES, TOO.

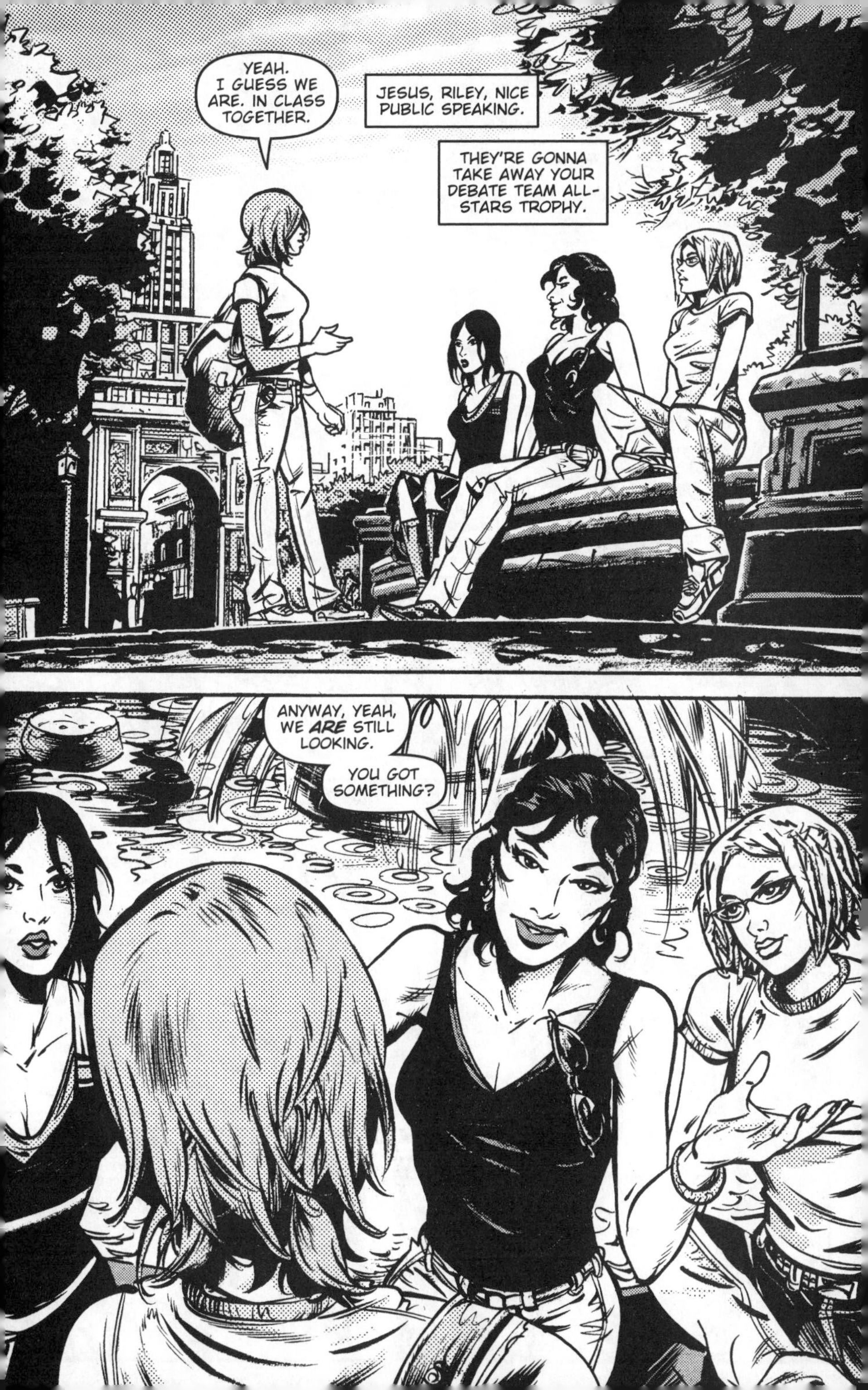
YEAH. I GUESS WE ARE. IN CLASS TOGETHER.
JESUS, RILEY, NICE PUBLIC SPEAKING.
THEY'RE GONNA TAKE AWAY YOUR DEBATE TEAM ALL-STARS TROPHY.
ANYWAY, YEAH, WE ARE STILL LOOKING.
YOU GOT SOMETHING?

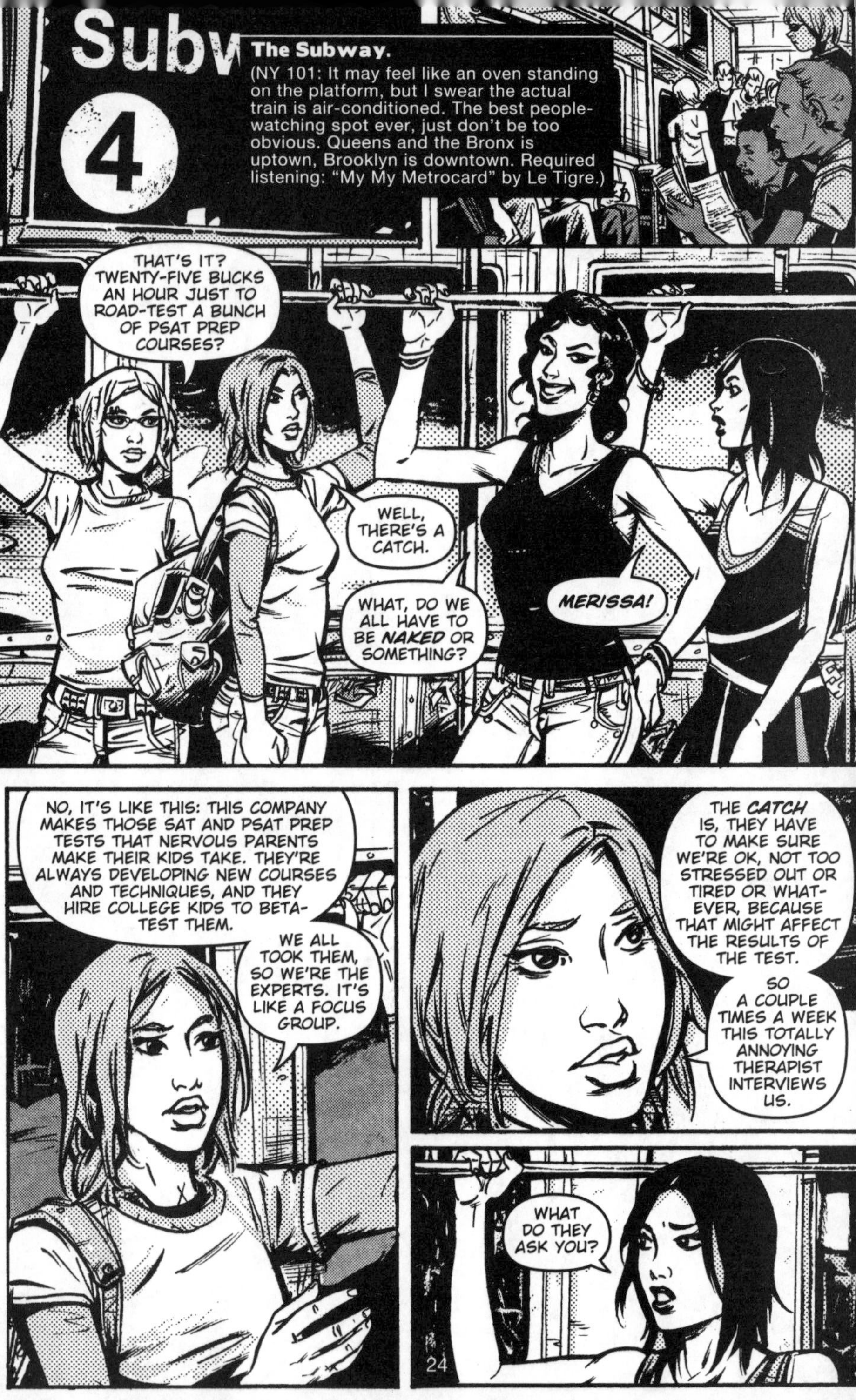
Subw
4
The Subway.
(NY 101: It may feel like an oven standing on the platform, but I swear the actual train is air-conditioned. The best people-watching spot ever, just don't be too obvious. Queens and the Bronx is uptown, Brooklyn is downtown. Required listening: "My My Metrocard" by Le Tigre.)
THAT'S IT? TWENTY-FIVE BUCKS AN HOUR JUST TO ROAD-TEST A BUNCH OF PSAT PREP COURSES?
WELL, THERE'S A CATCH.
WHAT, DO WE ALL HAVE TO BE ***NAKED*** OR SOMETHING?
MERISSA!
NO, IT'S LIKE THIS: THIS COMPANY MAKES THOSE SAT AND PSAT PREP TESTS THAT NERVOUS PARENTS MAKE THEIR KIDS TAKE. THEY'RE ALWAYS DEVELOPING NEW COURSES AND TECHNIQUES, AND THEY HIRE COLLEGE KIDS TO BETA-TEST THEM.
WE ALL TOOK THEM, SO WE'RE THE EXPERTS. IT'S LIKE A FOCUS GROUP.
THE ***CATCH*** IS, THEY HAVE TO MAKE SURE WE'RE OK, NOT TOO STRESSED OUT OR TIRED OR WHAT-EVER, BECAUSE THAT MIGHT AFFECT THE RESULTS OF THE TEST.
SO A COUPLE TIMES A WEEK THIS TOTALLY ANNOYING THERAPIST INTERVIEWS US.
WHAT DO THEY ASK YOU?

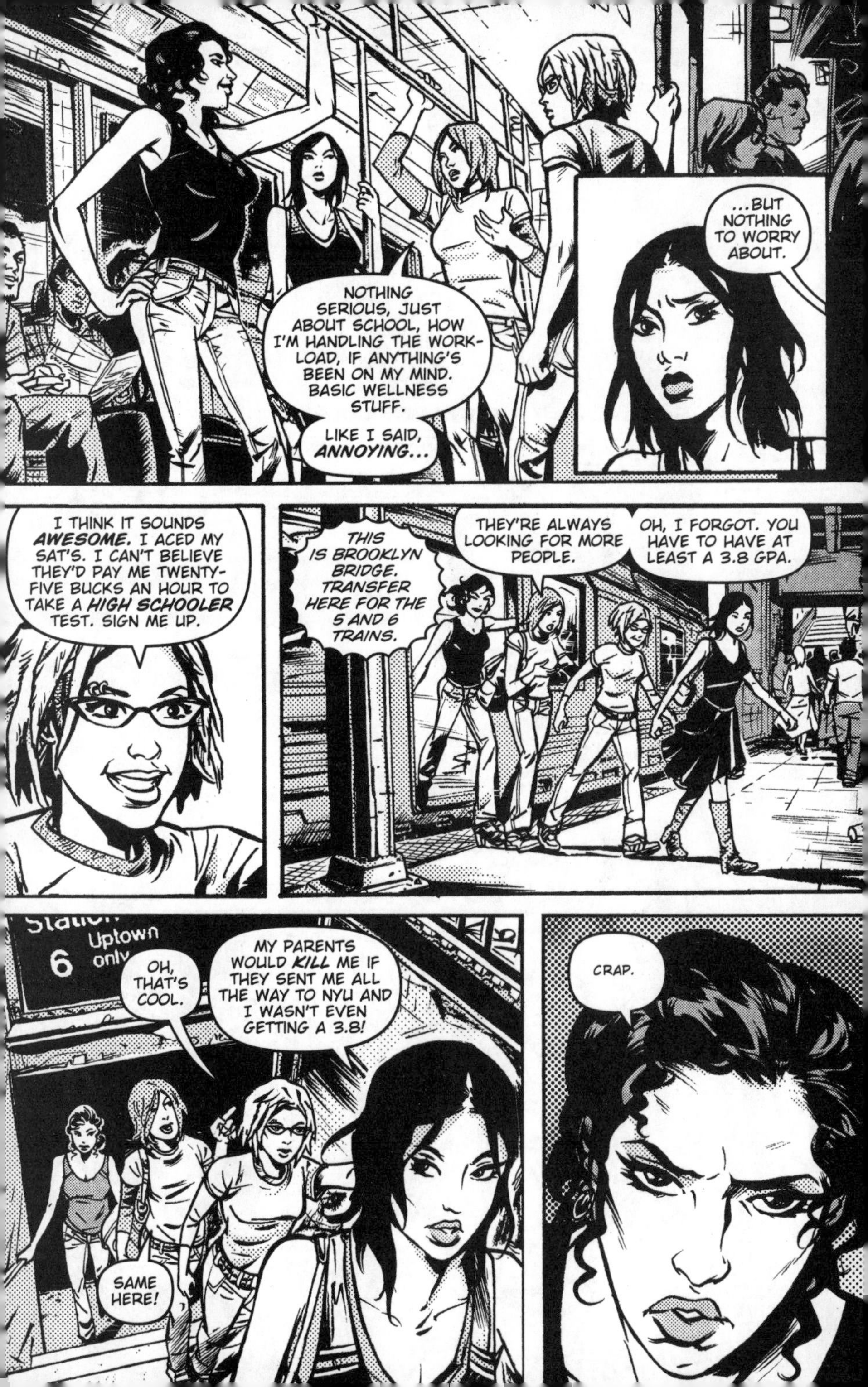
NOTHING SERIOUS, JUST ABOUT SCHOOL, HOW I'M HANDLING THE WORK-LOAD, IF ANYTHING'S BEEN ON MY MIND. BASIC WELLNESS STUFF.
LIKE I SAID, ANNOYING...
...BUT NOTHING TO WORRY ABOUT.
I THINK IT SOUNDS AWESOME. I ACED MY SAT'S. I CAN'T BELIEVE THEY'D PAY ME TWENTY-FIVE BUCKS AN HOUR TO TAKE A HIGH SCHOOLER TEST. SIGN ME UP.
THIS IS BROOKLYN BRIDGE. TRANSFER HERE FOR THE 5 AND 6 TRAINS.
THEY'RE ALWAYS LOOKING FOR MORE PEOPLE.
OH, I FORGOT. YOU HAVE TO HAVE AT LEAST A 3.8 GPA.
6 Uptown only
OH, THAT'S COOL.
MY PARENTS WOULD KILL ME IF THEY SENT ME ALL THE WAY TO NYU AND I WASN'T EVEN GETTING A 3.8!
SAME HERE!
CRAP.

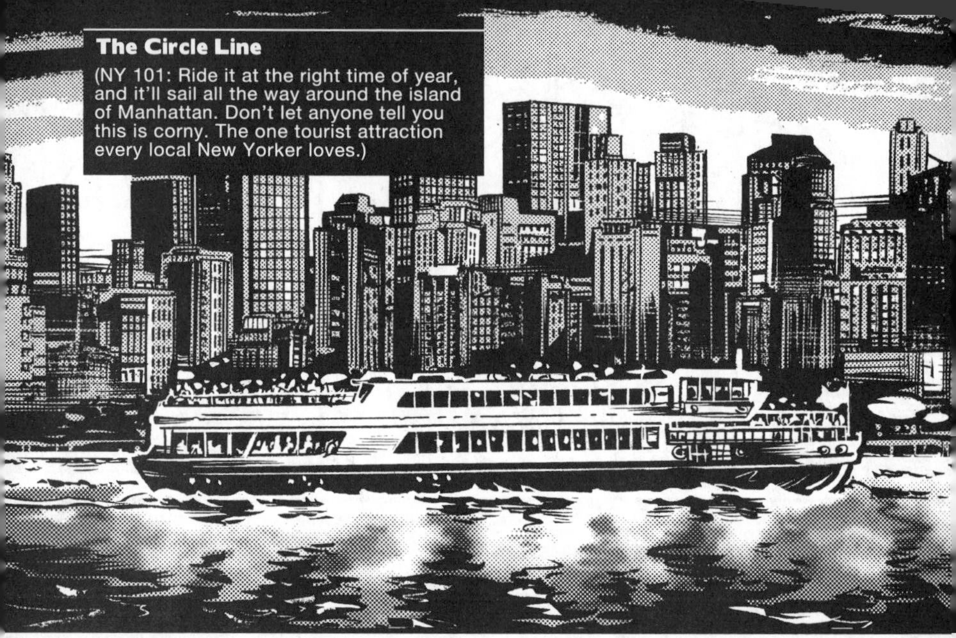
The Circle Line
(NY 101: Ride it at the right time of year, and it'll sail all the way around the island of Manhattan. Don't let anyone tell you this is corny. The one tourist attraction every local New Yorker loves.)

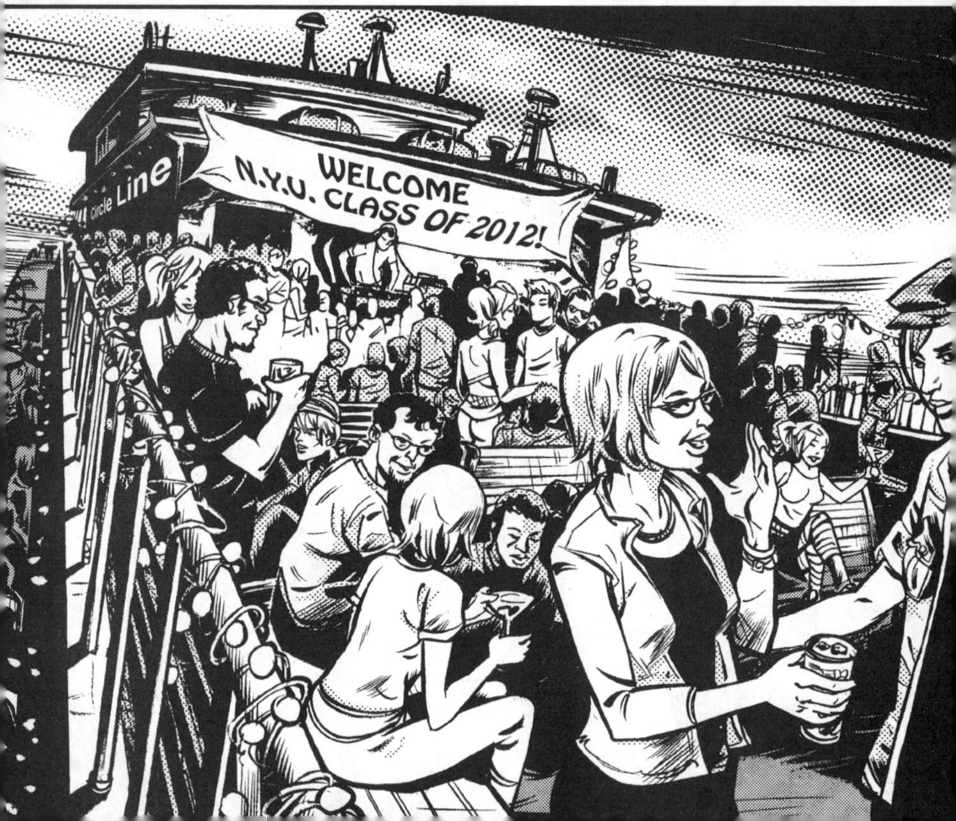
Circle Line
WELCOME
N.Y.U. CLASS OF 2012!

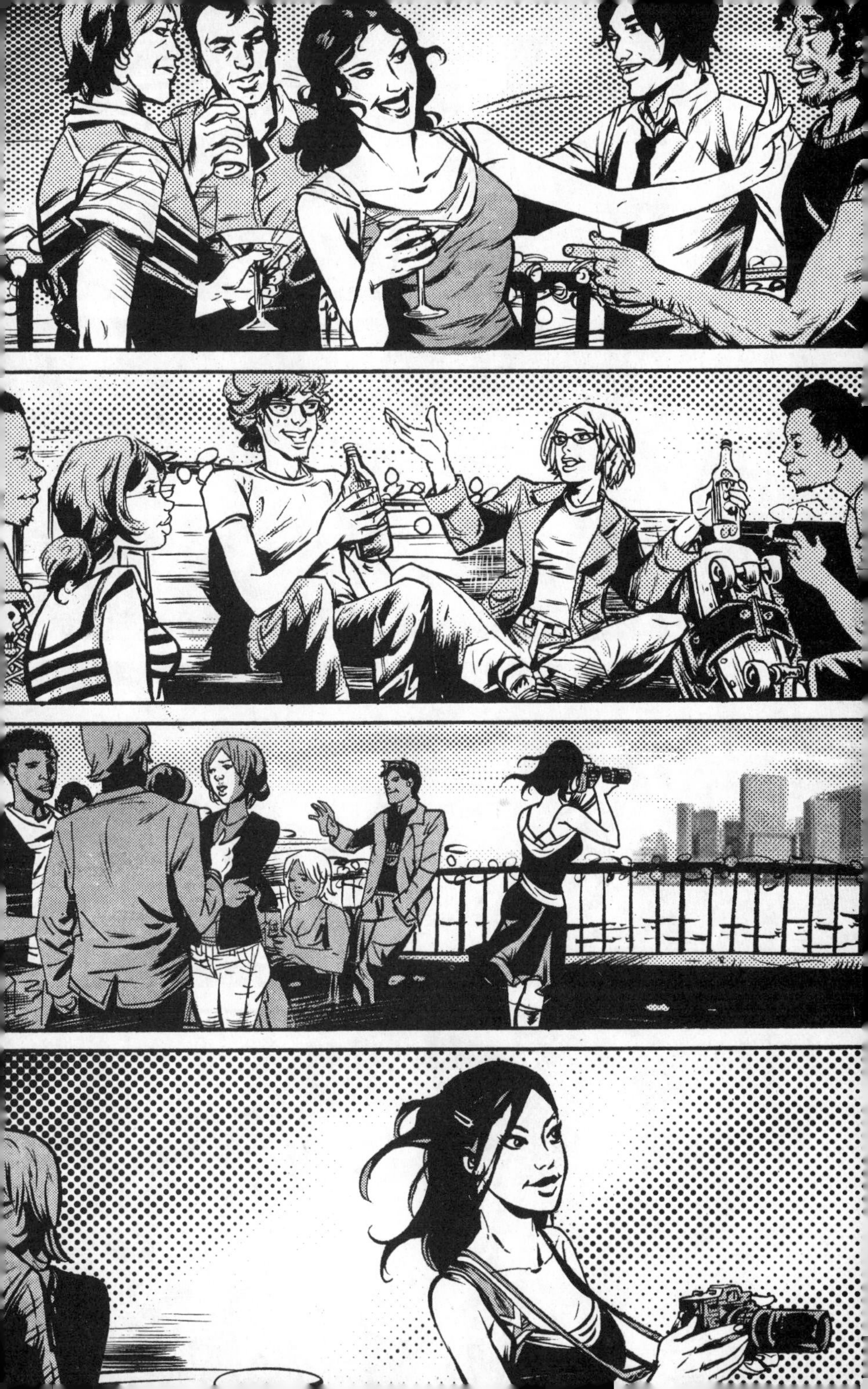

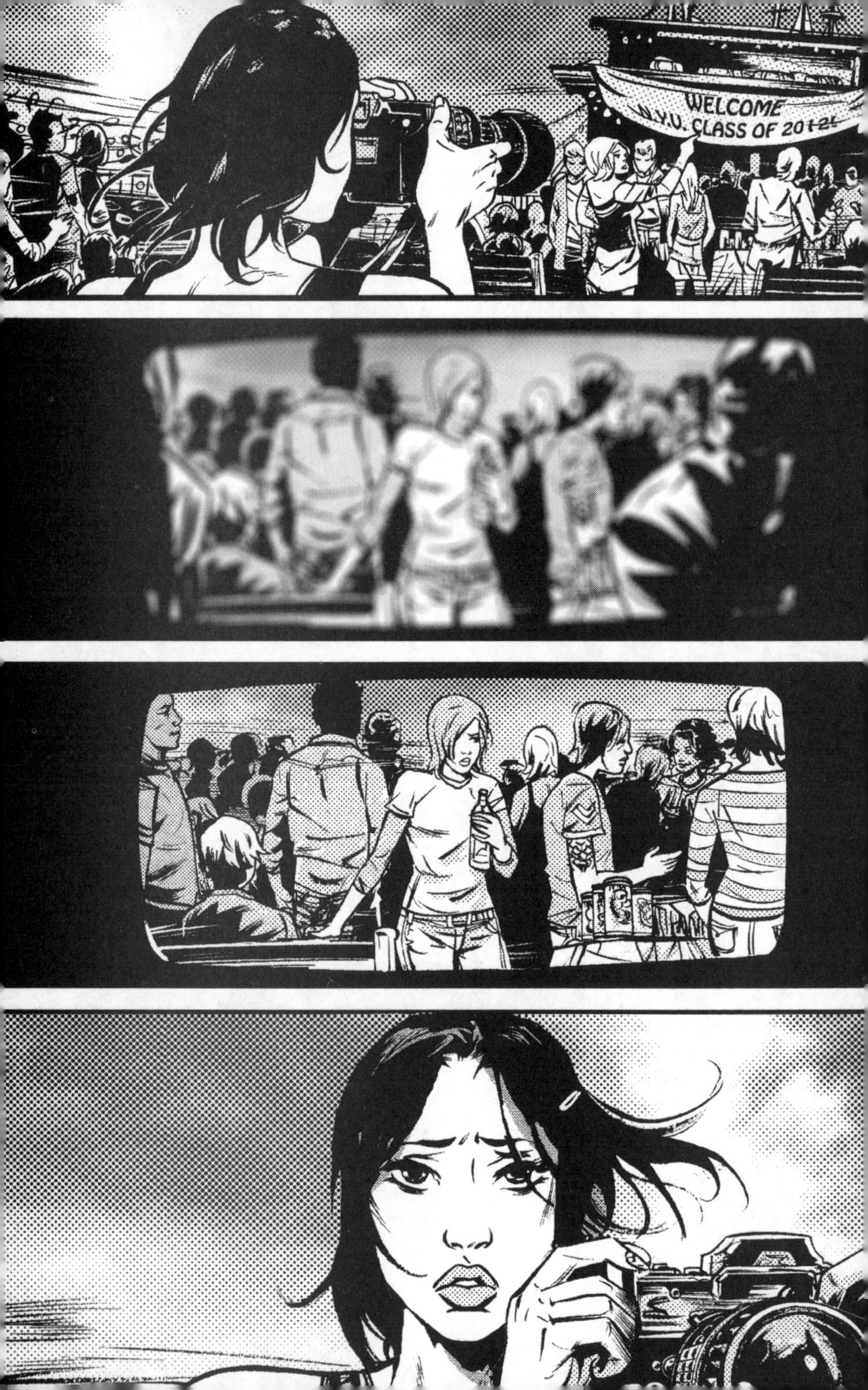
WELCOME
N.Y.U. CLASS OF 20

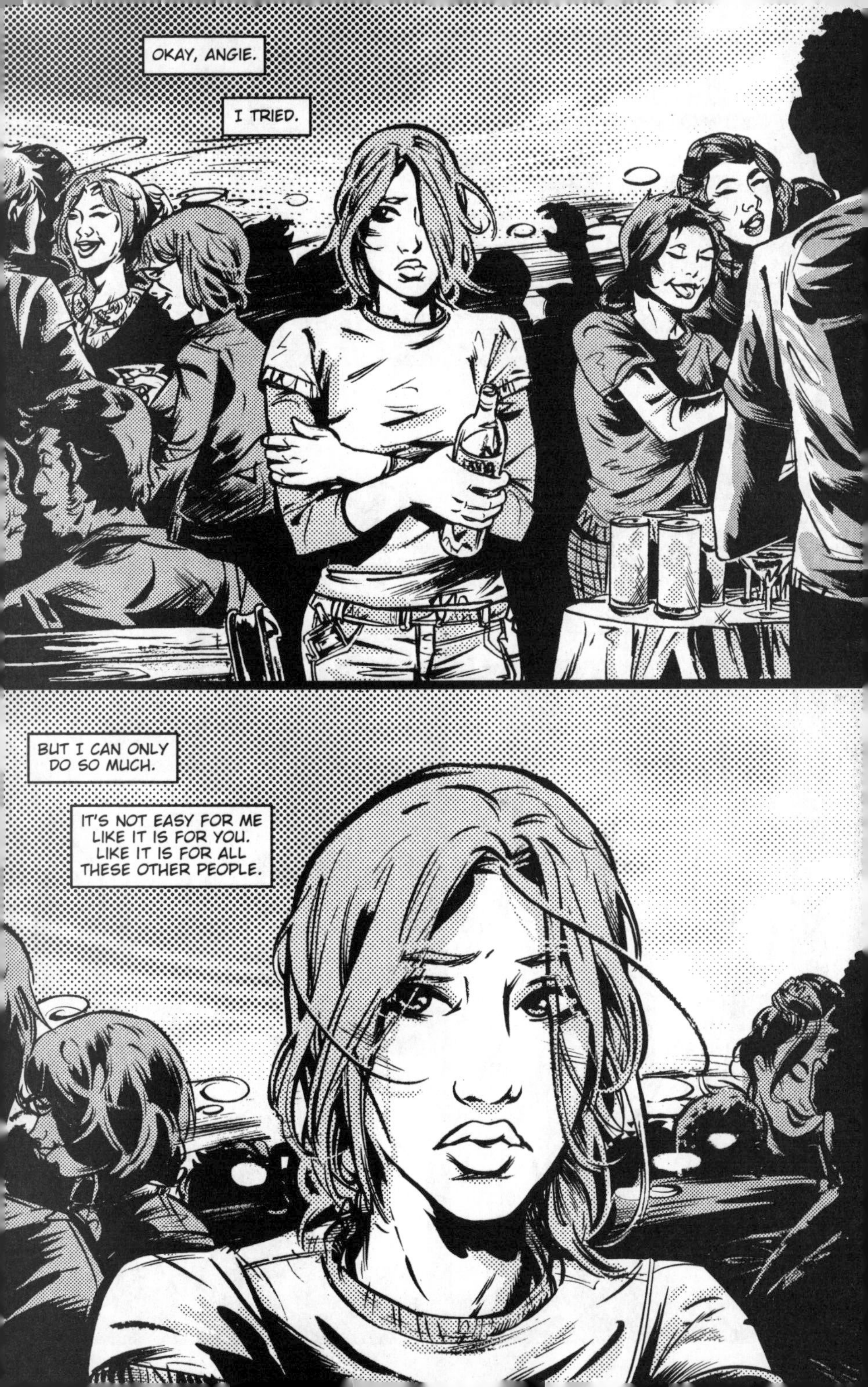
OKAY, ANGIE.
I TRIED.
BUT I CAN ONLY DO SO MUCH.
IT'S NOT EASY FOR ME LIKE IT IS FOR YOU. LIKE IT IS FOR ALL THESE OTHER PEOPLE.

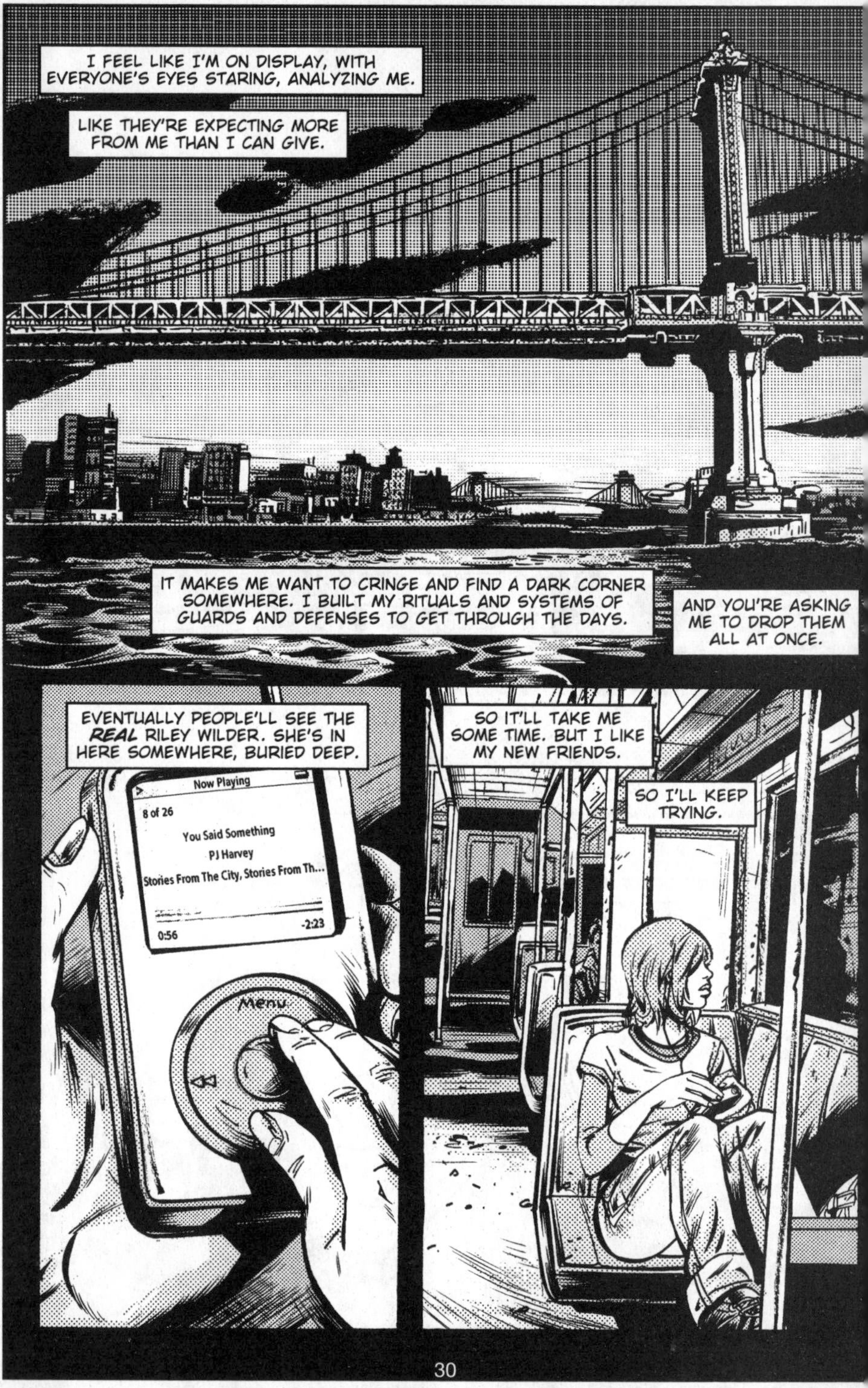
I FEEL LIKE I'M ON DISPLAY, WITH EVERYONE'S EYES STARING, ANALYZING ME.
LIKE THEY'RE EXPECTING MORE FROM ME THAN I CAN GIVE.
IT MAKES ME WANT TO CRINGE AND FIND A DARK CORNER SOMEWHERE. I BUILT MY RITUALS AND SYSTEMS OF GUARDS AND DEFENSES TO GET THROUGH THE DAYS.
AND YOU'RE ASKING ME TO DROP THEM ALL AT ONCE.
EVENTUALLY PEOPLE'LL SEE THE ***REAL*** RILEY WILDER. SHE'S IN HERE SOMEWHERE, BURIED DEEP.
Now Playing
8 of 26
You Said Something
PJ Harvey
Stories From The City, Stories From Th...
0:56
-2:23
Menu
SO IT'LL TAKE ME SOME TIME. BUT I LIKE MY NEW FRIENDS.
SO I'LL KEEP TRYING.

Chapter 2
Paths of Victory

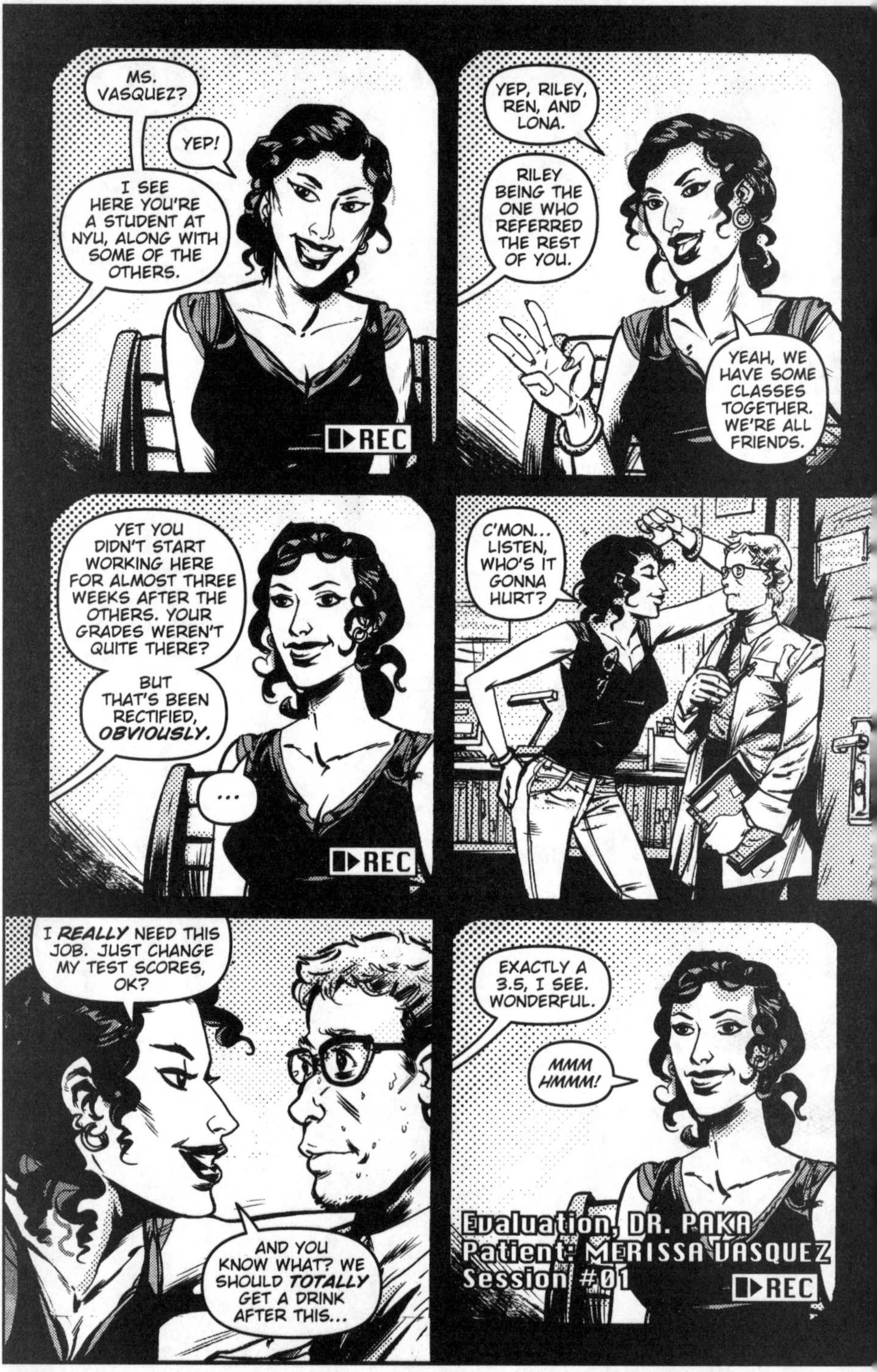
MS. VASQUEZ?
YEP!
I SEE HERE YOU'RE A STUDENT AT NYU, ALONG WITH SOME OF THE OTHERS.
REC
YEP, RILEY, REN, AND LONA.
RILEY BEING THE ONE WHO REFERRED THE REST OF YOU.
YEAH, WE HAVE SOME CLASSES TOGETHER. WE'RE ALL FRIENDS.
YET YOU DIDN'T START WORKING HERE FOR ALMOST THREE WEEKS AFTER THE OTHERS. YOUR GRADES WEREN'T QUITE THERE?
BUT THAT'S BEEN RECTIFIED, OBVIOUSLY.
...
REC
C'MON... LISTEN, WHO'S IT GONNA HURT?
I REALLY NEED THIS JOB. JUST CHANGE MY TEST SCORES, OK?
AND YOU KNOW WHAT? WE SHOULD TOTALLY GET A DRINK AFTER THIS...
EXACTLY A 3.5, I SEE. WONDERFUL.
MMM HMMM!
Evaluation, DR. PAKA
Patient: MERISSA VASQUEZ
Session #01
REC

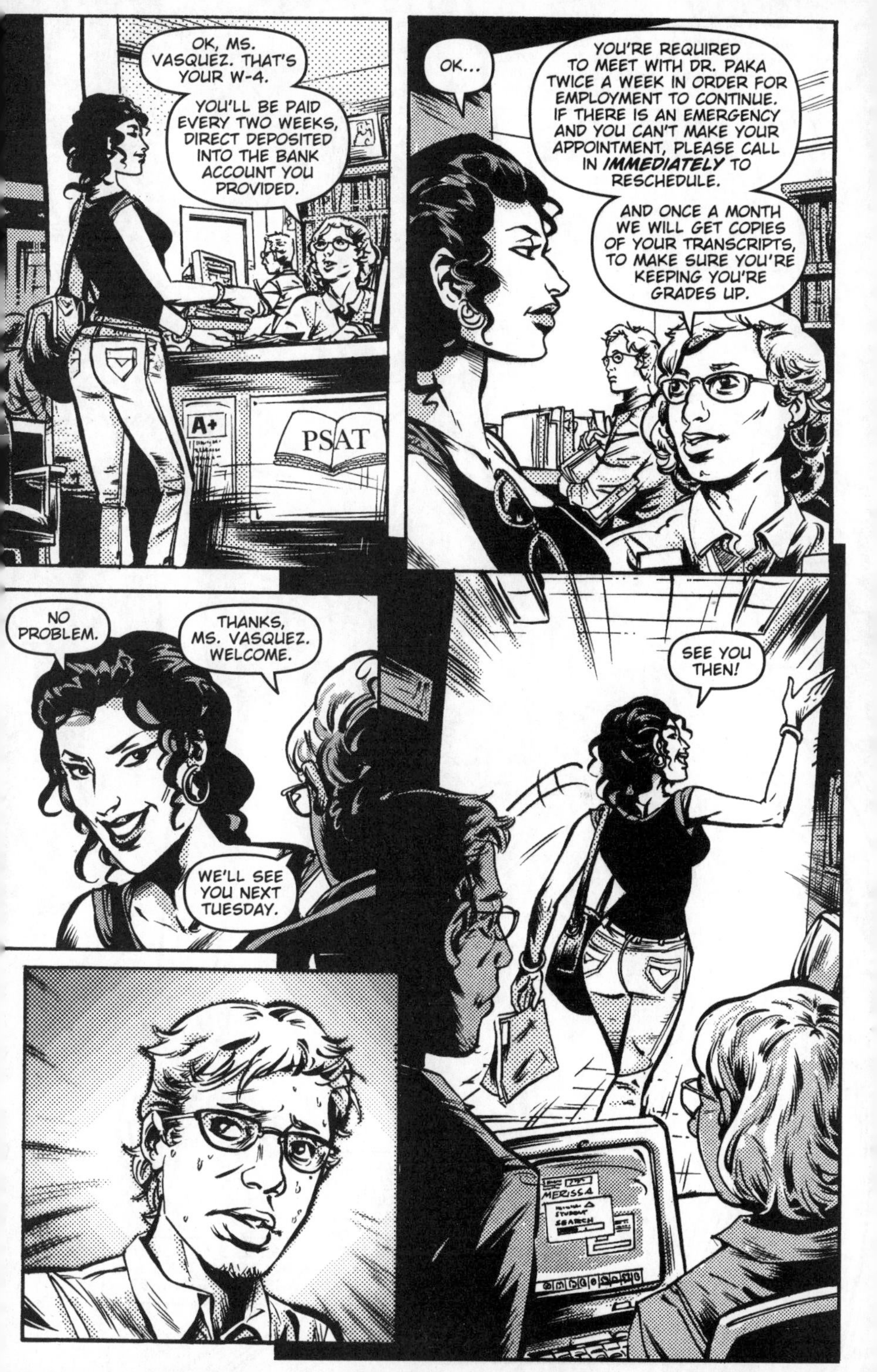
OK, MS. VASQUEZ. THAT'S YOUR W-4.
YOU'LL BE PAID EVERY TWO WEEKS, DIRECT DEPOSITED INTO THE BANK ACCOUNT YOU PROVIDED.
A+
PSAT
OK...
YOU'RE REQUIRED TO MEET WITH DR. PAKA TWICE A WEEK IN ORDER FOR EMPLOYMENT TO CONTINUE. IF THERE IS AN EMERGENCY AND YOU CAN'T MAKE YOUR APPOINTMENT, PLEASE CALL IN *IMMEDIATELY* TO RESCHEDULE.
AND ONCE A MONTH WE WILL GET COPIES OF YOUR TRANSCRIPTS, TO MAKE SURE YOU'RE KEEPING YOU'RE GRADES UP.
NO PROBLEM.
THANKS, MS. VASQUEZ. WELCOME.
WE'LL SEE YOU NEXT TUESDAY.
SEE YOU THEN!
MERISSA
STUDENT SEARCH

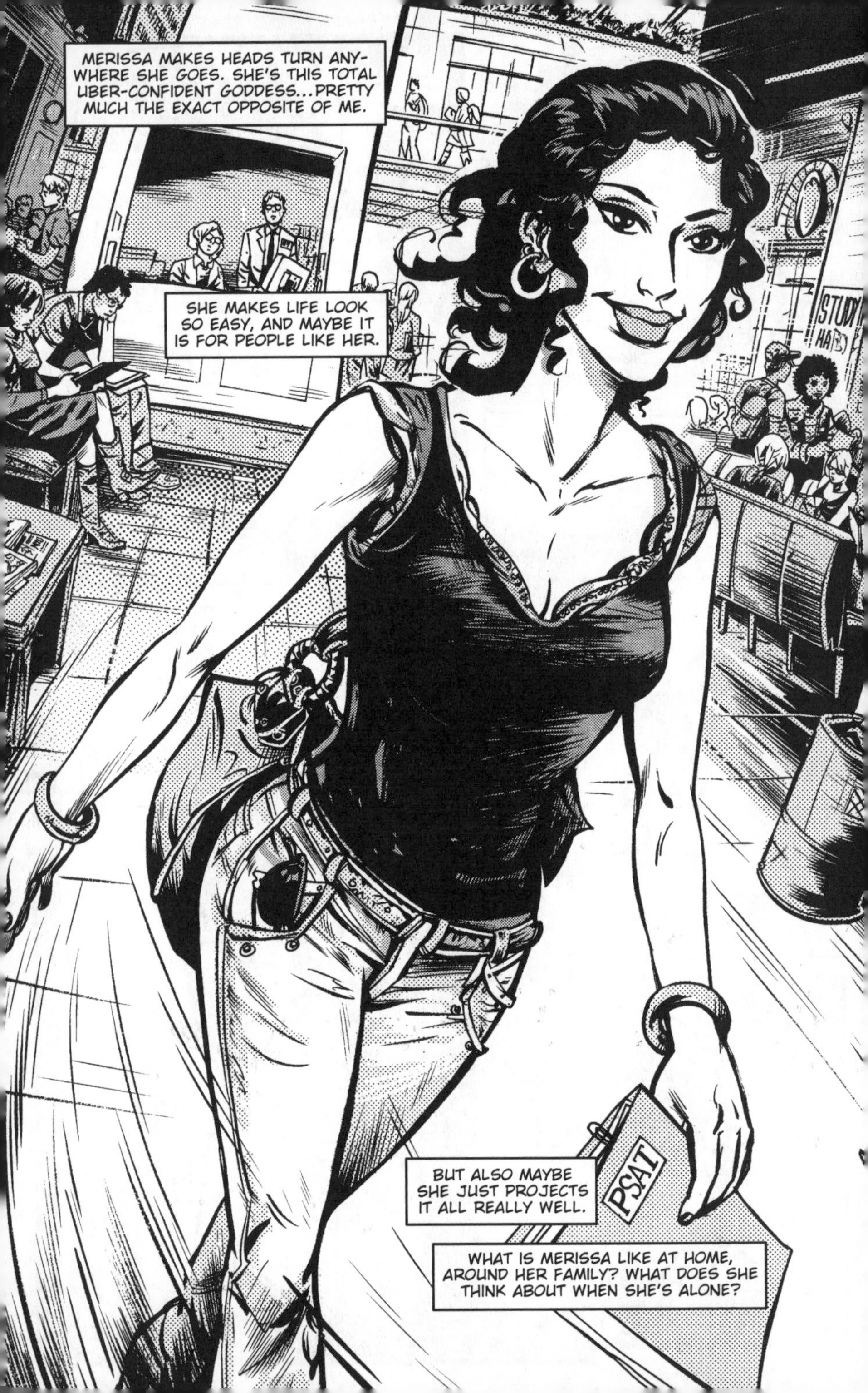
MERISSA MAKES HEADS TURN ANY-WHERE SHE GOES. SHE'S THIS TOTAL UBER-CONFIDENT GODDESS...PRETTY MUCH THE EXACT OPPOSITE OF ME.
SHE MAKES LIFE LOOK SO EASY, AND MAYBE IT IS FOR PEOPLE LIKE HER.
STUDY
BUT ALSO MAYBE SHE JUST PROJECTS IT ALL REALLY WELL.
PSAT
WHAT IS MERISSA LIKE AT HOME, AROUND HER FAMILY? WHAT DOES SHE THINK ABOUT WHEN SHE'S ALONE?

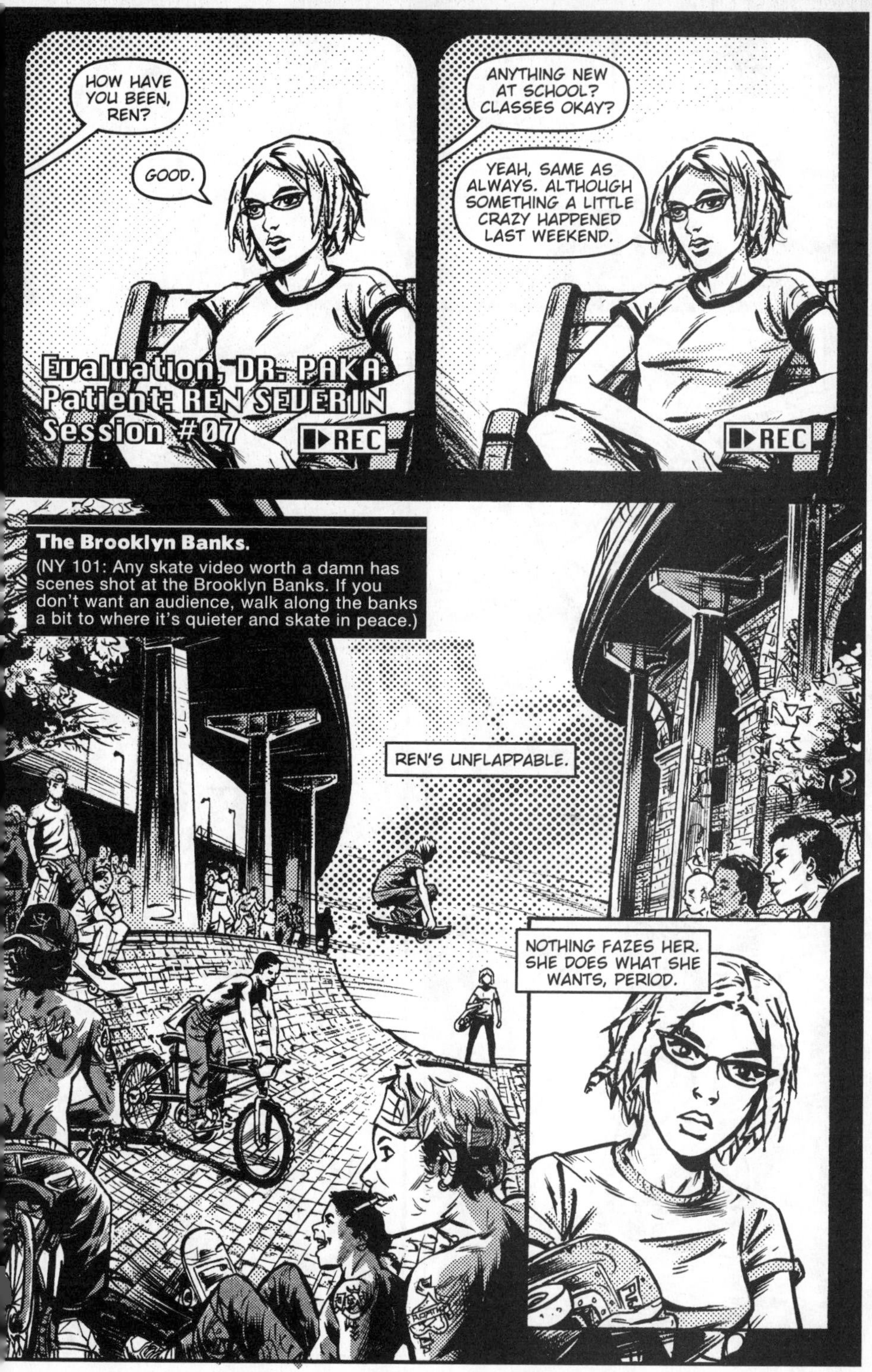
HOW HAVE YOU BEEN, REN?
GOOD.
Evaluation, DR. PAKA
Patient: REN SEVERIN
Session #07
REC
ANYTHING NEW AT SCHOOL? CLASSES OKAY?
YEAH, SAME AS ALWAYS. ALTHOUGH SOMETHING A LITTLE CRAZY HAPPENED LAST WEEKEND.
REC
The Brooklyn Banks.
(NY 101: Any skate video worth a damn has scenes shot at the Brooklyn Banks. If you don't want an audience, walk along the banks a bit to where it's quieter and skate in peace.)
REN'S UNFLAPPABLE.
NOTHING FAZES HER. SHE DOES WHAT SHE WANTS, PERIOD.

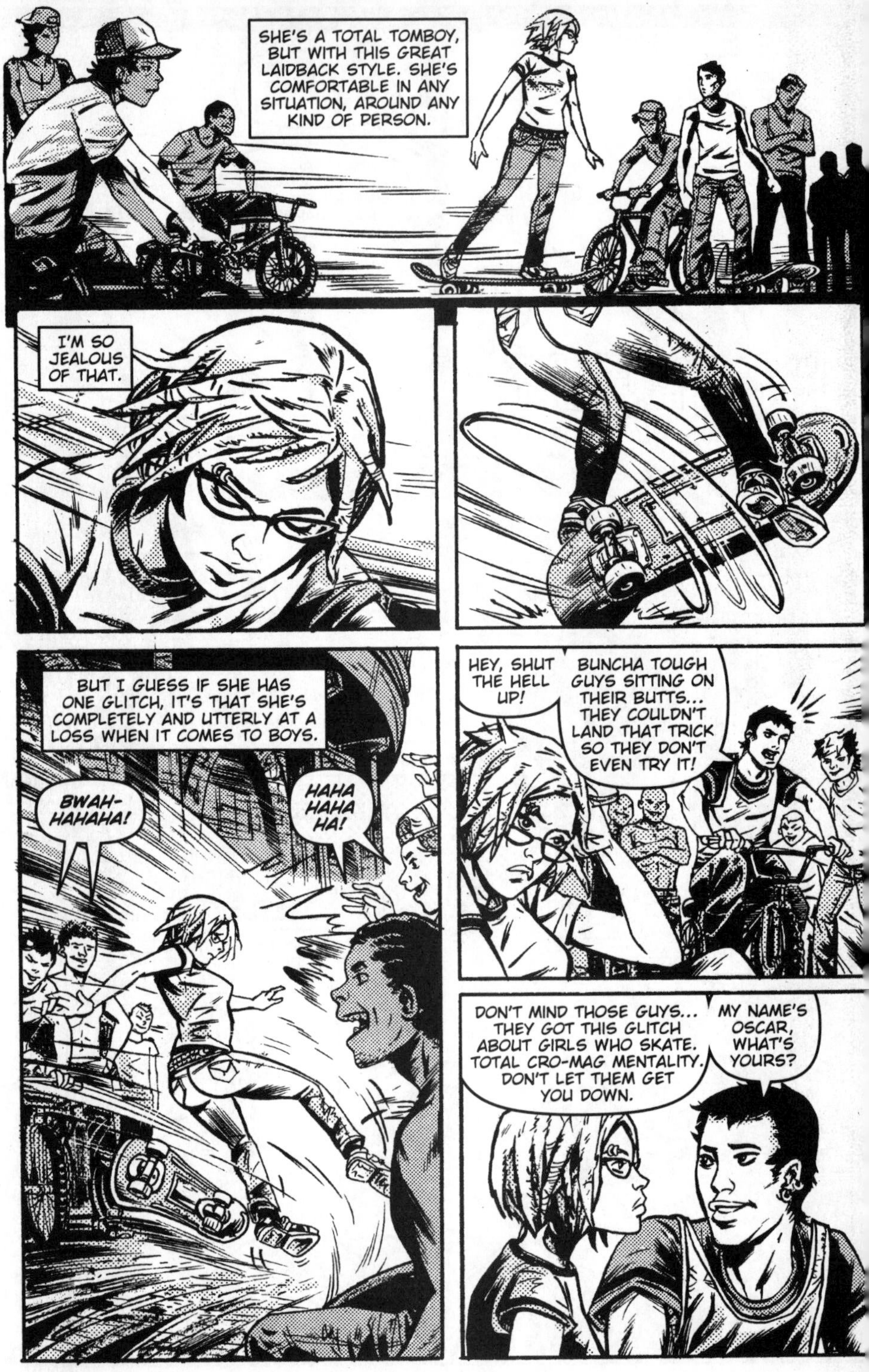
SHE'S A TOTAL TOMBOY, BUT WITH THIS GREAT LAIDBACK STYLE. SHE'S COMFORTABLE IN ANY SITUATION, AROUND ANY KIND OF PERSON.
I'M SO JEALOUS OF THAT.
BUT I GUESS IF SHE HAS ONE GLITCH, IT'S THAT SHE'S COMPLETELY AND UTTERLY AT A LOSS WHEN IT COMES TO BOYS.
BWAH-HAHAHA!
HAHA HAHA HA!
HEY, SHUT THE HELL UP!
BUNCHA TOUGH GUYS SITTING ON THEIR BUTTS... THEY COULDN'T LAND THAT TRICK SO THEY DON'T EVEN TRY IT!
DON'T MIND THOSE GUYS... THEY GOT THIS GLITCH ABOUT GIRLS WHO SKATE. TOTAL CRO-MAG MENTALITY. DON'T LET THEM GET YOU DOWN.
MY NAME'S OSCAR, WHAT'S YOURS?

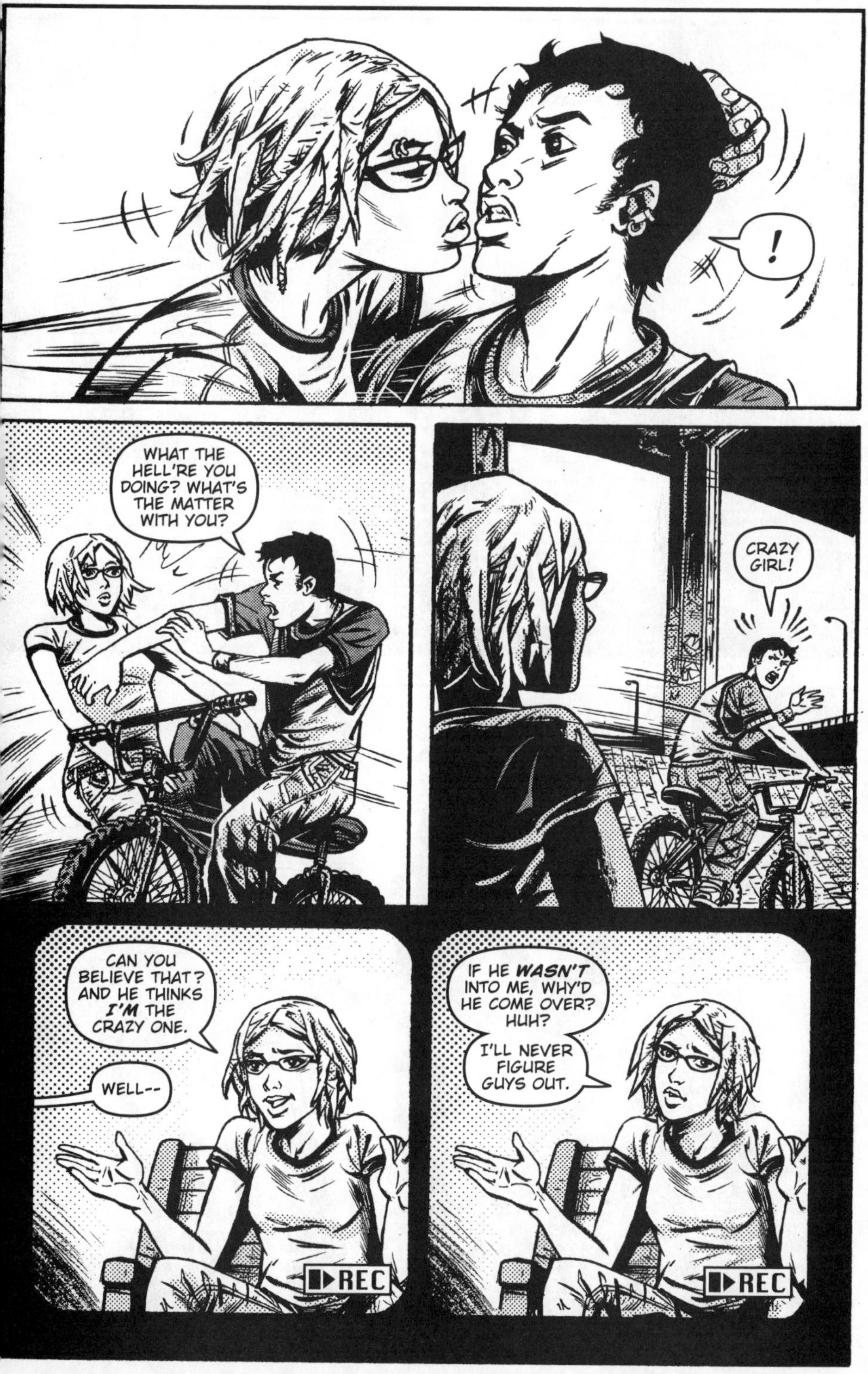
!
WHAT THE HELL'RE YOU DOING? WHAT'S THE MATTER WITH YOU?
CRAZY GIRL!
CAN YOU BELIEVE THAT? AND HE THINKS *I'M* THE CRAZY ONE.
WELL--
REC
IF HE ***WASN'T*** INTO ME, WHY'D HE COME OVER? HUH?
I'LL NEVER FIGURE GUYS OUT.
REC

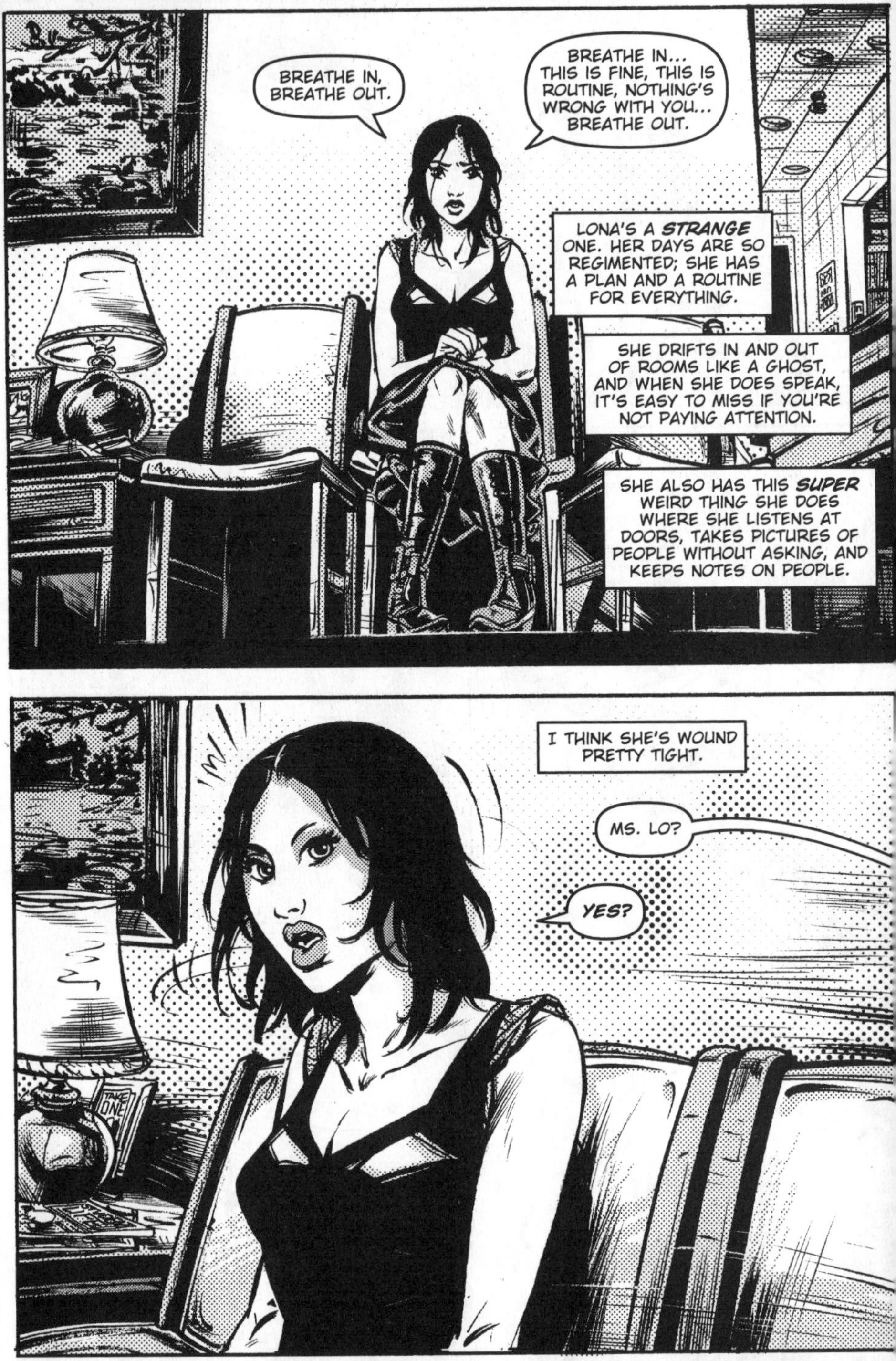
BREATHE IN, BREATHE OUT.
BREATHE IN... THIS IS FINE, THIS IS ROUTINE, NOTHING'S WRONG WITH YOU... BREATHE OUT.
LONA'S A STRANGE ONE. HER DAYS ARE SO REGIMENTED; SHE HAS A PLAN AND A ROUTINE FOR EVERYTHING.
SHE DRIFTS IN AND OUT OF ROOMS LIKE A GHOST, AND WHEN SHE DOES SPEAK, IT'S EASY TO MISS IF YOU'RE NOT PAYING ATTENTION.
SHE ALSO HAS THIS SUPER WEIRD THING SHE DOES WHERE SHE LISTENS AT DOORS, TAKES PICTURES OF PEOPLE WITHOUT ASKING, AND KEEPS NOTES ON PEOPLE.
I THINK SHE'S WOUND PRETTY TIGHT.
MS. LO?
YES?
TAKE ONE

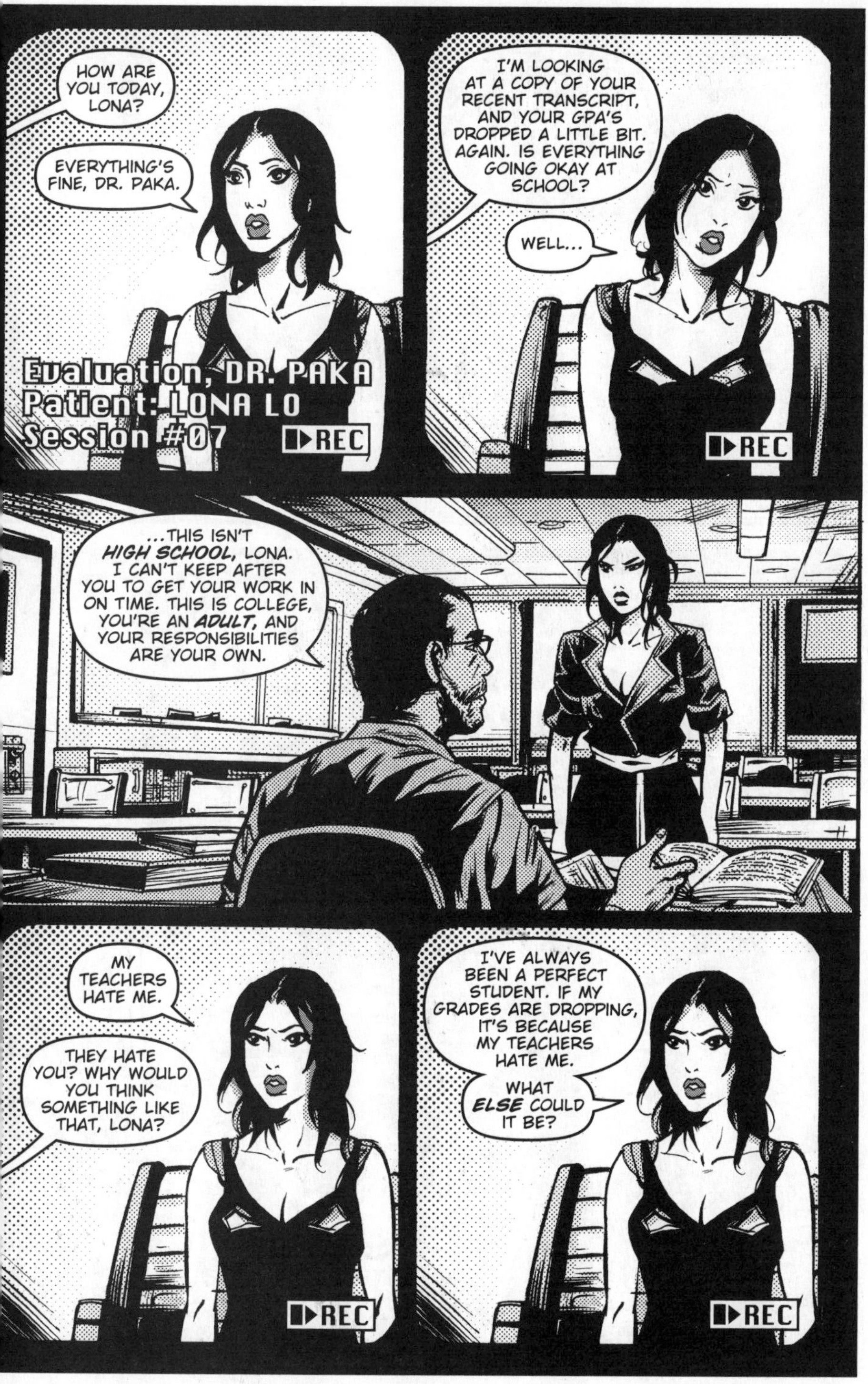
HOW ARE YOU TODAY, LONA?
EVERYTHING'S FINE, DR. PAKA.
Evaluation, DR. PAKA
Patient: LONA LO
Session #07
REC
I'M LOOKING AT A COPY OF YOUR RECENT TRANSCRIPT, AND YOUR GPA'S DROPPED A LITTLE BIT. AGAIN. IS EVERYTHING GOING OKAY AT SCHOOL?
WELL...
REC
...THIS ISN'T *HIGH SCHOOL,* LONA. I CAN'T KEEP AFTER YOU TO GET YOUR WORK IN ON TIME. THIS IS COLLEGE, YOU'RE AN *ADULT,* AND YOUR RESPONSIBILITIES ARE YOUR OWN.
MY TEACHERS HATE ME.
THEY HATE YOU? WHY WOULD YOU THINK SOMETHING LIKE THAT, LONA?
REC
I'VE ALWAYS BEEN A PERFECT STUDENT. IF MY GRADES ARE DROPPING, IT'S BECAUSE MY TEACHERS HATE ME.
WHAT *ELSE* COULD IT BE?
REC

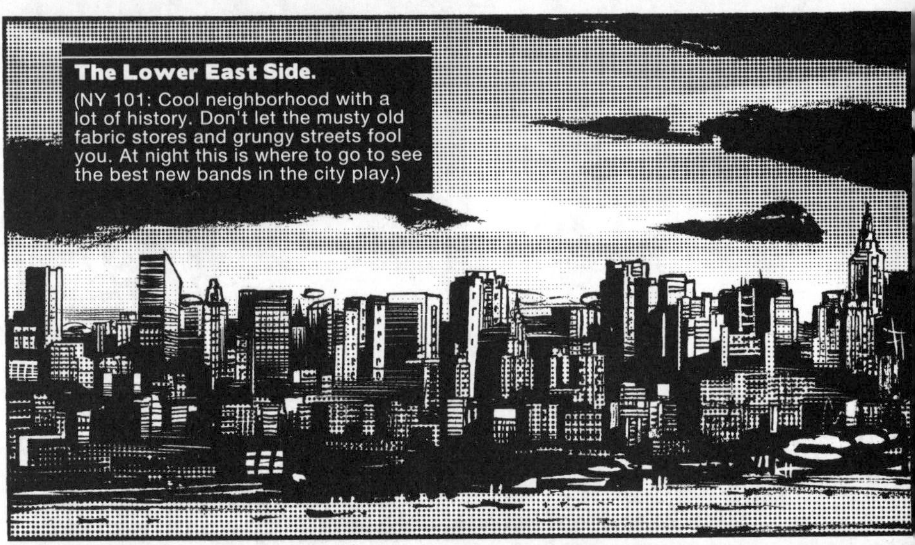
The Lower East Side.
(NY 101: Cool neighborhood with a lot of history. Don't let the musty old fabric stores and grungy streets fool you. At night this is where to go to see the best new bands in the city play.)

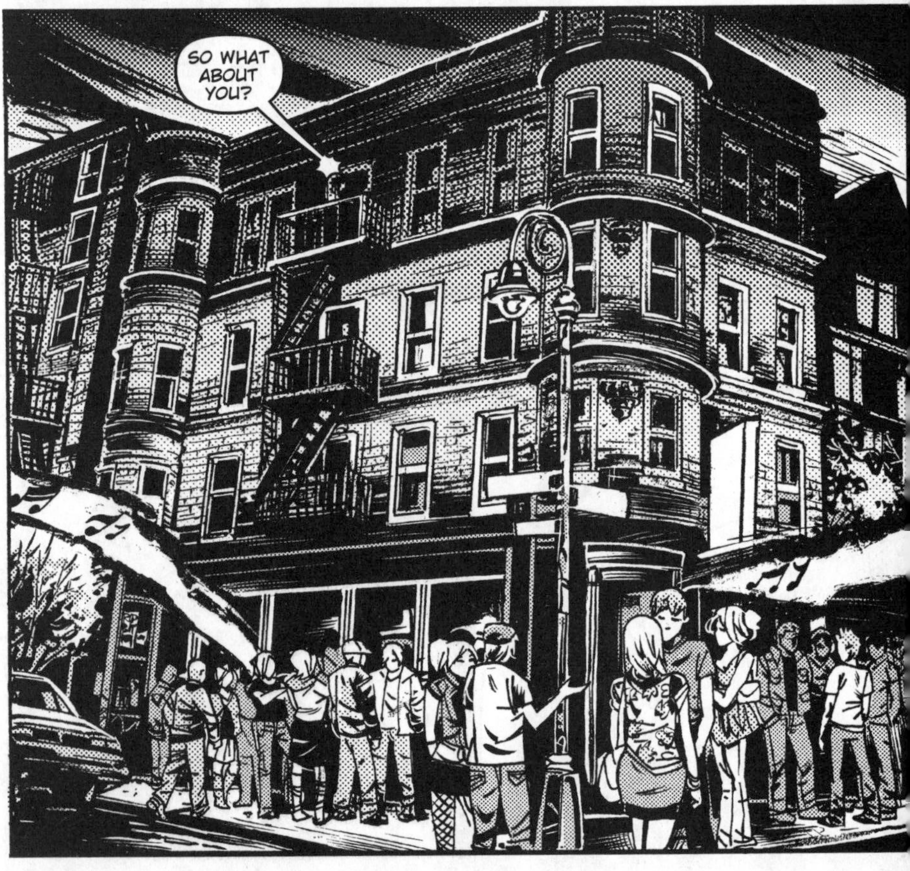
SO WHAT ABOUT YOU?

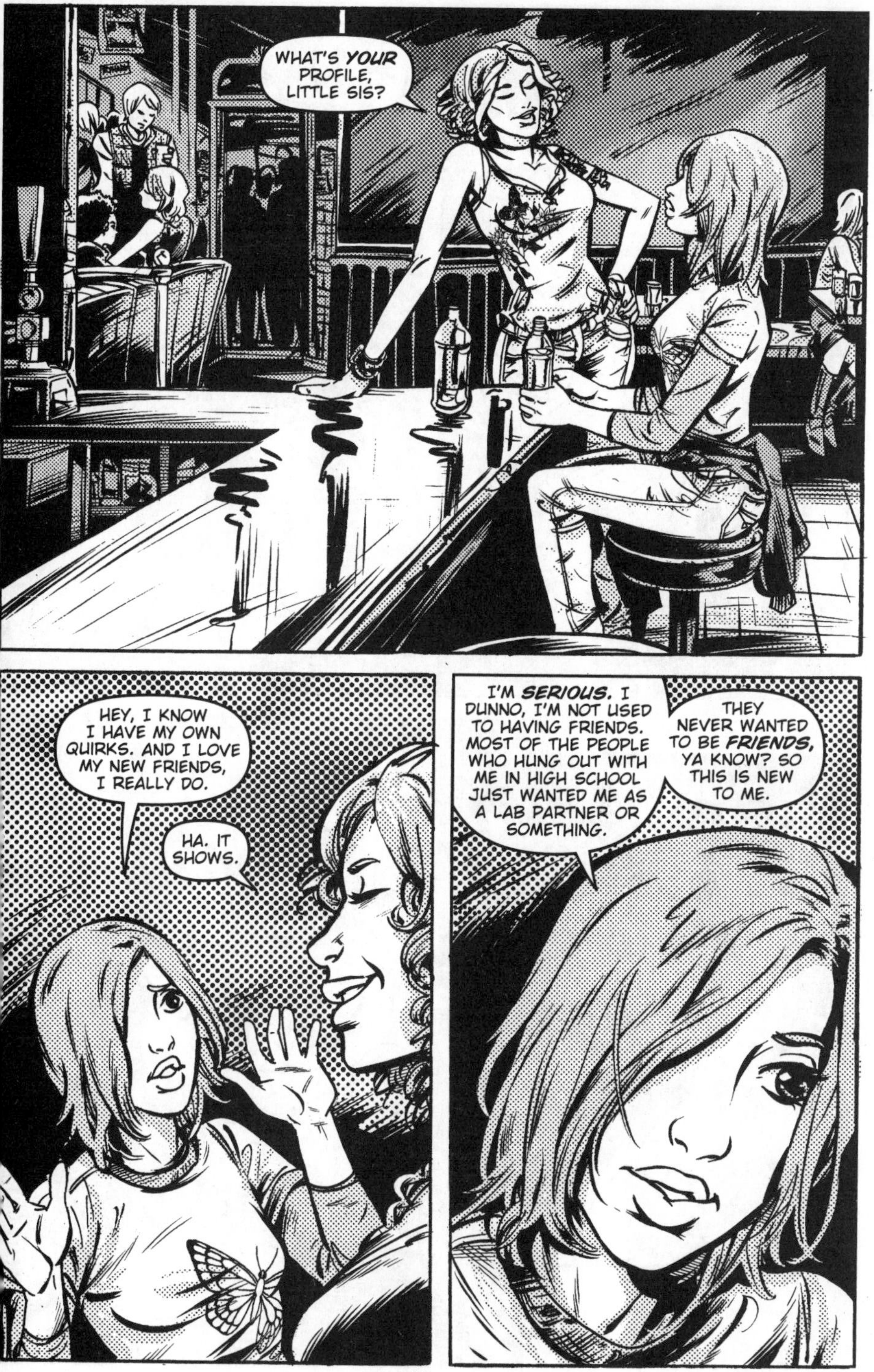
WHAT'S YOUR PROFILE, LITTLE SIS?
HEY, I KNOW I HAVE MY OWN QUIRKS. AND I LOVE MY NEW FRIENDS, I REALLY DO.
HA. IT SHOWS.
I'M SERIOUS. I DUNNO, I'M NOT USED TO HAVING FRIENDS. MOST OF THE PEOPLE WHO HUNG OUT WITH ME IN HIGH SCHOOL JUST WANTED ME AS A LAB PARTNER OR SOMETHING.
THEY NEVER WANTED TO BE FRIENDS, YA KNOW? SO THIS IS NEW TO ME.

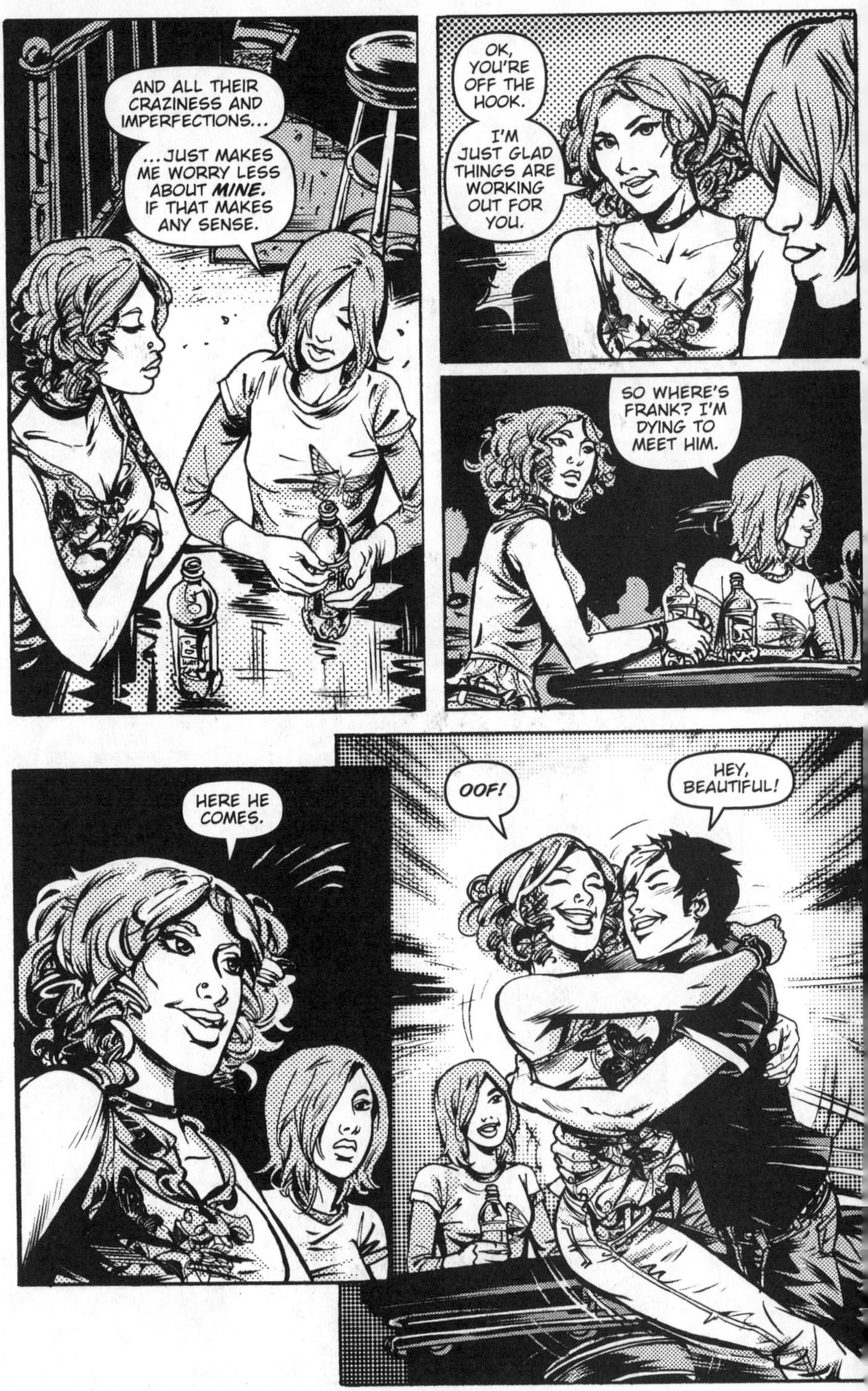
AND ALL THEIR CRAZINESS AND IMPERFECTIONS...
...JUST MAKES ME WORRY LESS ABOUT ***MINE.*** IF THAT MAKES ANY SENSE.
OK, YOU'RE OFF THE HOOK.
I'M JUST GLAD THINGS ARE WORKING OUT FOR YOU.
SO WHERE'S FRANK? I'M DYING TO MEET HIM.
HERE HE COMES.
OOF!
HEY, BEAUTIFUL!

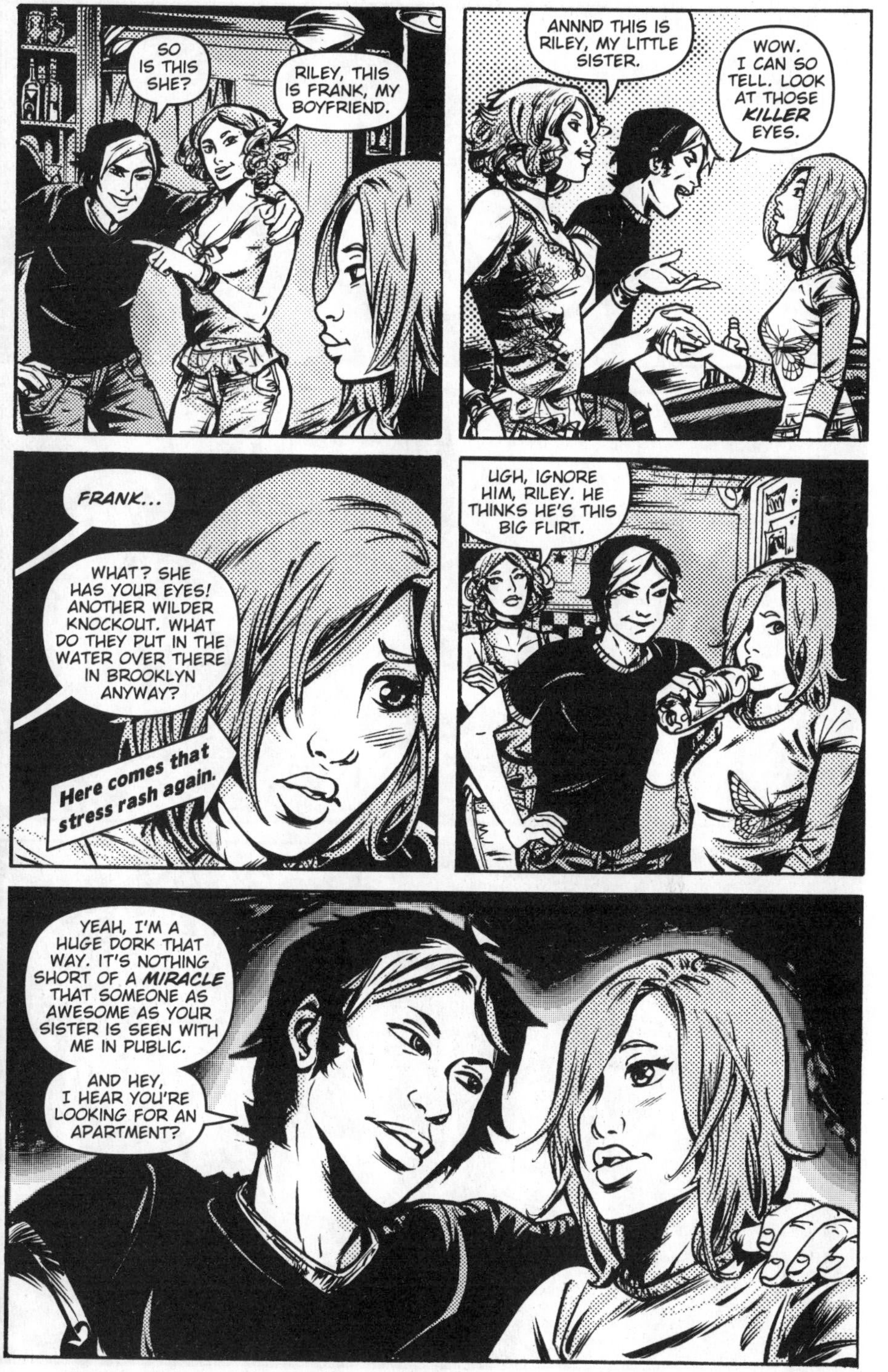
SO IS THIS SHE?
RILEY, THIS IS FRANK, MY BOYFRIEND.
ANNND THIS IS RILEY, MY LITTLE SISTER.
WOW. I CAN SO TELL. LOOK AT THOSE KILLER EYES.
FRANK...
WHAT? SHE HAS YOUR EYES! ANOTHER WILDER KNOCKOUT. WHAT DO THEY PUT IN THE WATER OVER THERE IN BROOKLYN ANYWAY?
Here comes that stress rash again.
UGH, IGNORE HIM, RILEY. HE THINKS HE'S THIS BIG FLIRT.
YEAH, I'M A HUGE DORK THAT WAY. IT'S NOTHING SHORT OF A MIRACLE THAT SOMEONE AS AWESOME AS YOUR SISTER IS SEEN WITH ME IN PUBLIC.
AND HEY, I HEAR YOU'RE LOOKING FOR AN APARTMENT?

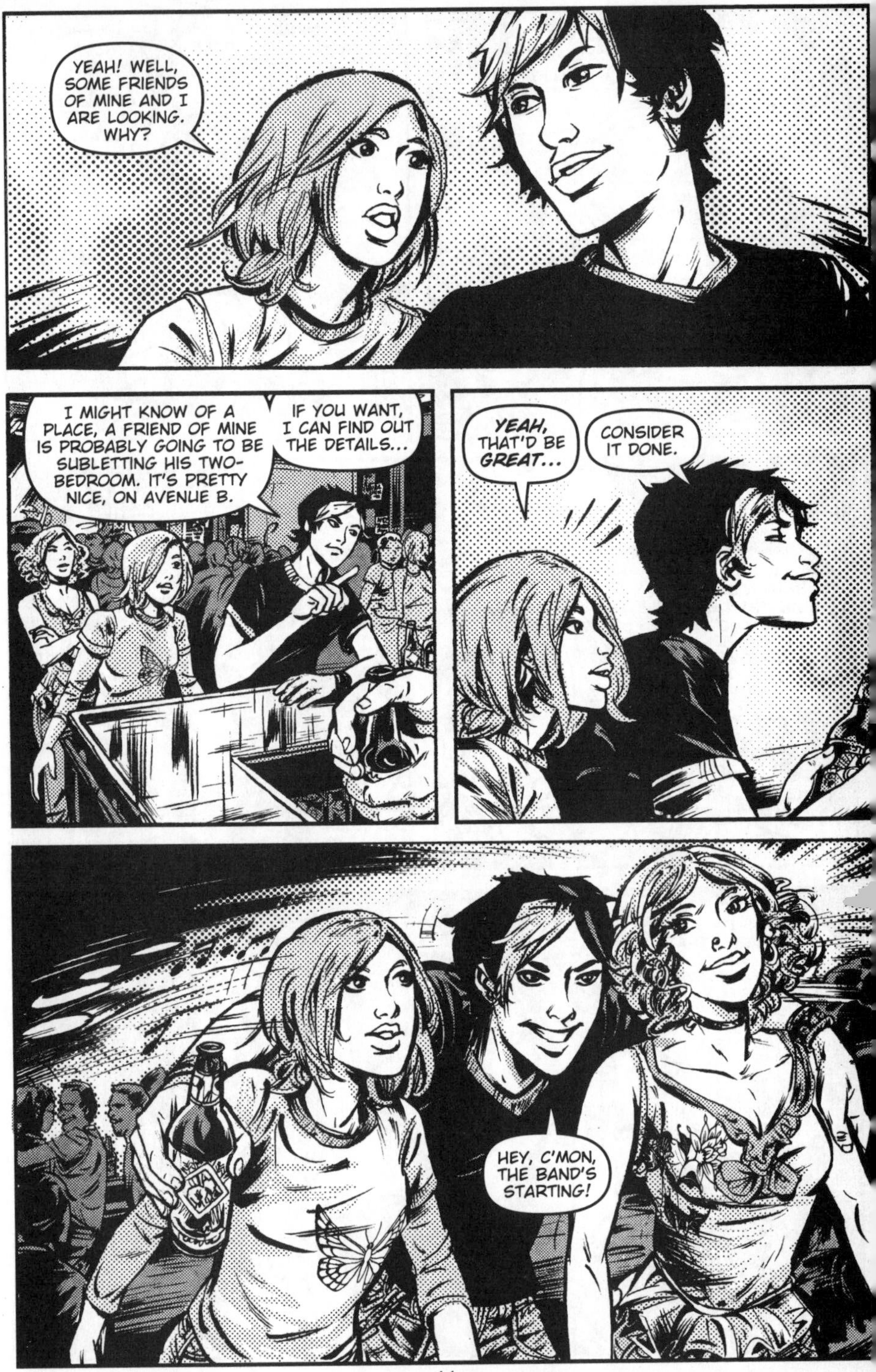
YEAH! WELL, SOME FRIENDS OF MINE AND I ARE LOOKING. WHY?
I MIGHT KNOW OF A PLACE, A FRIEND OF MINE IS PROBABLY GOING TO BE SUBLETTING HIS TWO-BEDROOM. IT'S PRETTY NICE, ON AVENUE B.
IF YOU WANT, I CAN FIND OUT THE DETAILS...
YEAH, THAT'D BE GREAT...
CONSIDER IT DONE.
HEY, C'MON, THE BAND'S STARTING!

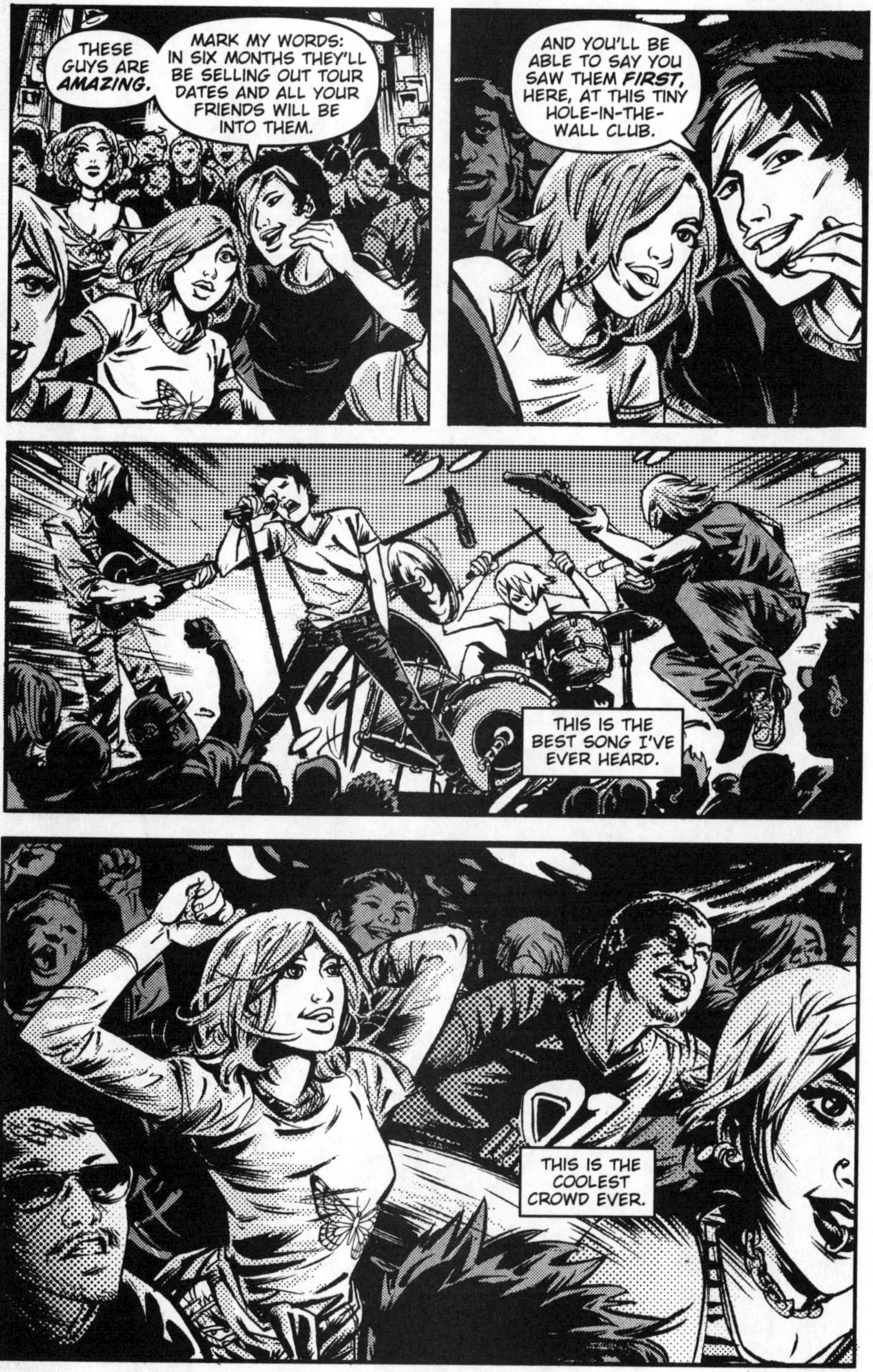
THESE GUYS ARE *AMAZING.*
MARK MY WORDS: IN SIX MONTHS THEY'LL BE SELLING OUT TOUR DATES AND ALL YOUR FRIENDS WILL BE INTO THEM.
AND YOU'LL BE ABLE TO SAY YOU SAW THEM *FIRST,* HERE, AT THIS TINY HOLE-IN-THE-WALL CLUB.
THIS IS THE BEST SONG I'VE EVER HEARD.
THIS IS THE COOLEST CROWD EVER.

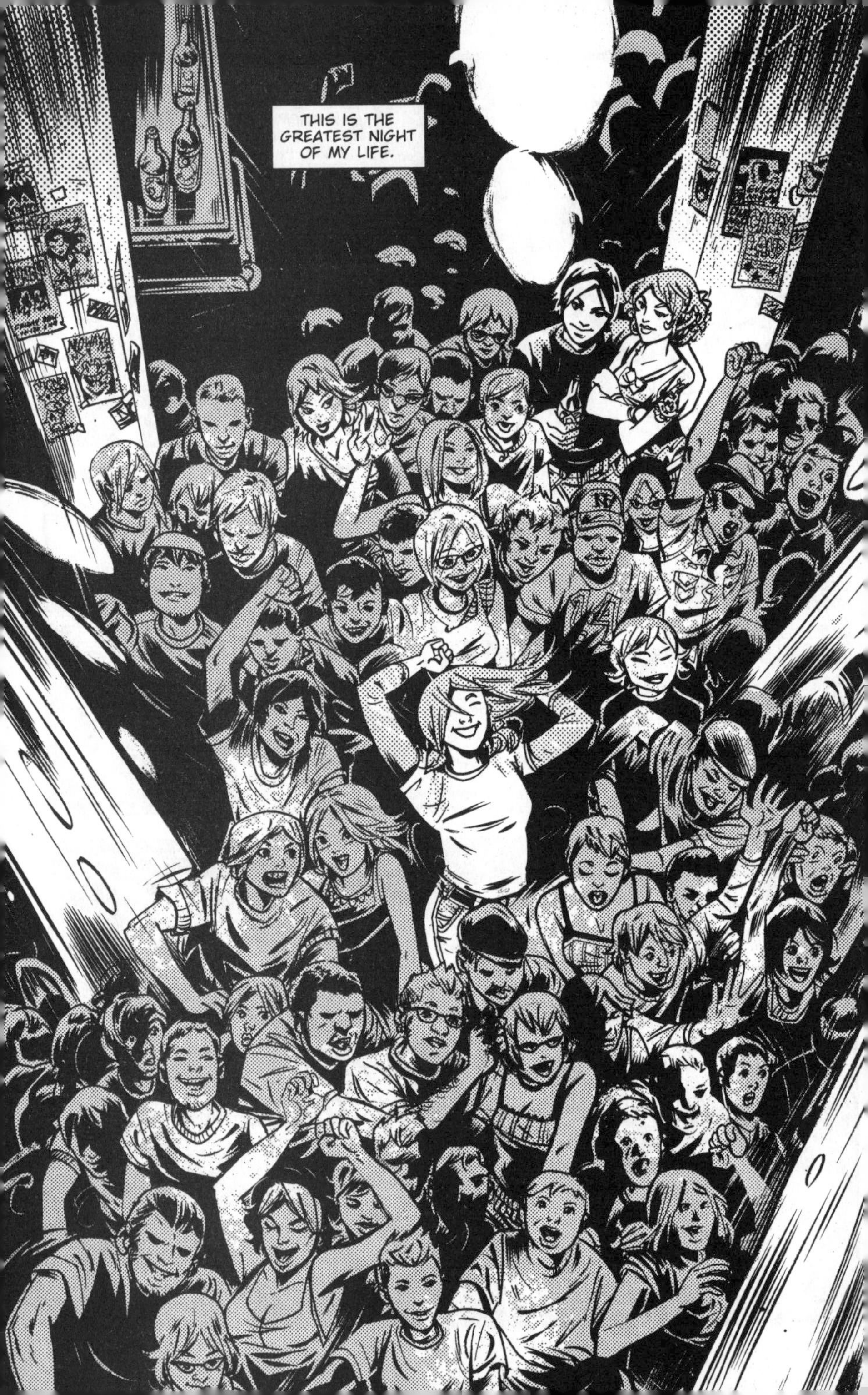
THIS IS THE GREATEST NIGHT OF MY LIFE.

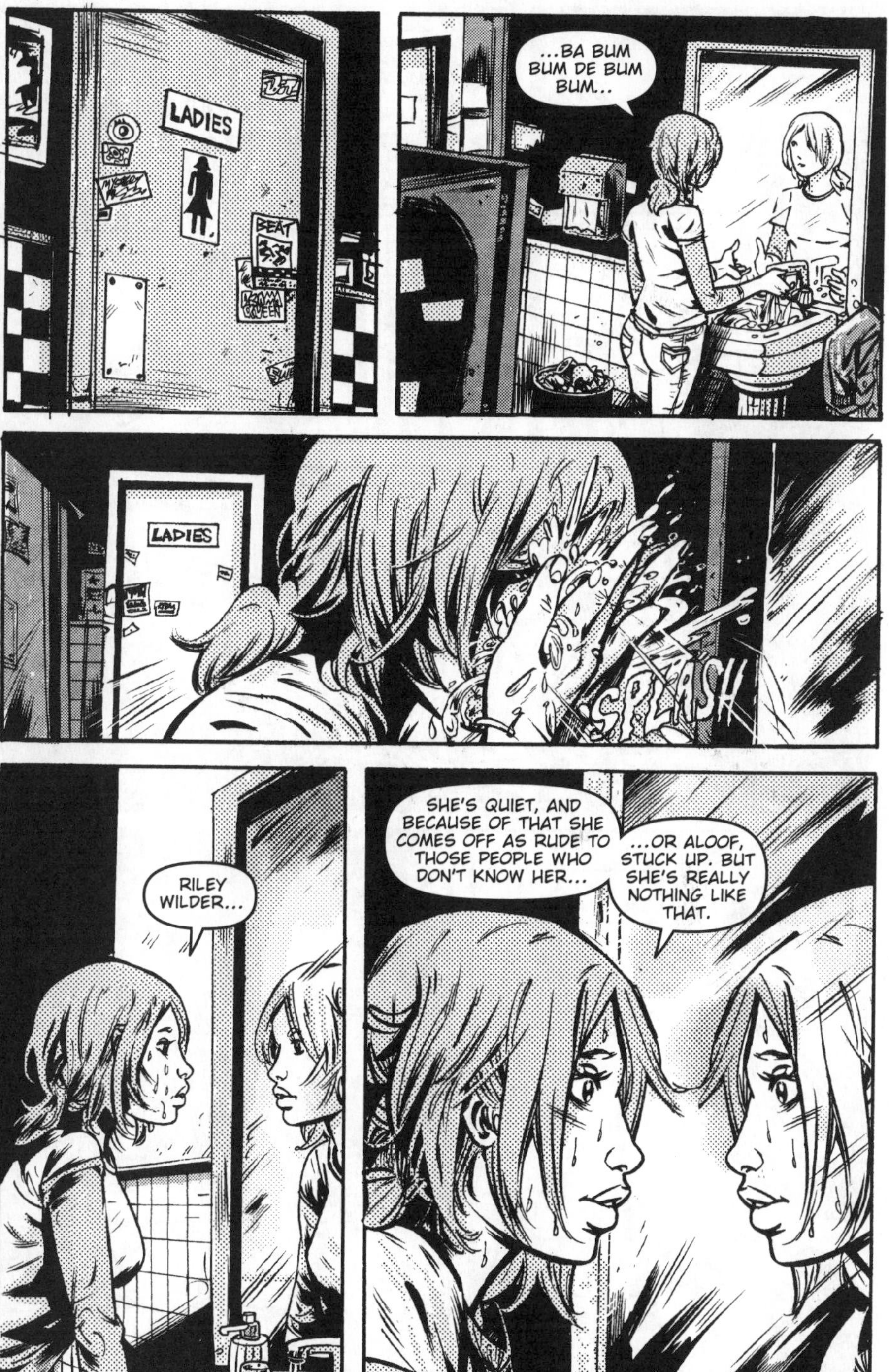
LADIES
BEAT
...BA BUM BUM DE BUM BUM...
LADIES
SPLASH
RILEY WILDER...
SHE'S QUIET, AND BECAUSE OF THAT SHE COMES OFF AS RUDE TO THOSE PEOPLE WHO DON'T KNOW HER...
...OR ALOOF, STUCK UP. BUT SHE'S REALLY NOTHING LIKE THAT.

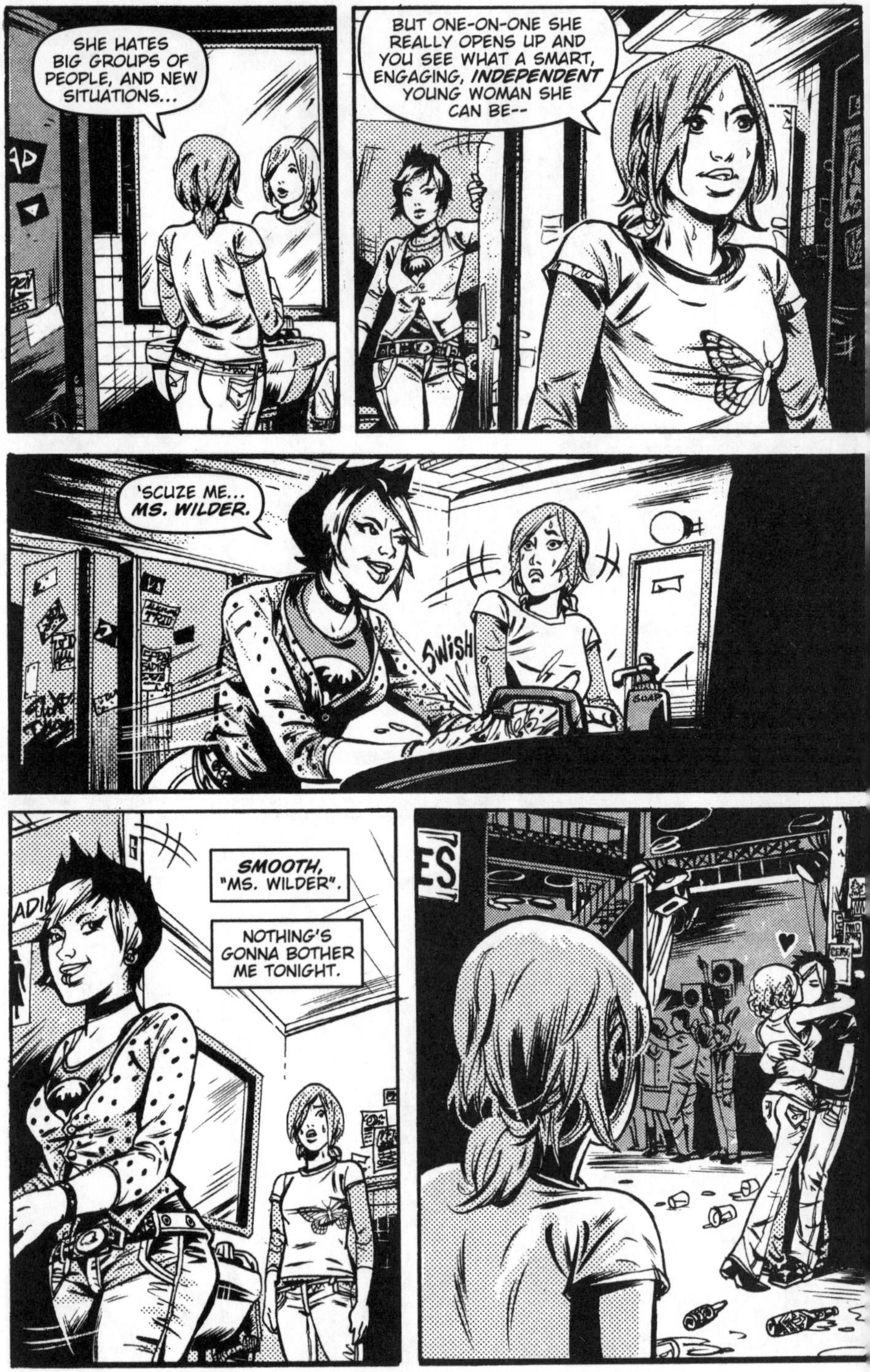
SHE HATES BIG GROUPS OF PEOPLE, AND NEW SITUATIONS...
BUT ONE-ON-ONE SHE REALLY OPENS UP AND YOU SEE WHAT A SMART, ENGAGING, *INDEPENDENT* YOUNG WOMAN SHE CAN BE--
'SCUZE ME... ***MS. WILDER.***
SWISH
SMOOTH, "MS. WILDER".
NOTHING'S GONNA BOTHER ME TONIGHT.

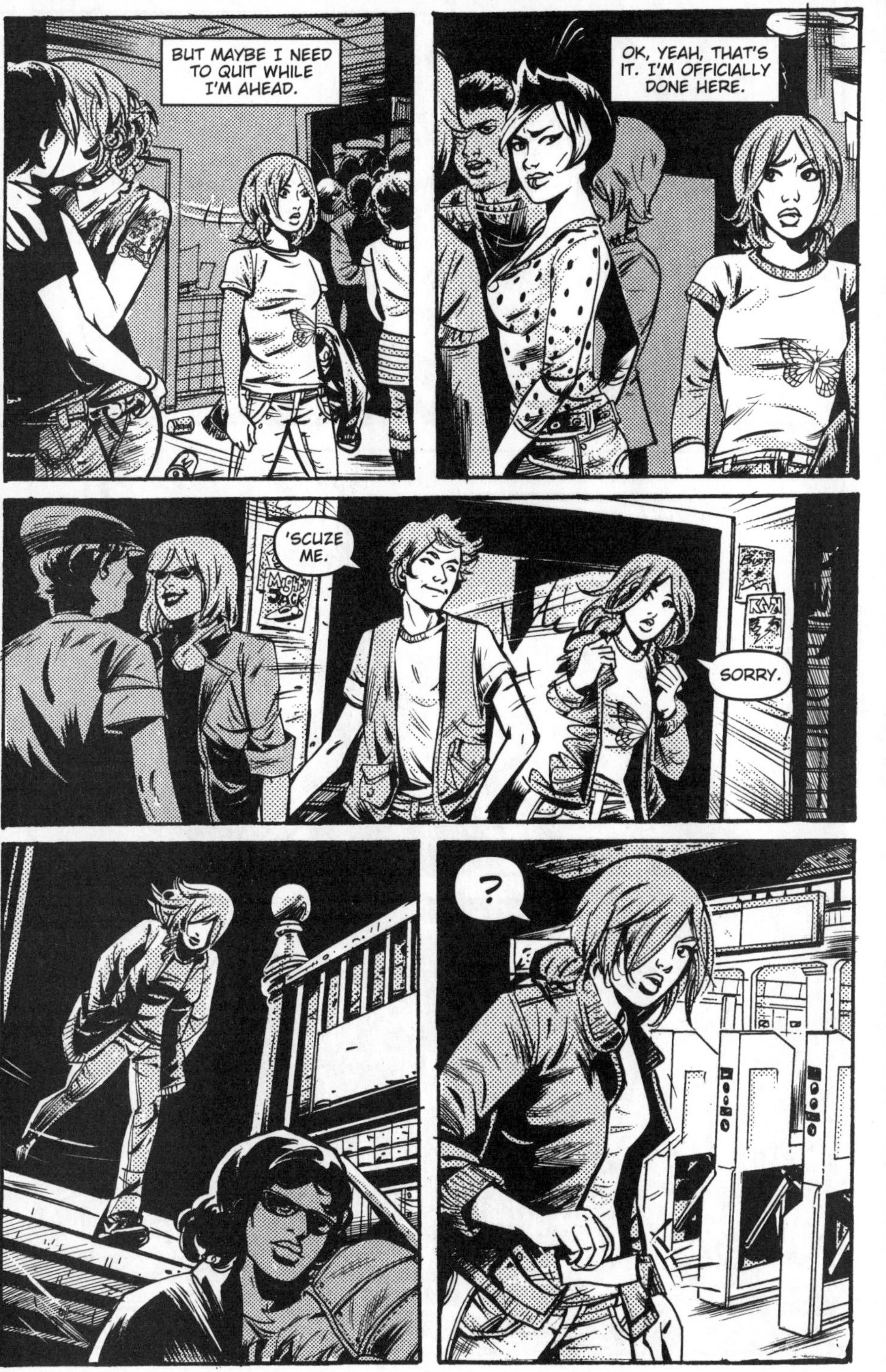
BUT MAYBE I NEED TO QUIT WHILE I'M AHEAD.
OK, YEAH, THAT'S IT. I'M OFFICIALLY DONE HERE.
'SCUZE ME.
SORRY.
?

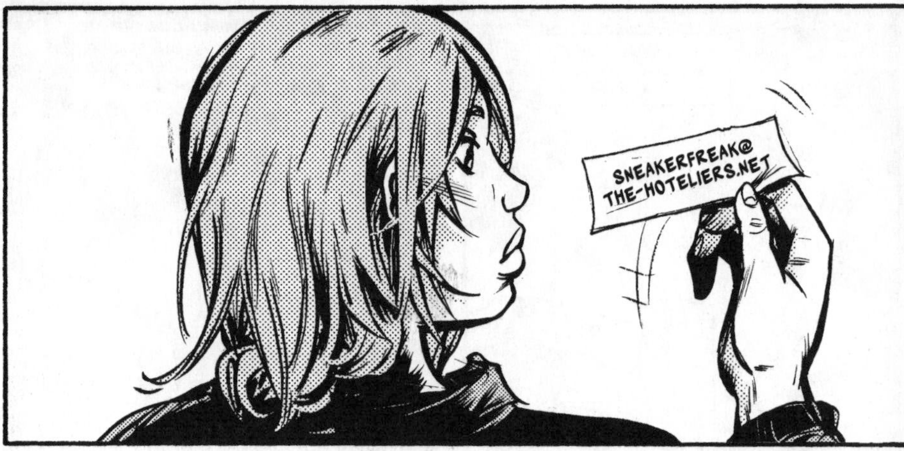
SNEAKERFREAK@
THE-HOTELIERS.NET

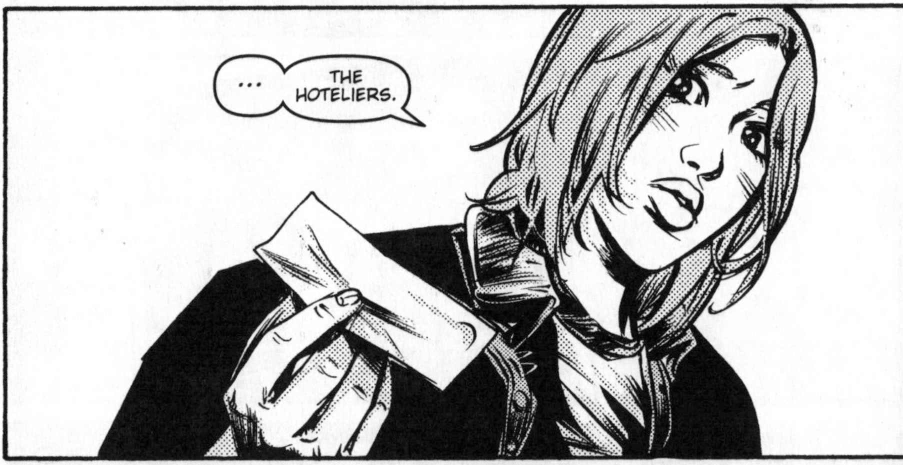
...
THE HOTELIERS.

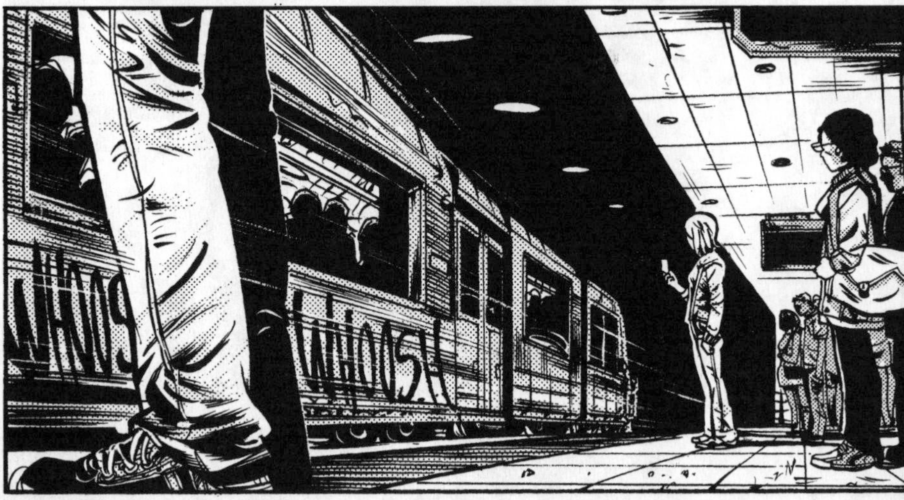

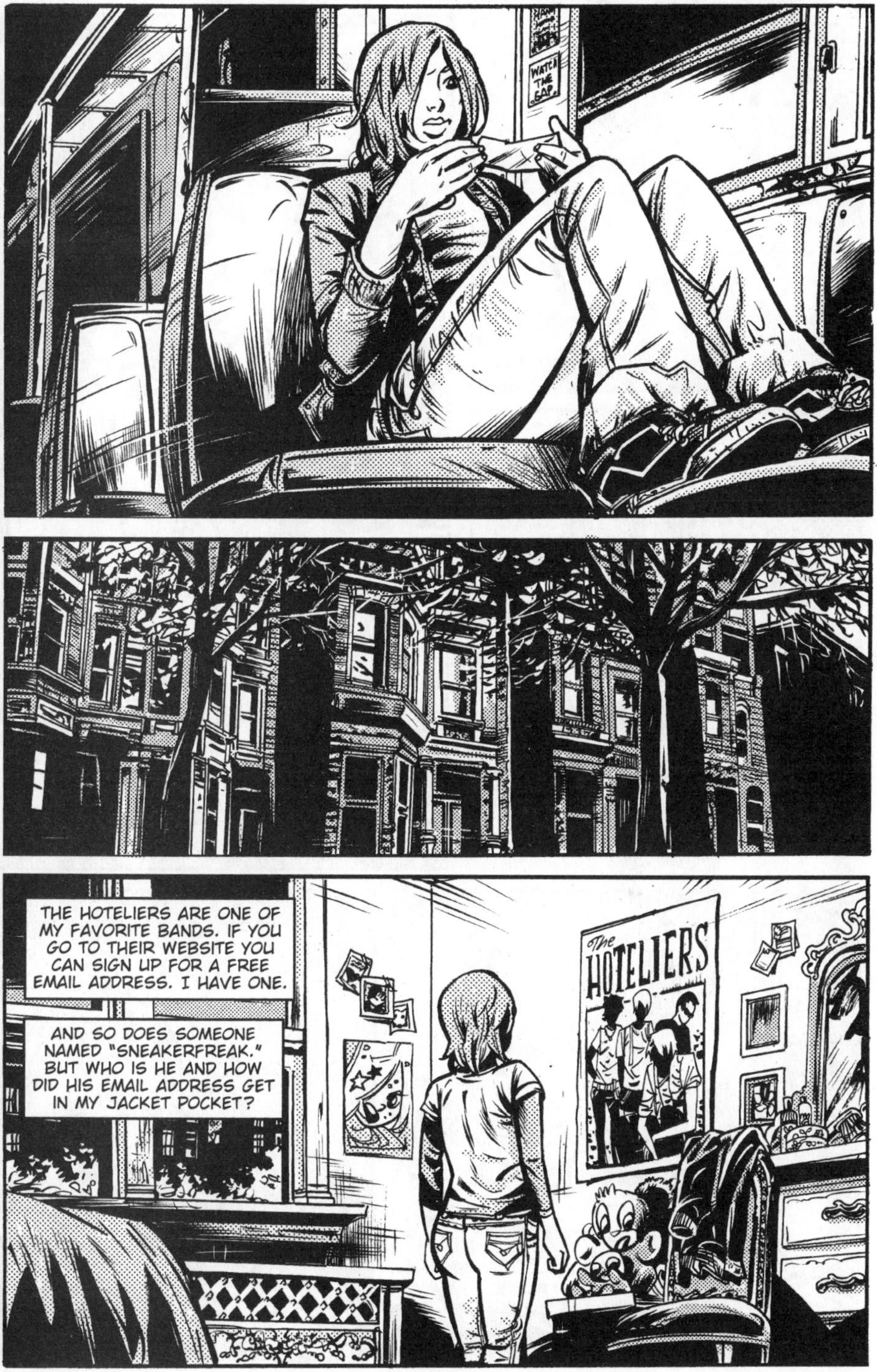
WATCH THE GAP
THE HOTELIERS ARE ONE OF MY FAVORITE BANDS. IF YOU GO TO THEIR WEBSITE YOU CAN SIGN UP FOR A FREE EMAIL ADDRESS. I HAVE ONE.
AND SO DOES SOMEONE NAMED "SNEAKERFREAK." BUT WHO IS HE AND HOW DID HIS EMAIL ADDRESS GET IN MY JACKET POCKET?
The HOTELIERS

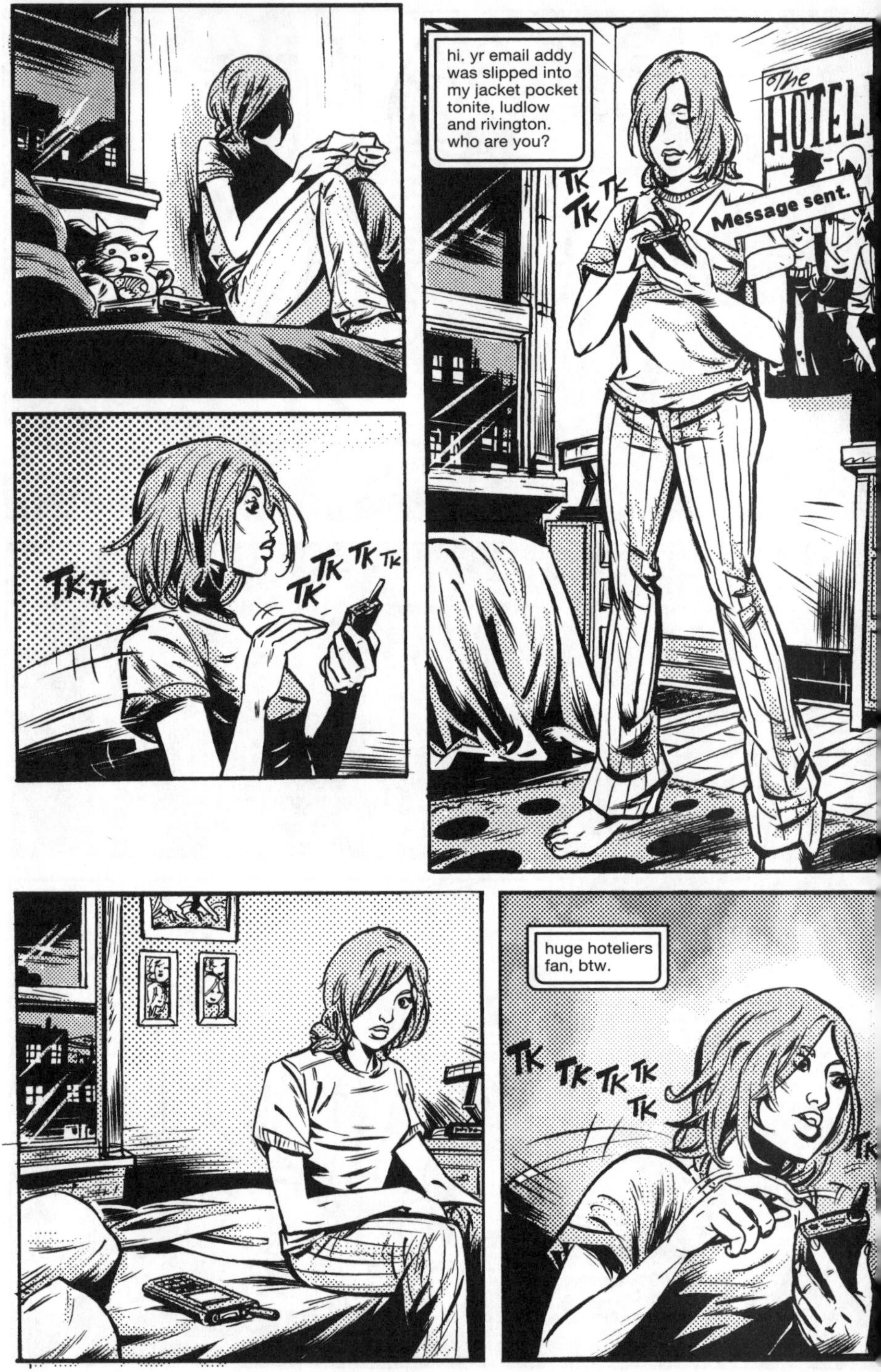
hi. yr email addy was slipped into my jacket pocket tonite, ludlow and rivington. who are you?
TK TK TK
Message sent.
The HOTEL
TK TK TK TK TK TK
huge hoteliers fan, btw.
TK TK TK TK TK

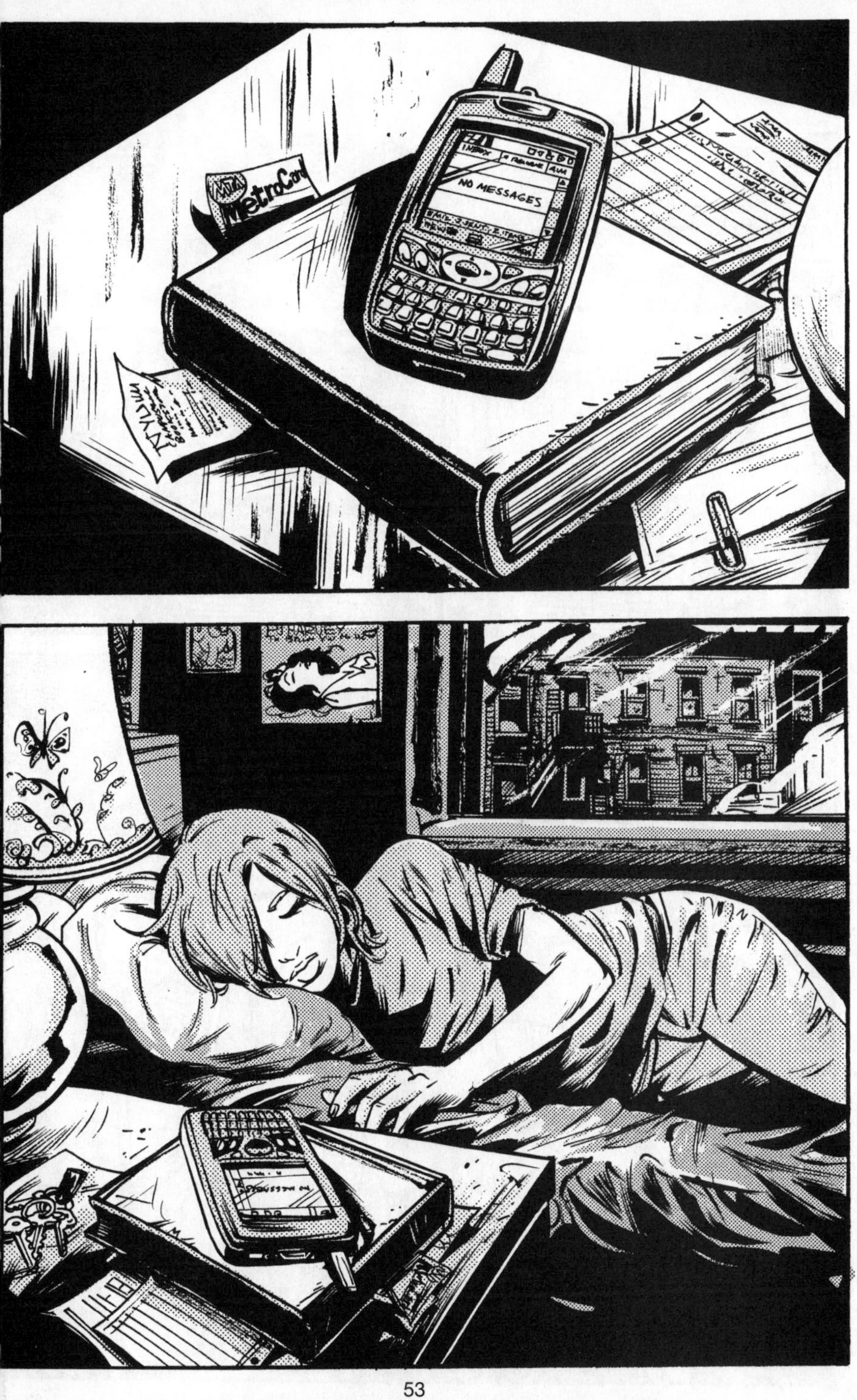
NO MESSAGES

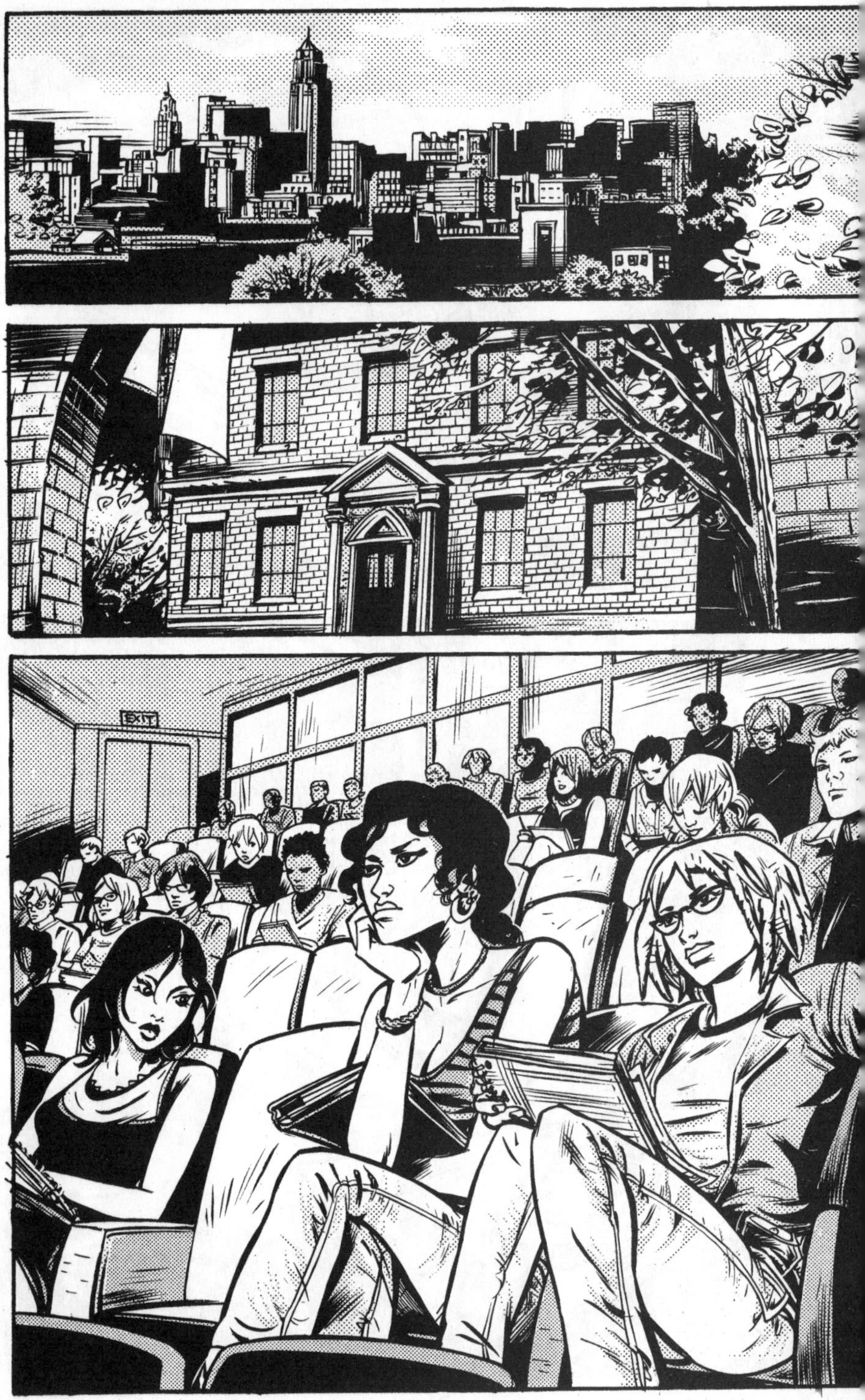
EXIT

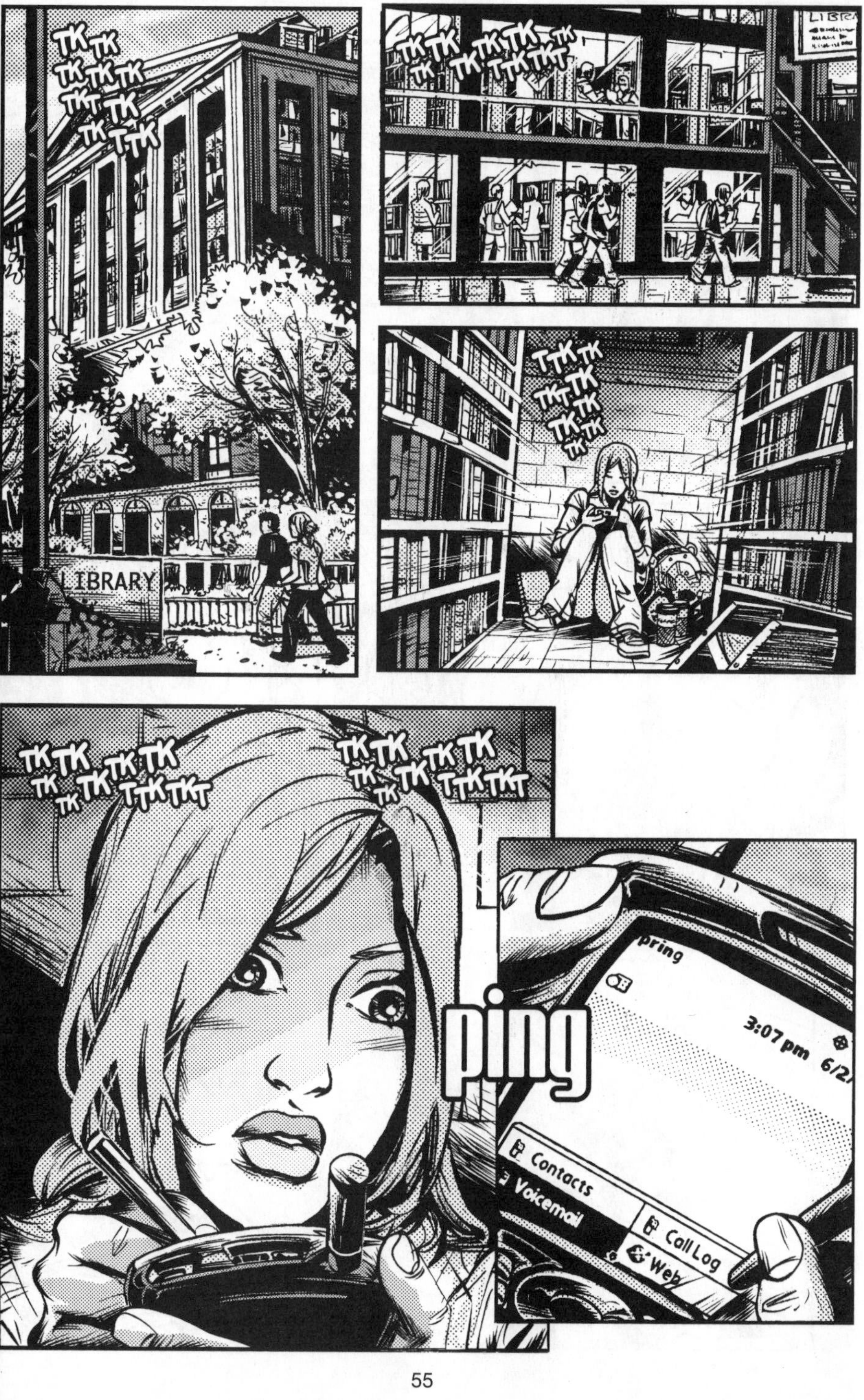
TK TK TK TK TK TKT TK TK TTK
LIBRARY
TK TK TK TK TK TK TK TK TTK TKT
LIBRA
TTK TK TKT TK TK TK TK TK
TK TK TK TK TK TK TK TK TTK TKT
TK TK TK TK TK TK TK TK TTK TKT
pring
3:07 pm
Contacts
Voicemail
Call Log
Web
ping

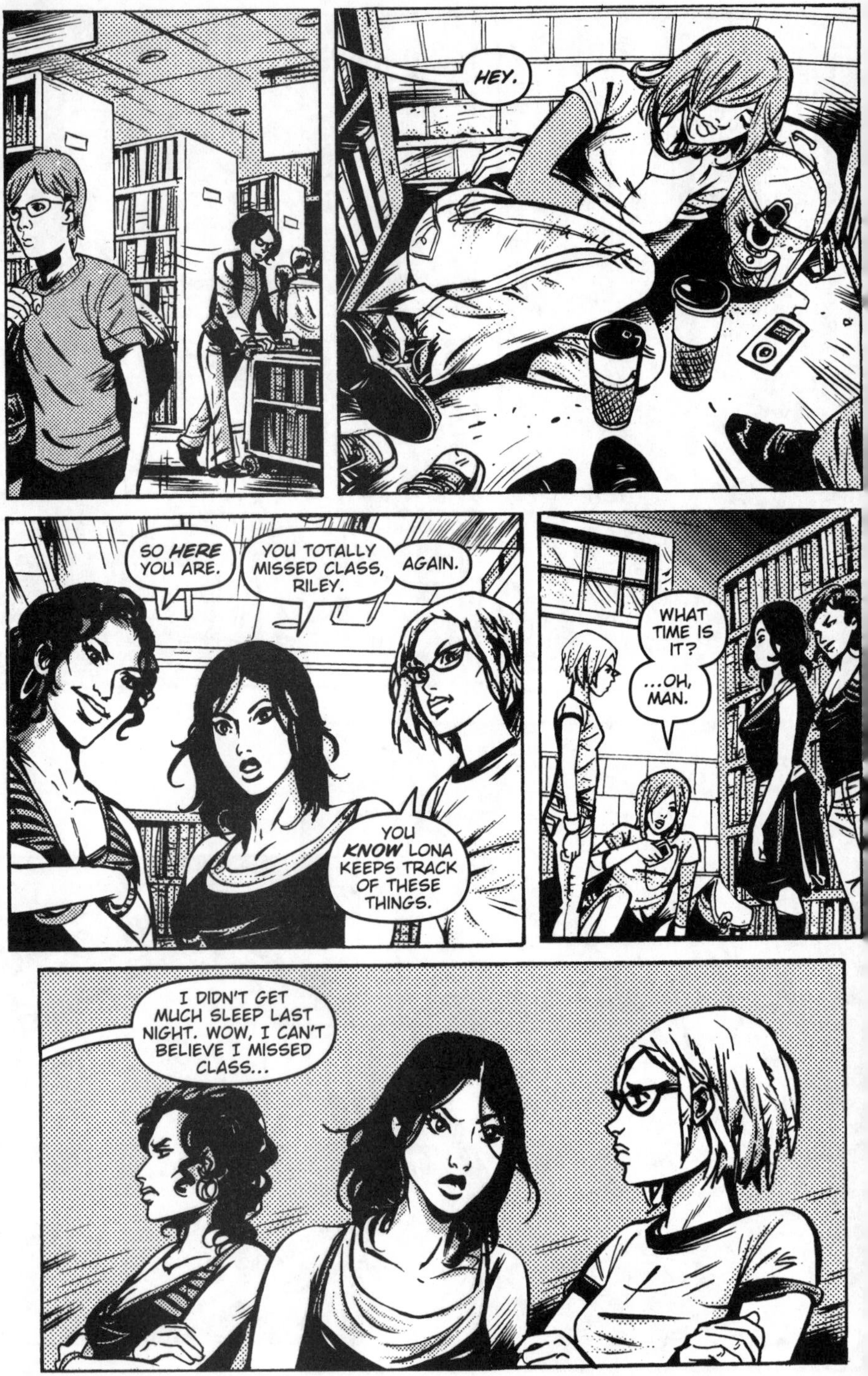
HEY.
SO HERE YOU ARE.
YOU TOTALLY MISSED CLASS, RILEY.
AGAIN.
YOU KNOW LONA KEEPS TRACK OF THESE THINGS.
WHAT TIME IS IT?
...OH, MAN.
I DIDN'T GET MUCH SLEEP LAST NIGHT. WOW, I CAN'T BELIEVE I MISSED CLASS...

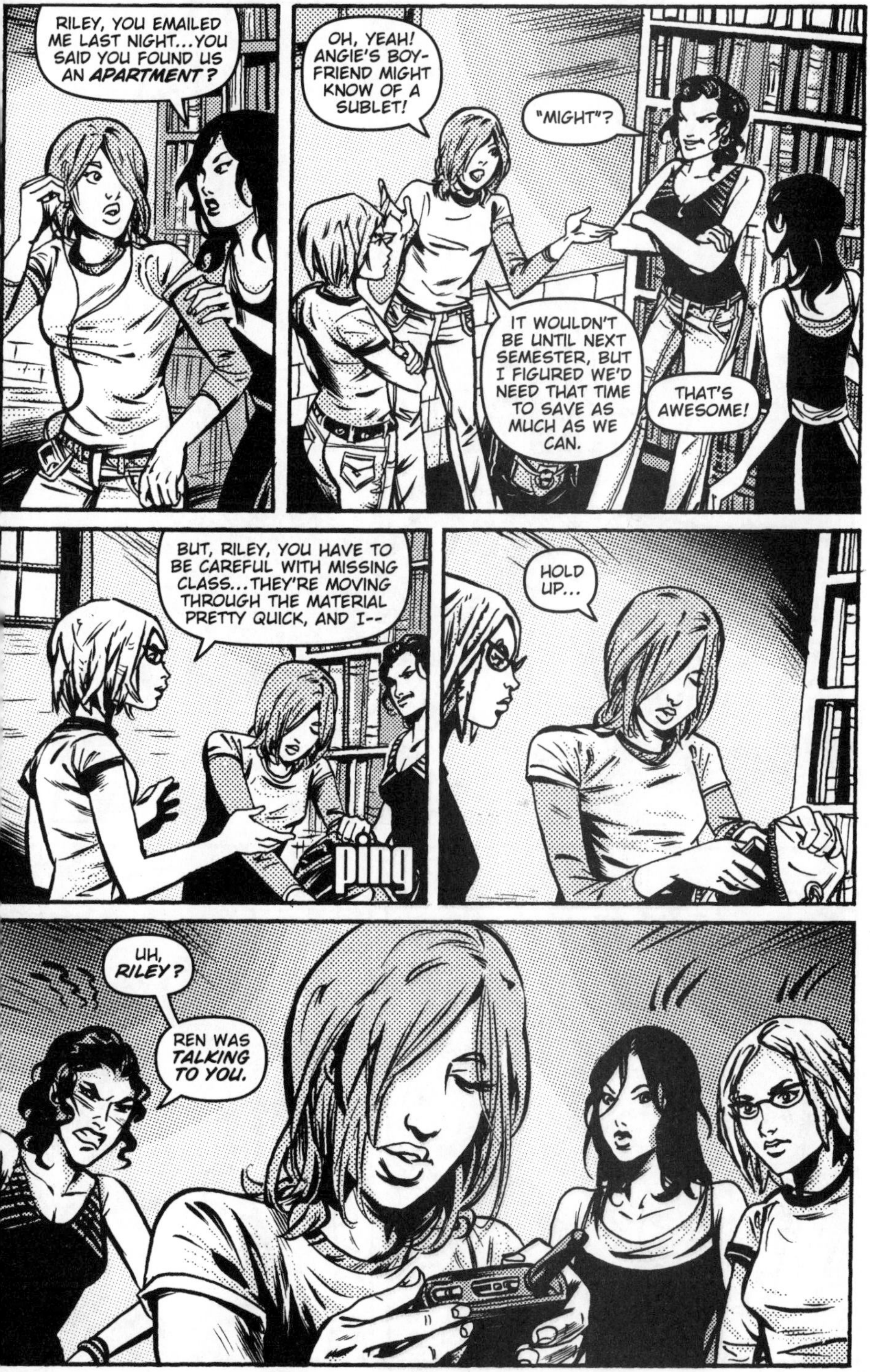
RILEY, YOU EMAILED ME LAST NIGHT...YOU SAID YOU FOUND US AN *APARTMENT*?
OH, YEAH! ANGIE'S BOY-FRIEND MIGHT KNOW OF A SUBLET!
"MIGHT"?
IT WOULDN'T BE UNTIL NEXT SEMESTER, BUT I FIGURED WE'D NEED THAT TIME TO SAVE AS MUCH AS WE CAN.
THAT'S AWESOME!
BUT, RILEY, YOU HAVE TO BE CAREFUL WITH MISSING CLASS...THEY'RE MOVING THROUGH THE MATERIAL PRETTY QUICK, AND I--
ping
HOLD UP...
UH, *RILEY*?
REN WAS *TALKING TO YOU.*

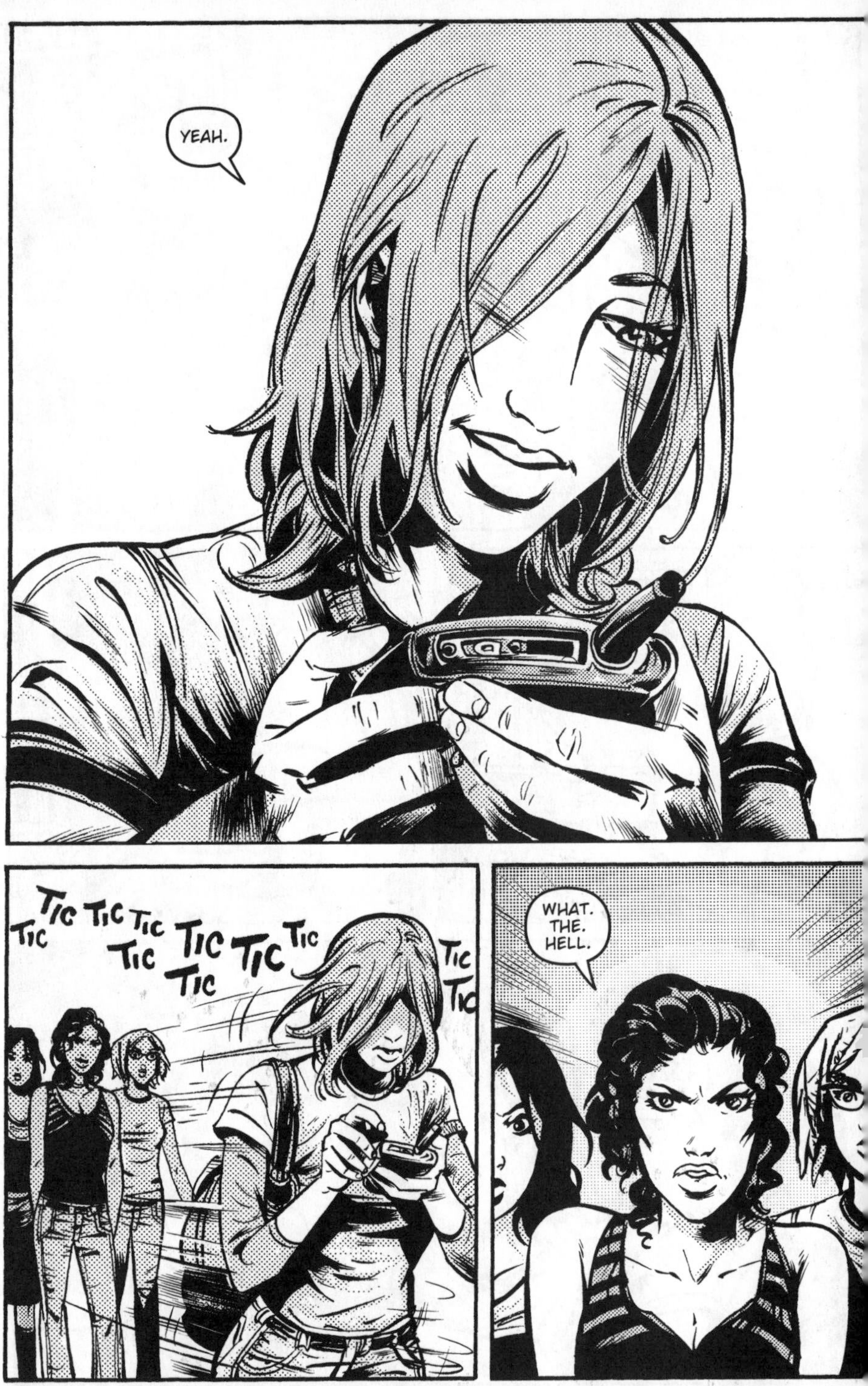
YEAH.
TIC TIC TIC TIC TIC TIC TIC TIC TIC TIC TIC TIC
WHAT. THE. HELL.

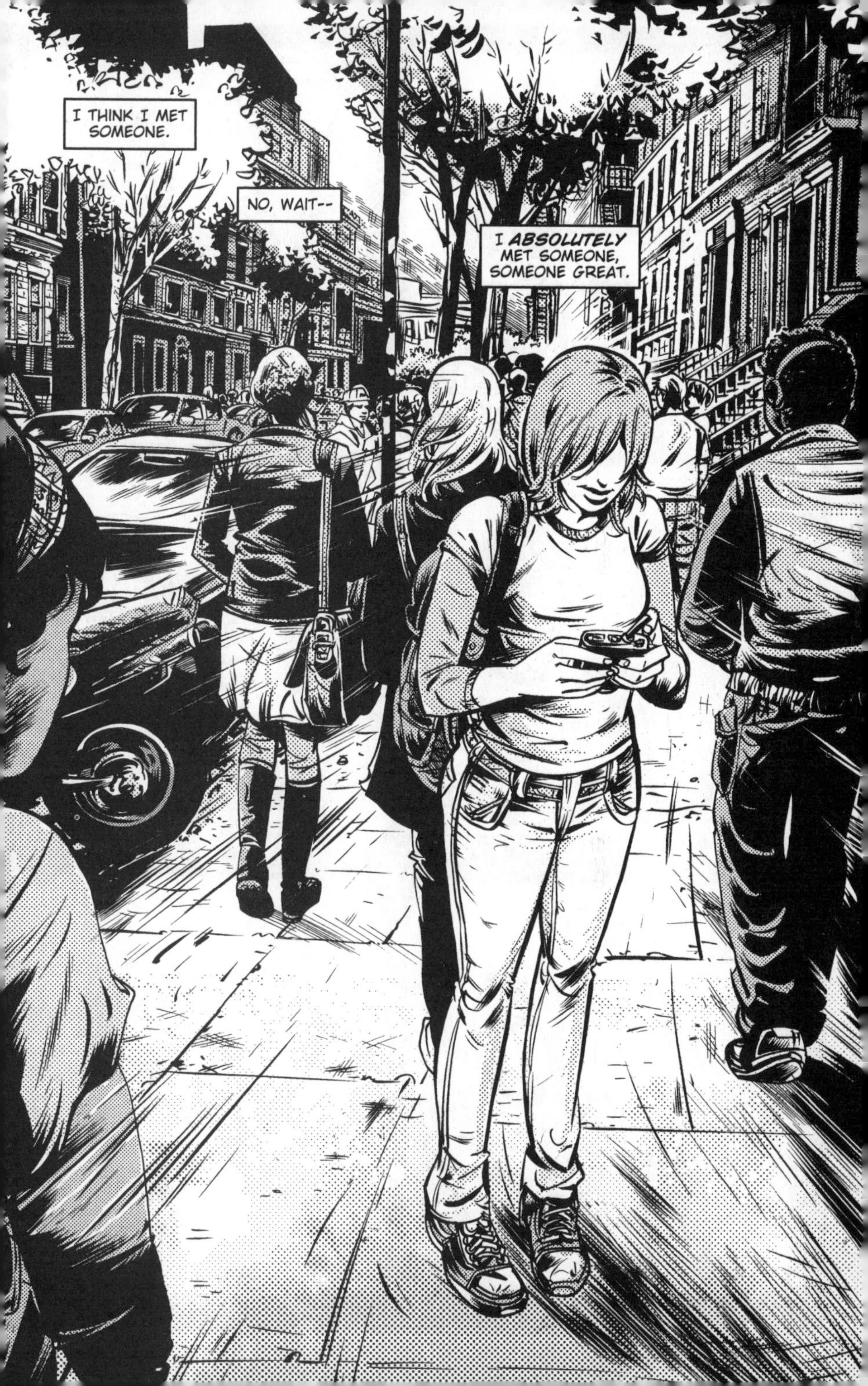
I THINK I MET SOMEONE.
NO, WAIT--
I ABSOLUTELY MET SOMEONE, SOMEONE GREAT.

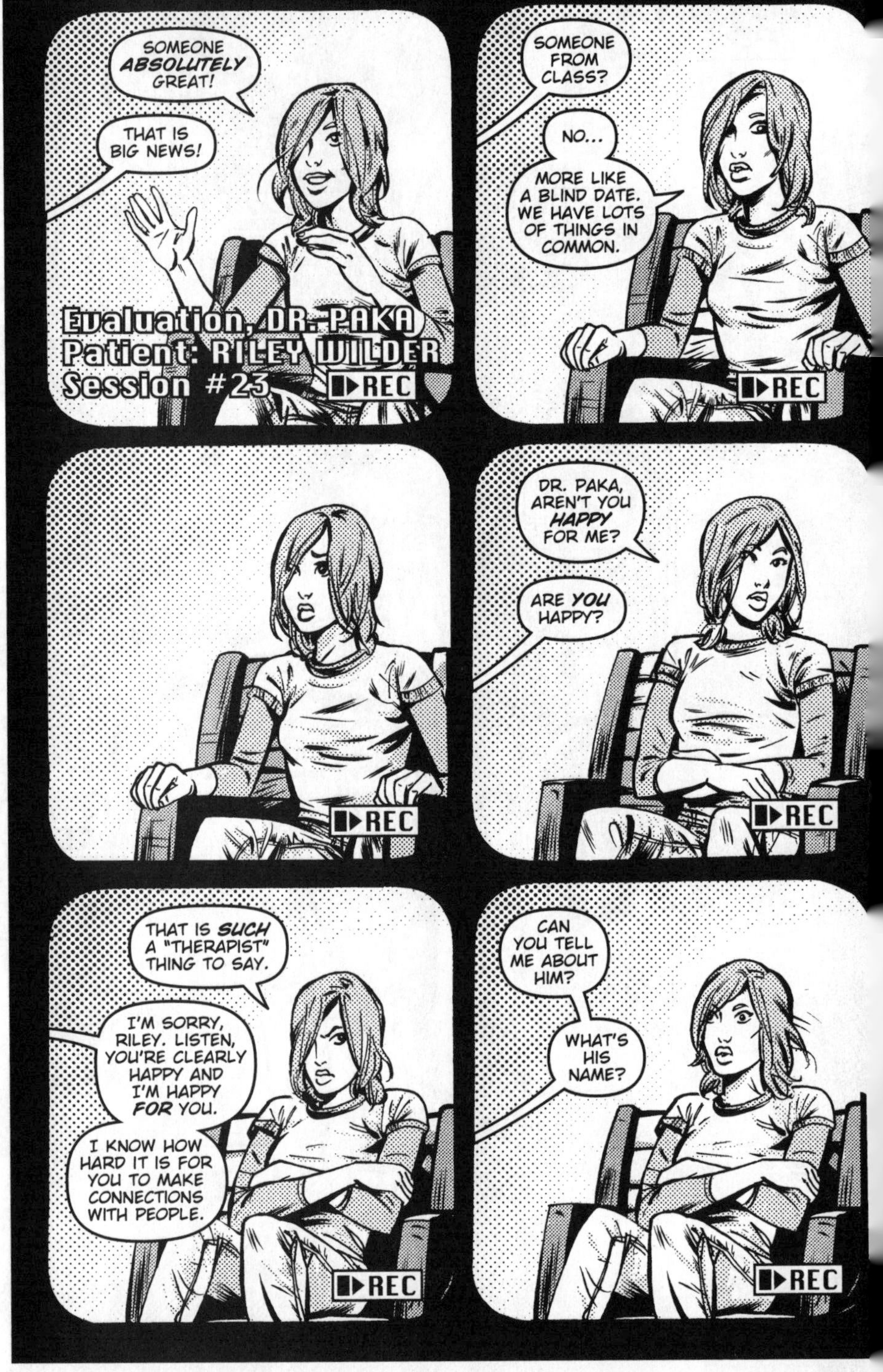
SOMEONE ABSOLUTELY GREAT!
THAT IS BIG NEWS!
Evaluation, DR. PAKA
Patient: RILEY WILDER
Session #23
REC
SOMEONE FROM CLASS?
NO...
MORE LIKE A BLIND DATE. WE HAVE LOTS OF THINGS IN COMMON.
REC
REC
DR. PAKA, AREN'T YOU HAPPY FOR ME?
ARE YOU HAPPY?
REC
THAT IS SUCH A "THERAPIST" THING TO SAY.
I'M SORRY, RILEY. LISTEN, YOU'RE CLEARLY HAPPY AND I'M HAPPY FOR YOU.
I KNOW HOW HARD IT IS FOR YOU TO MAKE CONNECTIONS WITH PEOPLE.
REC
CAN YOU TELL ME ABOUT HIM?
WHAT'S HIS NAME?
REC

Chapter 3
Love & Communication

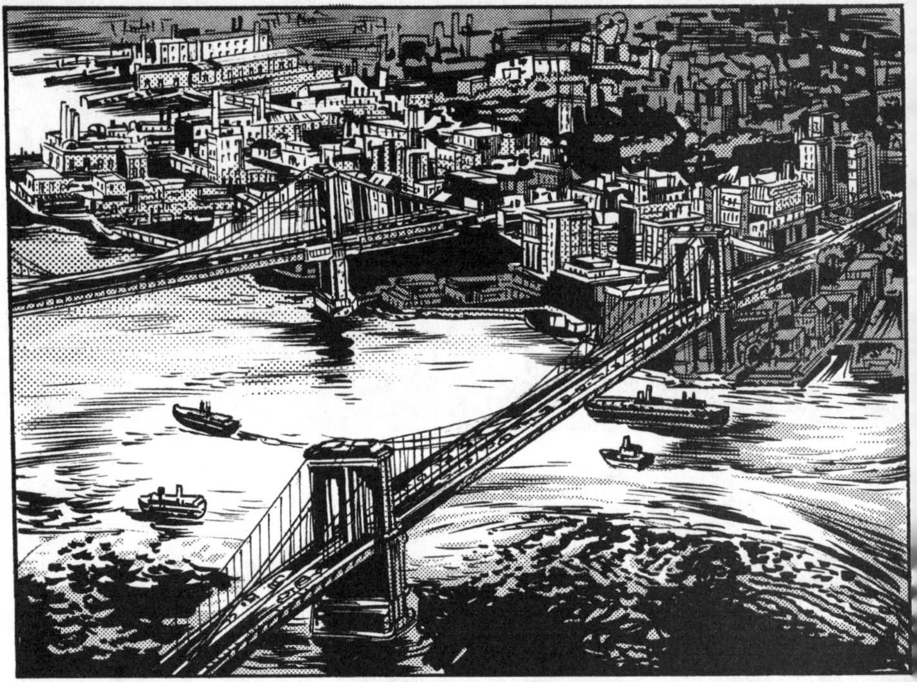

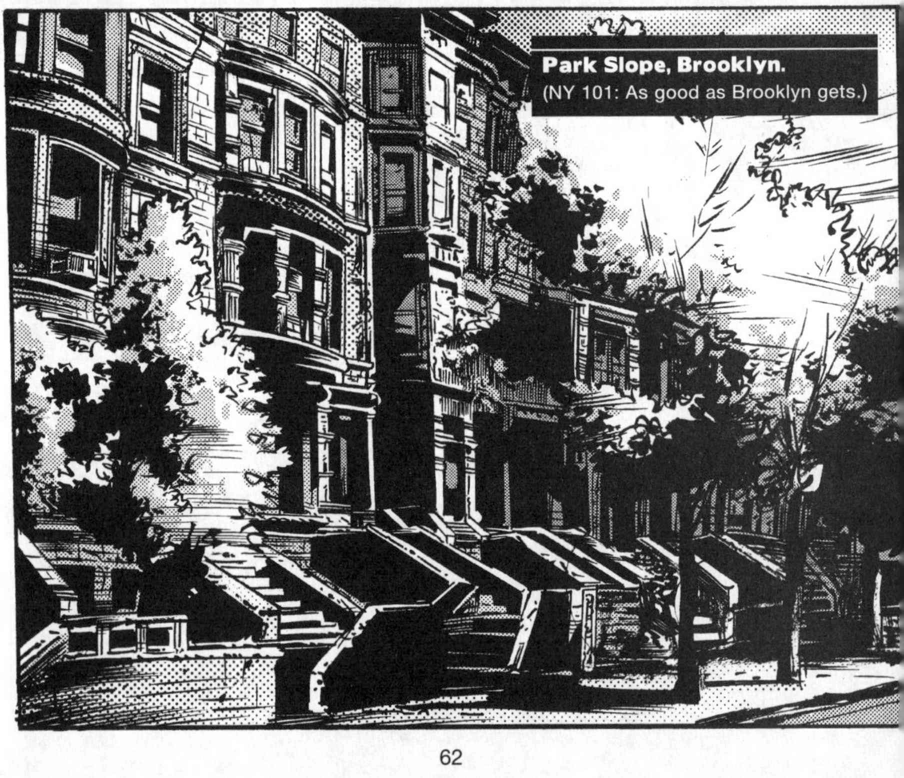
Park Slope, Brooklyn.
(NY 101: As good as Brooklyn gets.)

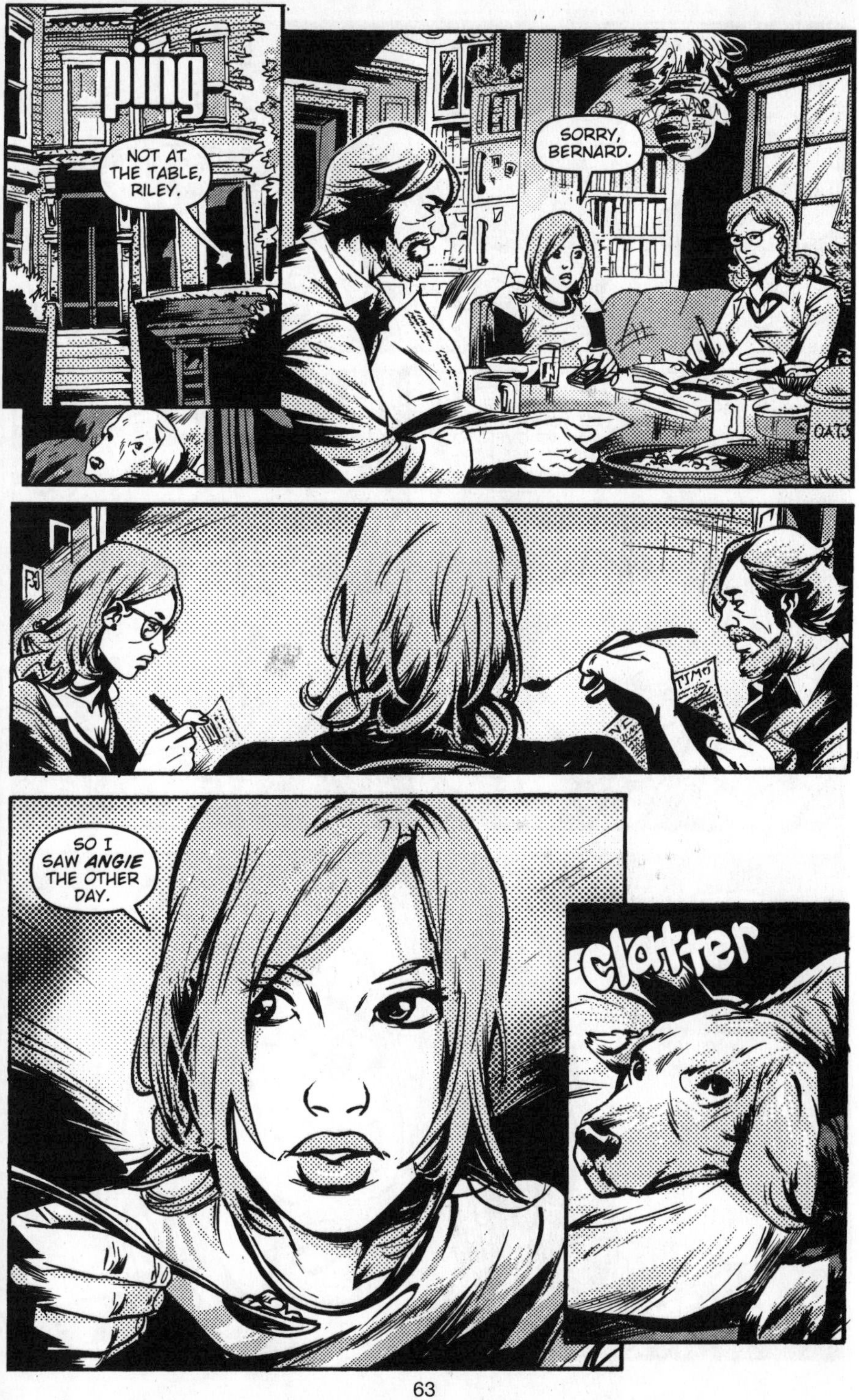
ping
NOT AT THE TABLE, RILEY.
SORRY, BERNARD.
OATS
SO I SAW ANGIE THE OTHER DAY.
clatter

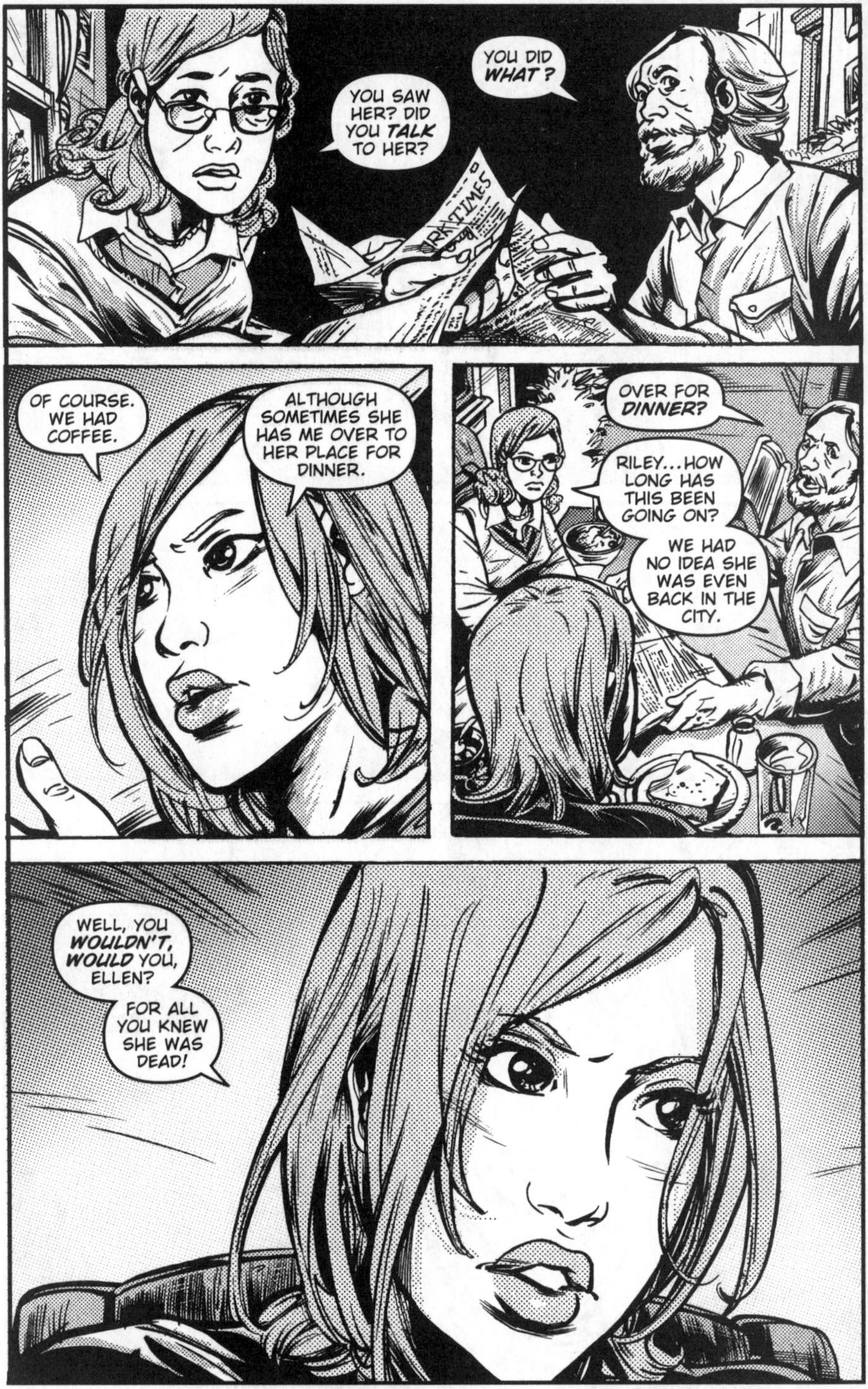
YOU SAW HER? DID YOU TALK TO HER?
YOU DID WHAT?
RA TIMES
OF COURSE. WE HAD COFFEE.
ALTHOUGH SOMETIMES SHE HAS ME OVER TO HER PLACE FOR DINNER.
OVER FOR DINNER?
RILEY...HOW LONG HAS THIS BEEN GOING ON?
WE HAD NO IDEA SHE WAS EVEN BACK IN THE CITY.
WELL, YOU WOULDN'T, WOULD YOU, ELLEN?
FOR ALL YOU KNEW SHE WAS DEAD!

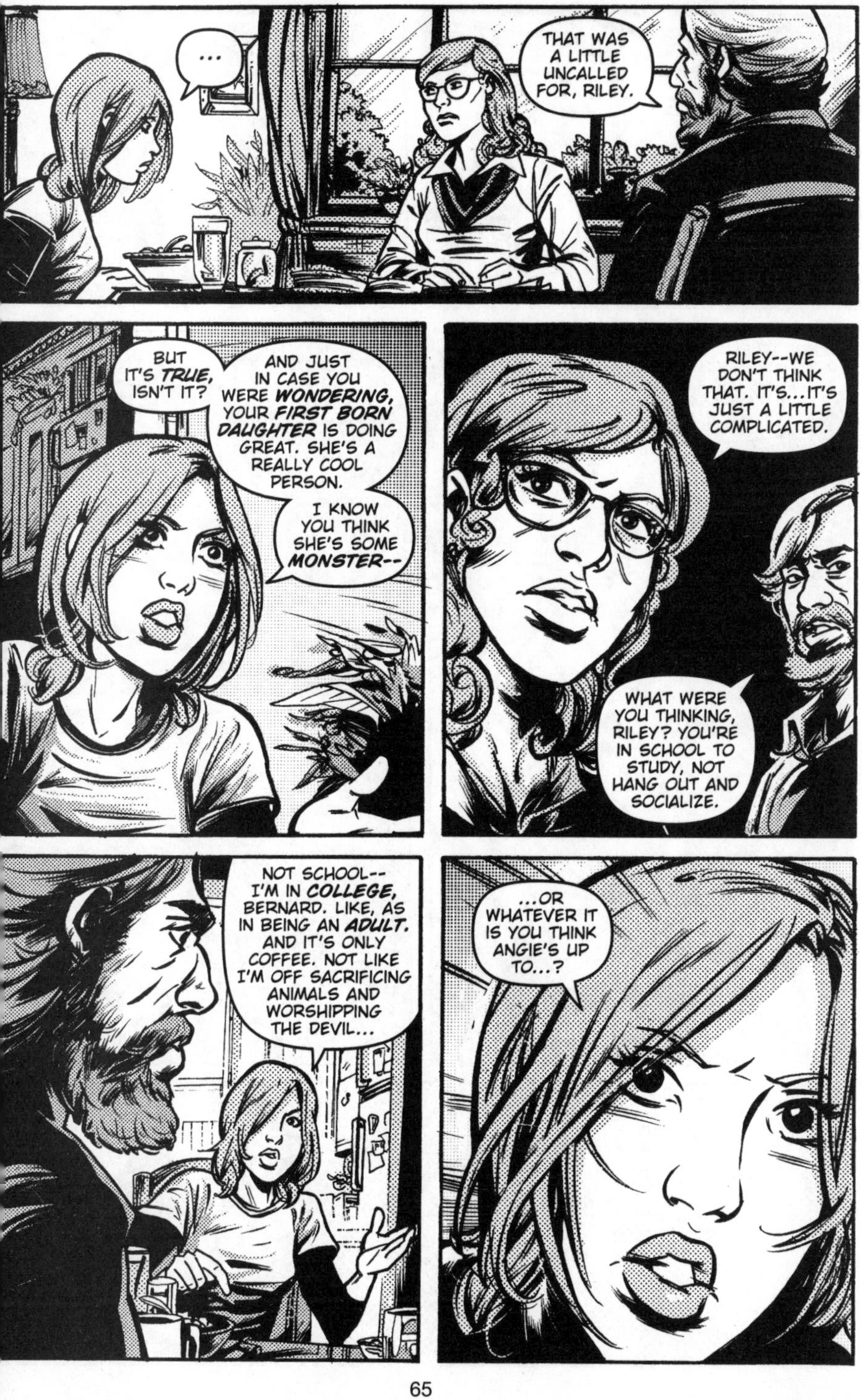
...
THAT WAS A LITTLE UNCALLED FOR, RILEY.
BUT IT'S *TRUE,* ISN'T IT?
AND JUST IN CASE YOU WERE *WONDERING,* YOUR *FIRST BORN DAUGHTER* IS DOING GREAT. SHE'S A REALLY COOL PERSON.
I KNOW YOU THINK SHE'S SOME *MONSTER--*
RILEY--WE DON'T THINK THAT. IT'S...IT'S JUST A LITTLE COMPLICATED.
WHAT WERE YOU THINKING, RILEY? YOU'RE IN SCHOOL TO STUDY, NOT HANG OUT AND SOCIALIZE.
NOT SCHOOL-- I'M IN *COLLEGE,* BERNARD. LIKE, AS IN BEING AN *ADULT.* AND IT'S ONLY COFFEE. NOT LIKE I'M OFF SACRIFICING ANIMALS AND WORSHIPPING THE DEVIL...
...OR WHATEVER IT IS YOU THINK ANGIE'S UP TO...?

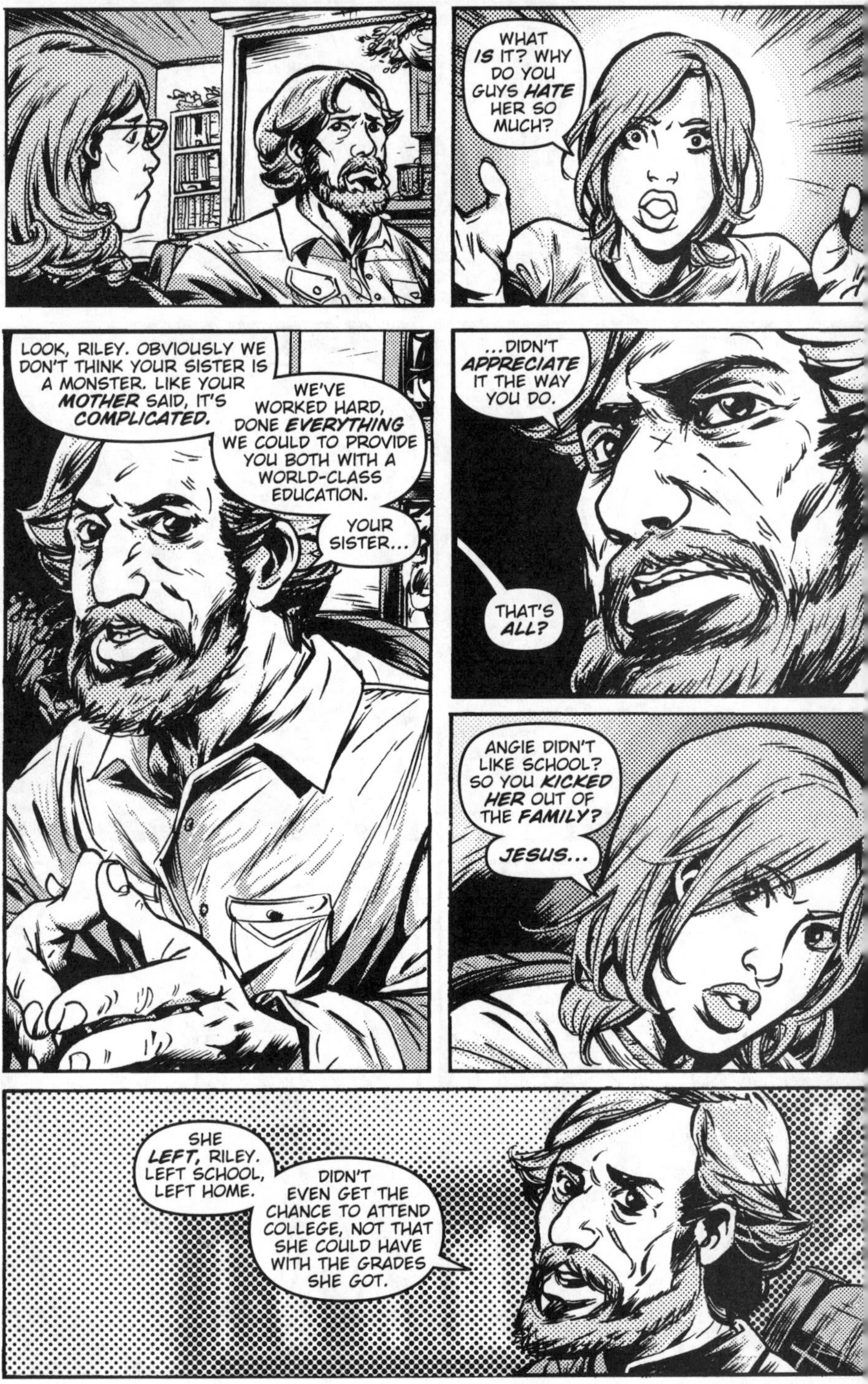
WHAT *IS* IT? WHY DO YOU GUYS *HATE* HER SO MUCH?
LOOK, RILEY. OBVIOUSLY WE DON'T THINK YOUR SISTER IS A MONSTER. LIKE YOUR *MOTHER* SAID, IT'S *COMPLICATED.*
WE'VE WORKED HARD, DONE *EVERYTHING* WE COULD TO PROVIDE YOU BOTH WITH A WORLD-CLASS EDUCATION.
YOUR SISTER...
...DIDN'T *APPRECIATE* IT THE WAY YOU DO.
THAT'S *ALL?*
ANGIE DIDN'T LIKE SCHOOL? SO YOU *KICKED HER* OUT OF THE *FAMILY?*
JESUS...
SHE *LEFT,* RILEY. LEFT SCHOOL, LEFT HOME.
DIDN'T EVEN GET THE CHANCE TO ATTEND COLLEGE, NOT THAT SHE COULD HAVE WITH THE GRADES SHE GOT.

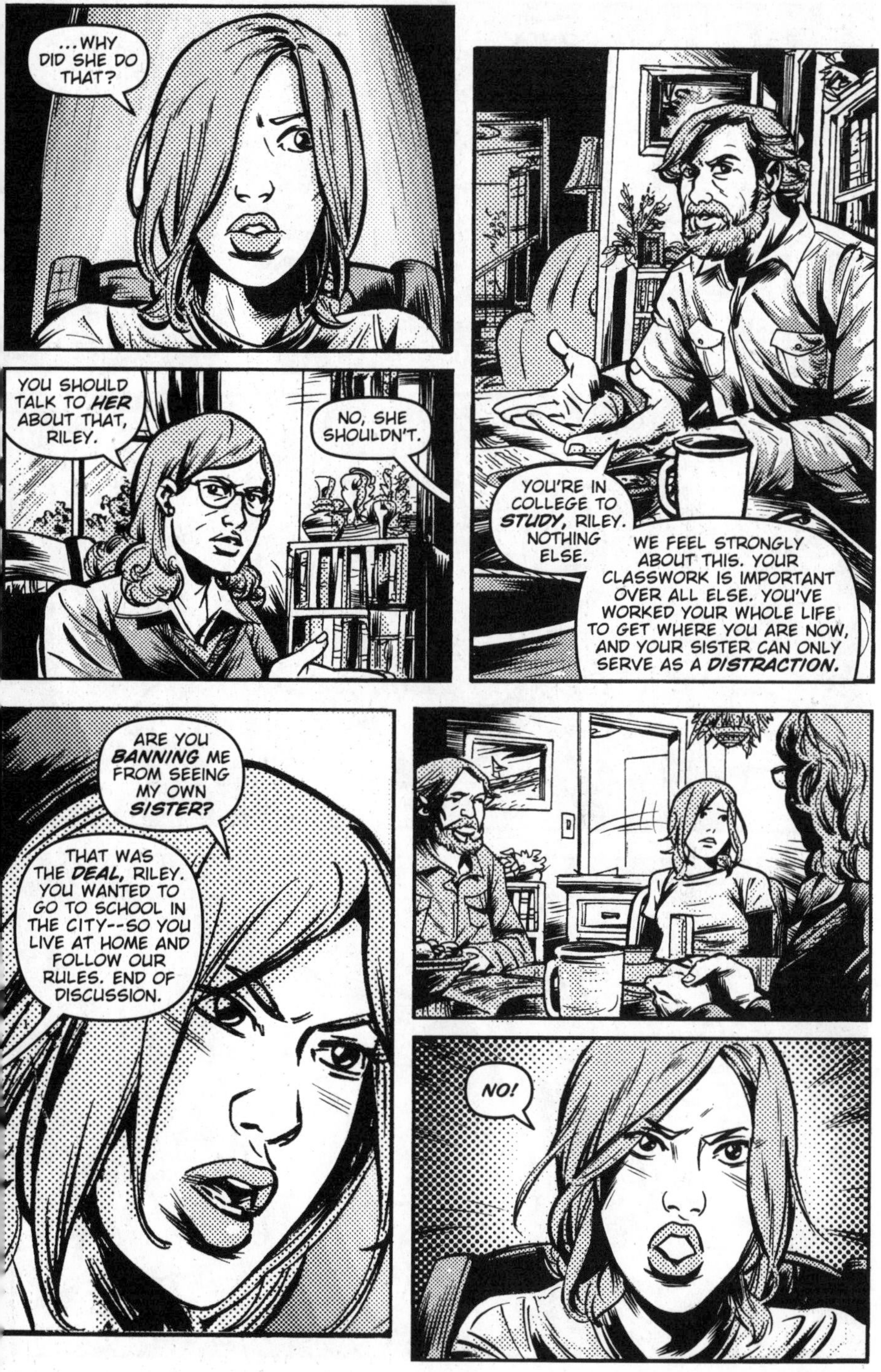
...WHY DID SHE DO THAT?
YOU SHOULD TALK TO HER ABOUT THAT, RILEY.
NO, SHE SHOULDN'T.
YOU'RE IN COLLEGE TO STUDY, RILEY. NOTHING ELSE.
WE FEEL STRONGLY ABOUT THIS. YOUR CLASSWORK IS IMPORTANT OVER ALL ELSE. YOU'VE WORKED YOUR WHOLE LIFE TO GET WHERE YOU ARE NOW, AND YOUR SISTER CAN ONLY SERVE AS A DISTRACTION.
ARE YOU BANNING ME FROM SEEING MY OWN SISTER?
THAT WAS THE DEAL, RILEY. YOU WANTED TO GO TO SCHOOL IN THE CITY--SO YOU LIVE AT HOME AND FOLLOW OUR RULES. END OF DISCUSSION.
NO!

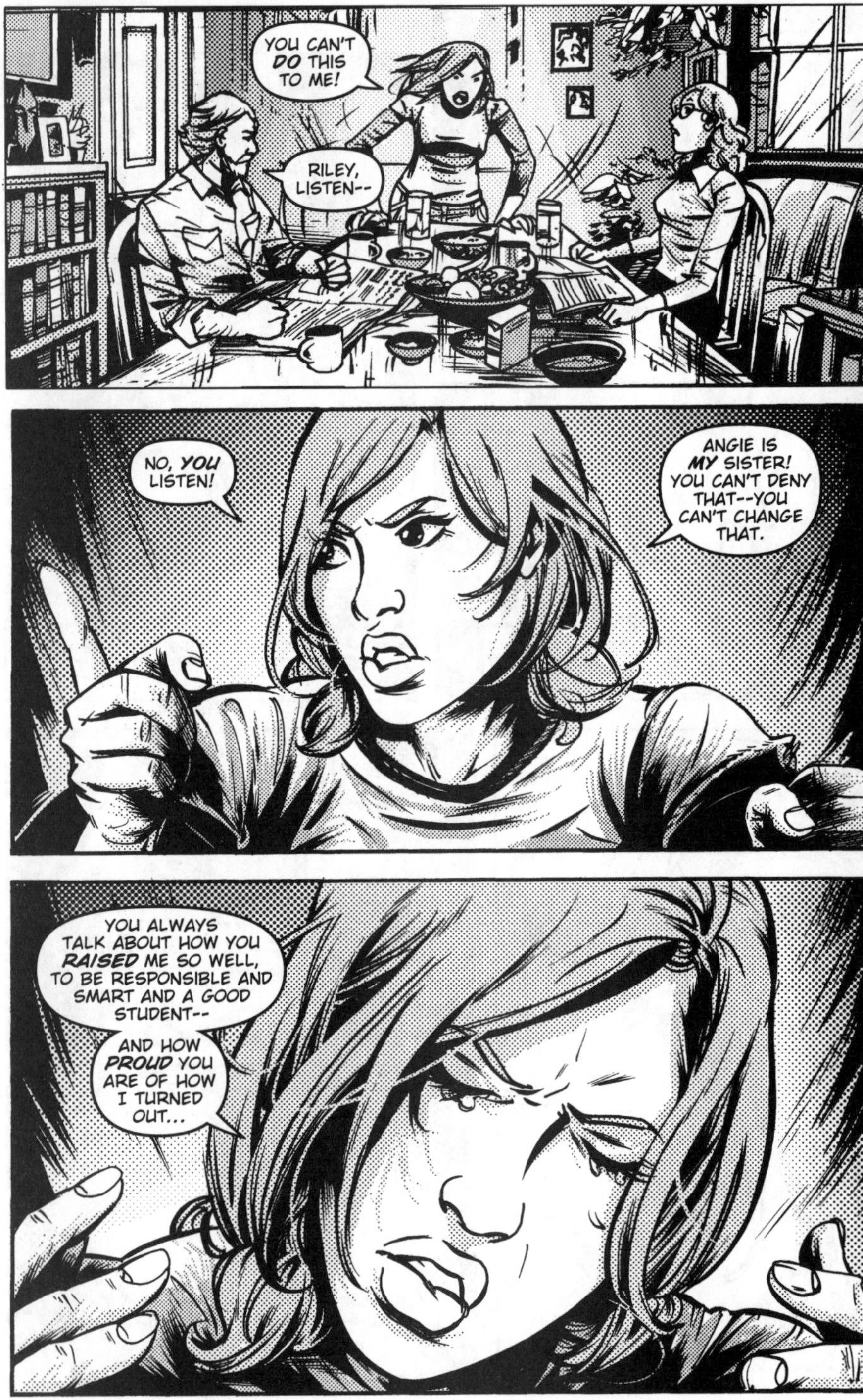
YOU CAN'T DO THIS TO ME!
RILEY, LISTEN--
NO, YOU LISTEN!
ANGIE IS MY SISTER! YOU CAN'T DENY THAT--YOU CAN'T CHANGE THAT.
YOU ALWAYS TALK ABOUT HOW YOU RAISED ME SO WELL, TO BE RESPONSIBLE AND SMART AND A GOOD STUDENT--
AND HOW PROUD YOU ARE OF HOW I TURNED OUT...

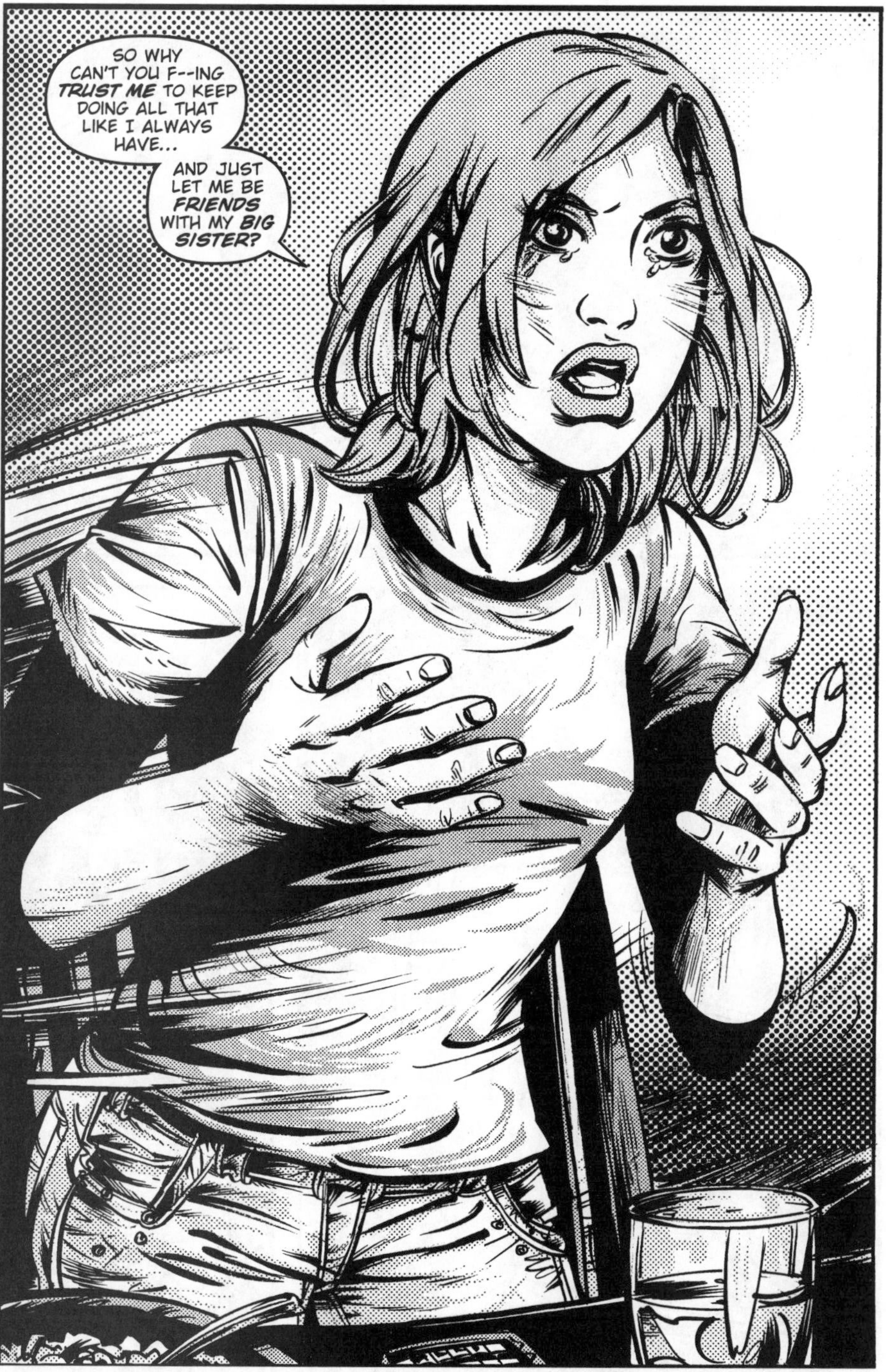
SO WHY CAN'T YOU F--ING TRUST ME TO KEEP DOING ALL THAT LIKE I ALWAYS HAVE...
AND JUST LET ME BE FRIENDS WITH MY BIG SISTER?

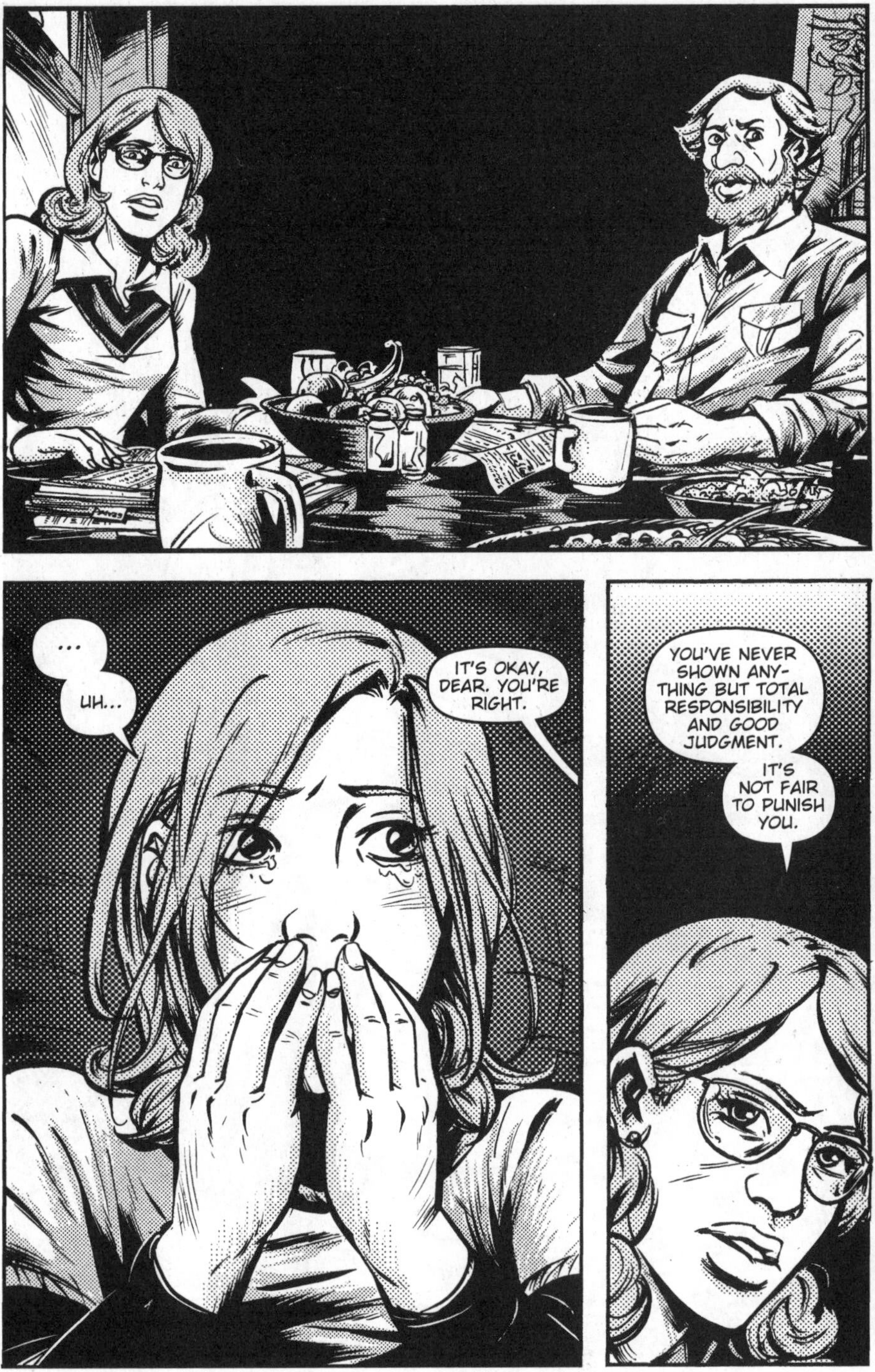
...
UH...
IT'S OKAY, DEAR. YOU'RE RIGHT.
YOU'VE NEVER SHOWN ANY-THING BUT TOTAL RESPONSIBILITY AND GOOD JUDGMENT.
IT'S NOT FAIR TO PUNISH YOU.

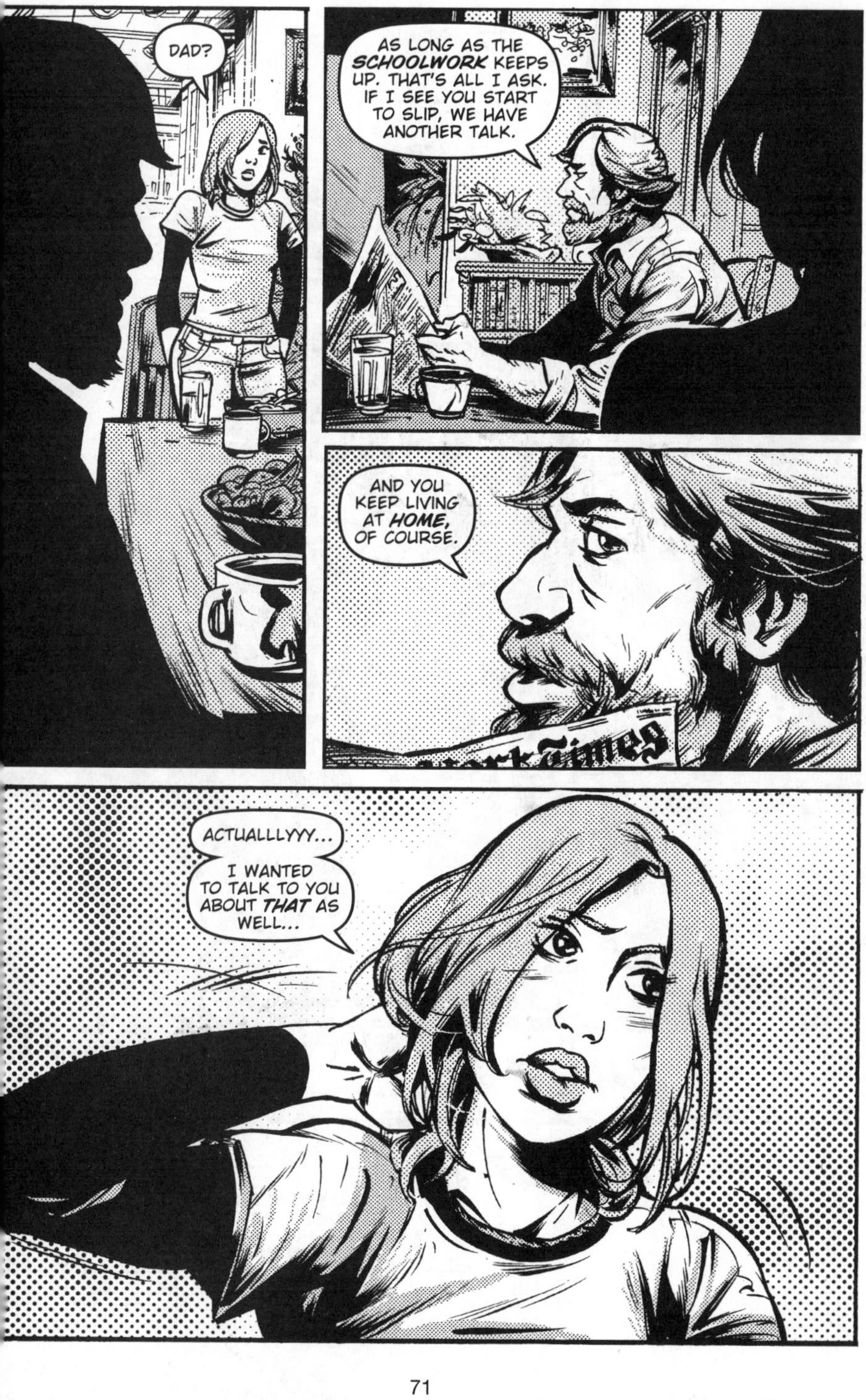
DAD?
AS LONG AS THE SCHOOLWORK KEEPS UP. THAT'S ALL I ASK. IF I SEE YOU START TO SLIP, WE HAVE ANOTHER TALK.
AND YOU KEEP LIVING AT HOME, OF COURSE.
ACTUALLLYYY...
I WANTED TO TALK TO YOU ABOUT THAT AS WELL...

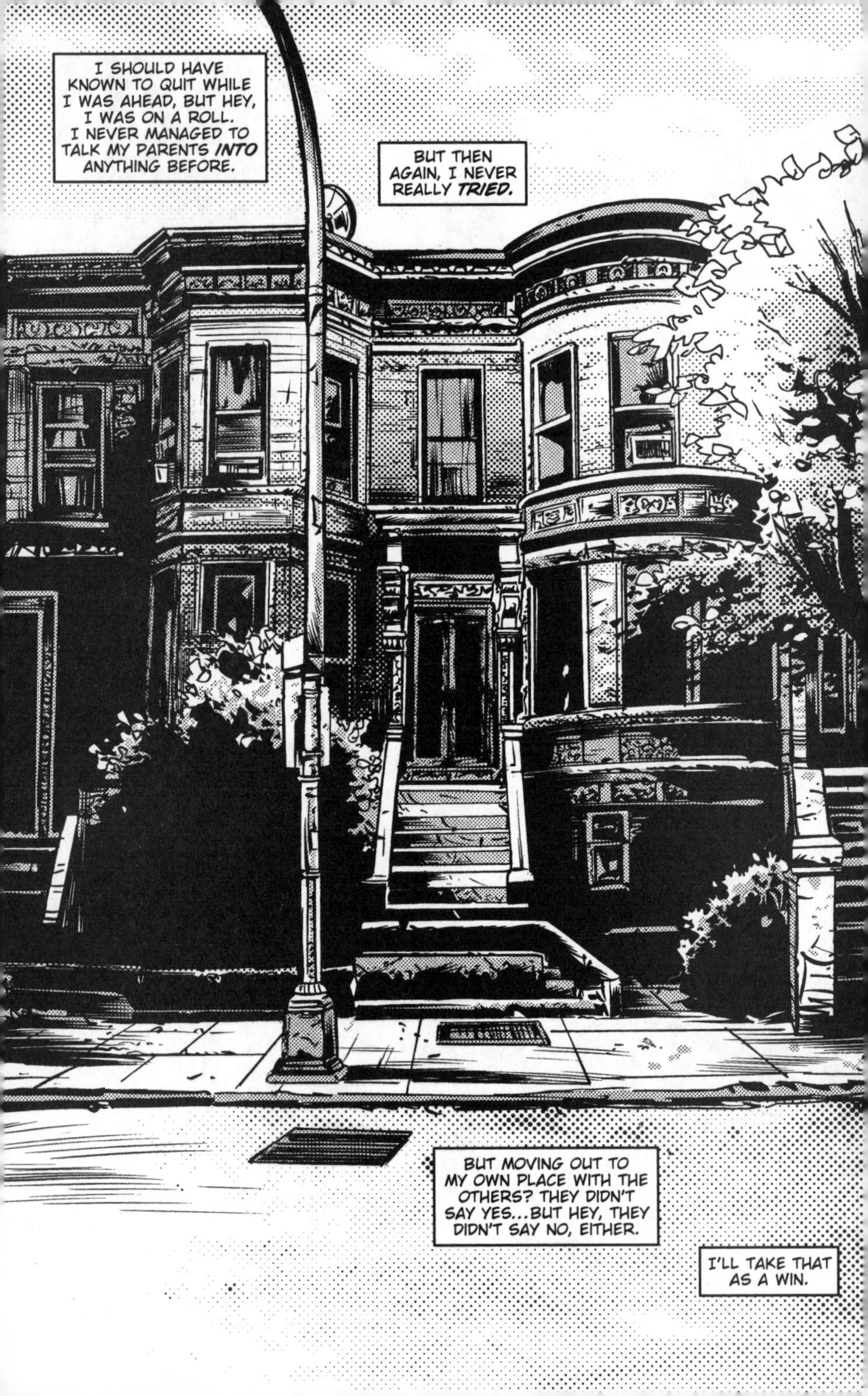
I SHOULD HAVE KNOWN TO QUIT WHILE I WAS AHEAD, BUT HEY, I WAS ON A ROLL. I NEVER MANAGED TO TALK MY PARENTS *INTO* ANYTHING BEFORE.
BUT THEN AGAIN, I NEVER REALLY *TRIED.*
BUT MOVING OUT TO MY OWN PLACE WITH THE OTHERS? THEY DIDN'T SAY YES...BUT HEY, THEY DIDN'T SAY NO, EITHER.
I'LL TAKE THAT AS A WIN.

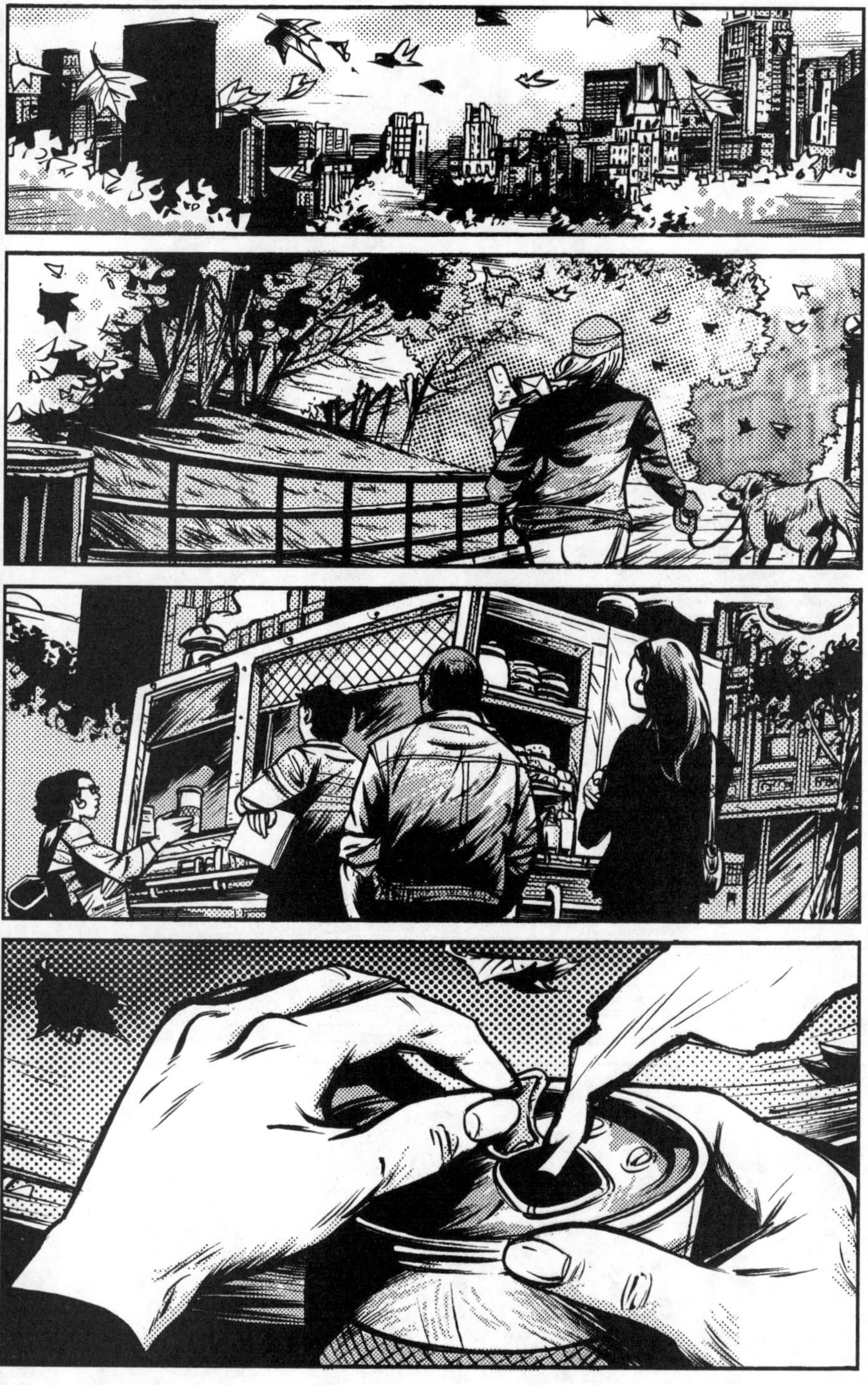

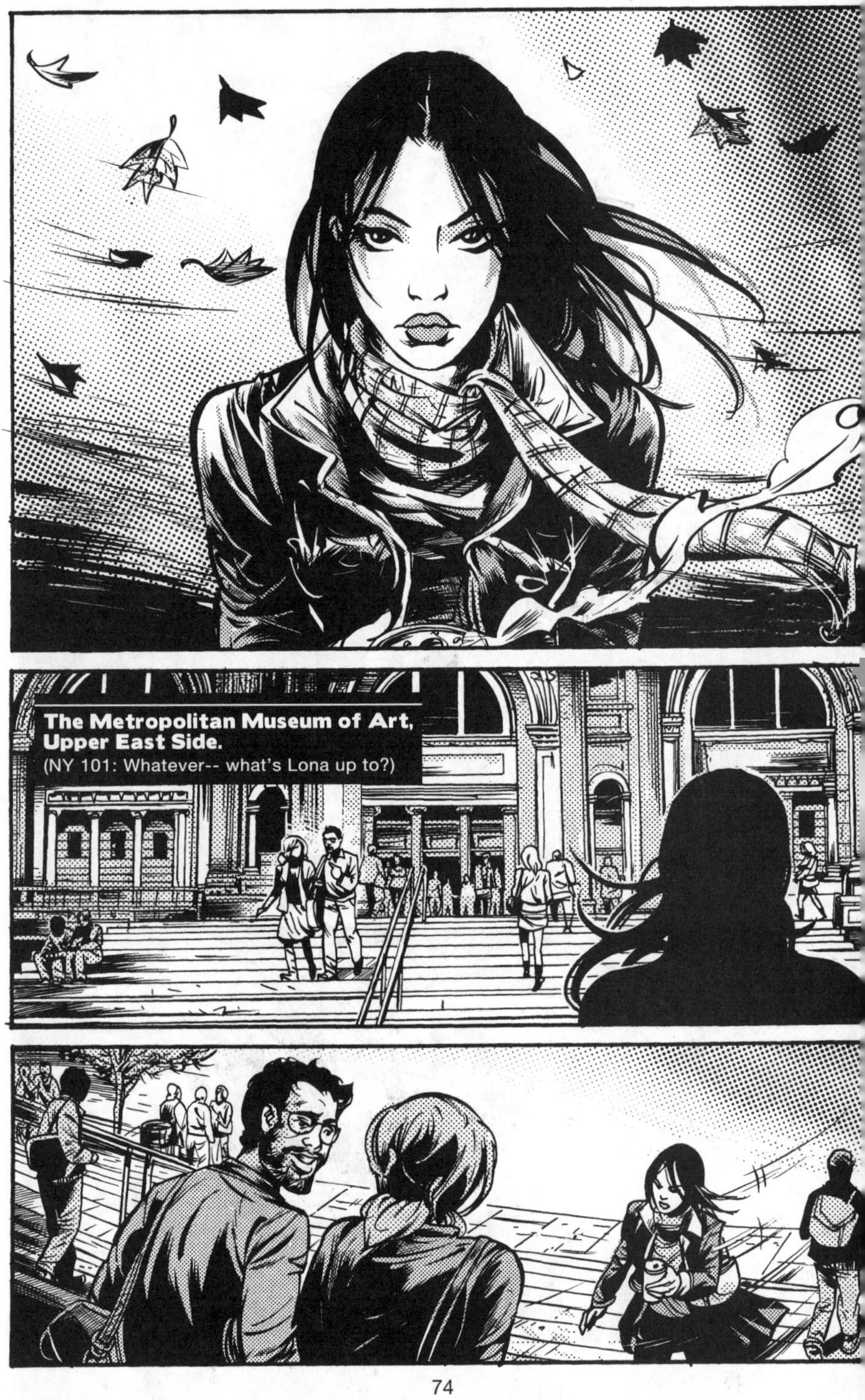
The Metropolitan Museum of Art, Upper East Side.
(NY 101: Whatever-- what's Lona up to?)

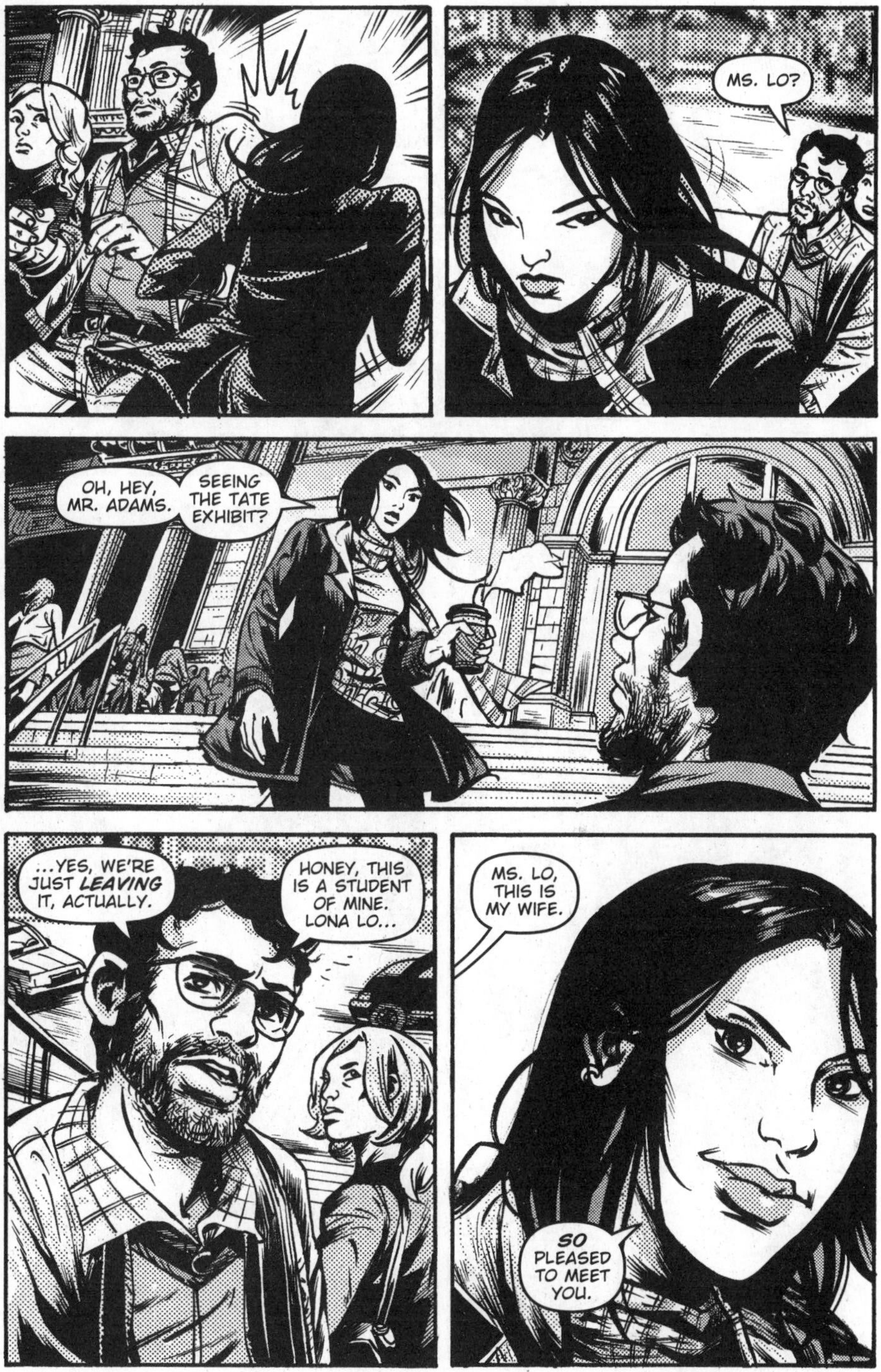
MS. LO?
OH, HEY, MR. ADAMS.
SEEING THE TATE EXHIBIT?
...YES, WE'RE JUST *LEAVING* IT, ACTUALLY.
HONEY, THIS IS A STUDENT OF MINE. LONA LO...
MS. LO, THIS IS MY WIFE.
SO PLEASED TO MEET YOU.

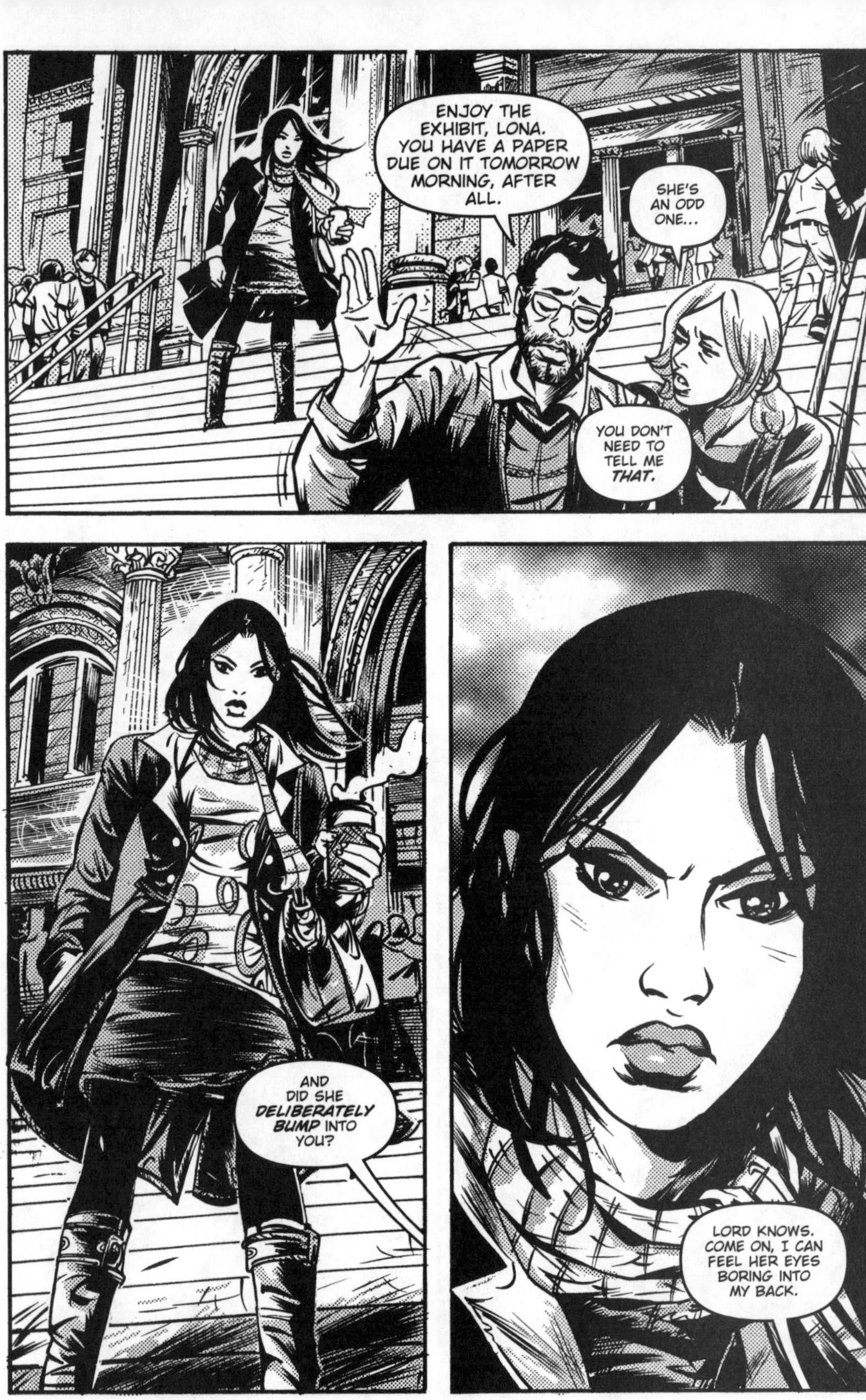
ENJOY THE EXHIBIT, LONA. YOU HAVE A PAPER DUE ON IT TOMORROW MORNING, AFTER ALL.
SHE'S AN ODD ONE...
YOU DON'T NEED TO TELL ME *THAT.*
AND DID SHE *DELIBERATELY BUMP* INTO YOU?
LORD KNOWS. COME ON, I CAN FEEL HER EYES BORING INTO MY BACK.

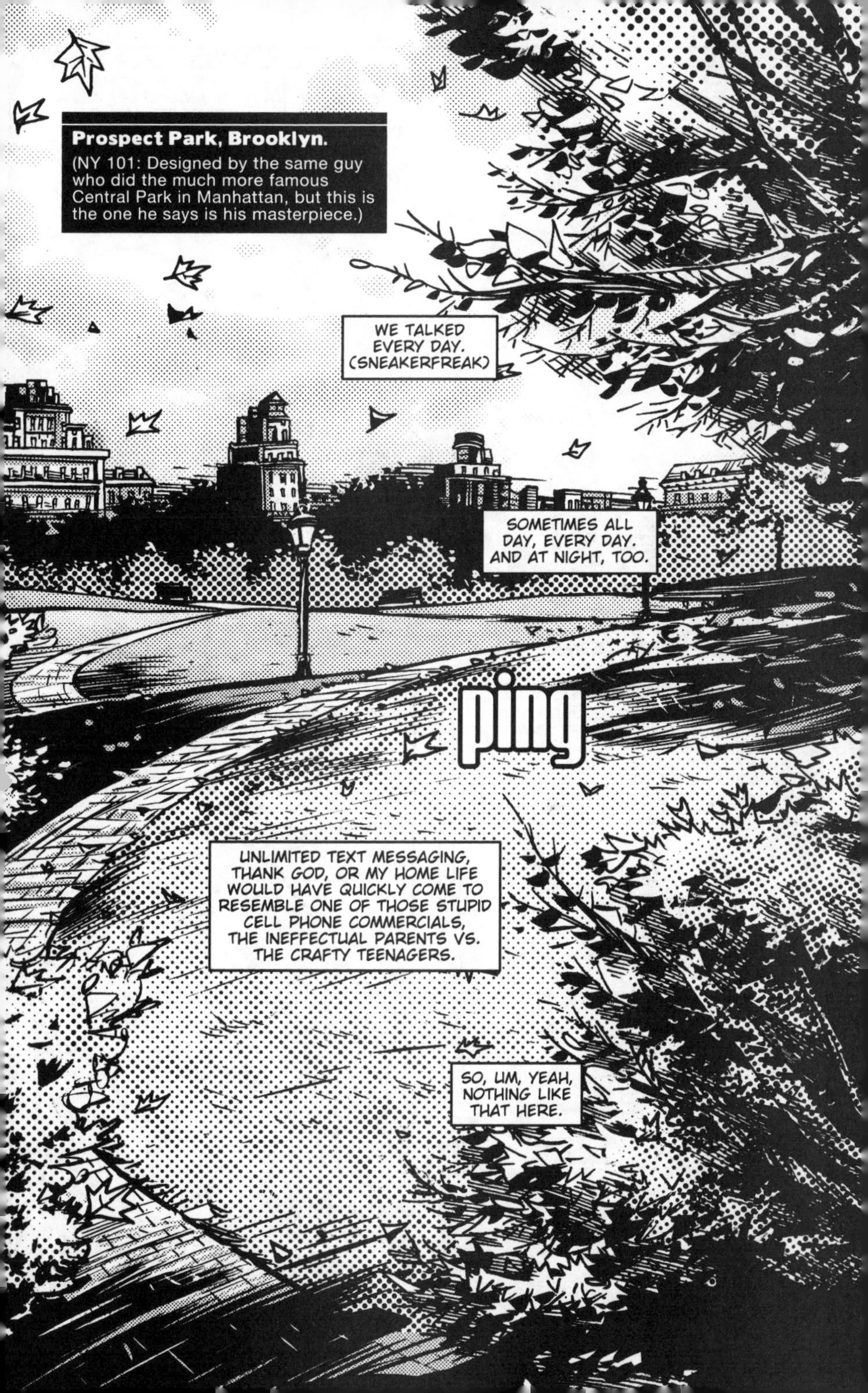
Prospect Park, Brooklyn.
(NY 101: Designed by the same guy who did the much more famous Central Park in Manhattan, but this is the one he says is his masterpiece.)
WE TALKED EVERY DAY. (SNEAKERFREAK)
SOMETIMES ALL DAY, EVERY DAY. AND AT NIGHT, TOO.
ping
UNLIMITED TEXT MESSAGING, THANK GOD, OR MY HOME LIFE WOULD HAVE QUICKLY COME TO RESEMBLE ONE OF THOSE STUPID CELL PHONE COMMERCIALS, THE INEFFECTUAL PARENTS VS. THE CRAFTY TEENAGERS.
SO, UM, YEAH, NOTHING LIKE THAT HERE.

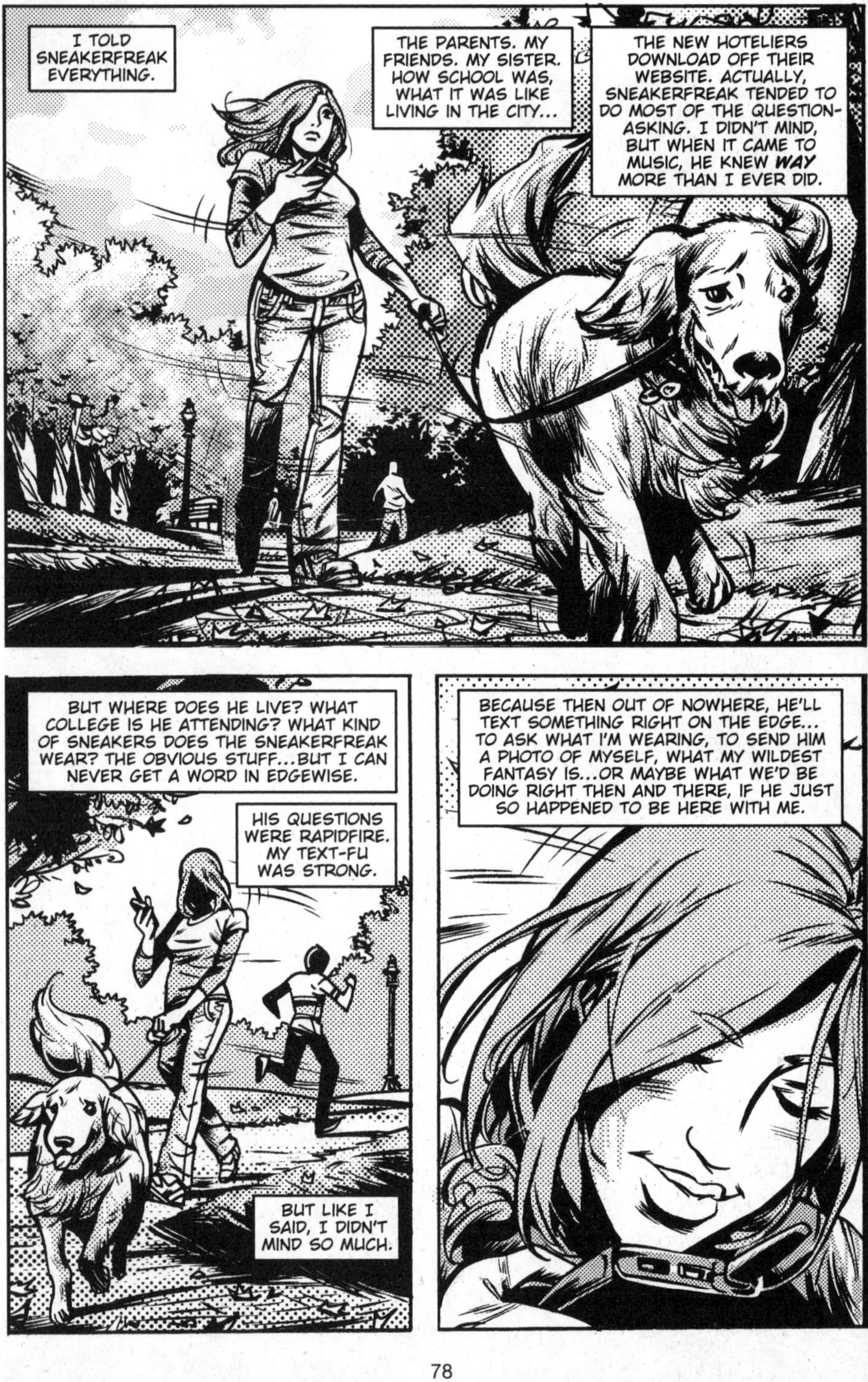
I TOLD SNEAKERFREAK EVERYTHING.
THE PARENTS. MY FRIENDS. MY SISTER. HOW SCHOOL WAS, WHAT IT WAS LIKE LIVING IN THE CITY...
THE NEW HOTELIERS DOWNLOAD OFF THEIR WEBSITE. ACTUALLY, SNEAKERFREAK TENDED TO DO MOST OF THE QUESTION-ASKING. I DIDN'T MIND, BUT WHEN IT CAME TO MUSIC, HE KNEW ***WAY*** MORE THAN I EVER DID.
BUT WHERE DOES HE LIVE? WHAT COLLEGE IS HE ATTENDING? WHAT KIND OF SNEAKERS DOES THE SNEAKERFREAK WEAR? THE OBVIOUS STUFF...BUT I CAN NEVER GET A WORD IN EDGEWISE.
HIS QUESTIONS WERE RAPIDFIRE. MY TEXT-FU WAS STRONG.
BUT LIKE I SAID, I DIDN'T MIND SO MUCH.
BECAUSE THEN OUT OF NOWHERE, HE'LL TEXT SOMETHING RIGHT ON THE EDGE... TO ASK WHAT I'M WEARING, TO SEND HIM A PHOTO OF MYSELF, WHAT MY WILDEST FANTASY IS...OR MAYBE WHAT WE'D BE DOING RIGHT THEN AND THERE, IF HE JUST SO HAPPENED TO BE HERE WITH ME.

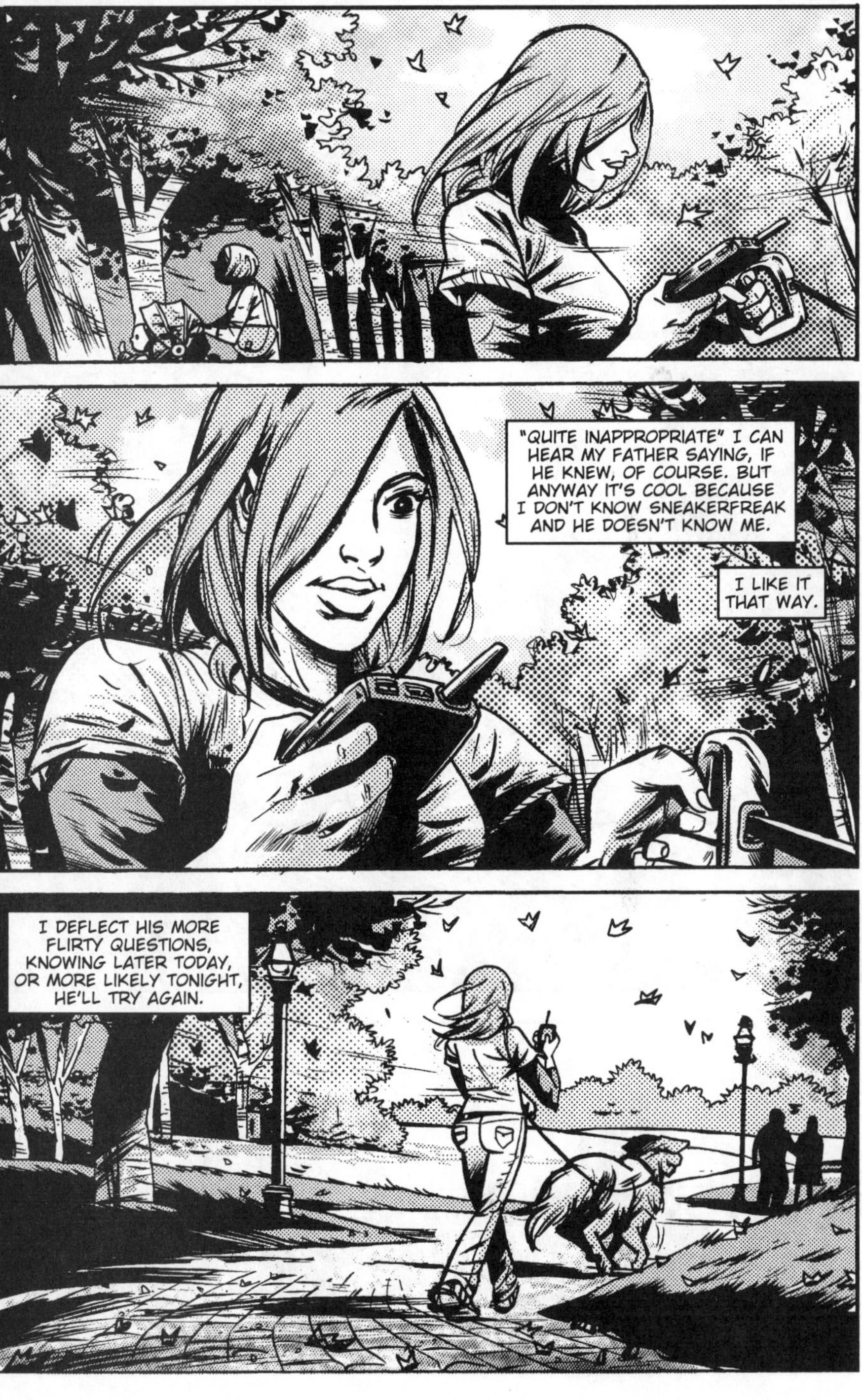
"QUITE INAPPROPRIATE" I CAN HEAR MY FATHER SAYING, IF HE KNEW, OF COURSE. BUT ANYWAY IT'S COOL BECAUSE I DON'T KNOW SNEAKERFREAK AND HE DOESN'T KNOW ME.
I LIKE IT THAT WAY.
I DEFLECT HIS MORE FLIRTY QUESTIONS, KNOWING LATER TODAY, OR MORE LIKELY TONIGHT, HE'LL TRY AGAIN.

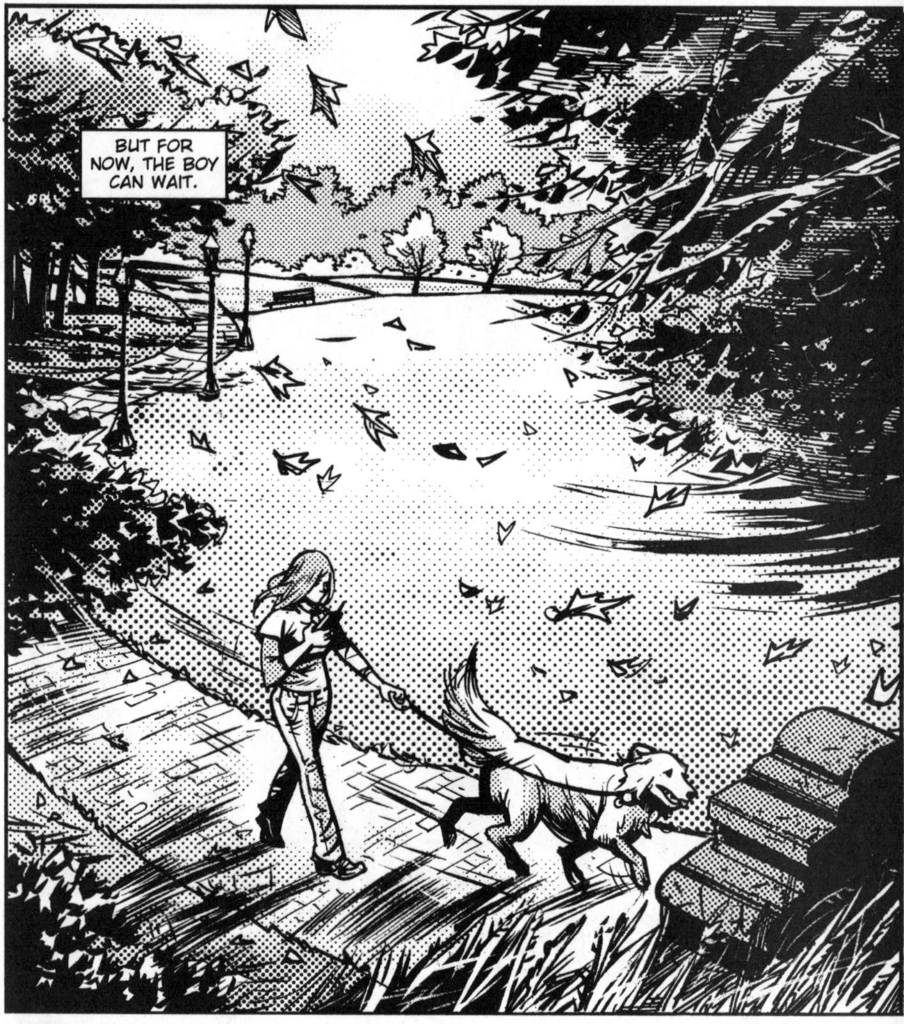
BUT FOR NOW, THE BOY CAN WAIT.

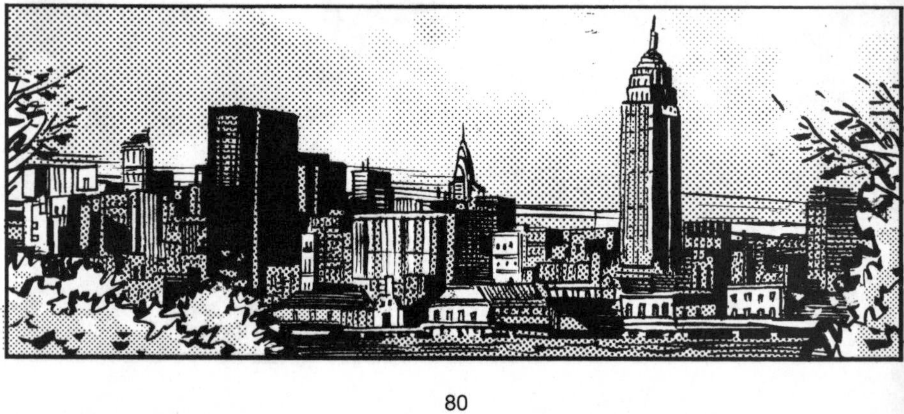

Chapter 4

Disown, Delete

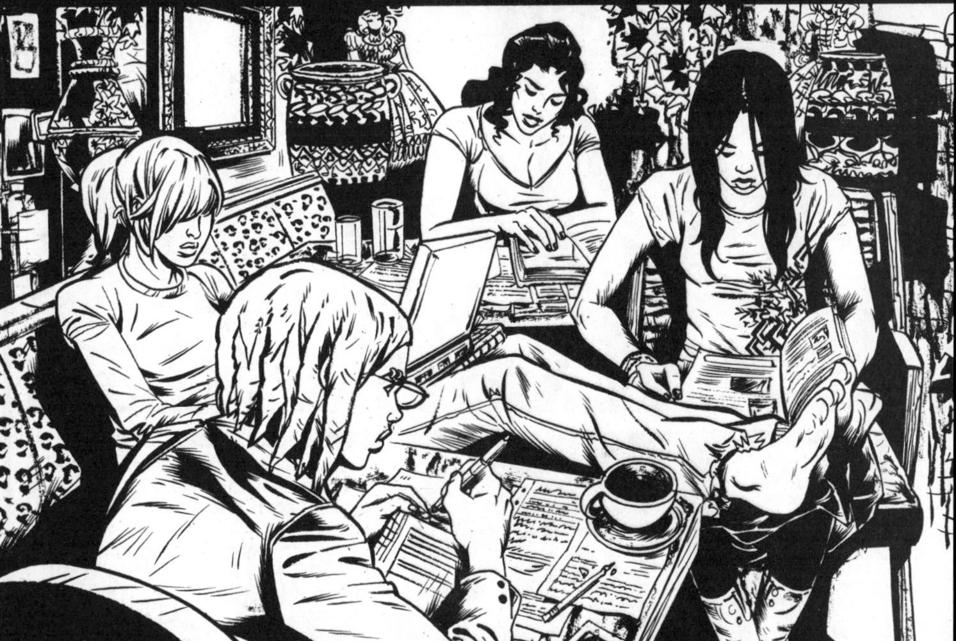

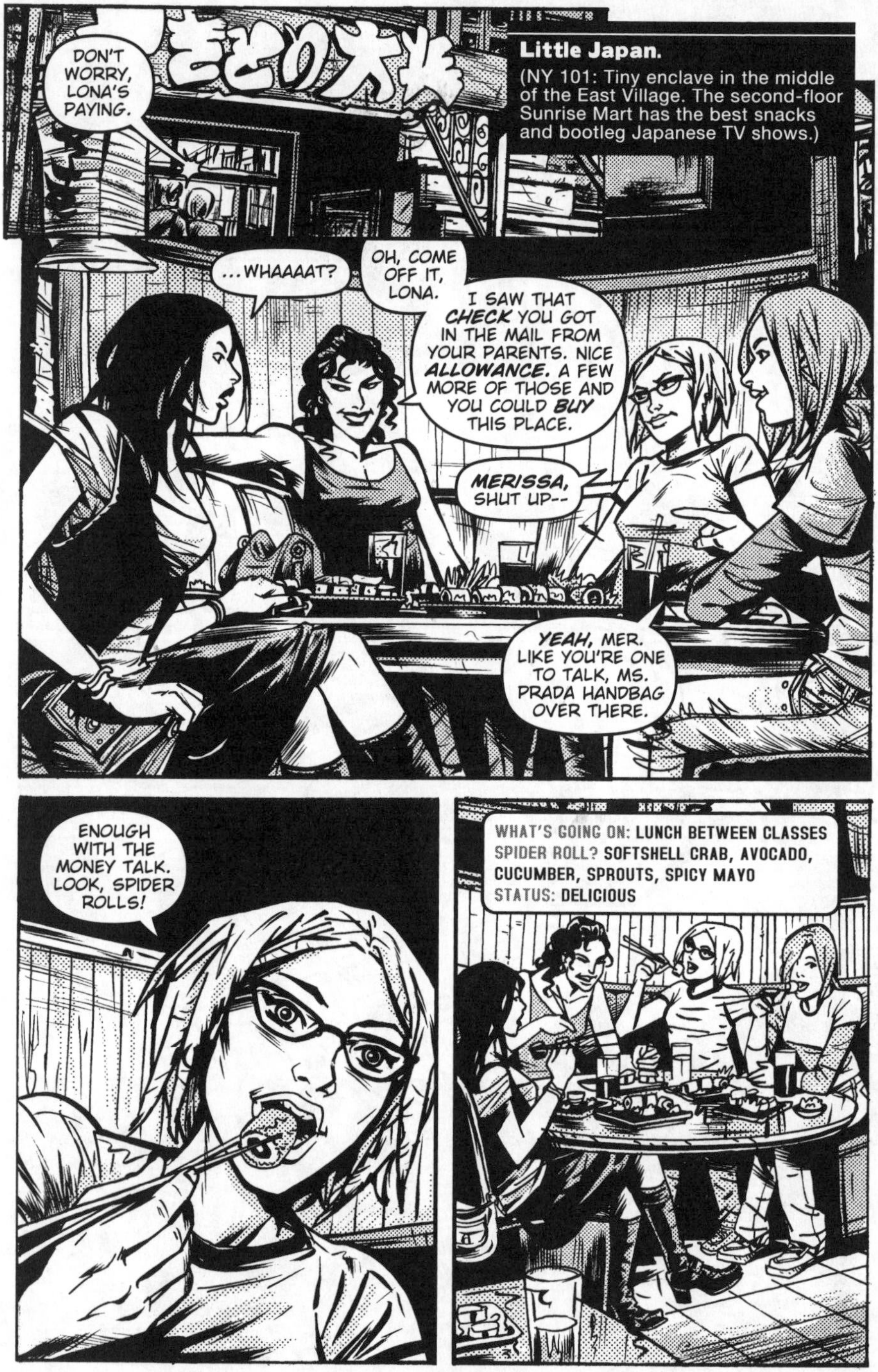
DON'T WORRY, LONA'S PAYING.
Little Japan.
(NY 101: Tiny enclave in the middle of the East Village. The second-floor Sunrise Mart has the best snacks and bootleg Japanese TV shows.)
...WHAAAAT?
OH, COME OFF IT, LONA.
I SAW THAT CHECK YOU GOT IN THE MAIL FROM YOUR PARENTS. NICE ALLOWANCE. A FEW MORE OF THOSE AND YOU COULD BUY THIS PLACE.
MERISSA, SHUT UP--
YEAH, MER. LIKE YOU'RE ONE TO TALK, MS. PRADA HANDBAG OVER THERE.
ENOUGH WITH THE MONEY TALK. LOOK, SPIDER ROLLS!
WHAT'S GOING ON: LUNCH BETWEEN CLASSES
SPIDER ROLL? SOFTSHELL CRAB, AVOCADO, CUCUMBER, SPROUTS, SPICY MAYO
STATUS: DELICIOUS

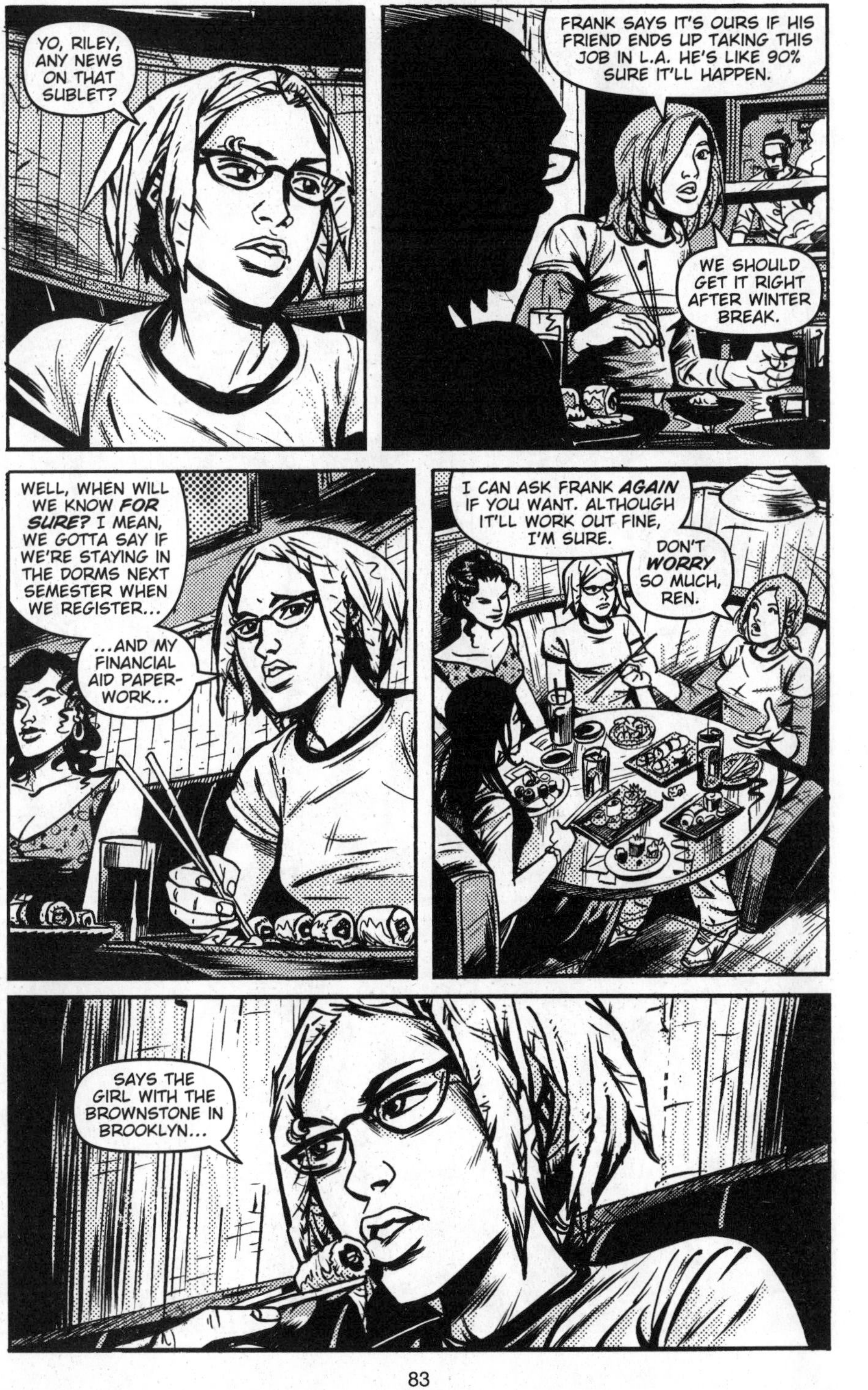
YO, RILEY, ANY NEWS ON THAT SUBLET?
FRANK SAYS IT'S OURS IF HIS FRIEND ENDS UP TAKING THIS JOB IN L.A. HE'S LIKE 90% SURE IT'LL HAPPEN.
WE SHOULD GET IT RIGHT AFTER WINTER BREAK.
WELL, WHEN WILL WE KNOW *FOR SURE?* I MEAN, WE GOTTA SAY IF WE'RE STAYING IN THE DORMS NEXT SEMESTER WHEN WE REGISTER...
...AND MY FINANCIAL AID PAPER-WORK...
I CAN ASK FRANK *AGAIN* IF YOU WANT. ALTHOUGH IT'LL WORK OUT FINE, I'M SURE.
DON'T *WORRY* SO MUCH, REN.
SAYS THE GIRL WITH THE BROWNSTONE IN BROOKLYN...

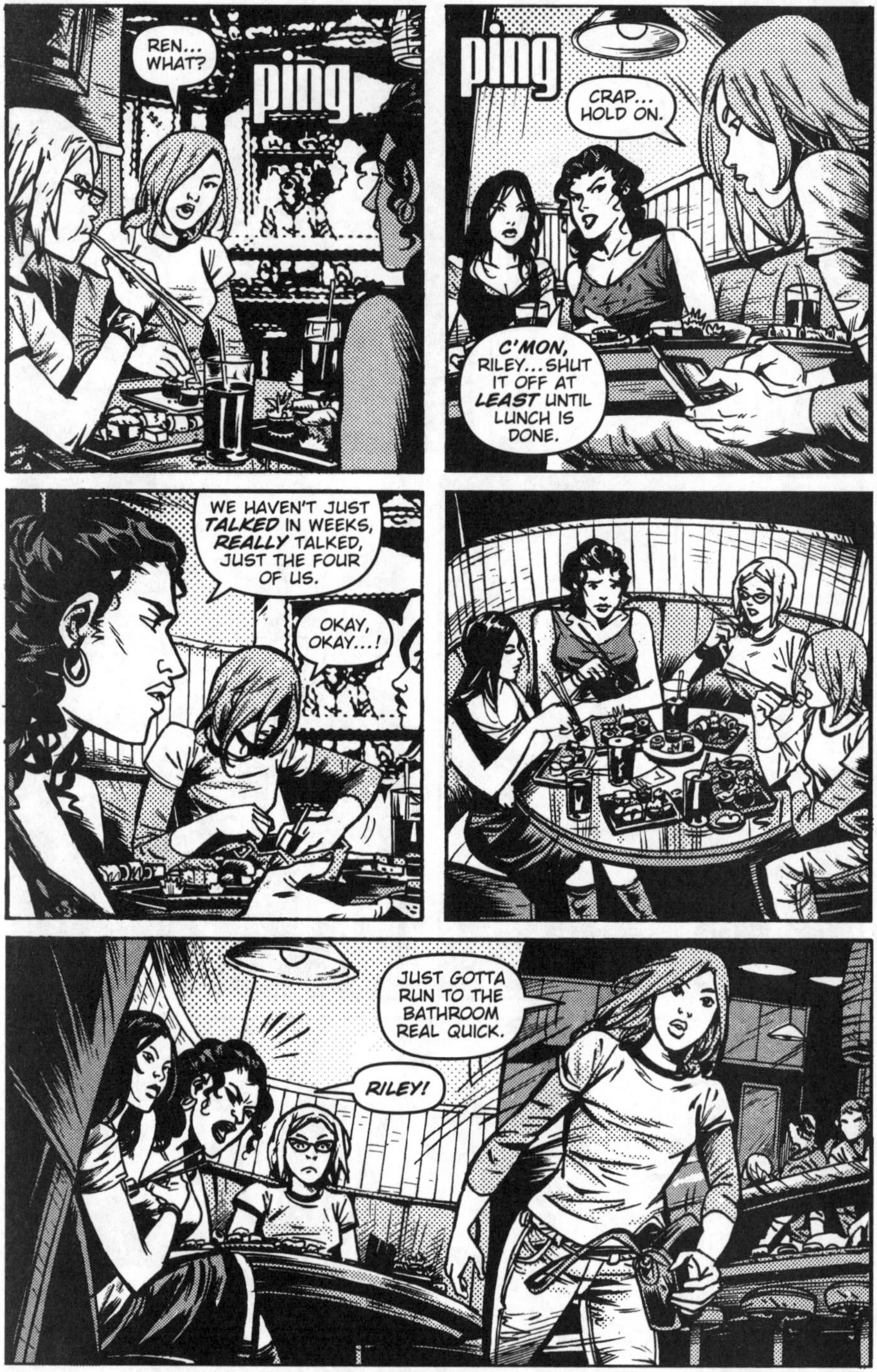
REN... WHAT?
ping
ping
CRAP... HOLD ON.
C'MON, RILEY... SHUT IT OFF AT LEAST UNTIL LUNCH IS DONE.
WE HAVEN'T JUST TALKED IN WEEKS, REALLY TALKED, JUST THE FOUR OF US.
OKAY, OKAY...!
JUST GOTTA RUN TO THE BATHROOM REAL QUICK.
RILEY!

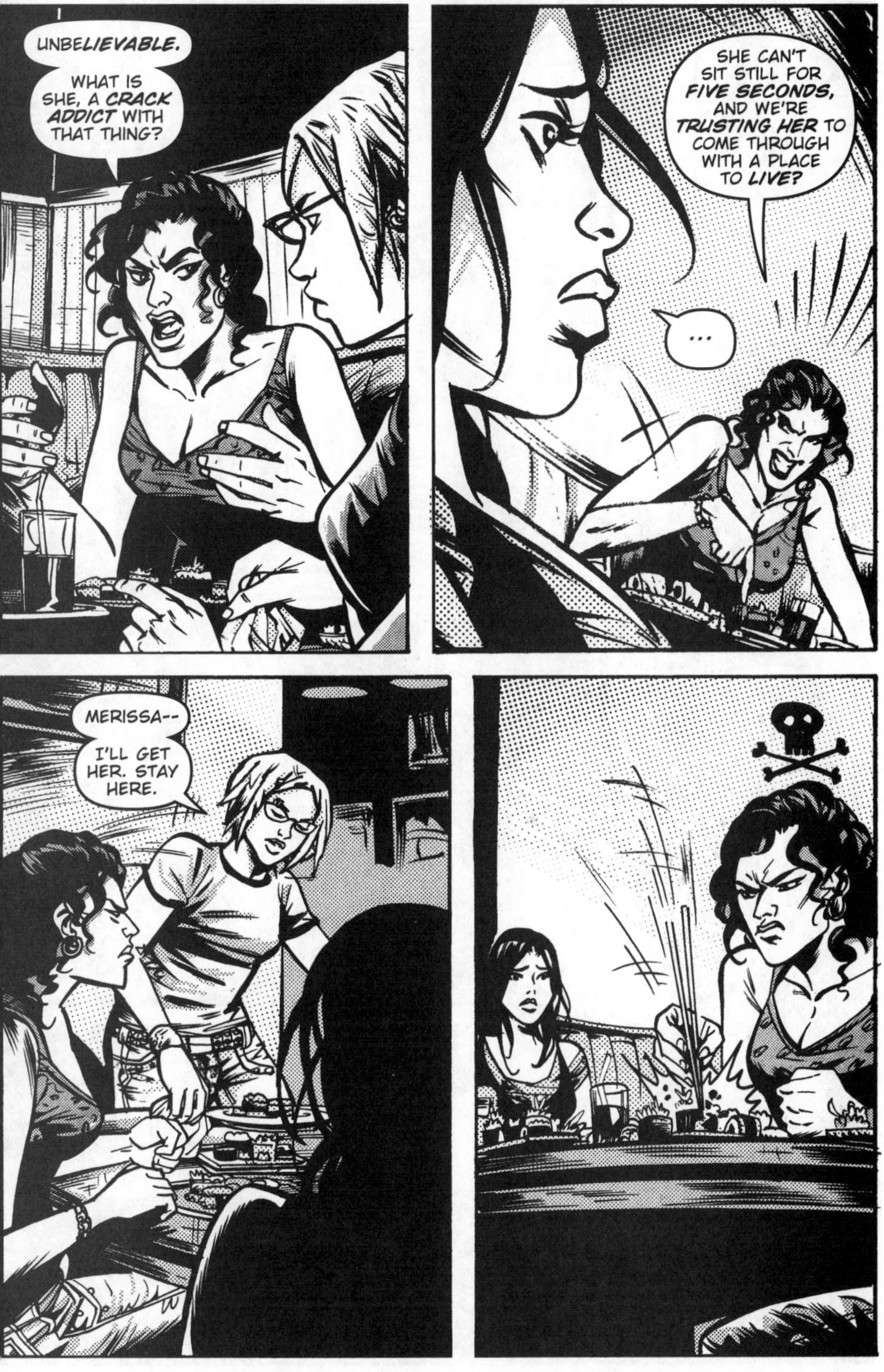
UNBELIEVABLE.
WHAT IS SHE, A CRACK ADDICT WITH THAT THING?
SHE CAN'T SIT STILL FOR FIVE SECONDS, AND WE'RE TRUSTING HER TO COME THROUGH WITH A PLACE TO LIVE?
...
MERISSA--
I'LL GET HER. STAY HERE.

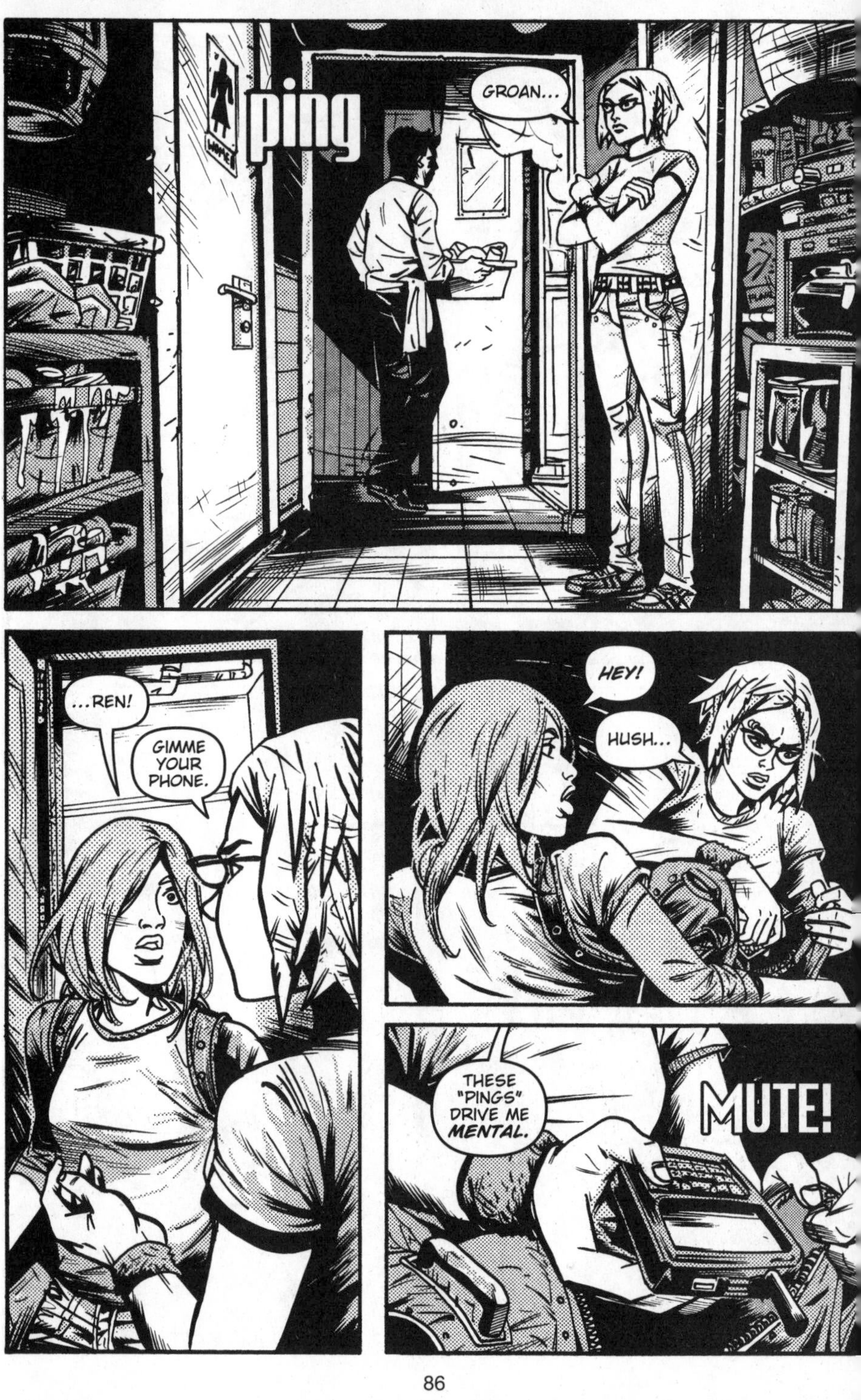
ping
GROAN...
...REN!
GIMME YOUR PHONE.
HEY!
HUSH...
THESE "PINGS" DRIVE ME *MENTAL*.
MUTE!

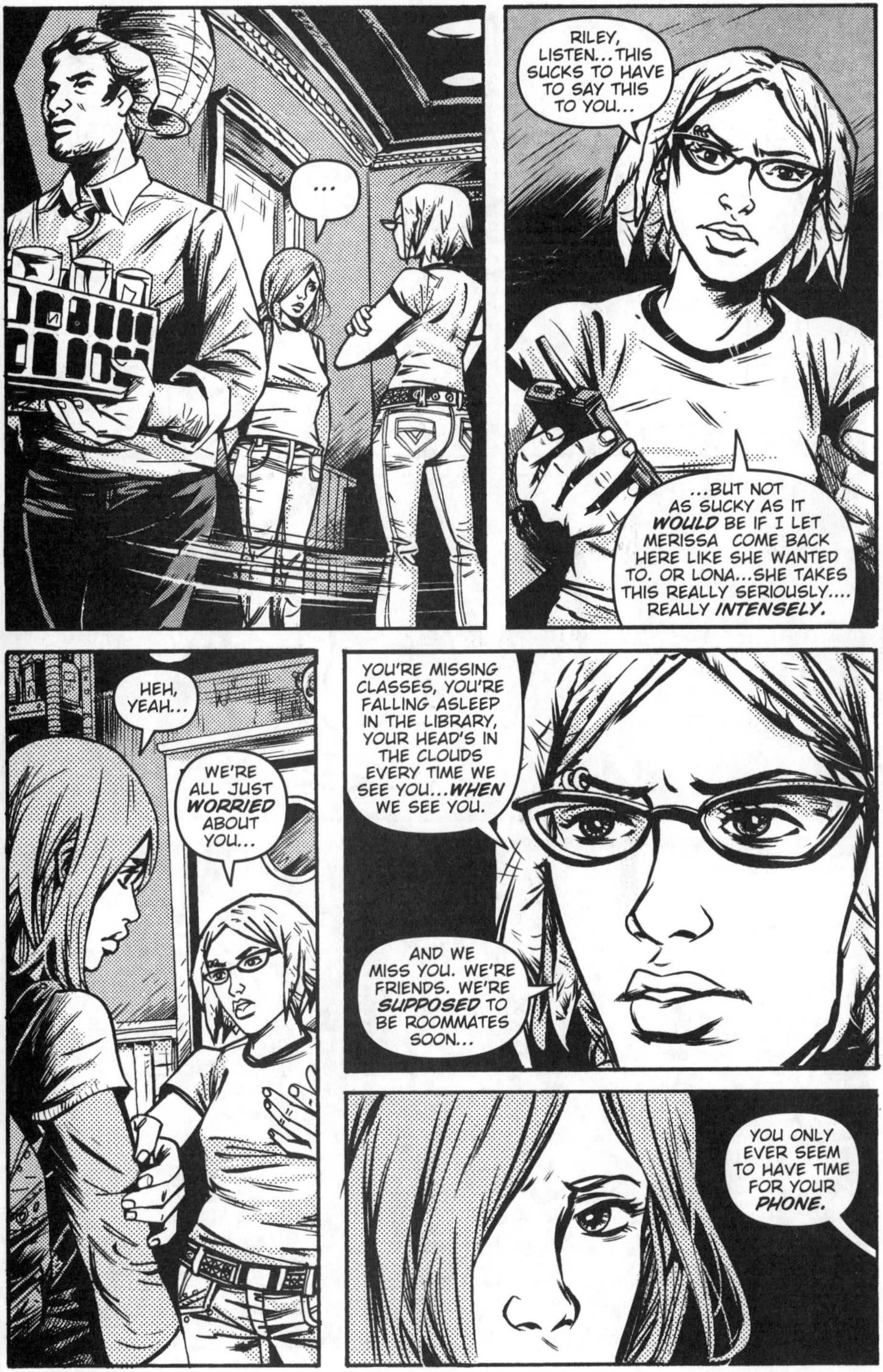
...
RILEY, LISTEN... THIS SUCKS TO HAVE TO SAY THIS TO YOU...
...BUT NOT AS SUCKY AS IT WOULD BE IF I LET MERISSA COME BACK HERE LIKE SHE WANTED TO. OR LONA...SHE TAKES THIS REALLY SERIOUSLY.... REALLY INTENSELY.
HEH, YEAH...
WE'RE ALL JUST WORRIED ABOUT YOU...
YOU'RE MISSING CLASSES, YOU'RE FALLING ASLEEP IN THE LIBRARY, YOUR HEAD'S IN THE CLOUDS EVERY TIME WE SEE YOU...WHEN WE SEE YOU.
AND WE MISS YOU. WE'RE FRIENDS. WE'RE SUPPOSED TO BE ROOMMATES SOON...
YOU ONLY EVER SEEM TO HAVE TIME FOR YOUR PHONE.

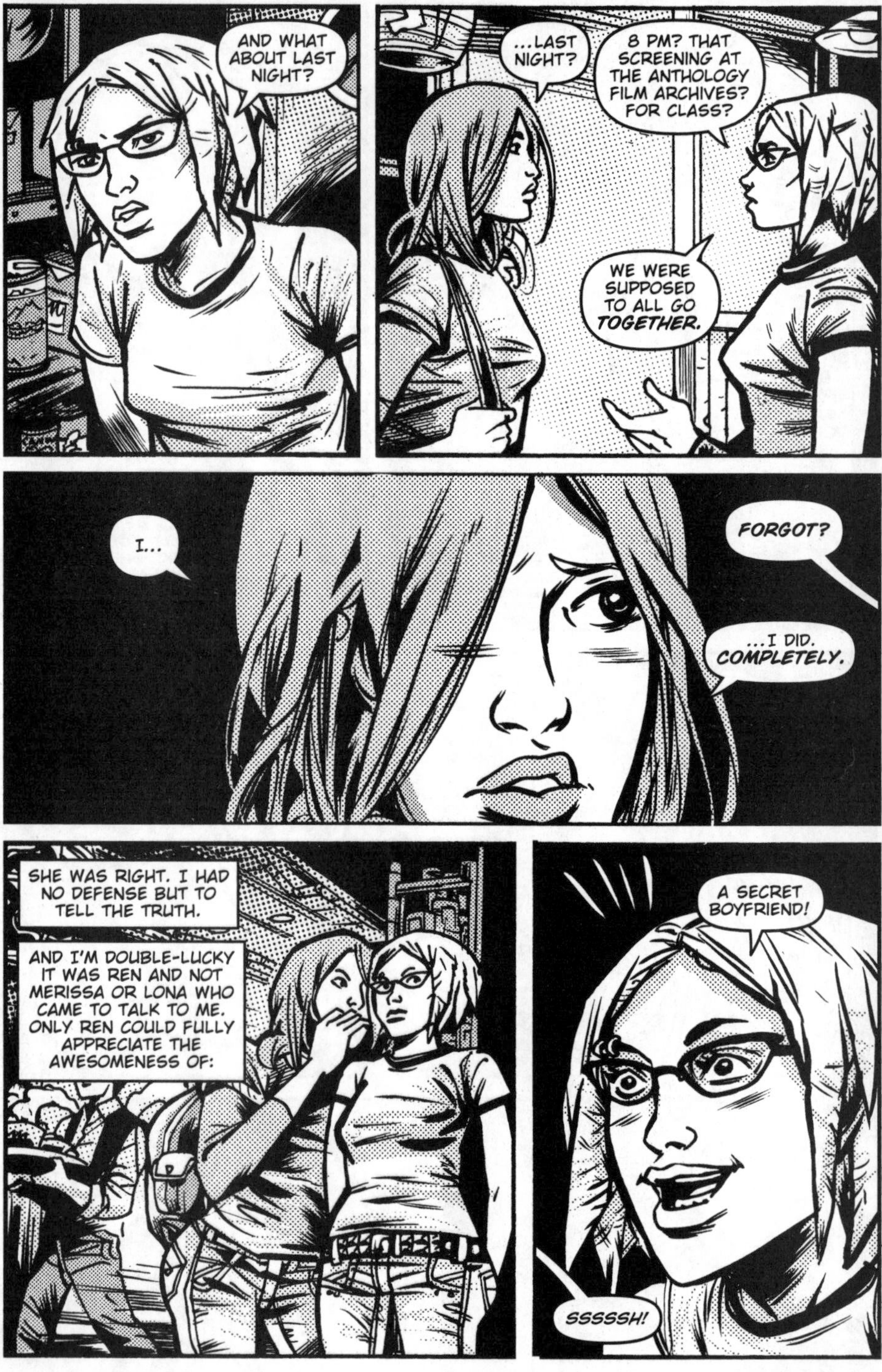
AND WHAT ABOUT LAST NIGHT?
...LAST NIGHT?
8 PM? THAT SCREENING AT THE ANTHOLOGY FILM ARCHIVES? FOR CLASS?
WE WERE SUPPOSED TO ALL GO TOGETHER.
I...
FORGOT?
...I DID. COMPLETELY.
SHE WAS RIGHT. I HAD NO DEFENSE BUT TO TELL THE TRUTH.
AND I'M DOUBLE-LUCKY IT WAS REN AND NOT MERISSA OR LONA WHO CAME TO TALK TO ME. ONLY REN COULD FULLY APPRECIATE THE AWESOMENESS OF:
A SECRET BOYFRIEND!
SSSSSH!

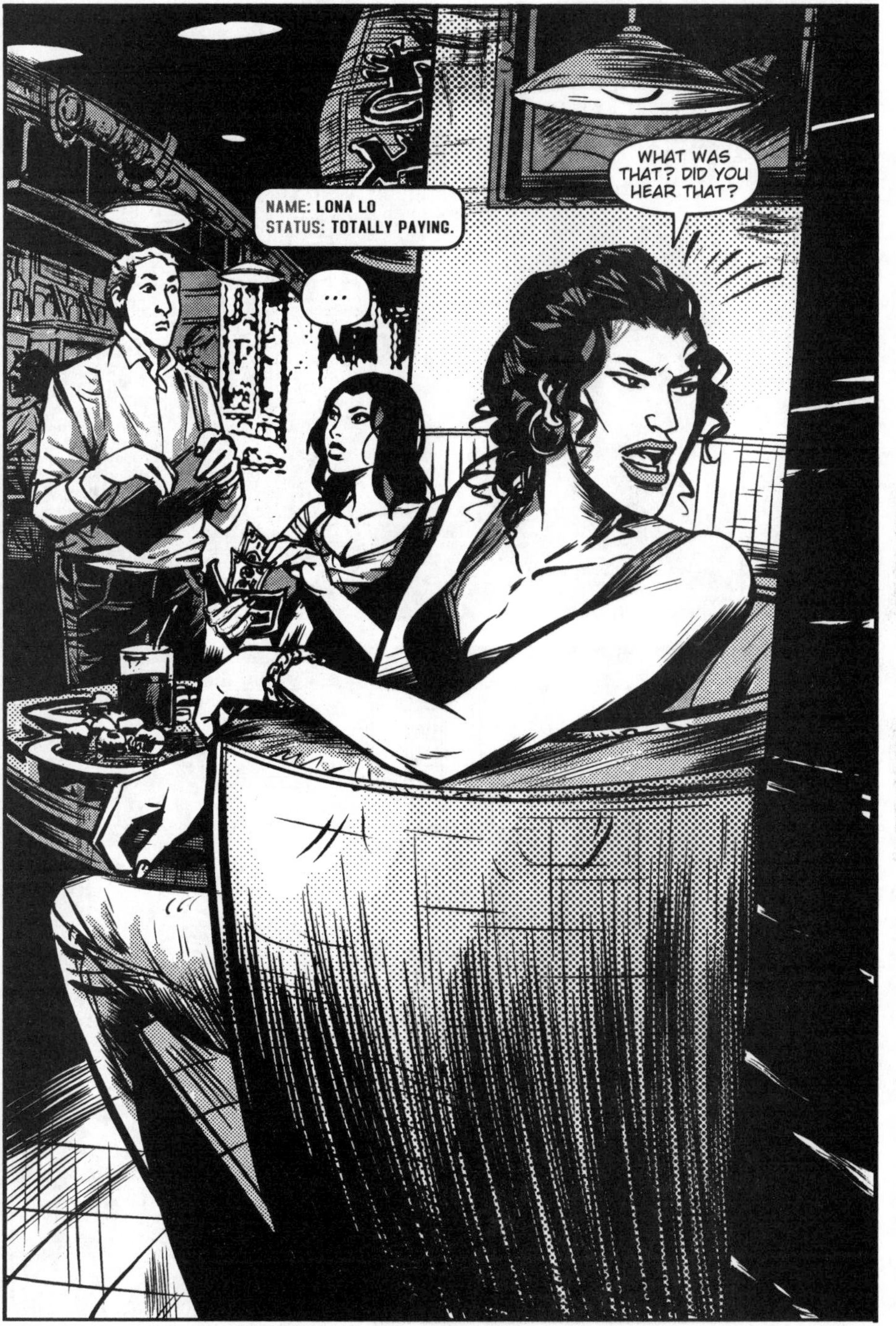
NAME: LONA LO
STATUS: TOTALLY PAYING.
...
WHAT WAS THAT? DID YOU HEAR THAT?

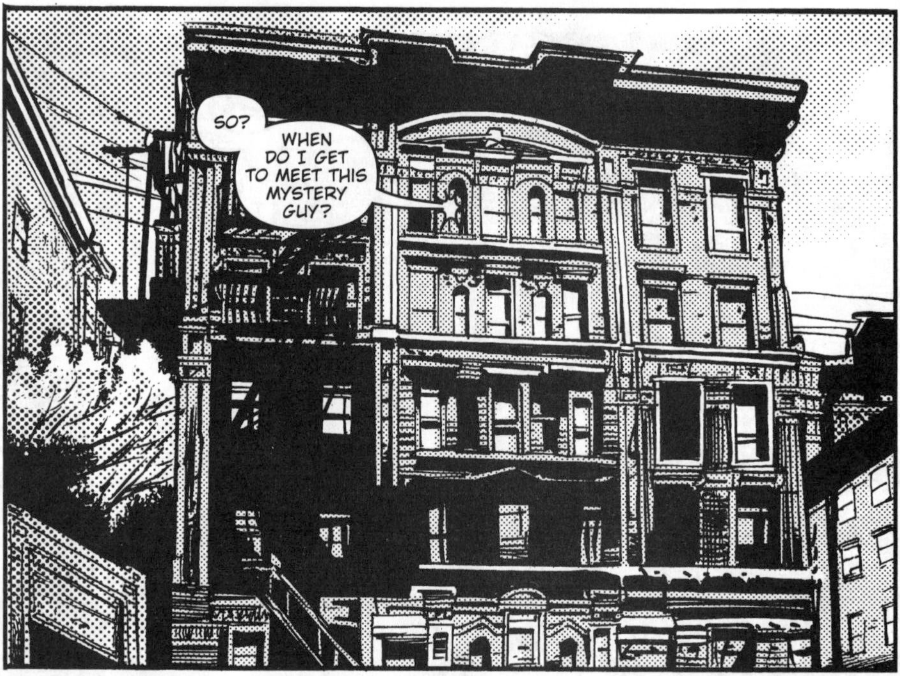
SO?
WHEN DO I GET TO MEET THIS MYSTERY GUY?

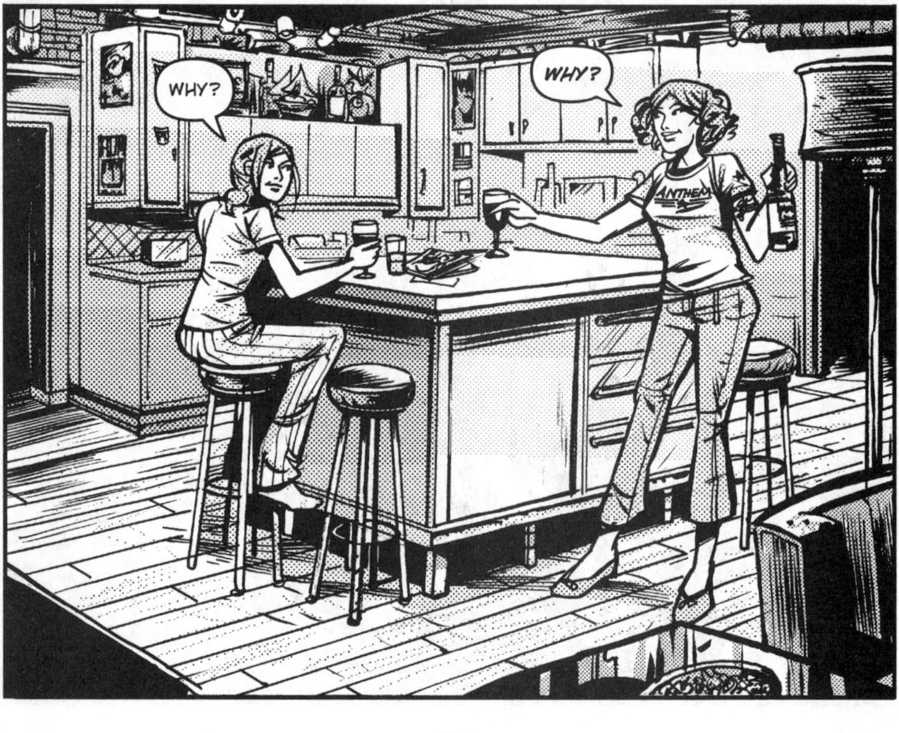
WHY?
WHY?
ANTHEM

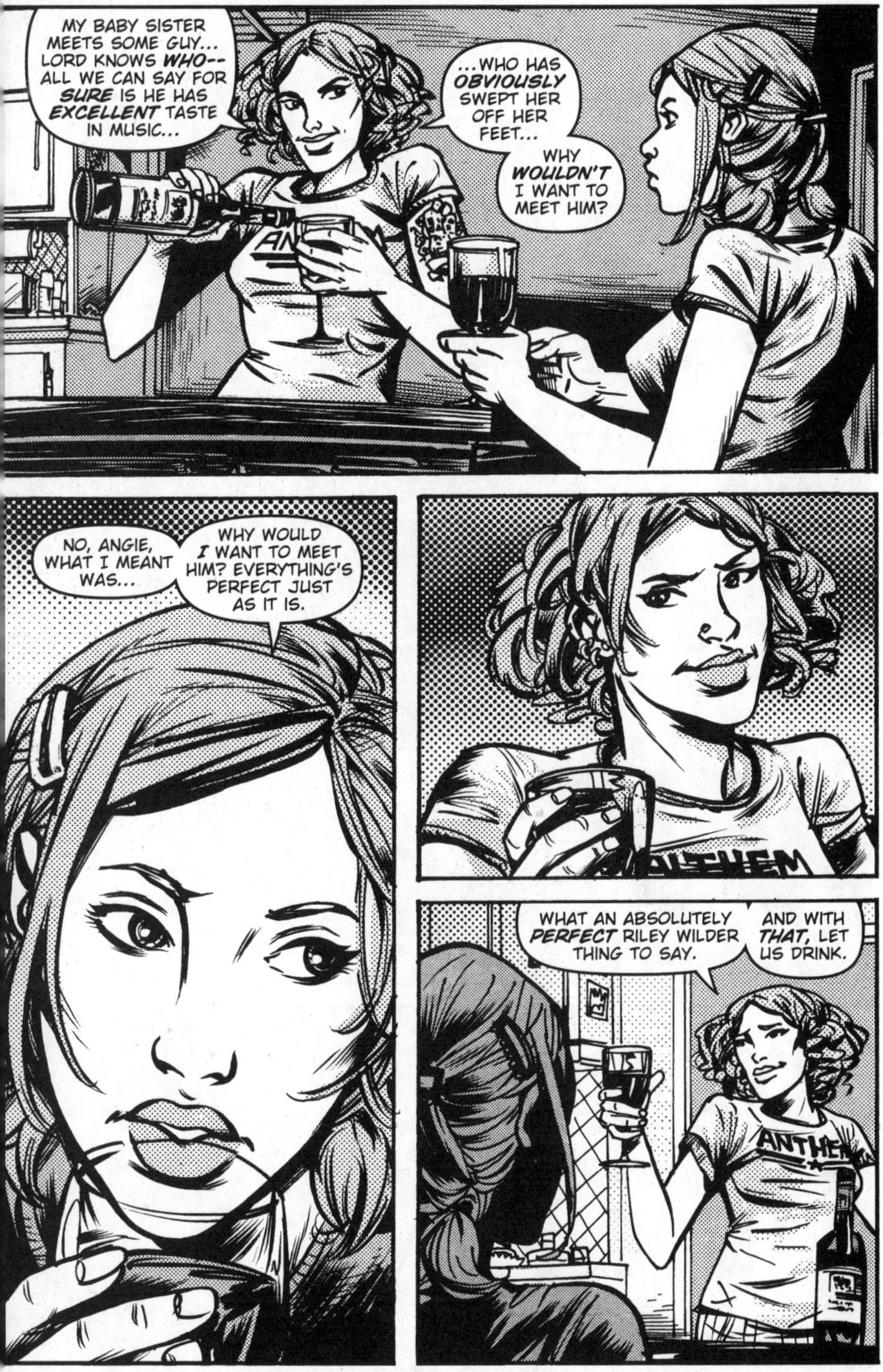
MY BABY SISTER MEETS SOME GUY... LORD KNOWS *WHO*-- ALL WE CAN SAY FOR *SURE* IS HE HAS *EXCELLENT* TASTE IN MUSIC...
...WHO HAS *OBVIOUSLY* SWEPT HER OFF HER FEET...
WHY *WOULDN'T* I WANT TO MEET HIM?
NO, ANGIE, WHAT I MEANT WAS...
WHY WOULD *I* WANT TO MEET HIM? EVERYTHING'S PERFECT JUST AS IT IS.
ANTHEM
WHAT AN ABSOLUTELY *PERFECT* RILEY WILDER THING TO SAY.
AND WITH *THAT*, LET US DRINK.

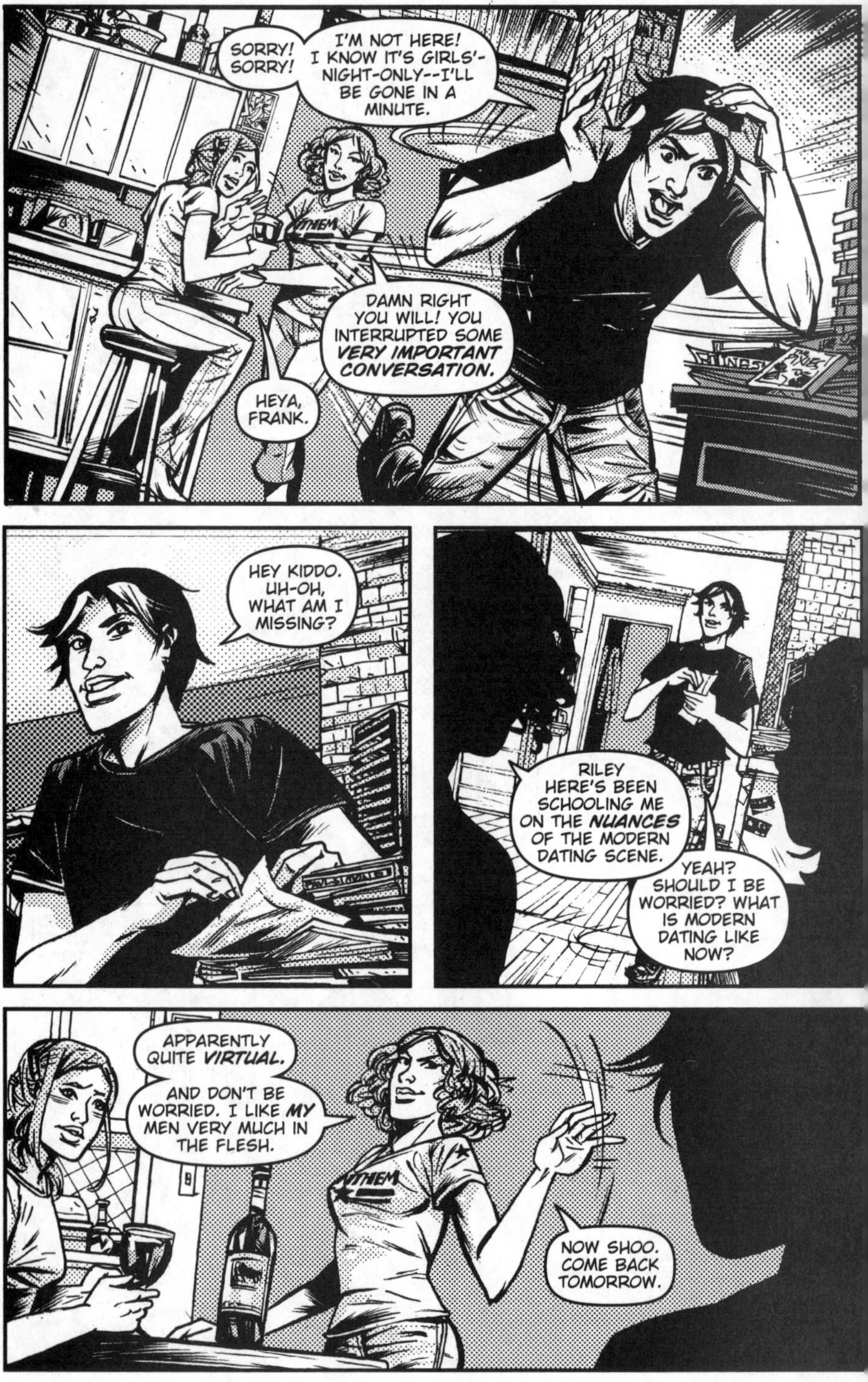
SORRY! SORRY!
I'M NOT HERE! I KNOW IT'S GIRLS'-NIGHT-ONLY--I'LL BE GONE IN A MINUTE.
DAMN RIGHT YOU WILL! YOU INTERRUPTED SOME **VERY IMPORTANT CONVERSATION.**
HEYA, FRANK.
HEY KIDDO. UH-OH, WHAT AM I MISSING?
RILEY HERE'S BEEN SCHOOLING ME ON THE **NUANCES** OF THE MODERN DATING SCENE.
YEAH? SHOULD I BE WORRIED? WHAT IS MODERN DATING LIKE NOW?
APPARENTLY QUITE **VIRTUAL.**
AND DON'T BE WORRIED. I LIKE **MY** MEN VERY MUCH IN THE FLESH.
NOW SHOO. COME BACK TOMORROW.

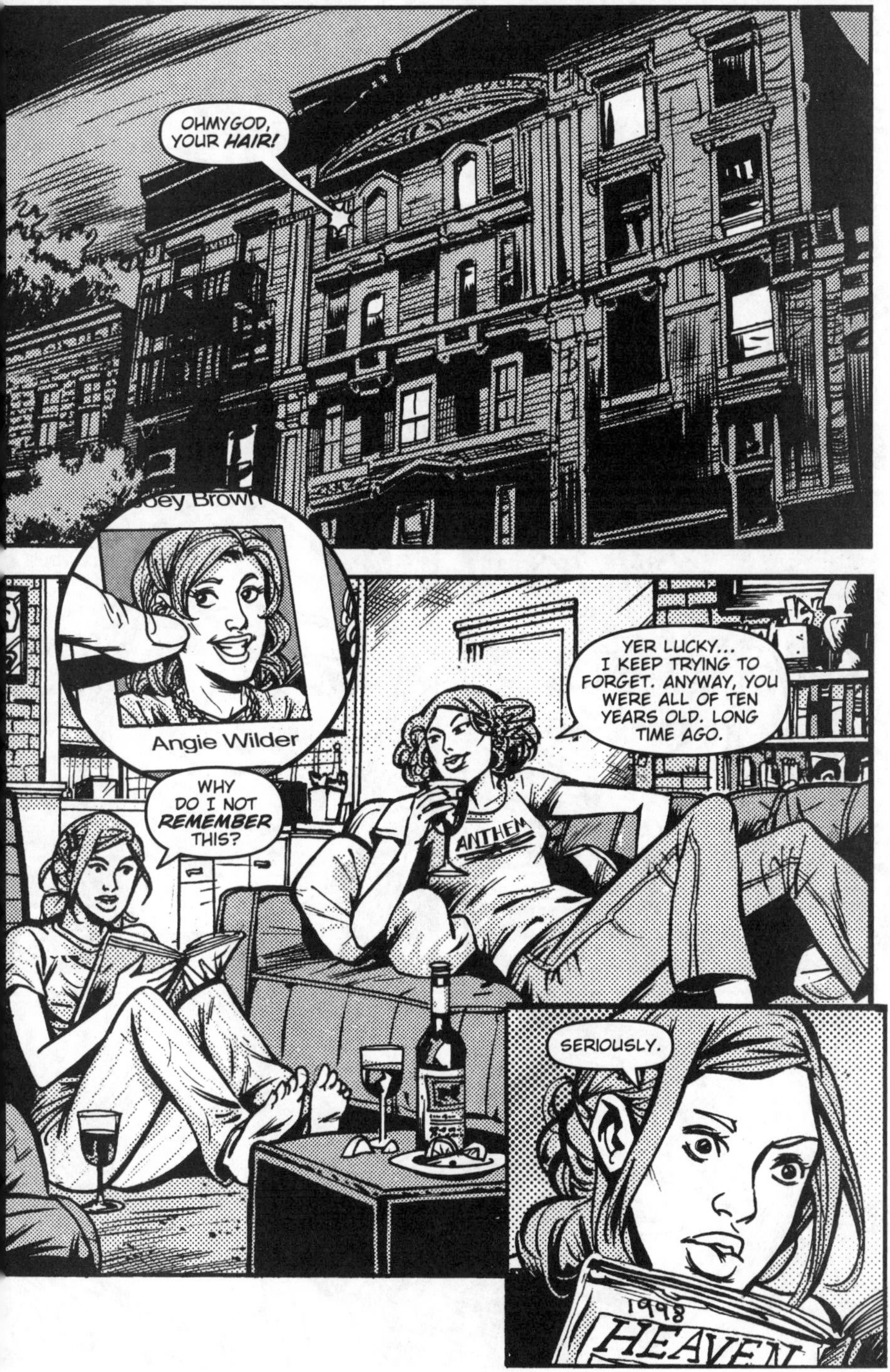
OHMYGOD, YOUR HAIR!
Angie Wilder
WHY DO I NOT REMEMBER THIS?
YER LUCKY... I KEEP TRYING TO FORGET. ANYWAY, YOU WERE ALL OF TEN YEARS OLD. LONG TIME AGO.
ANTHEM
SERIOUSLY.
1998
HEAVEN

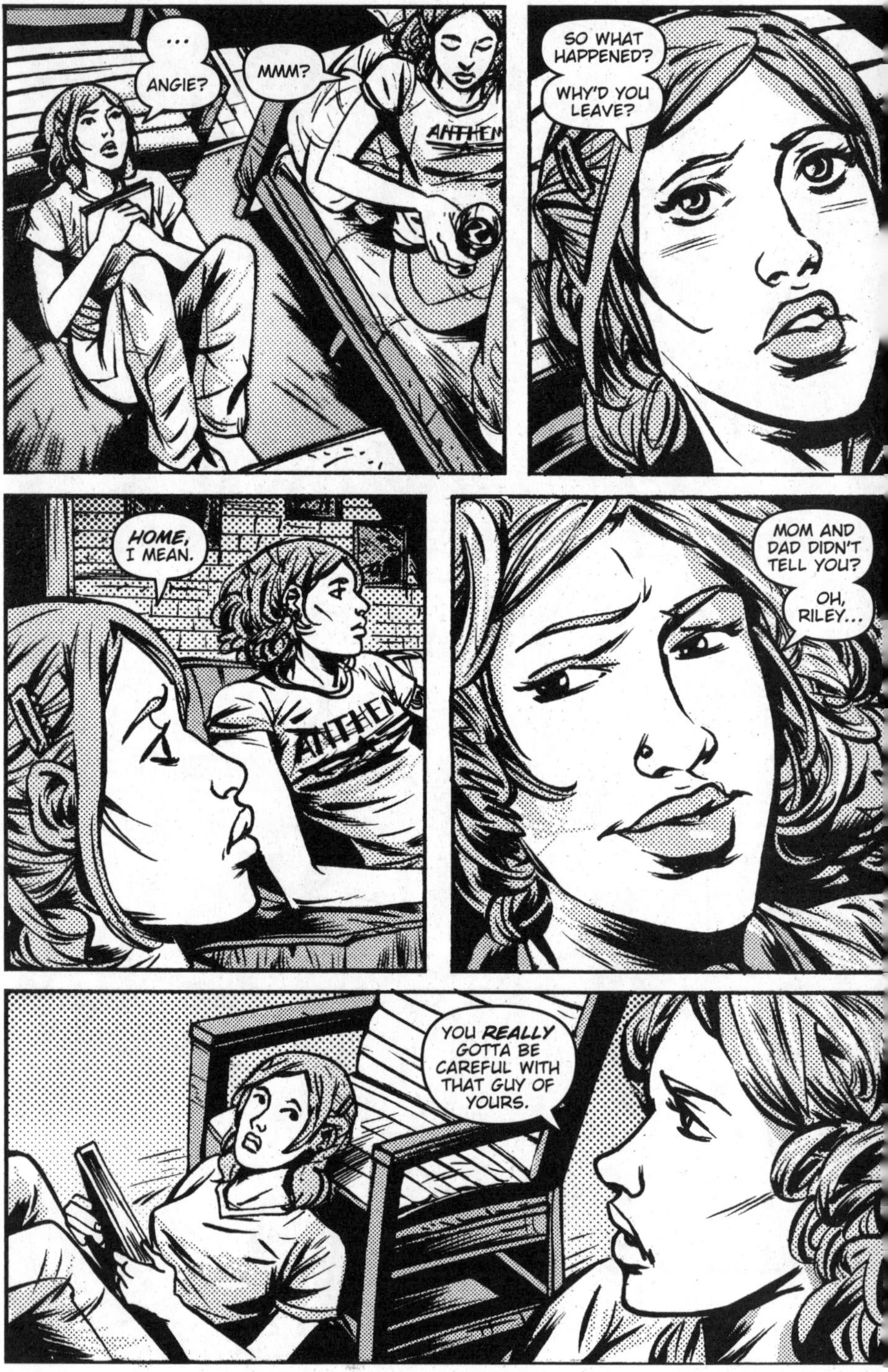
...
ANGIE?
MMM?
SO WHAT HAPPENED?
WHY'D YOU LEAVE?
HOME, I MEAN.
MOM AND DAD DIDN'T TELL YOU?
OH, RILEY...
YOU *REALLY* GOTTA BE CAREFUL WITH THAT GUY OF YOURS.

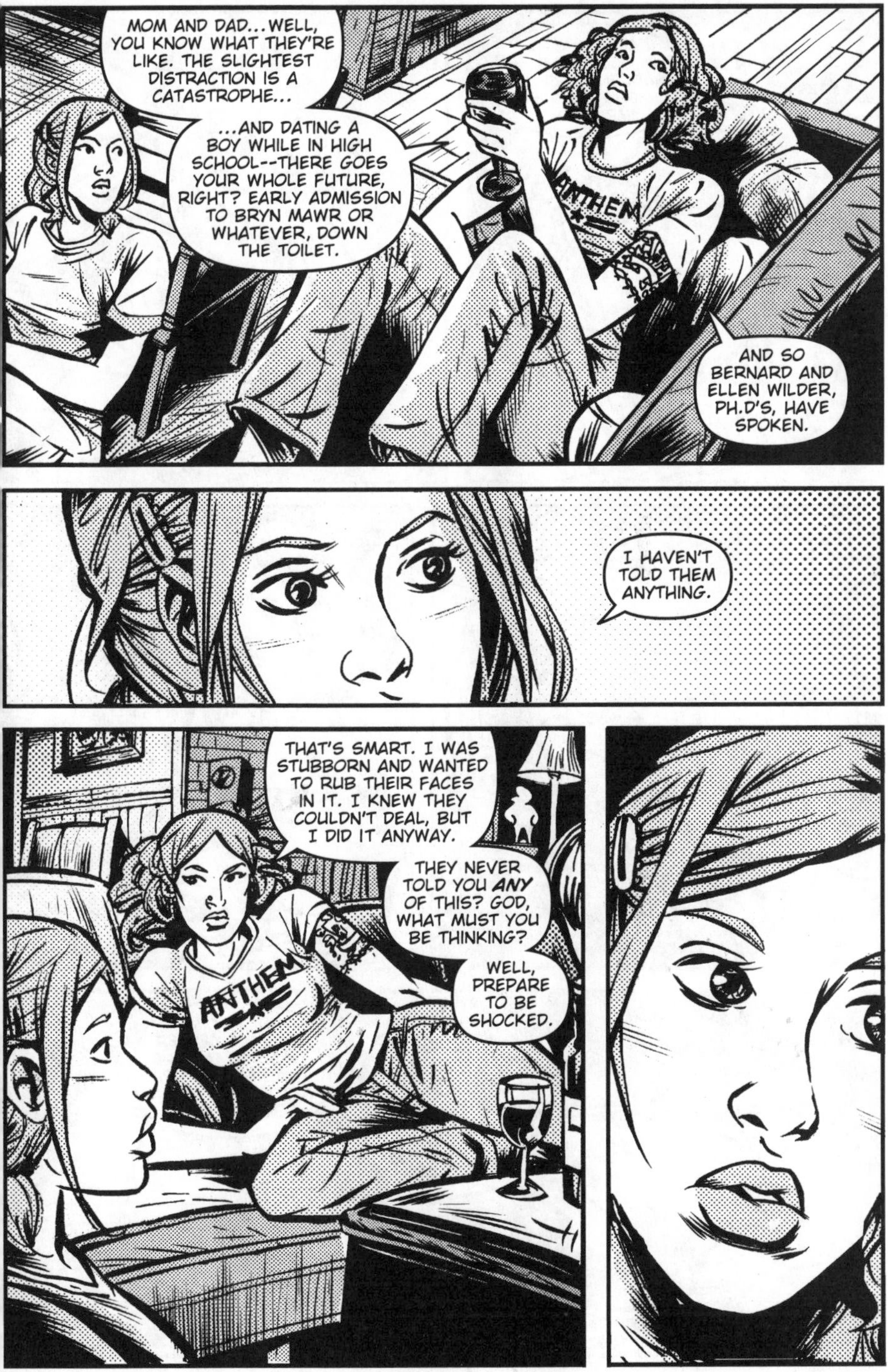
MOM AND DAD...WELL, YOU KNOW WHAT THEY'RE LIKE. THE SLIGHTEST DISTRACTION IS A CATASTROPHE...
...AND DATING A BOY WHILE IN HIGH SCHOOL--THERE GOES YOUR WHOLE FUTURE, RIGHT? EARLY ADMISSION TO BRYN MAWR OR WHATEVER, DOWN THE TOILET.
AND SO BERNARD AND ELLEN WILDER, PH.D'S, HAVE SPOKEN.
I HAVEN'T TOLD THEM ANYTHING.
THAT'S SMART. I WAS STUBBORN AND WANTED TO RUB THEIR FACES IN IT. I KNEW THEY COULDN'T DEAL, BUT I DID IT ANYWAY.
THEY NEVER TOLD YOU *ANY* OF THIS? GOD, WHAT MUST YOU BE THINKING?
WELL, PREPARE TO BE SHOCKED.

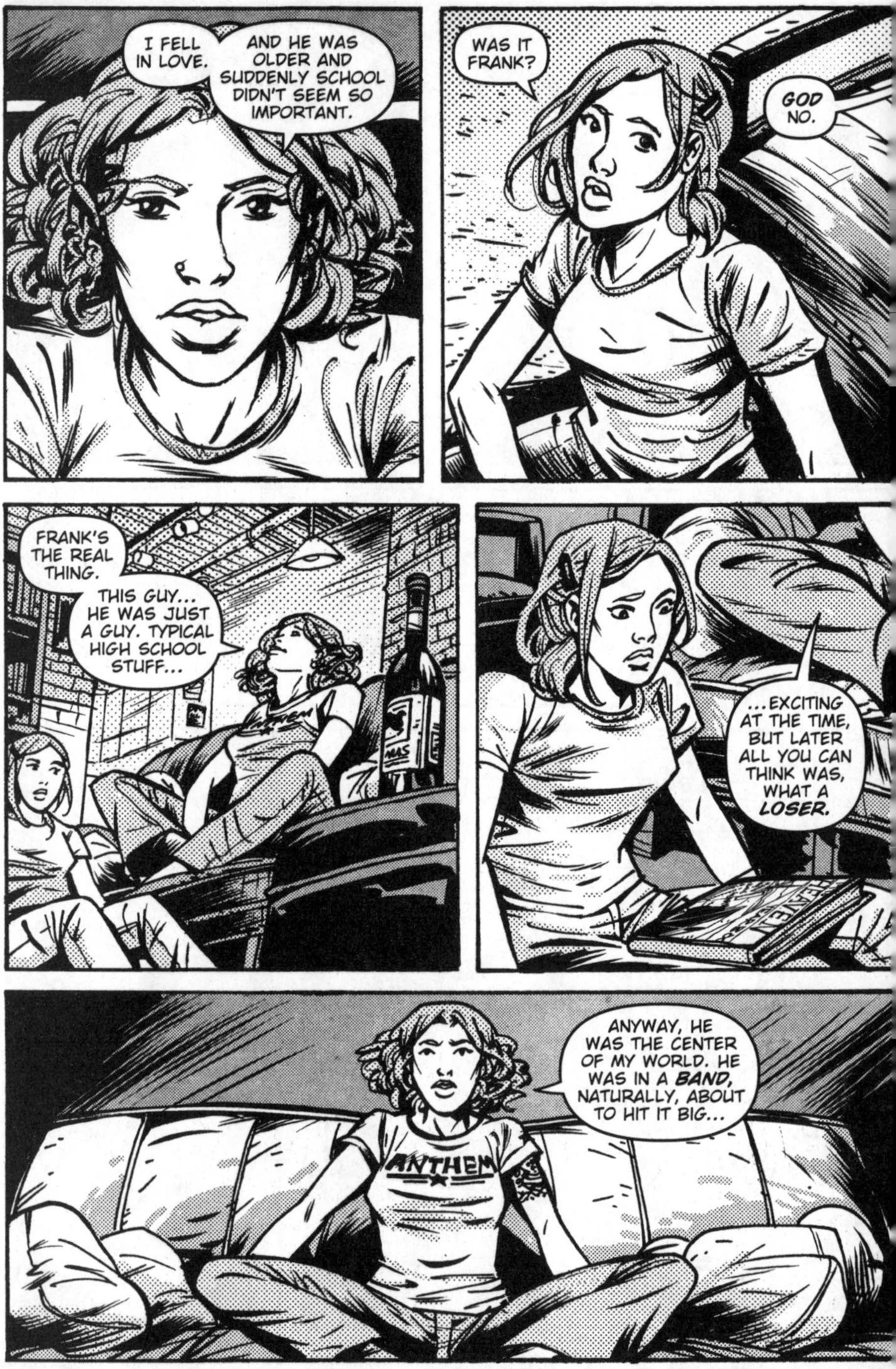
I FELL IN LOVE.
AND HE WAS OLDER AND SUDDENLY SCHOOL DIDN'T SEEM SO IMPORTANT.
WAS IT FRANK?
GOD NO.
FRANK'S THE REAL THING.
THIS GUY... HE WAS JUST A GUY. TYPICAL HIGH SCHOOL STUFF...
...EXCITING AT THE TIME, BUT LATER ALL YOU CAN THINK WAS, WHAT A LOSER.
ANYWAY, HE WAS THE CENTER OF MY WORLD. HE WAS IN A BAND, NATURALLY, ABOUT TO HIT IT BIG...
ANTHEM

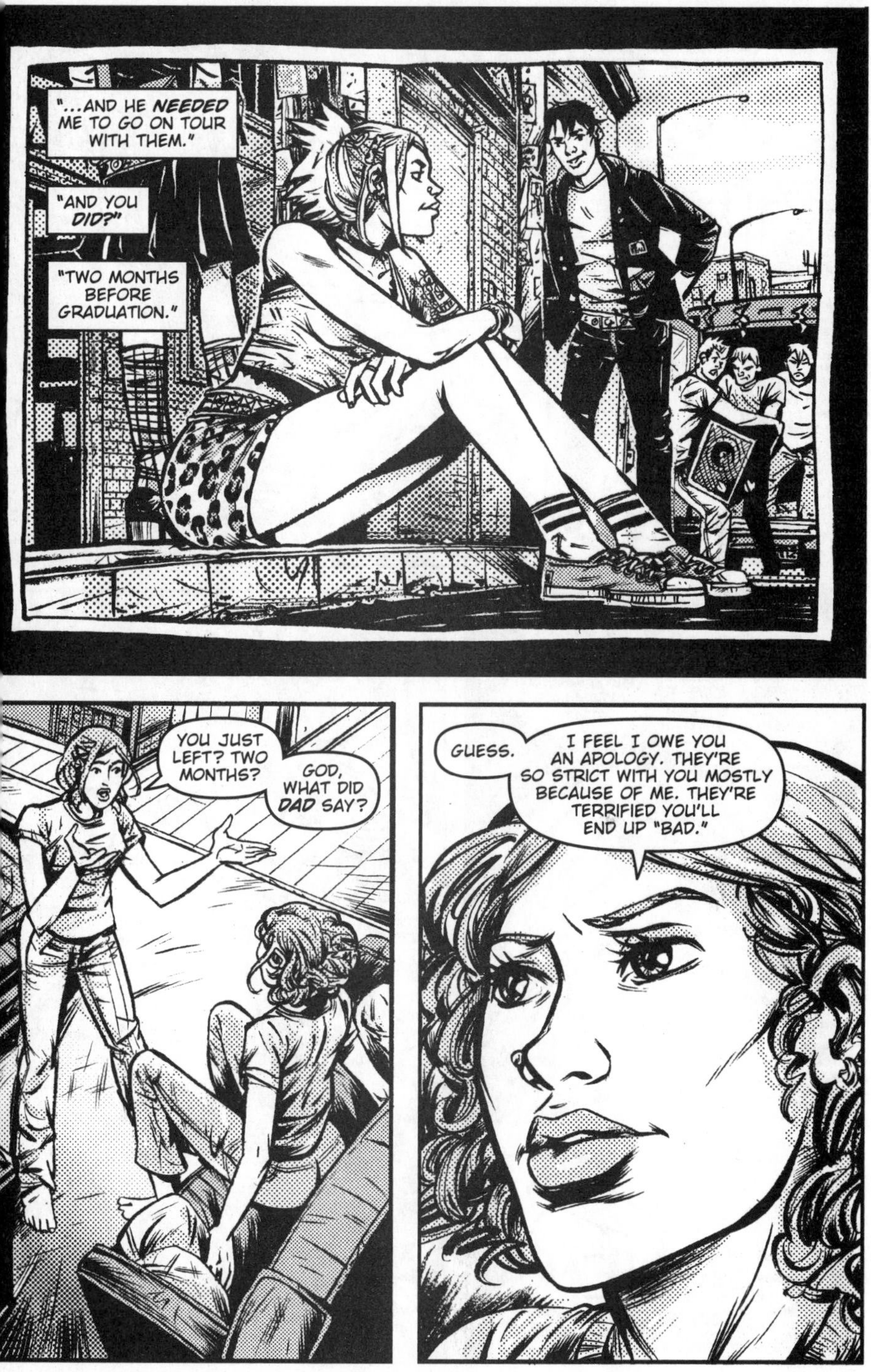
"...AND HE NEEDED ME TO GO ON TOUR WITH THEM."
"AND YOU DID?"
"TWO MONTHS BEFORE GRADUATION."
YOU JUST LEFT? TWO MONTHS?
GOD, WHAT DID DAD SAY?
GUESS.
I FEEL I OWE YOU AN APOLOGY. THEY'RE SO STRICT WITH YOU MOSTLY BECAUSE OF ME. THEY'RE TERRIFIED YOU'LL END UP "BAD."

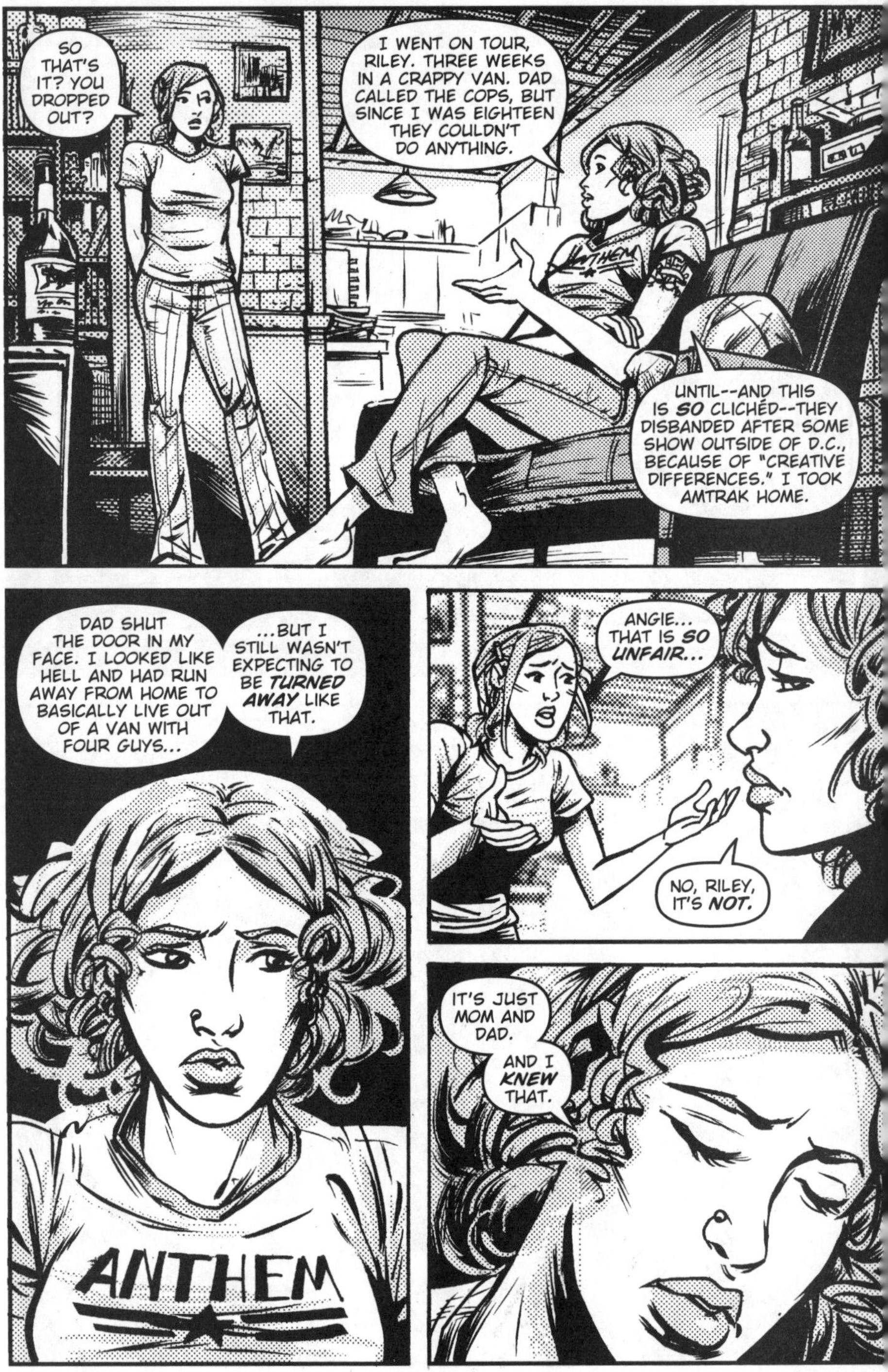
SO THAT'S IT? YOU DROPPED OUT?
I WENT ON TOUR, RILEY. THREE WEEKS IN A CRAPPY VAN. DAD CALLED THE COPS, BUT SINCE I WAS EIGHTEEN THEY COULDN'T DO ANYTHING.
ANTHEM
UNTIL--AND THIS IS **SO** CLICHÉD--THEY DISBANDED AFTER SOME SHOW OUTSIDE OF D.C., BECAUSE OF "CREATIVE DIFFERENCES." I TOOK AMTRAK HOME.
DAD SHUT THE DOOR IN MY FACE. I LOOKED LIKE HELL AND HAD RUN AWAY FROM HOME TO BASICALLY LIVE OUT OF A VAN WITH FOUR GUYS...
...BUT I STILL WASN'T EXPECTING TO BE ***TURNED AWAY*** LIKE THAT.
ANTHEM
ANGIE... THAT IS ***SO UNFAIR...***
NO, RILEY, IT'S ***NOT.***
IT'S JUST MOM AND DAD.
AND I ***KNEW*** THAT.

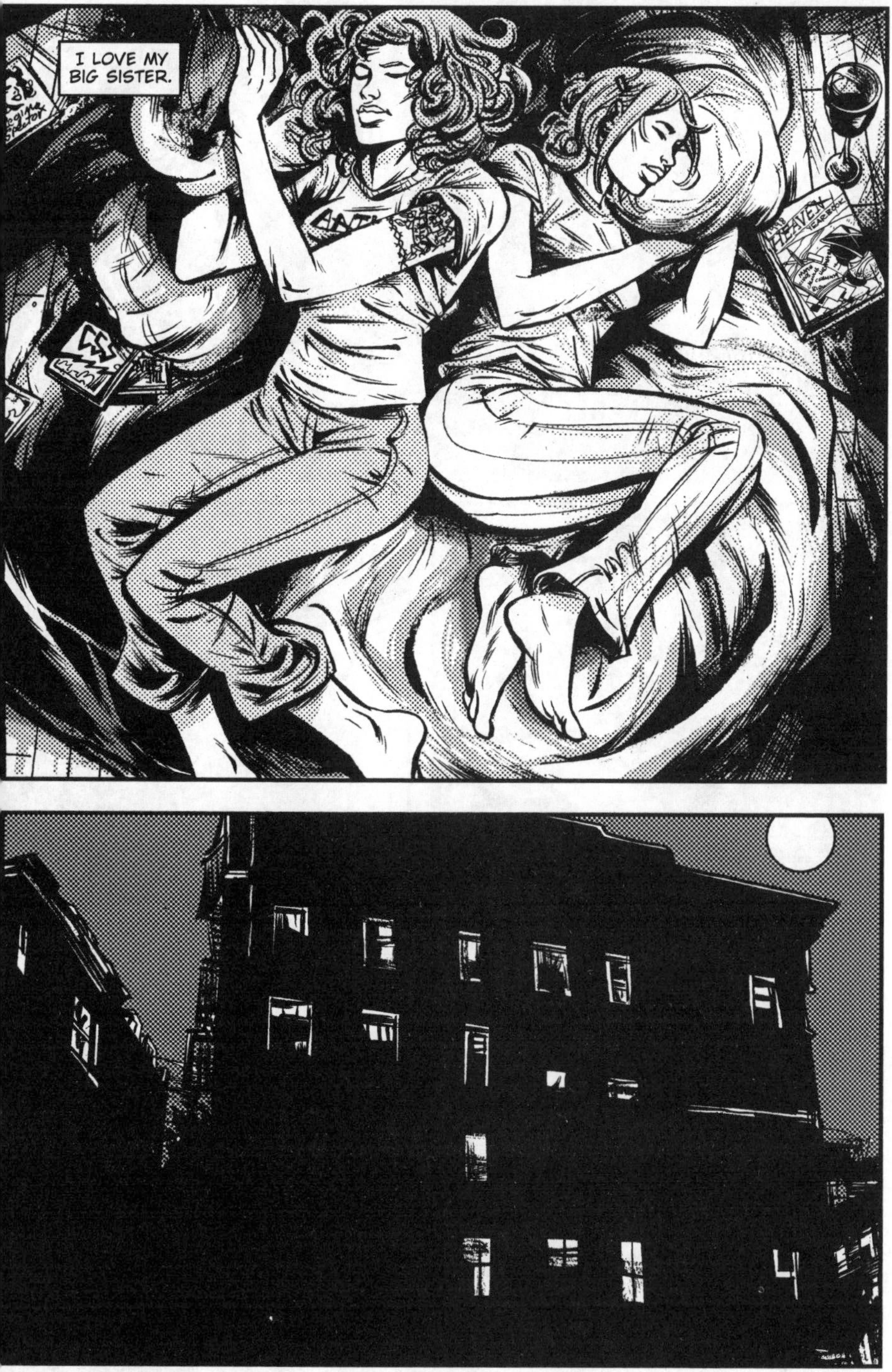
I LOVE MY BIG SISTER.

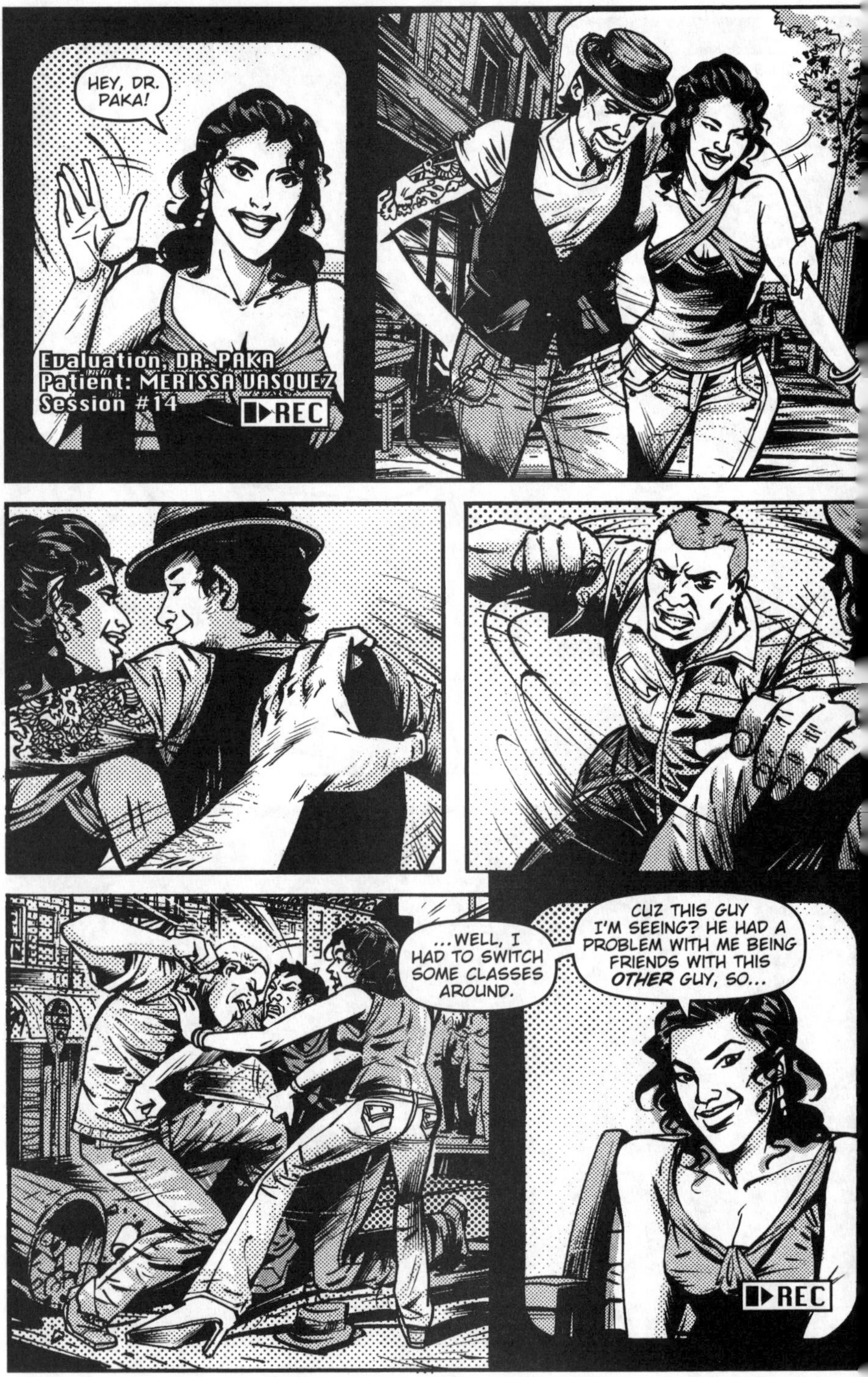
HEY, DR. PAKA!
Evaluation, DR. PAKA
Patient: MERISSA VASQUEZ
Session #14
REC
...WELL, I HAD TO SWITCH SOME CLASSES AROUND.
CUZ THIS GUY I'M SEEING? HE HAD A PROBLEM WITH ME BEING FRIENDS WITH THIS OTHER GUY, SO...
REC

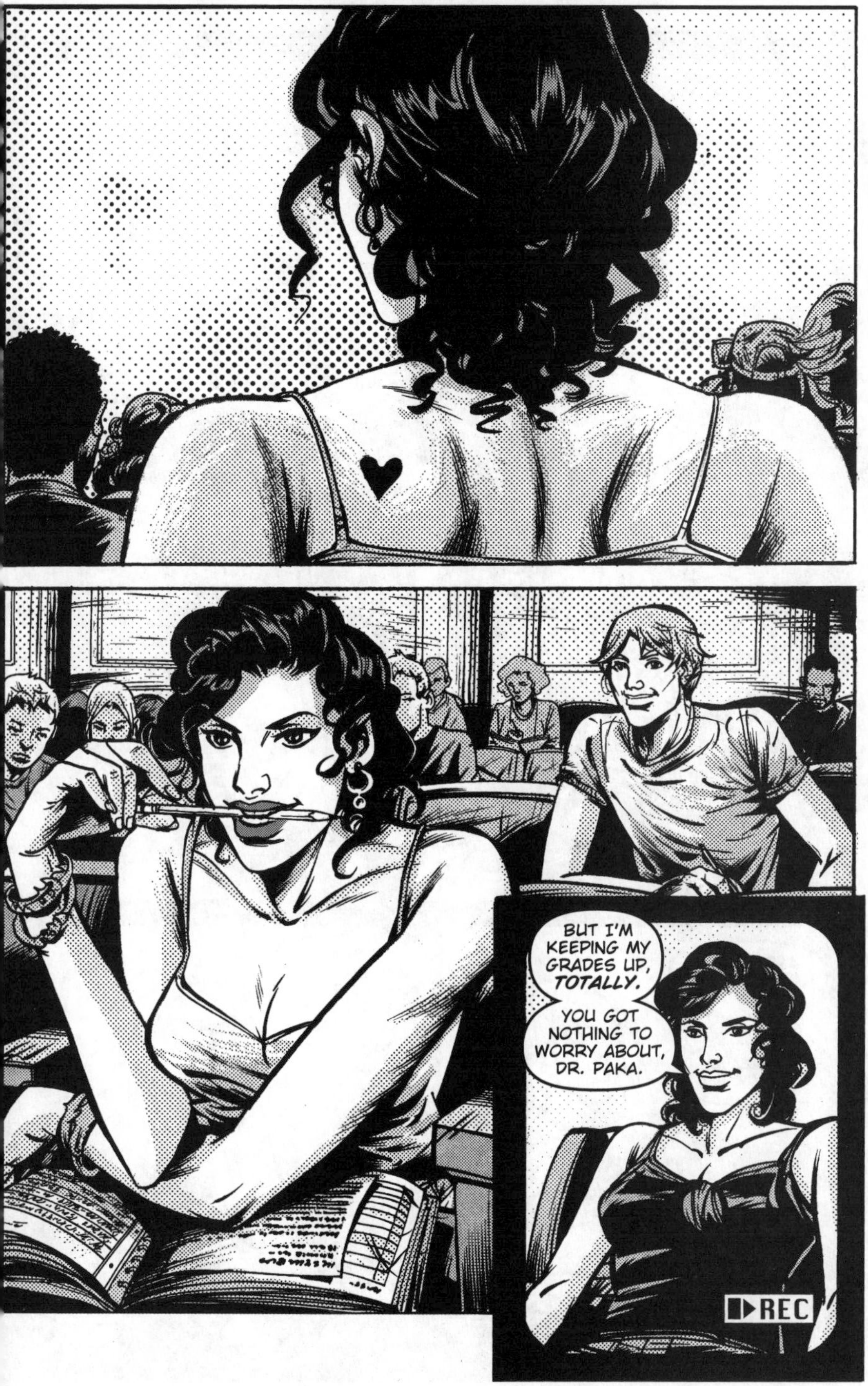
BUT I'M KEEPING MY GRADES UP, *TOTALLY.*
YOU GOT NOTHING TO WORRY ABOUT, DR. PAKA.
REC

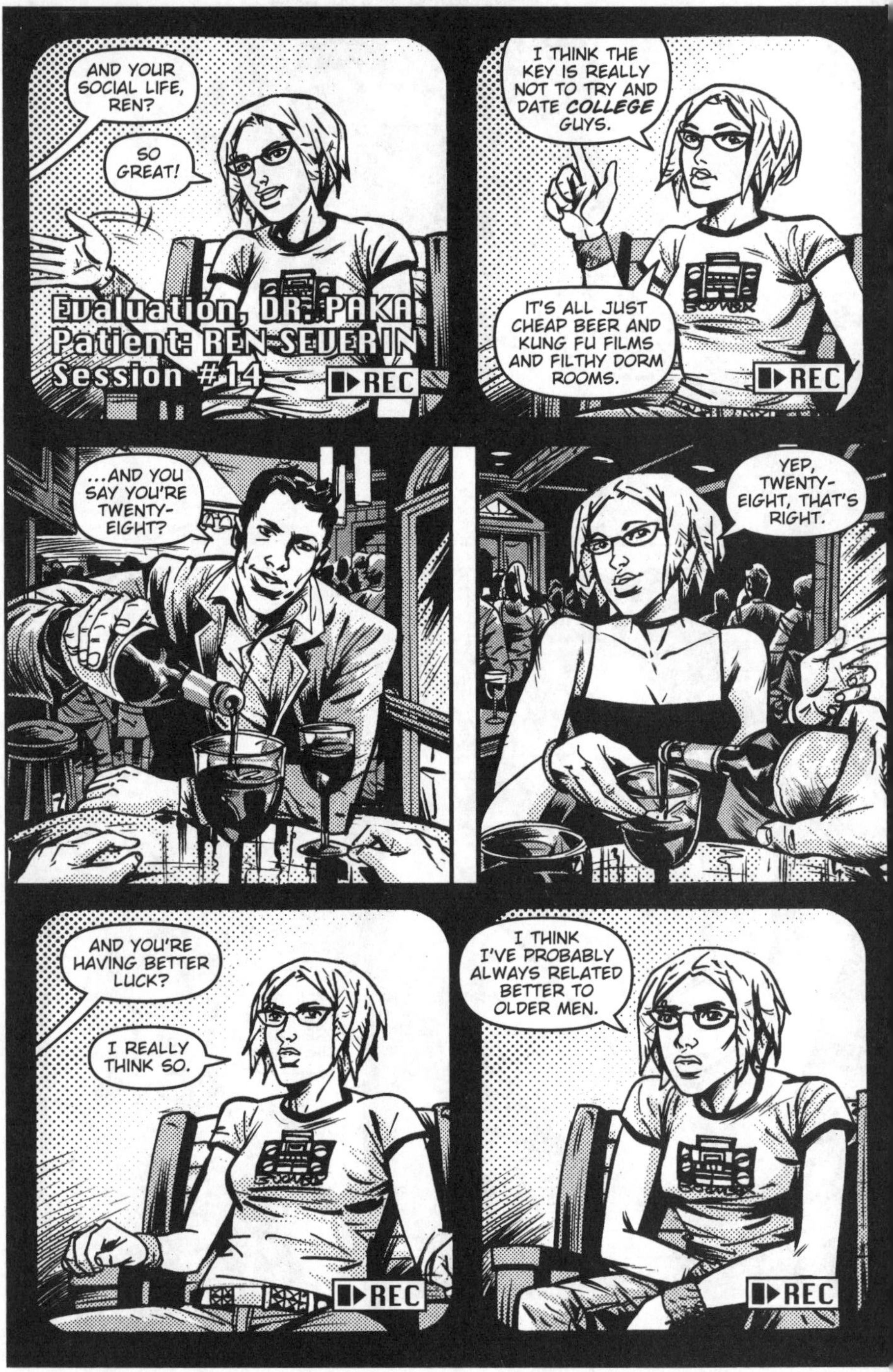
AND YOUR SOCIAL LIFE, REN?
SO GREAT!
Evaluation, DR. PAKA
Patient: REN SEVERIN
Session #14
REC
I THINK THE KEY IS REALLY NOT TO TRY AND DATE COLLEGE GUYS.
IT'S ALL JUST CHEAP BEER AND KUNG FU FILMS AND FILTHY DORM ROOMS.
REC
...AND YOU SAY YOU'RE TWENTY-EIGHT?
YEP, TWENTY-EIGHT, THAT'S RIGHT.
AND YOU'RE HAVING BETTER LUCK?
I REALLY THINK SO.
REC
I THINK I'VE PROBABLY ALWAYS RELATED BETTER TO OLDER MEN.
REC

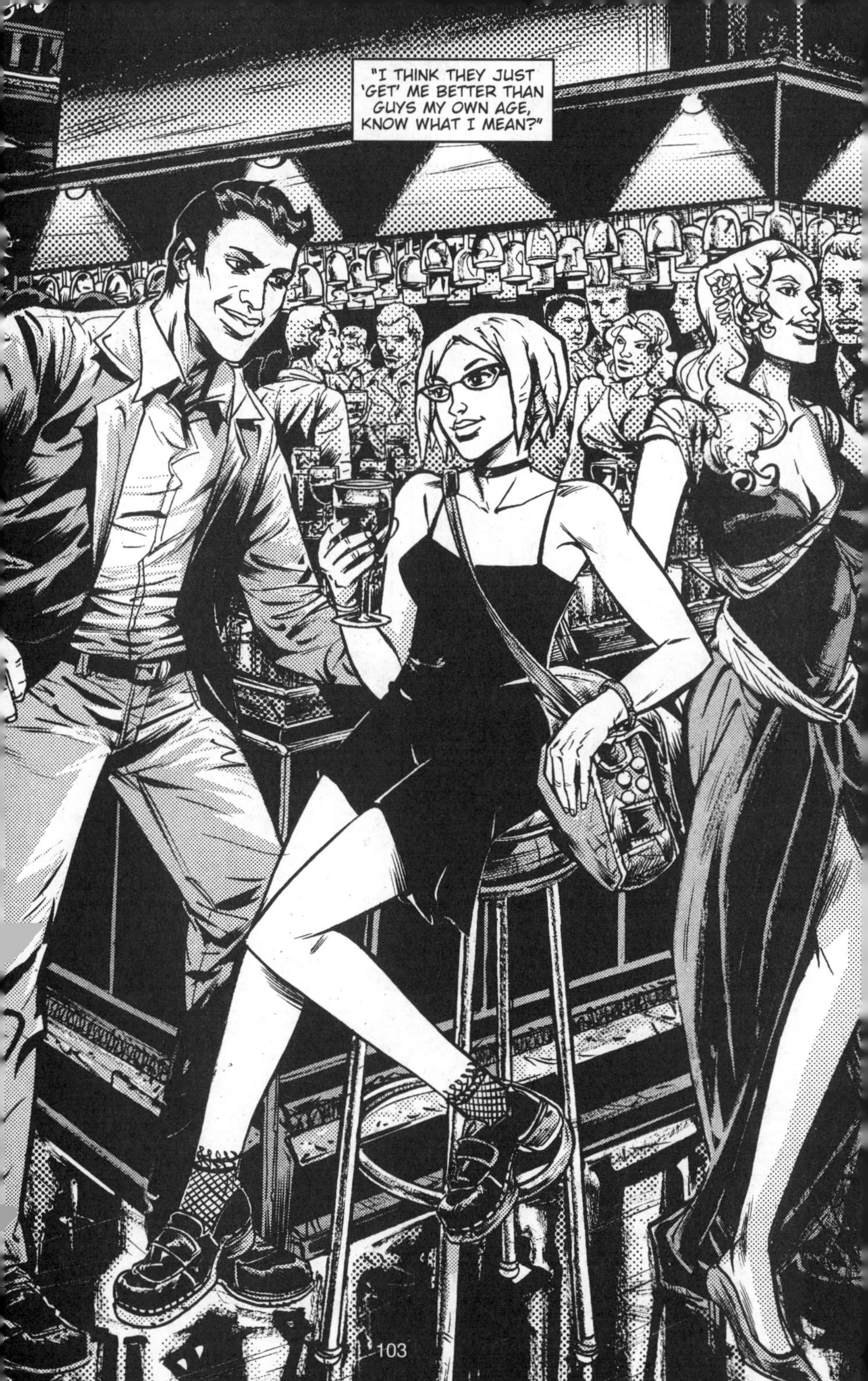
"I THINK THEY JUST 'GET' ME BETTER THAN GUYS MY OWN AGE, KNOW WHAT I MEAN?"

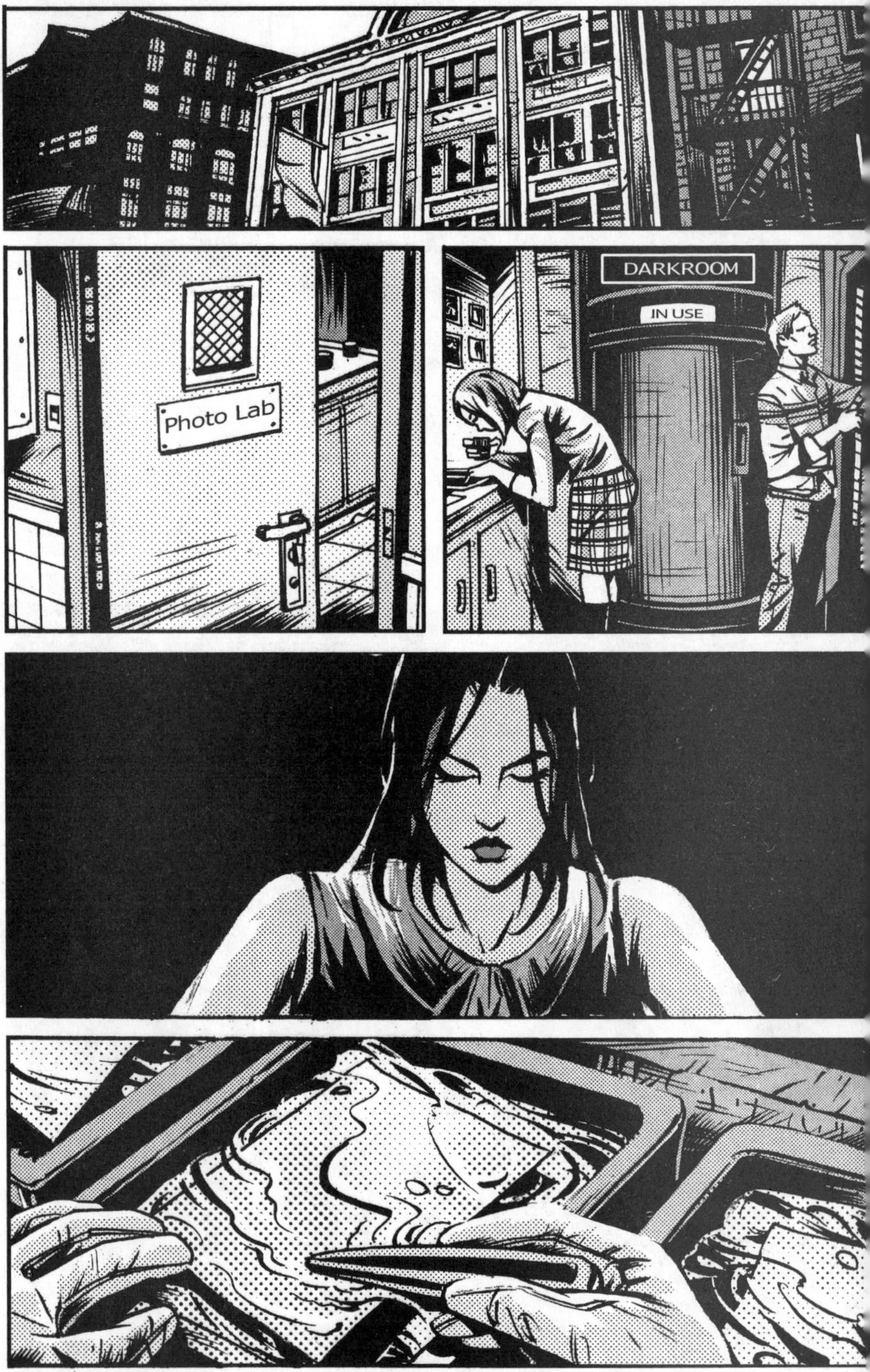
Photo Lab
DARKROOM
IN USE

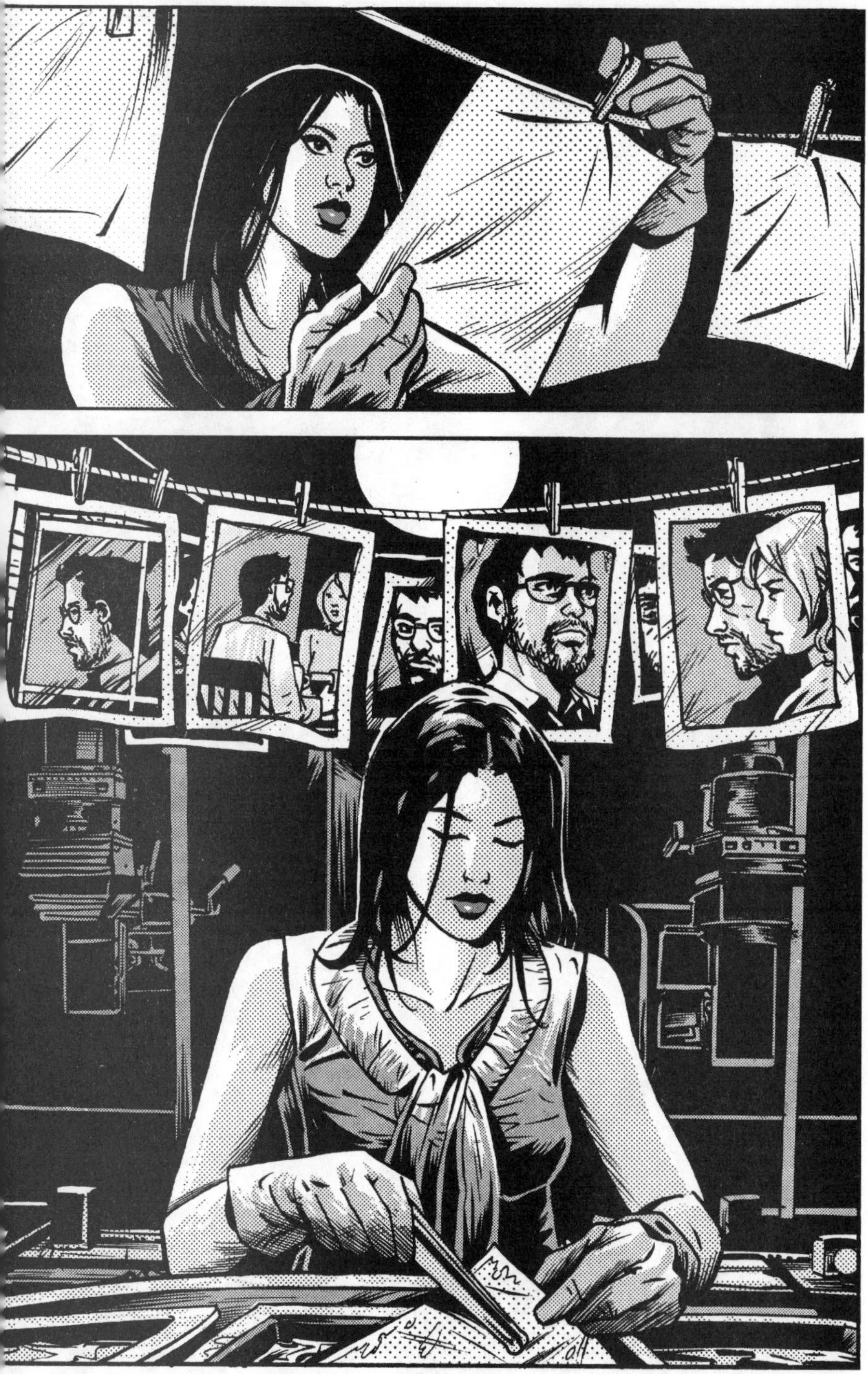

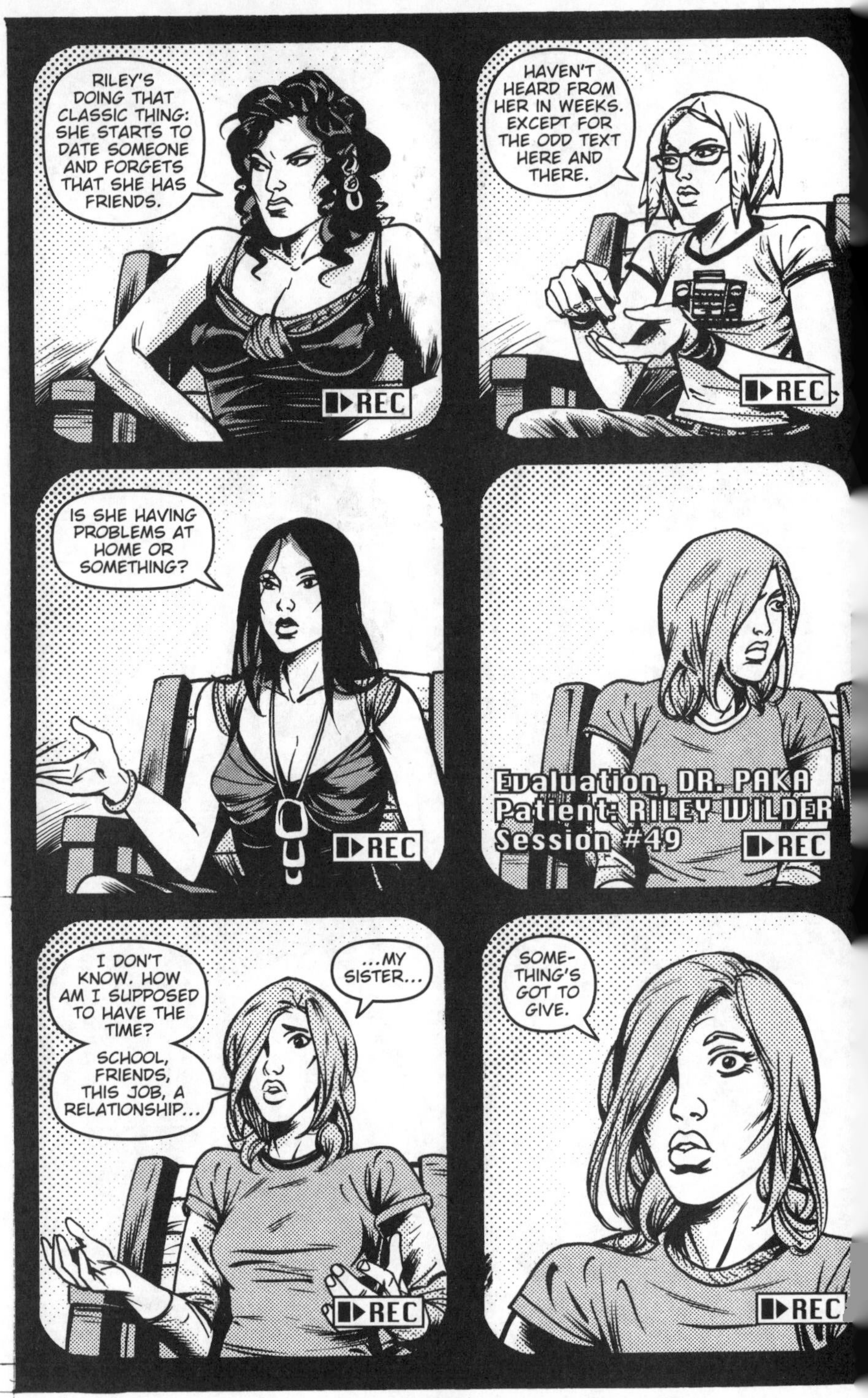
RILEY'S DOING THAT CLASSIC THING: SHE STARTS TO DATE SOMEONE AND FORGETS THAT SHE HAS FRIENDS.
REC
HAVEN'T HEARD FROM HER IN WEEKS. EXCEPT FOR THE ODD TEXT HERE AND THERE.
REC
IS SHE HAVING PROBLEMS AT HOME OR SOMETHING?
REC
Evaluation, DR. PAKA
Patient: RILEY WILDER
Session #49
REC
I DON'T KNOW. HOW AM I SUPPOSED TO HAVE THE TIME?
SCHOOL, FRIENDS, THIS JOB, A RELATIONSHIP...
...MY SISTER...
REC
SOME-THING'S GOT TO GIVE.
REC

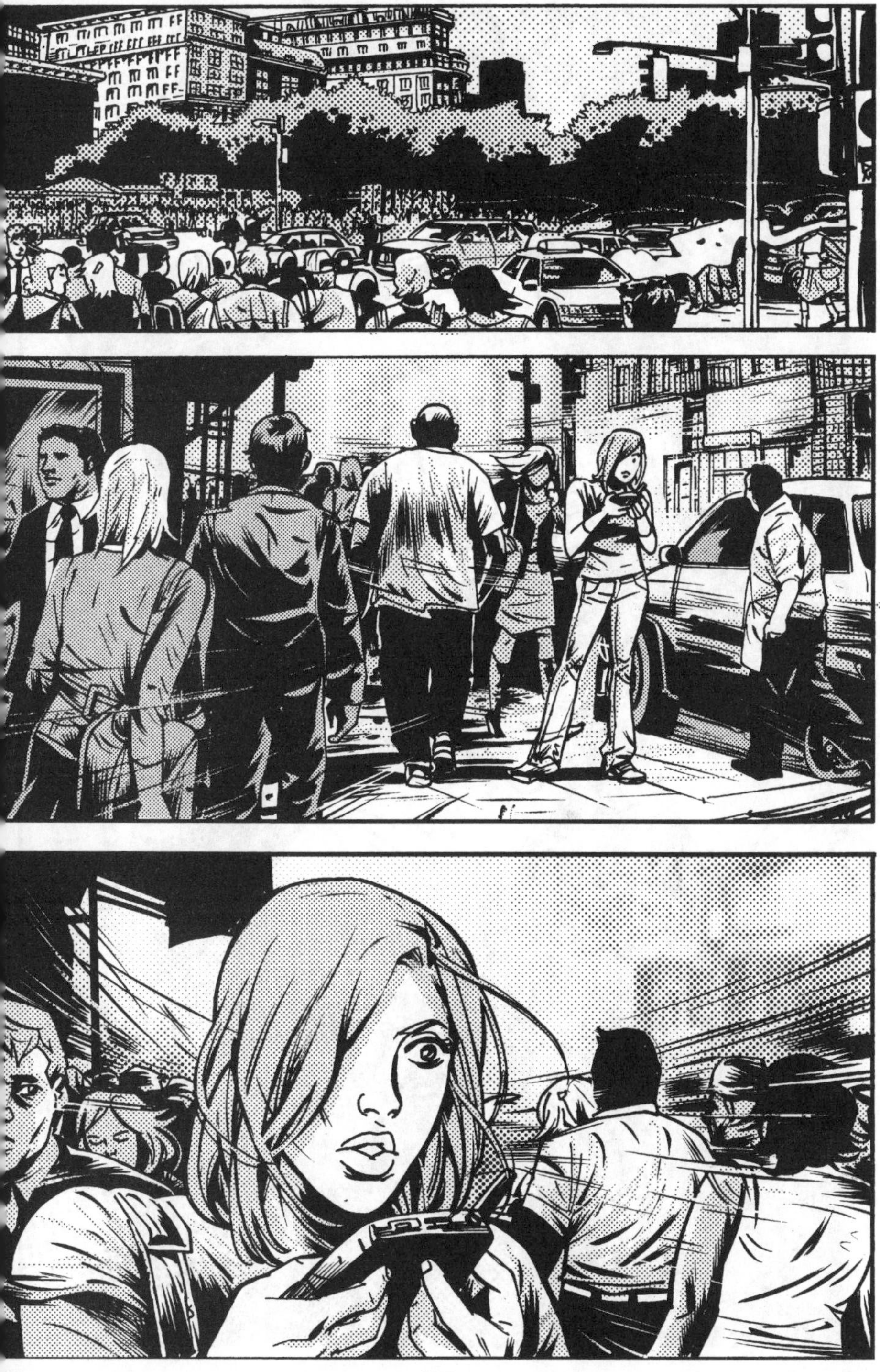

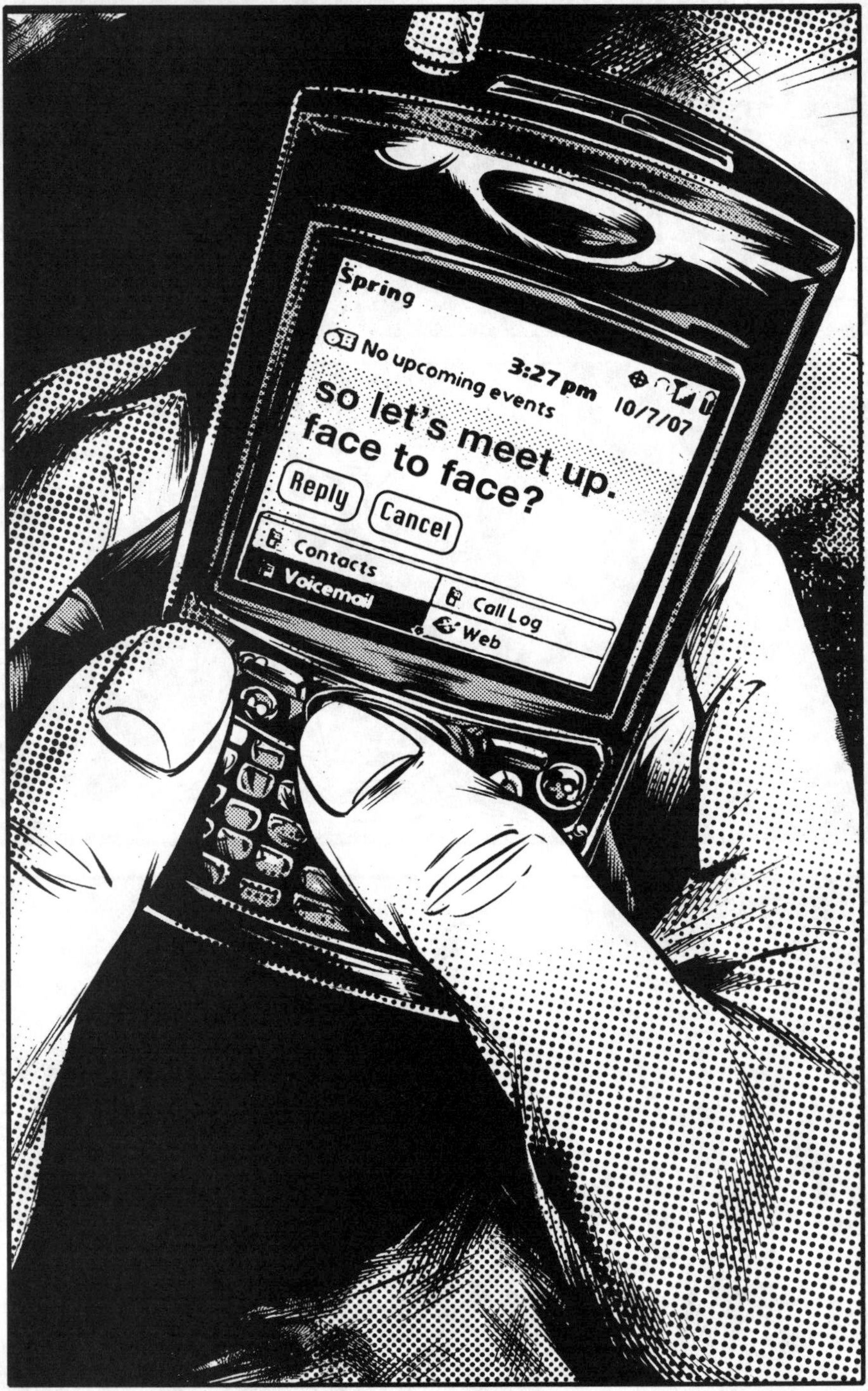
Spring
No upcoming events
3:27 pm
10/7/07
so let's meet up.
face to face?
Reply
Cancel
Contacts
Voicemail
Call Log
Web

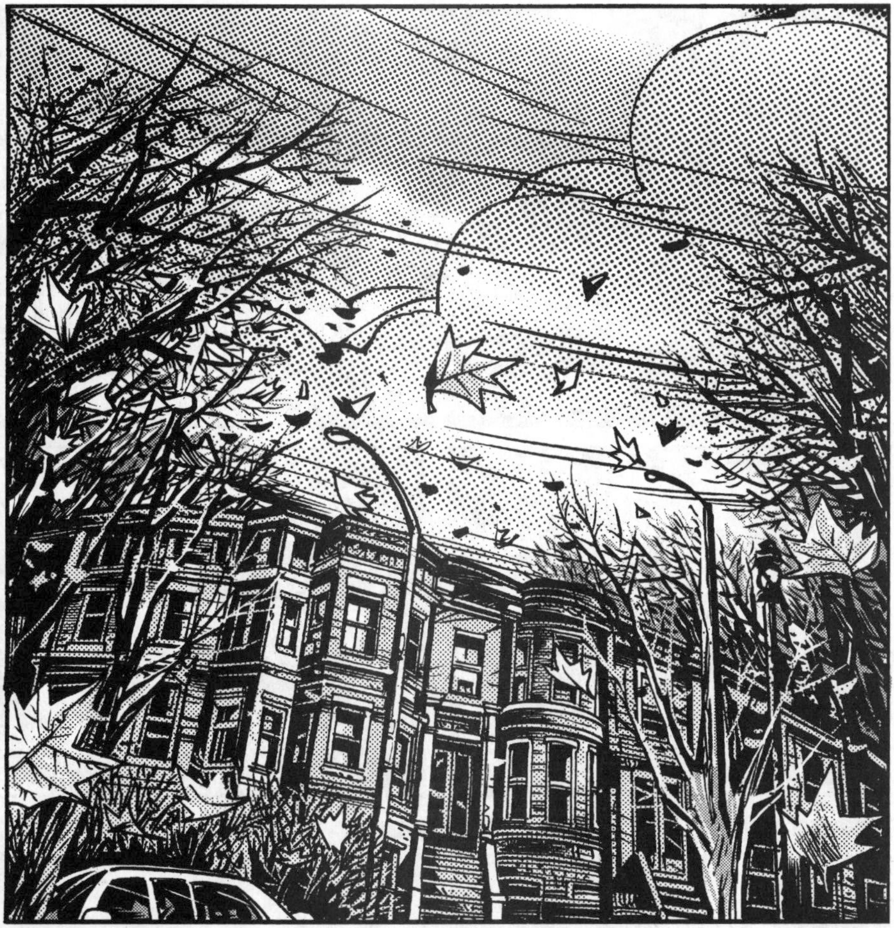

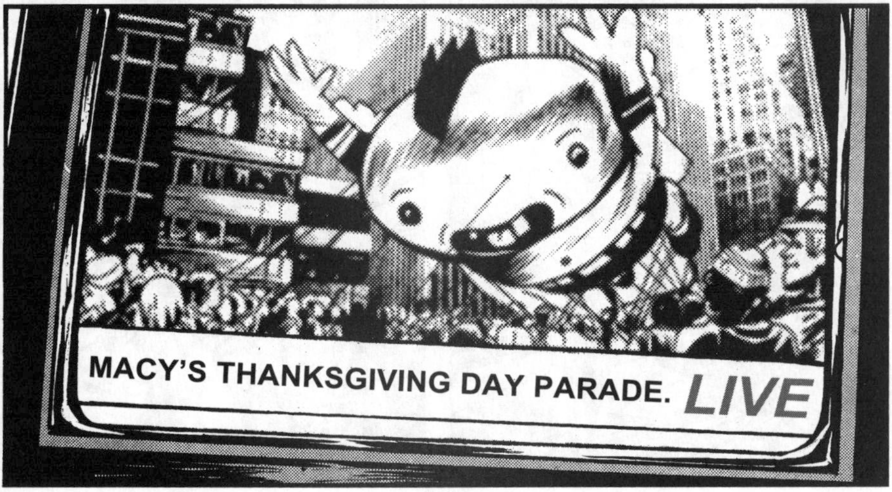
MACY'S THANKSGIVING DAY PARADE. LIVE

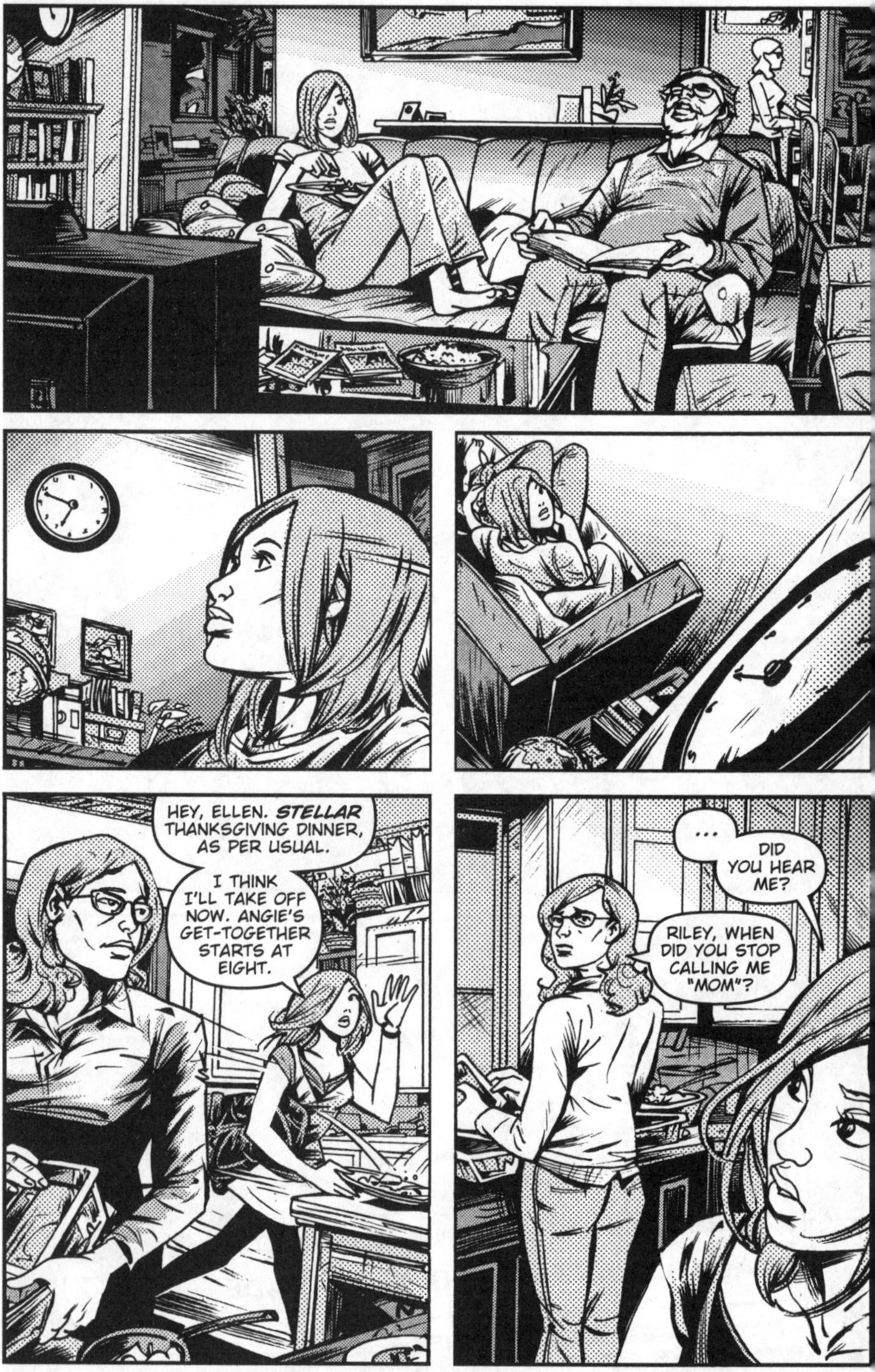
HEY, ELLEN. *STELLAR* THANKSGIVING DINNER, AS PER USUAL.
I THINK I'LL TAKE OFF NOW. ANGIE'S GET-TOGETHER STARTS AT EIGHT.
...
DID YOU HEAR ME?
RILEY, WHEN DID YOU STOP CALLING ME "MOM"?

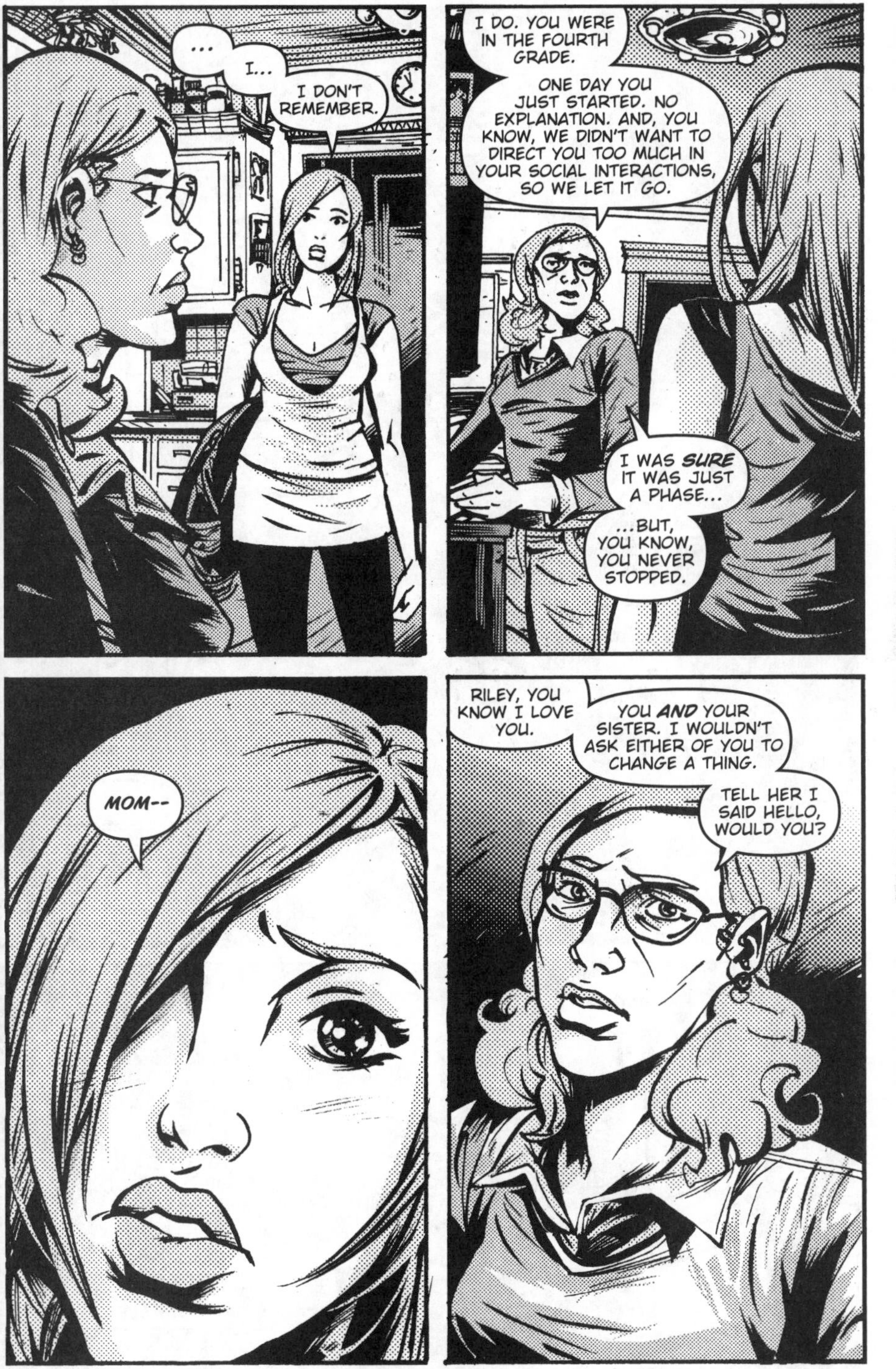
...
I...
I DON'T REMEMBER.
I DO. YOU WERE IN THE FOURTH GRADE.
ONE DAY YOU JUST STARTED. NO EXPLANATION. AND, YOU KNOW, WE DIDN'T WANT TO DIRECT YOU TOO MUCH IN YOUR SOCIAL INTERACTIONS, SO WE LET IT GO.
I WAS SURE IT WAS JUST A PHASE...
...BUT, YOU KNOW, YOU NEVER STOPPED.
MOM--
RILEY, YOU KNOW I LOVE YOU.
YOU AND YOUR SISTER. I WOULDN'T ASK EITHER OF YOU TO CHANGE A THING.
TELL HER I SAID HELLO, WOULD YOU?

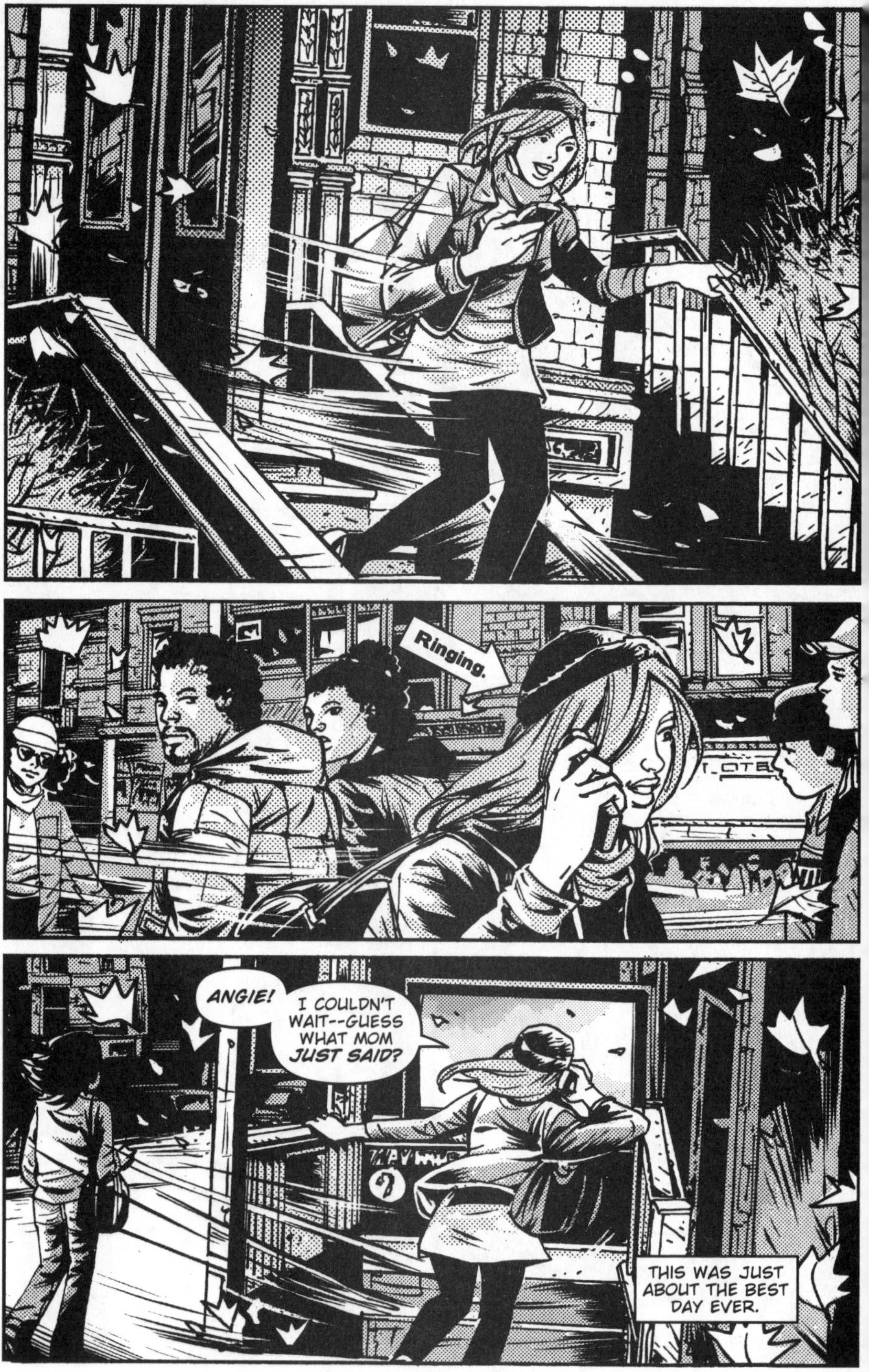
Ringing.
ANGIE!
I COULDN'T WAIT--GUESS WHAT MOM JUST SAID?
THIS WAS JUST ABOUT THE BEST DAY EVER.

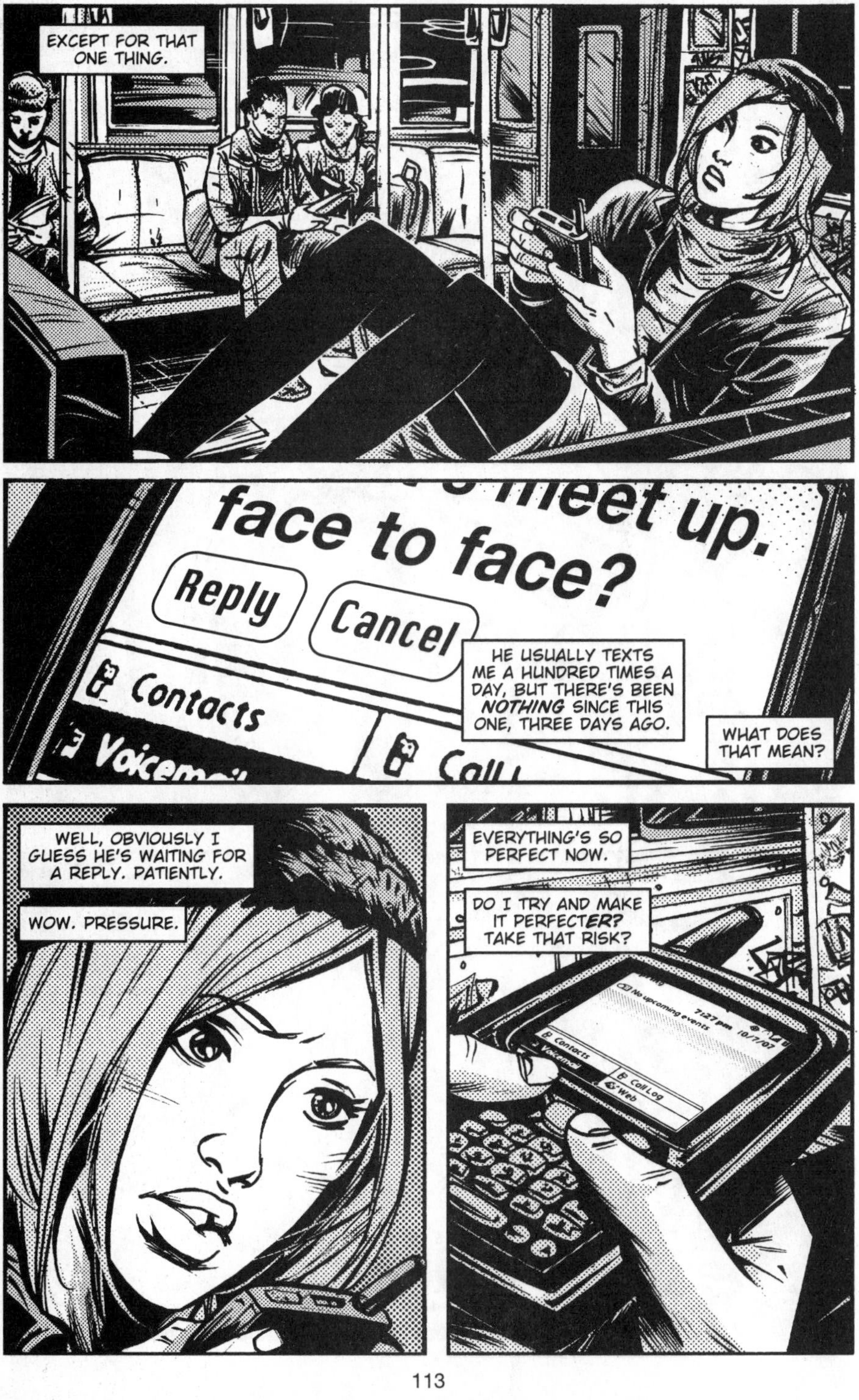
EXCEPT FOR THAT ONE THING.
meet up.
face to face?
Reply
Cancel
Contacts
HE USUALLY TEXTS ME A HUNDRED TIMES A DAY, BUT THERE'S BEEN ***NOTHING*** SINCE THIS ONE, THREE DAYS AGO.
WHAT DOES THAT MEAN?
WELL, OBVIOUSLY I GUESS HE'S WAITING FOR A REPLY. PATIENTLY.
WOW. PRESSURE.
EVERYTHING'S SO PERFECT NOW.
DO I TRY AND MAKE IT PERFECT***ER?*** TAKE THAT RISK?
No upcoming events
7:27 pm
10/7/07
Contacts
Call Log
Web

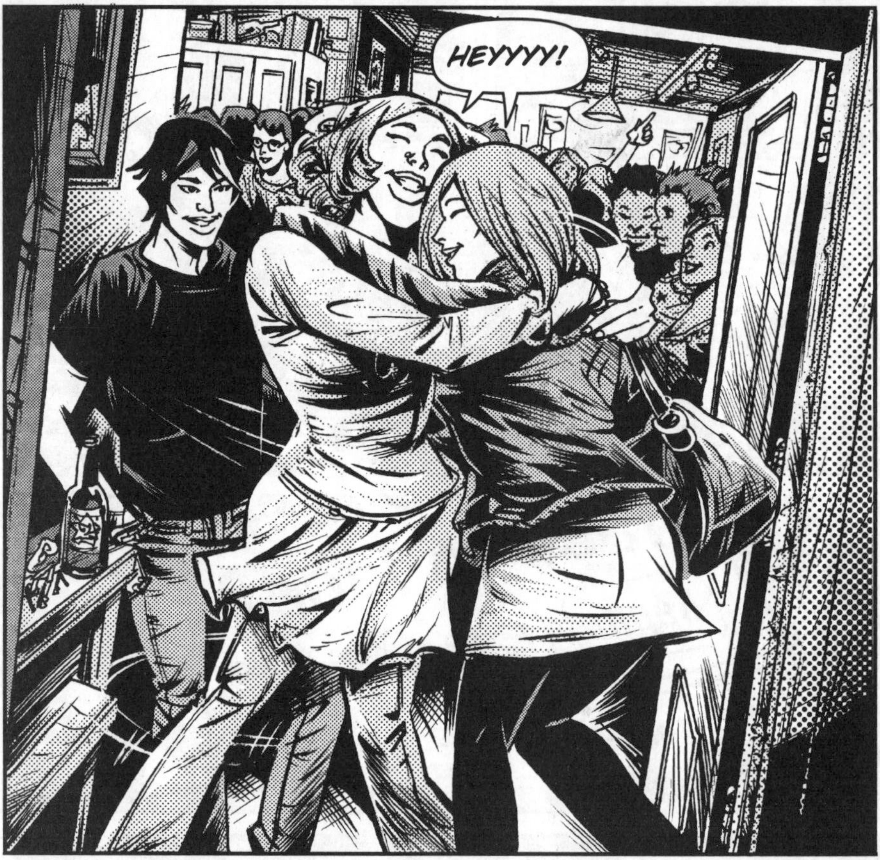
HEYYYY!

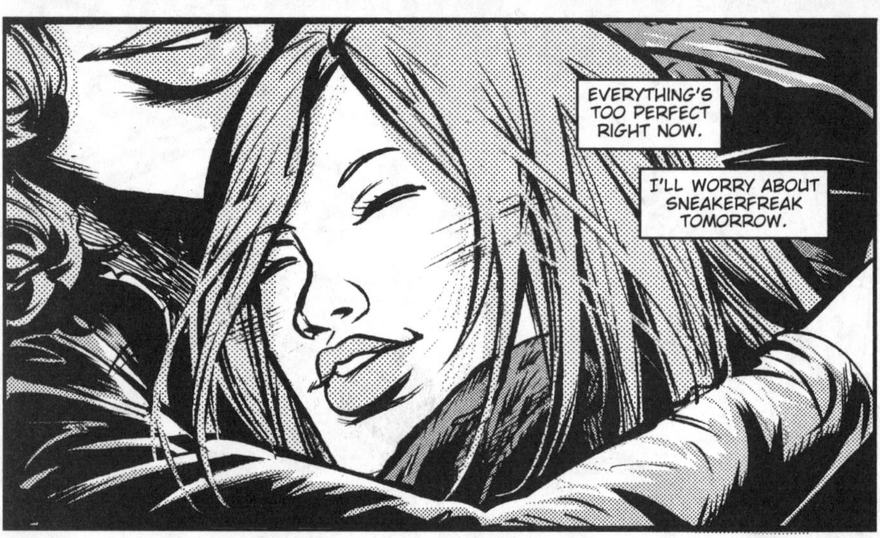
EVERYTHING'S TOO PERFECT RIGHT NOW.
I'LL WORRY ABOUT SNEAKERFREAK TOMORROW.

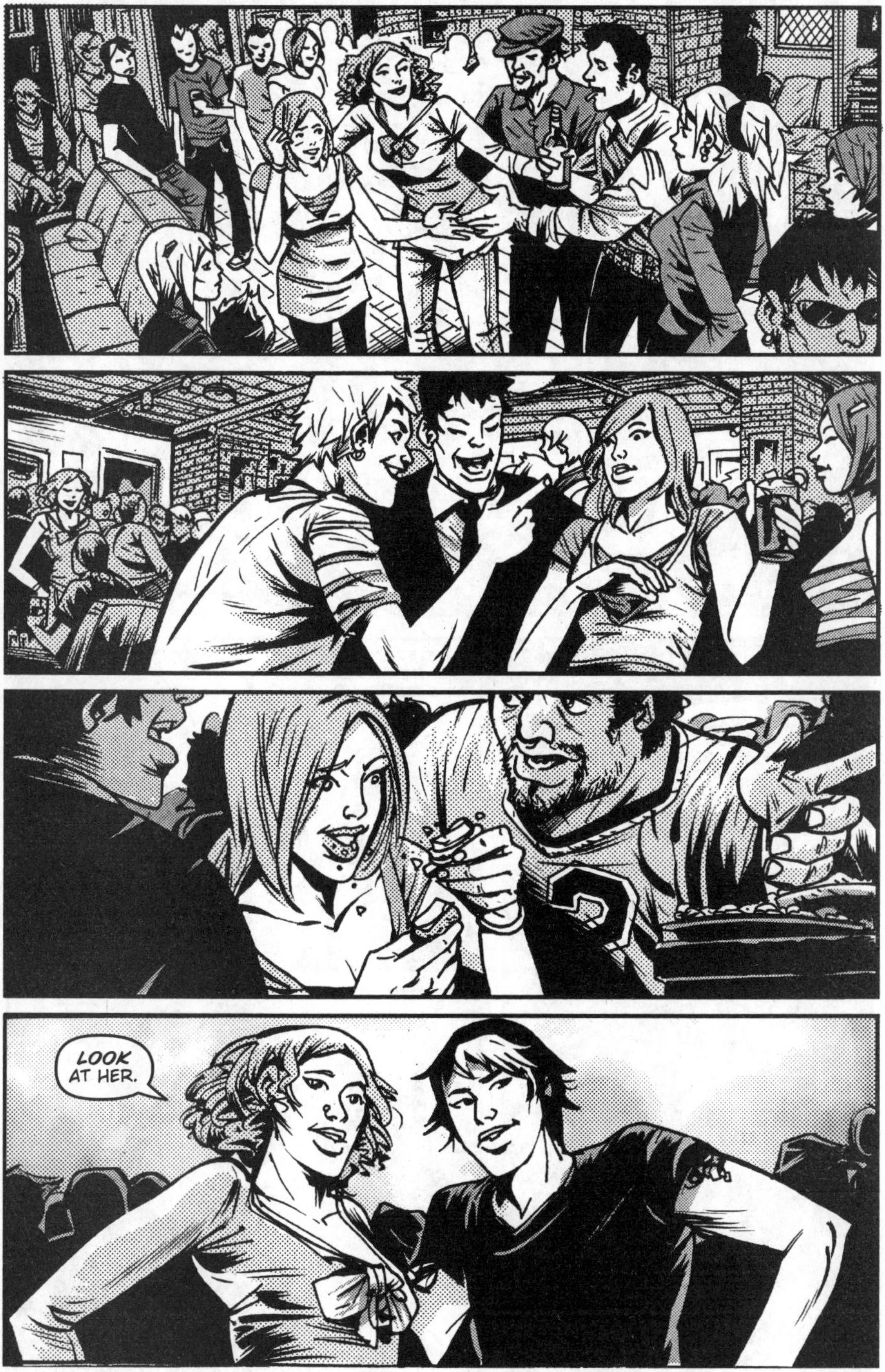
LOOK AT HER.

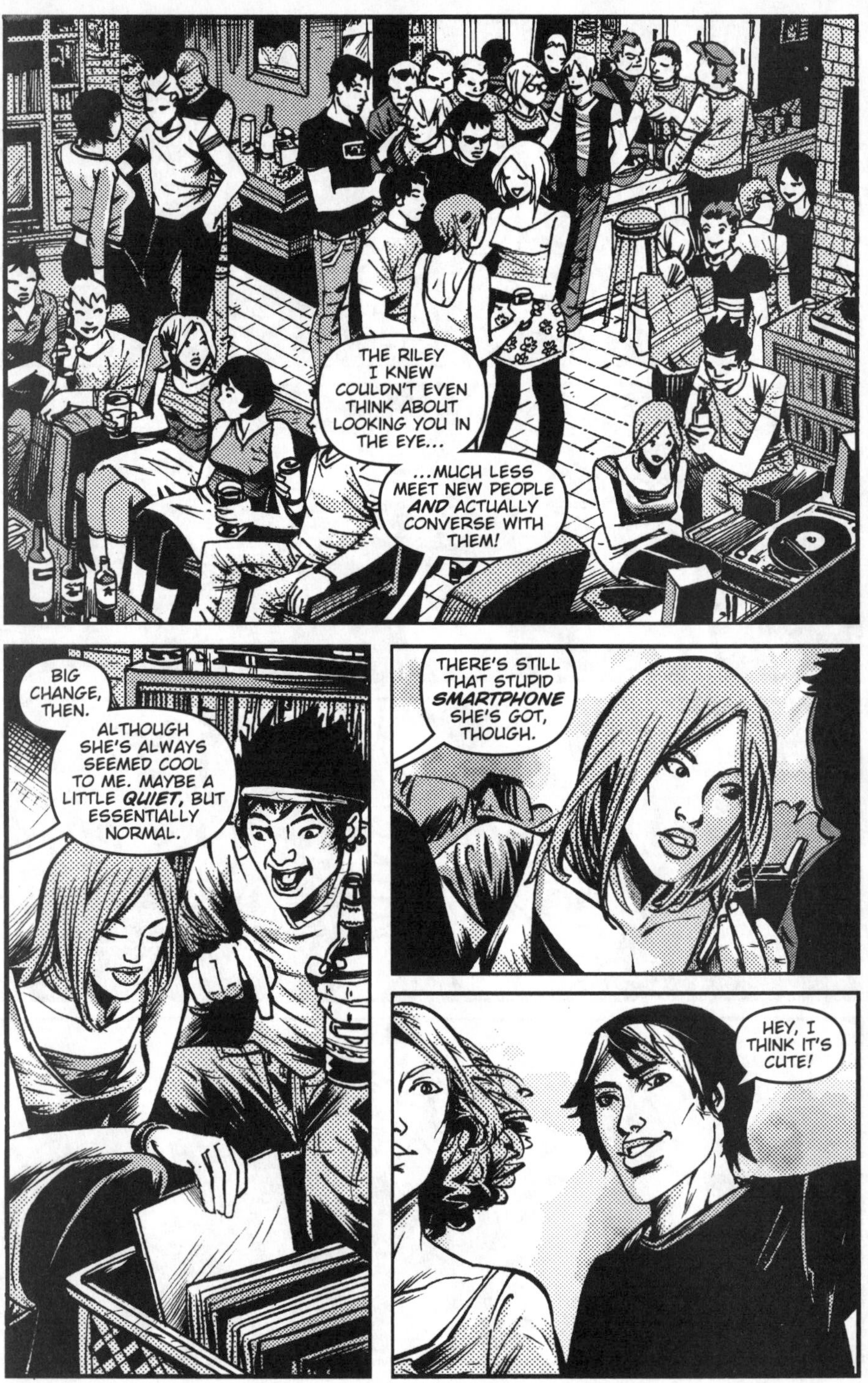
THE RILEY I KNEW COULDN'T EVEN THINK ABOUT LOOKING YOU IN THE EYE...
...MUCH LESS MEET NEW PEOPLE AND ACTUALLY CONVERSE WITH THEM!
BIG CHANGE, THEN.
ALTHOUGH SHE'S ALWAYS SEEMED COOL TO ME. MAYBE A LITTLE QUIET, BUT ESSENTIALLY NORMAL.
THERE'S STILL THAT STUPID SMARTPHONE SHE'S GOT, THOUGH.
HEY, I THINK IT'S CUTE!

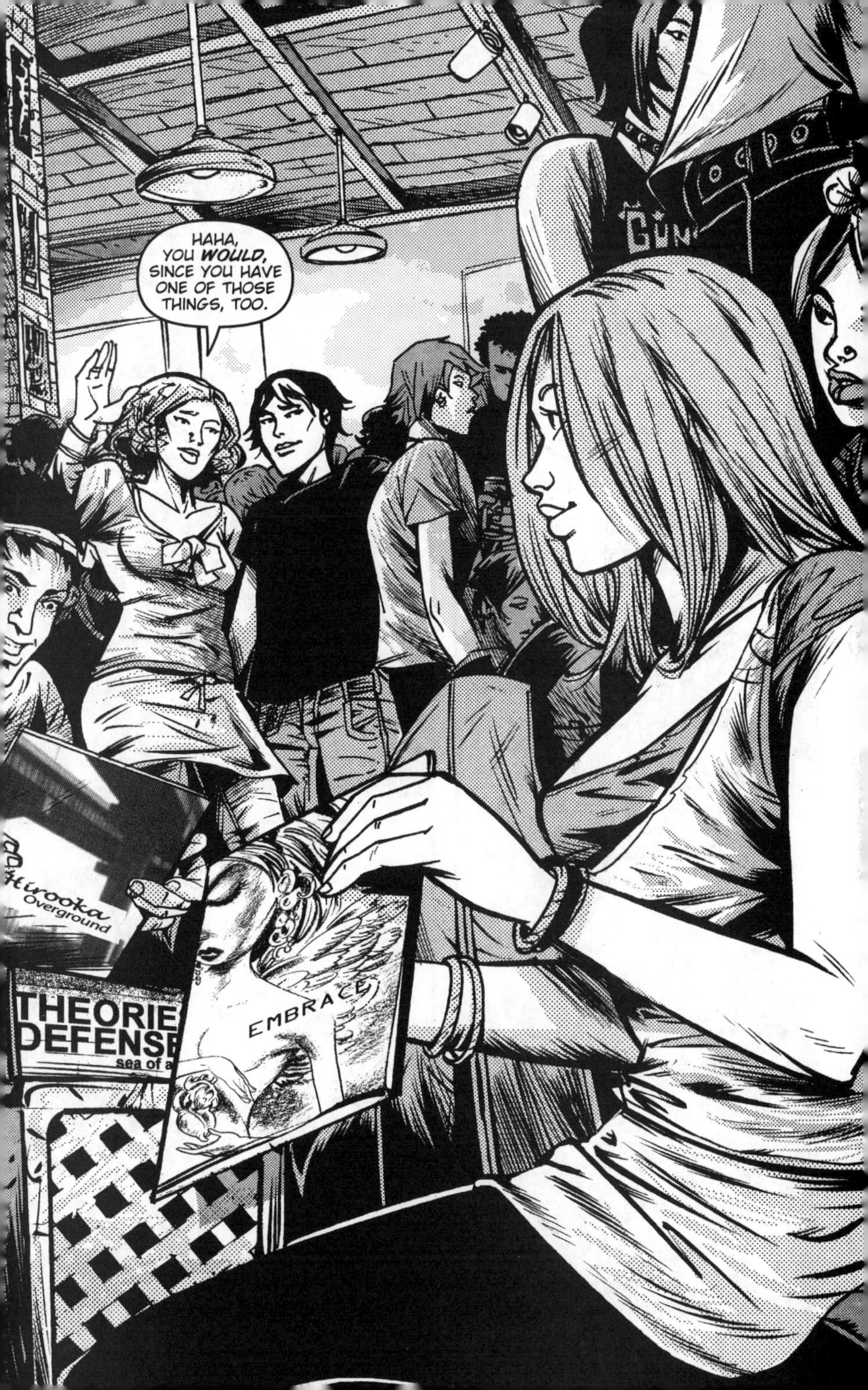
HAHA, YOU **WOULD,** SINCE YOU HAVE ONE OF THOSE THINGS, TOO.
GUN
Hirooka Overground
THEORIE DEFENSE sea of a
EMBRACE

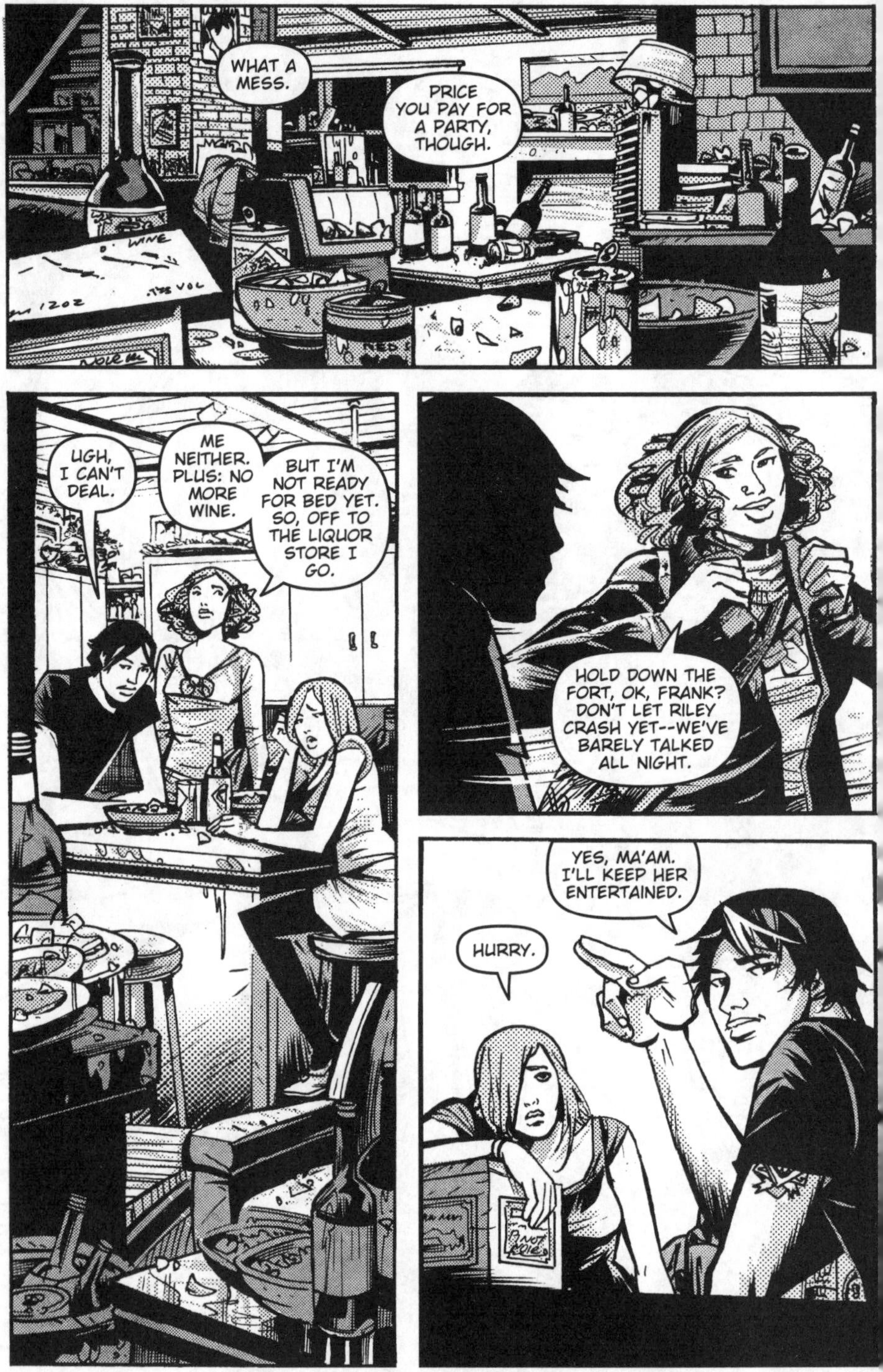
WHAT A MESS.
PRICE YOU PAY FOR A PARTY, THOUGH.
UGH, I CAN'T DEAL.
ME NEITHER. PLUS: NO MORE WINE.
BUT I'M NOT READY FOR BED YET. SO, OFF TO THE LIQUOR STORE I GO.
HOLD DOWN THE FORT, OK, FRANK? DON'T LET RILEY CRASH YET--WE'VE BARELY TALKED ALL NIGHT.
YES, MA'AM. I'LL KEEP HER ENTERTAINED.
HURRY.

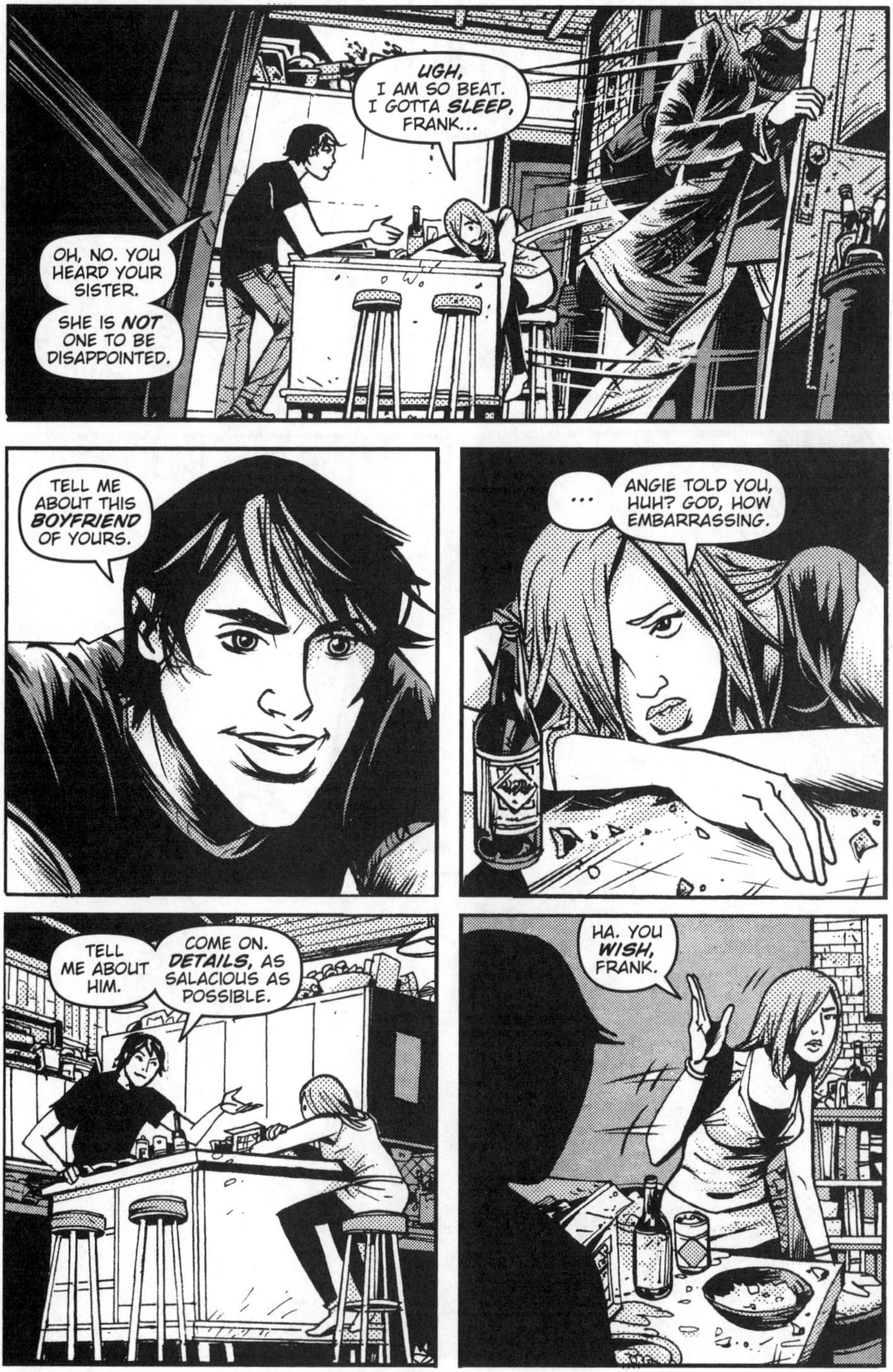
UGH, I AM SO BEAT. I GOTTA SLEEP, FRANK...
OH, NO. YOU HEARD YOUR SISTER.
SHE IS NOT ONE TO BE DISAPPOINTED.
TELL ME ABOUT THIS BOYFRIEND OF YOURS.
...
ANGIE TOLD YOU, HUH? GOD, HOW EMBARRASSING.
TELL ME ABOUT HIM.
COME ON. DETAILS, AS SALACIOUS AS POSSIBLE.
HA. YOU WISH, FRANK.

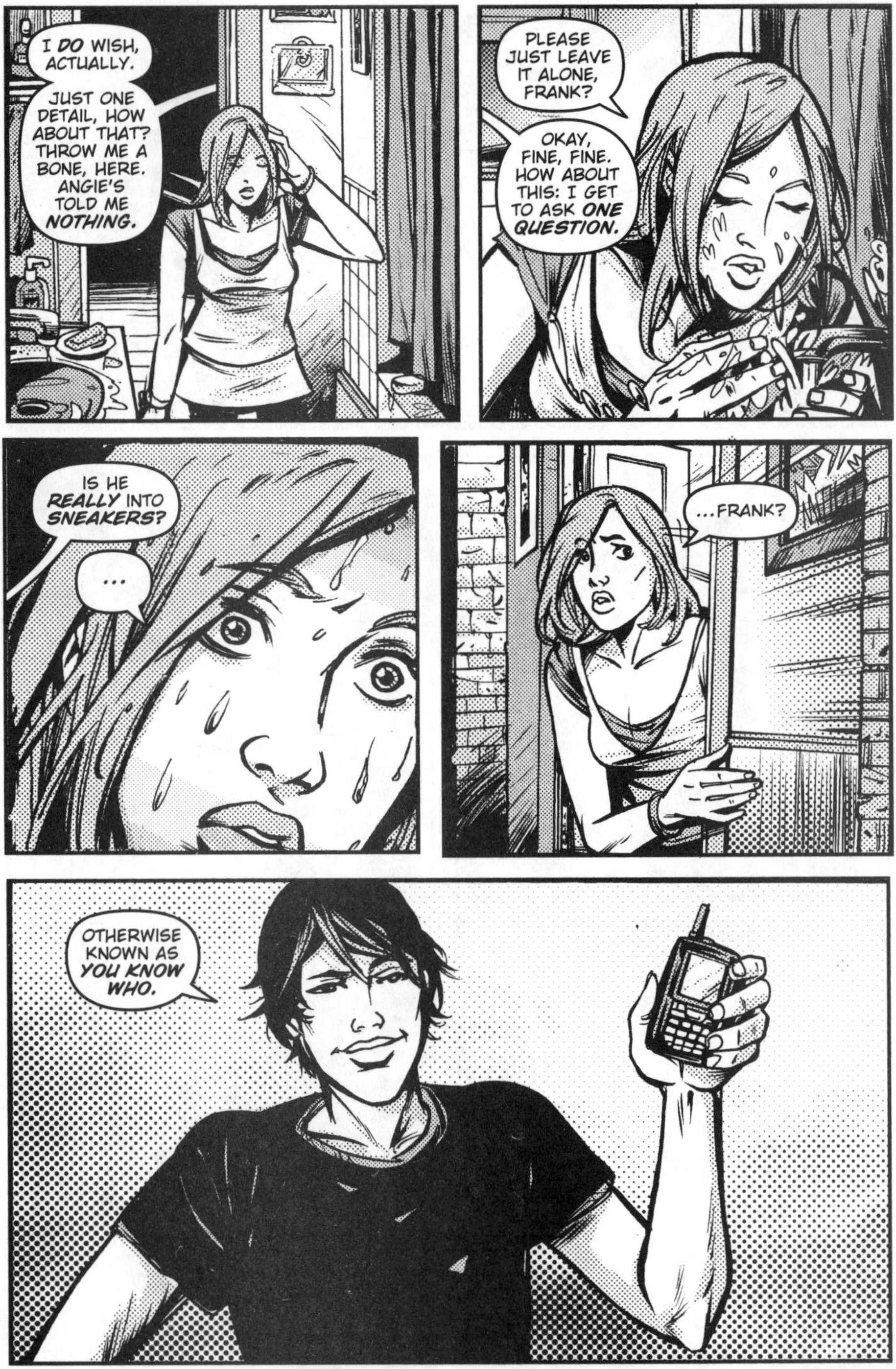
I *DO* WISH, ACTUALLY.
JUST ONE DETAIL, HOW ABOUT THAT? THROW ME A BONE, HERE. ANGIE'S TOLD ME ***NOTHING.***
PLEASE JUST LEAVE IT ALONE, FRANK?
OKAY, FINE, FINE. HOW ABOUT THIS: I GET TO ASK ***ONE QUESTION.***
IS HE ***REALLY*** INTO ***SNEAKERS?***
...
...FRANK?
OTHERWISE KNOWN AS ***YOU KNOW WHO.***

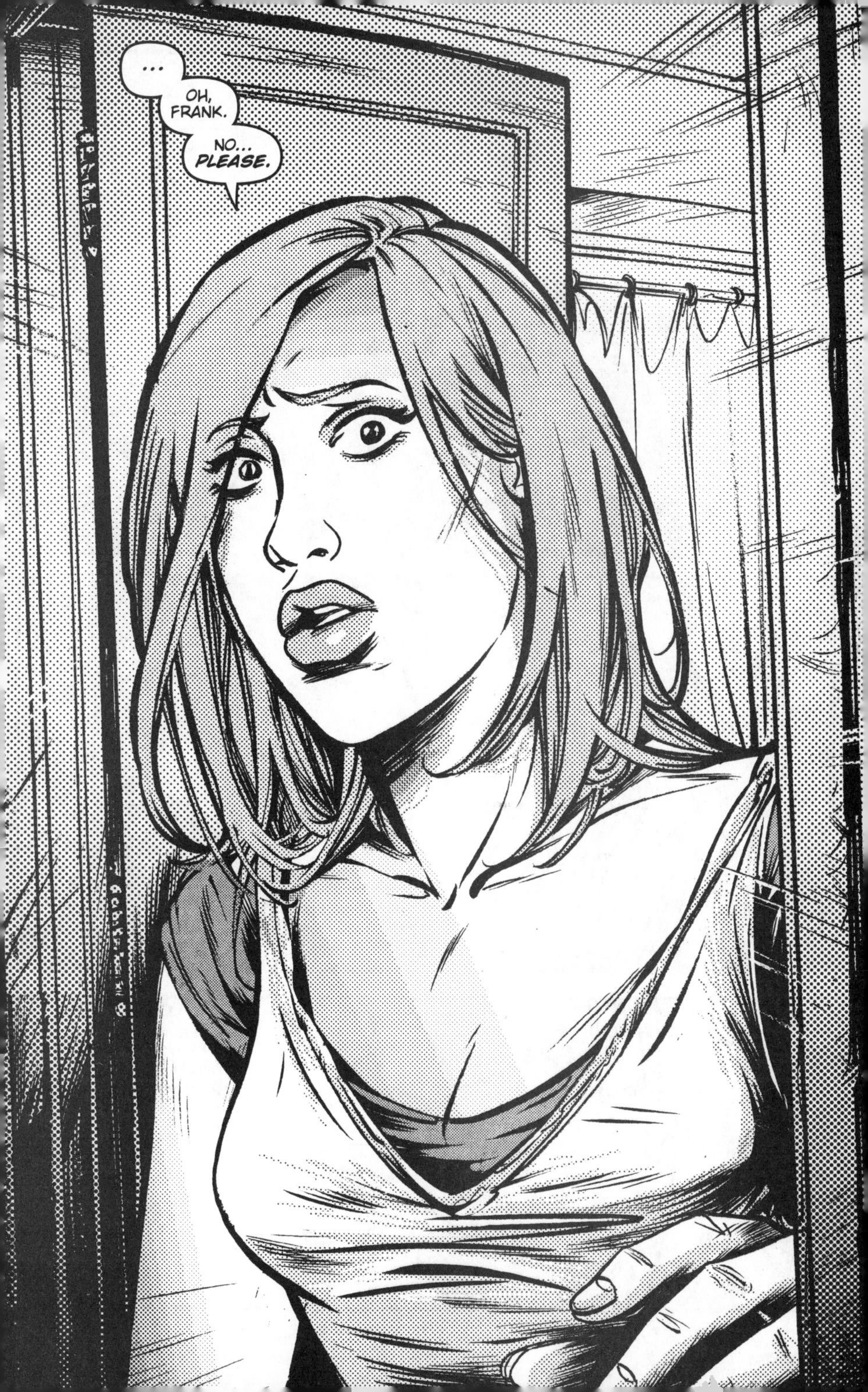
...
OH, FRANK.
NO... PLEASE.

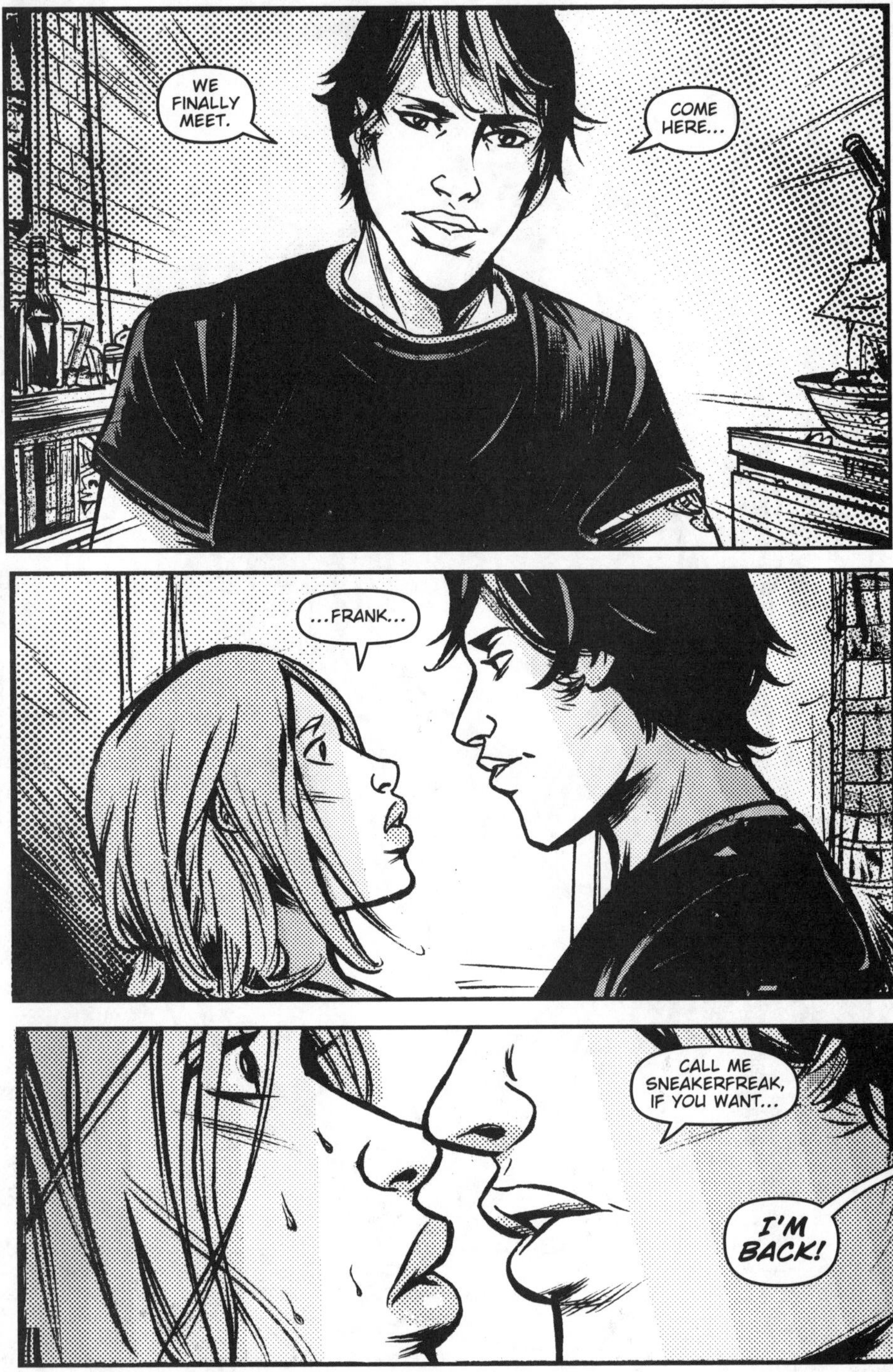
WE FINALLY MEET.
COME HERE...
...FRANK...
CALL ME SNEAKERFREAK, IF YOU WANT...
I'M BACK!

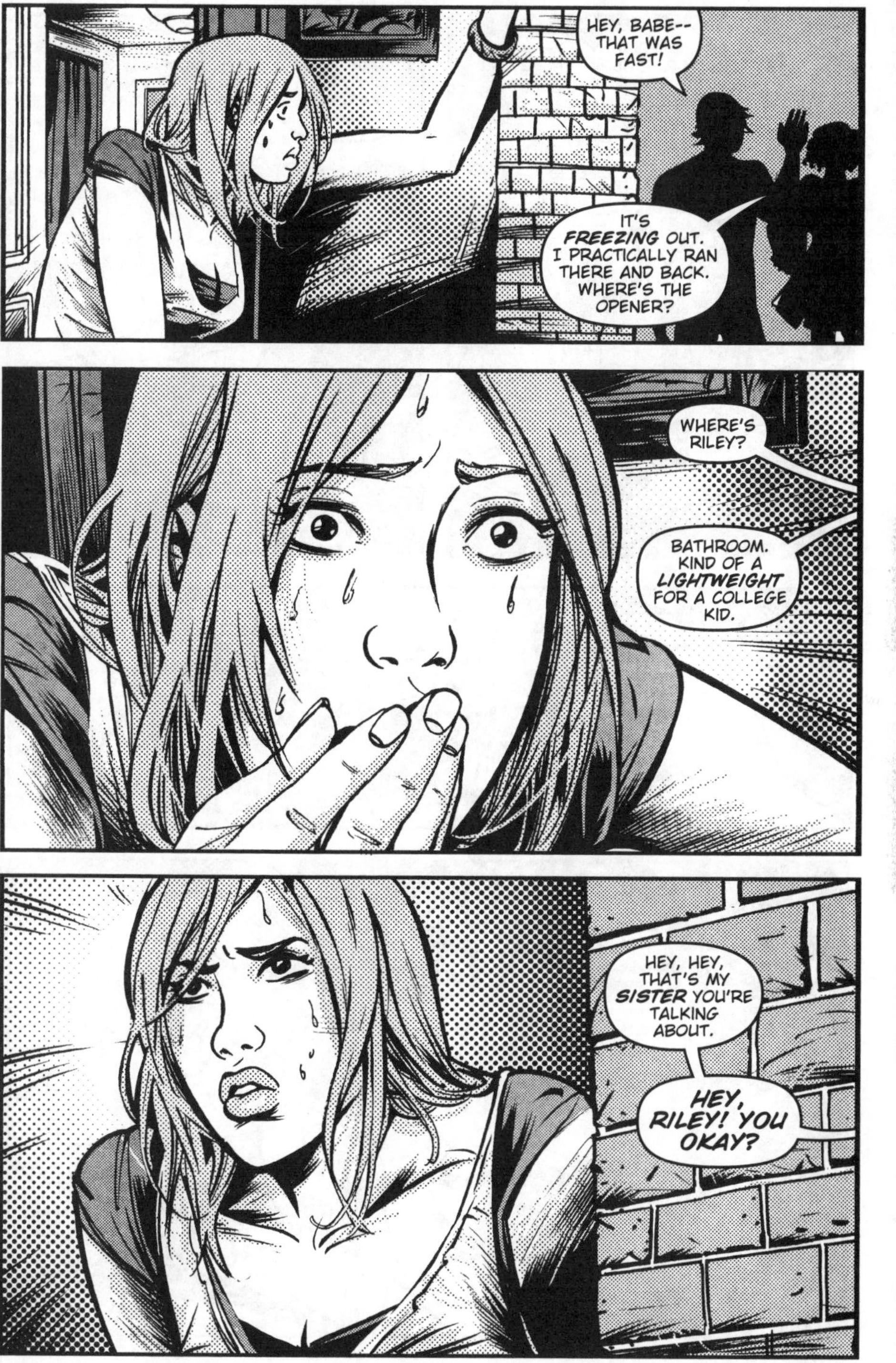
HEY, BABE-- THAT WAS FAST!
IT'S FREEZING OUT. I PRACTICALLY RAN THERE AND BACK. WHERE'S THE OPENER?
WHERE'S RILEY?
BATHROOM. KIND OF A LIGHTWEIGHT FOR A COLLEGE KID.
HEY, HEY, THAT'S MY SISTER YOU'RE TALKING ABOUT.
HEY, RILEY! YOU OKAY?

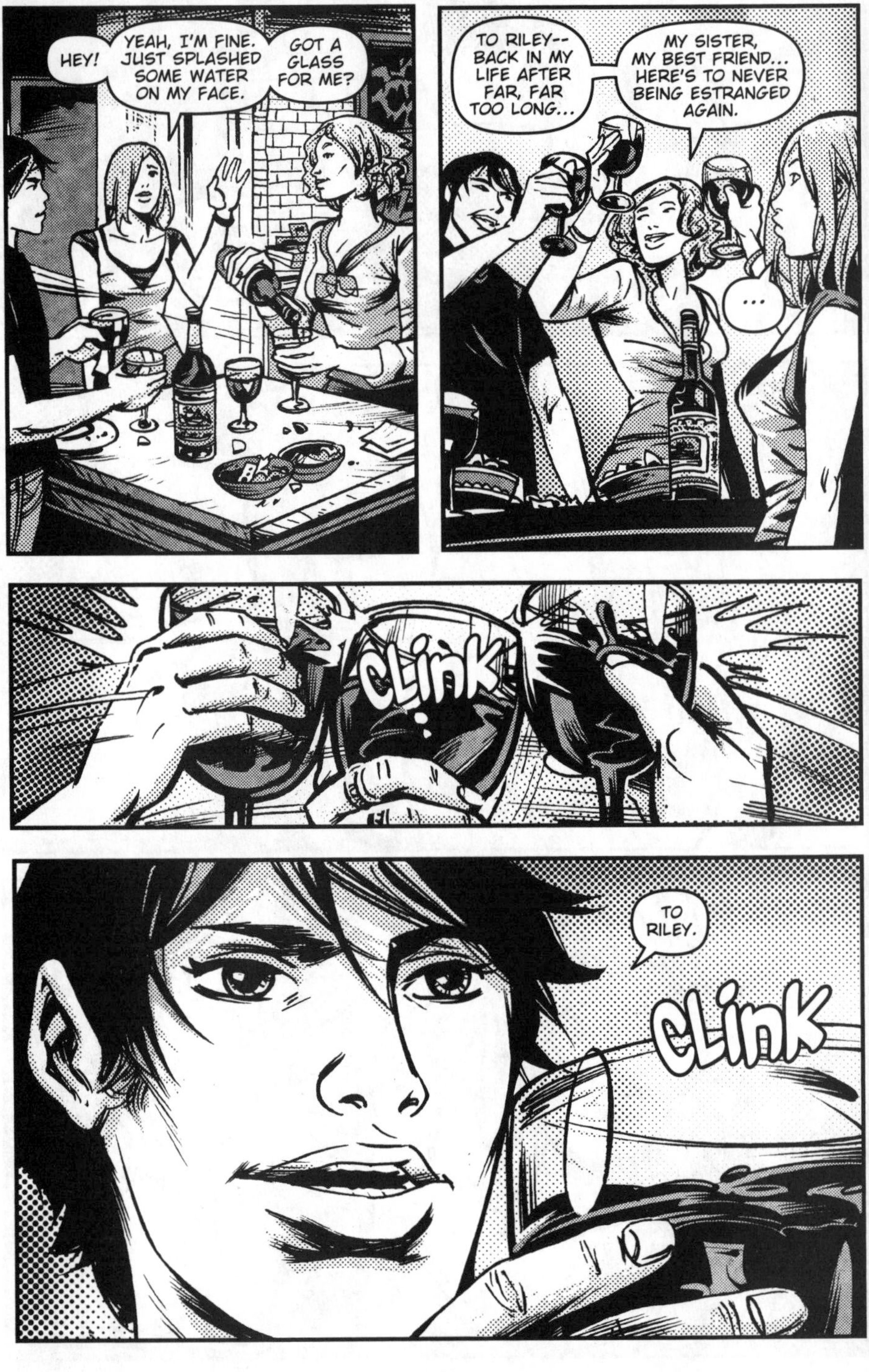
HEY!
YEAH, I'M FINE. JUST SPLASHED SOME WATER ON MY FACE.
GOT A GLASS FOR ME?
TO RILEY-- BACK IN MY LIFE AFTER FAR, FAR TOO LONG...
MY SISTER, MY BEST FRIEND... HERE'S TO NEVER BEING ESTRANGED AGAIN.
...
CLINK
TO RILEY.
CLINK

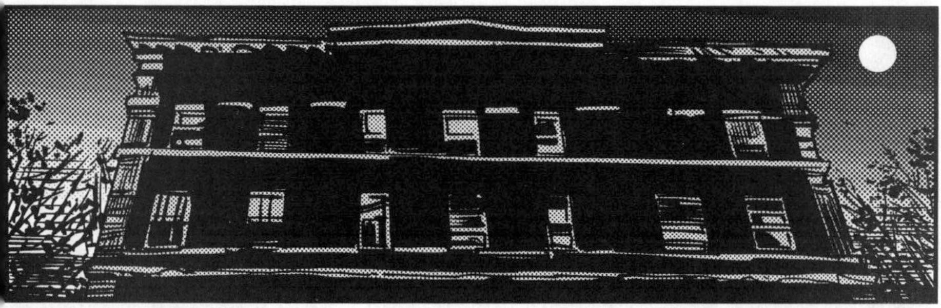

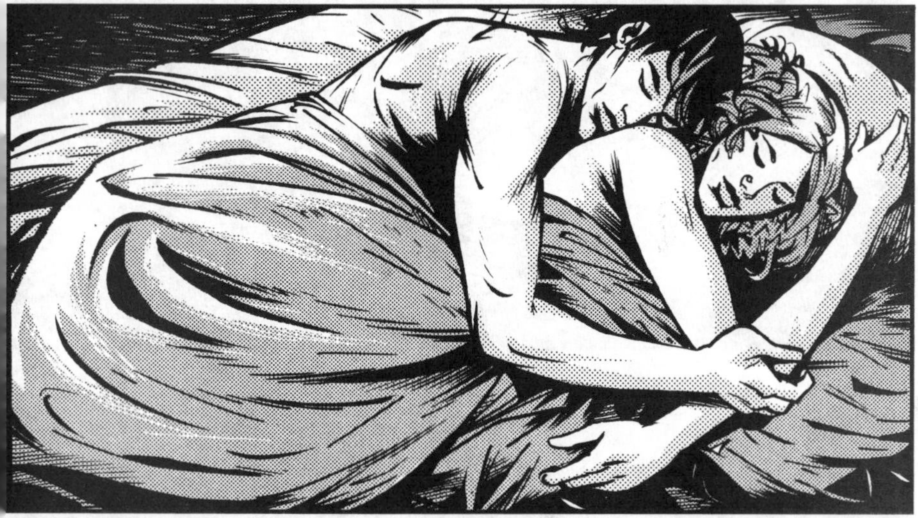

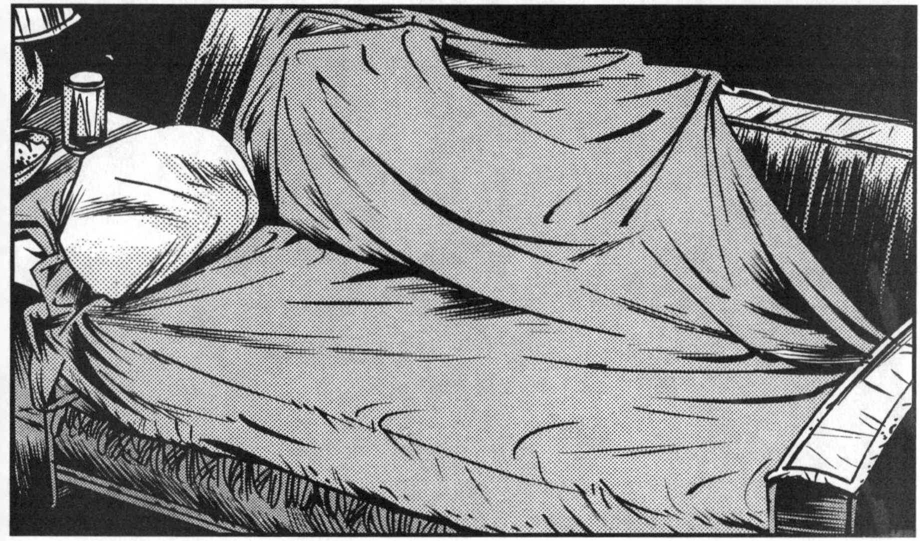

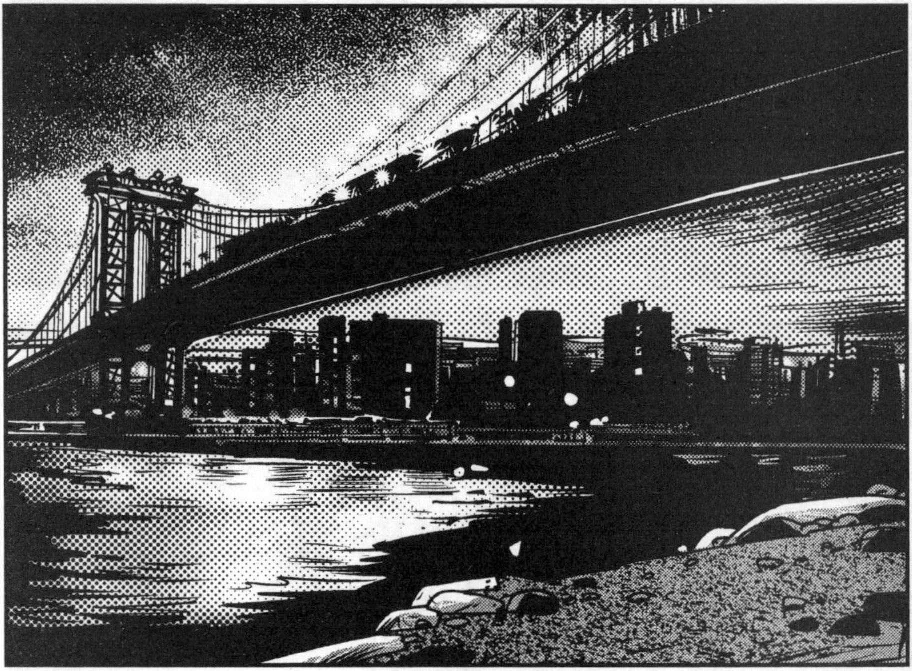

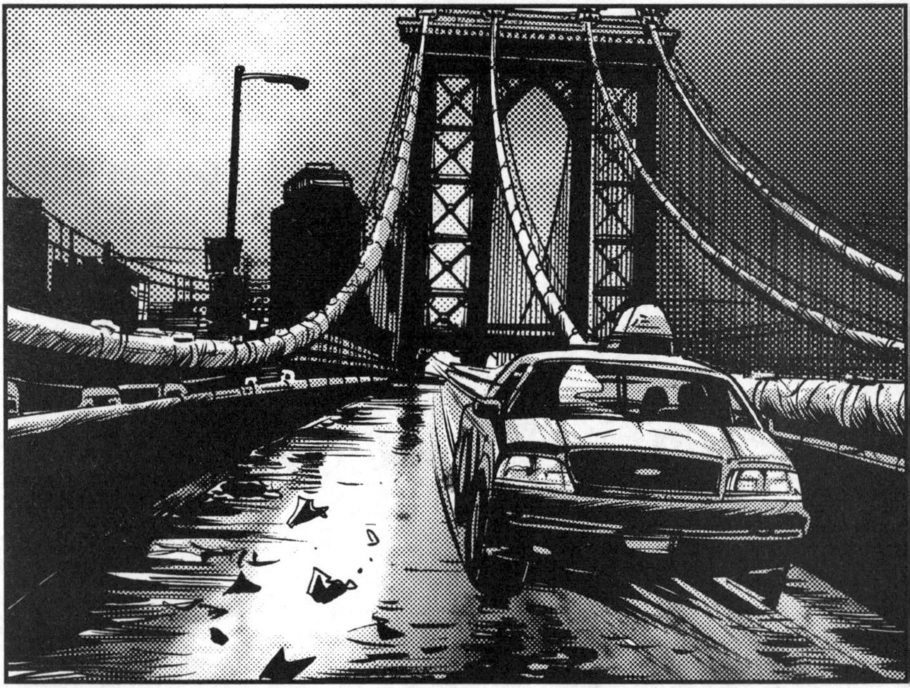

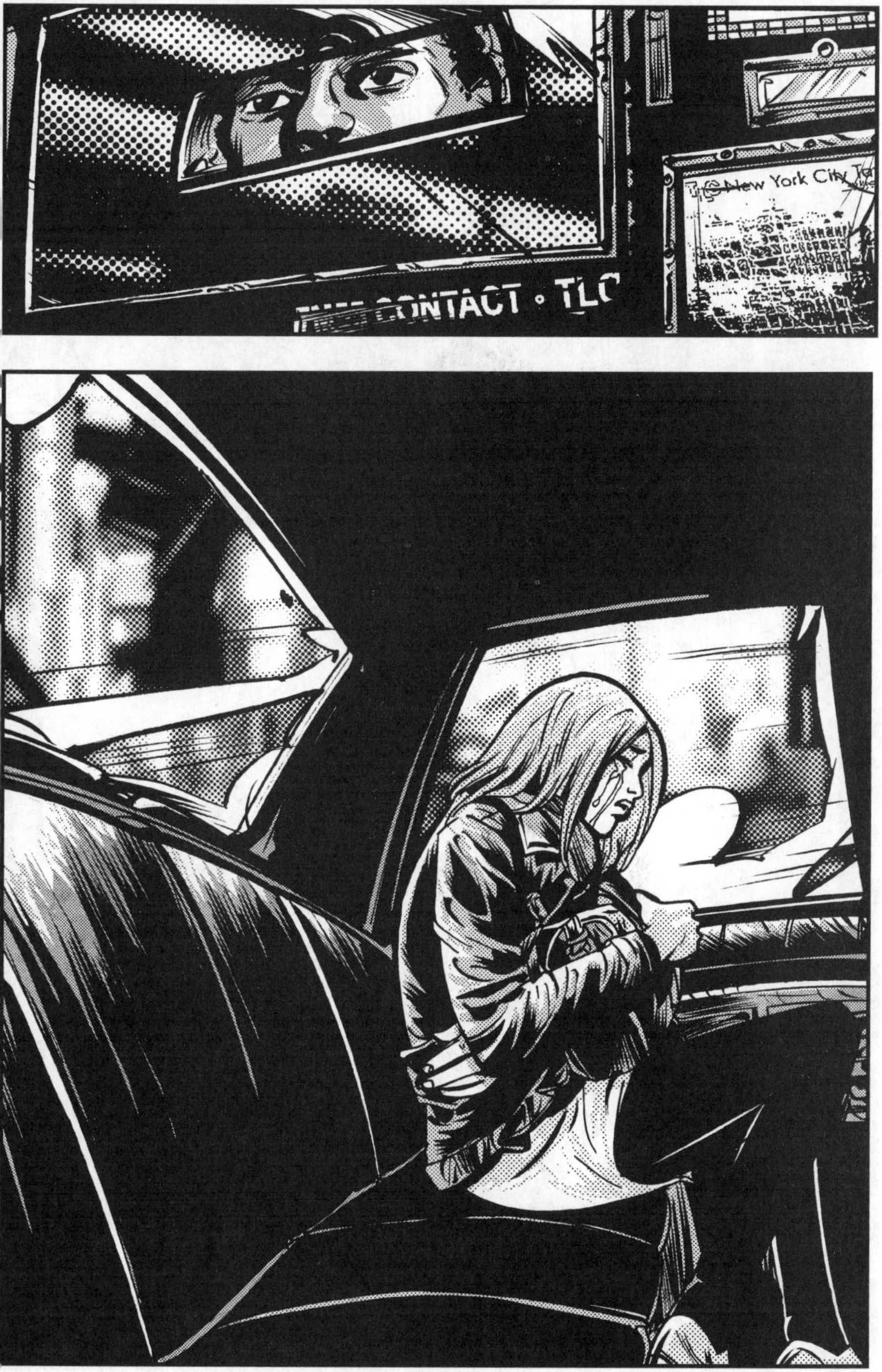
New York City
CONTACT • TLC

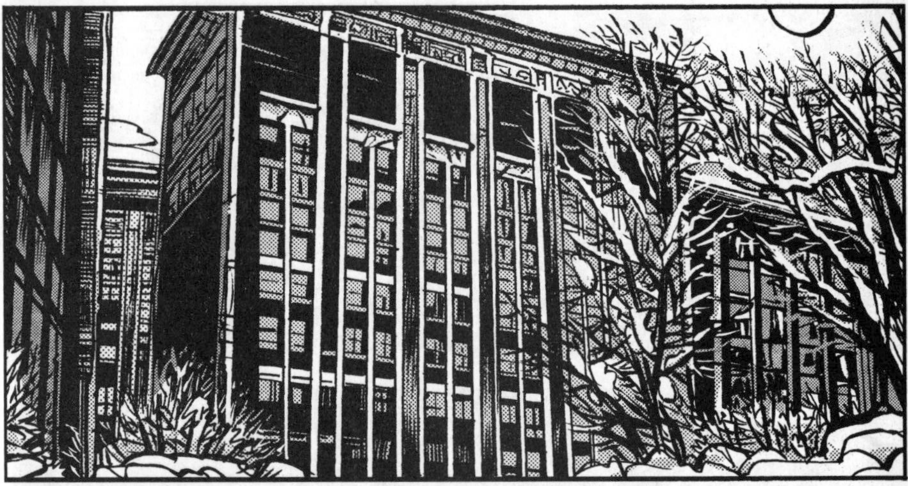

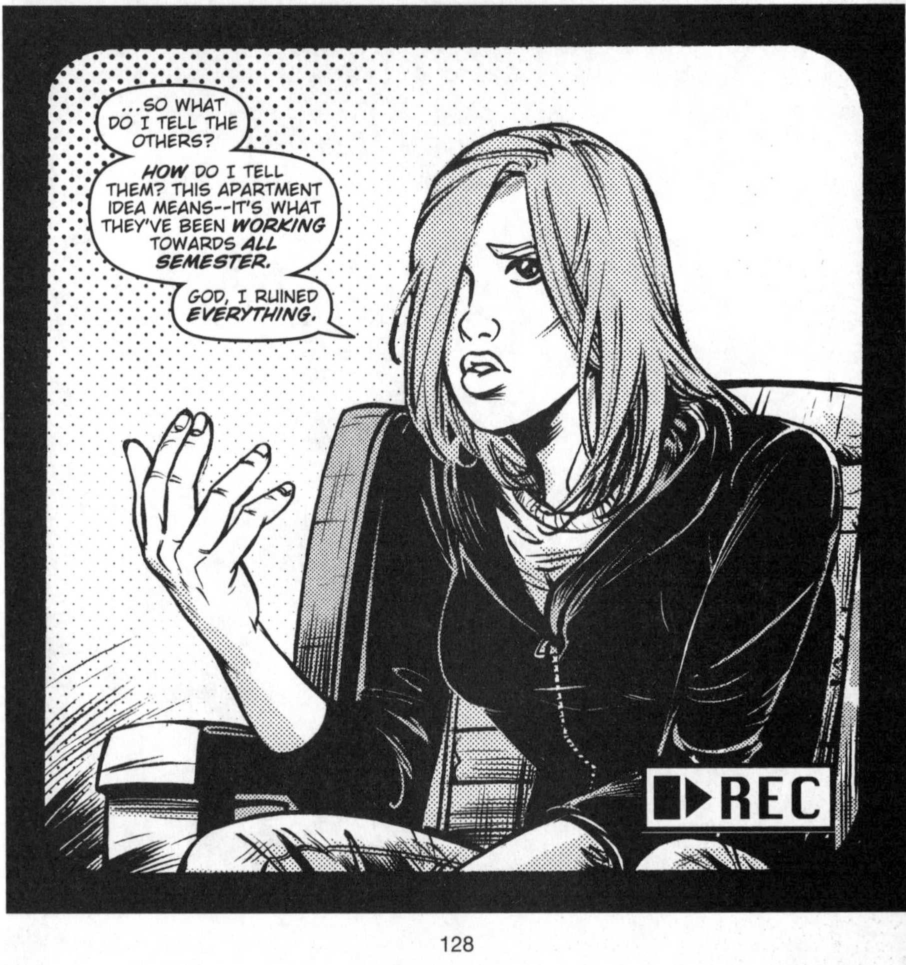
...SO WHAT DO I TELL THE OTHERS?
HOW DO I TELL THEM? THIS APARTMENT IDEA MEANS--IT'S WHAT THEY'VE BEEN WORKING TOWARDS ALL SEMESTER.
GOD, I RUINED EVERYTHING.
REC

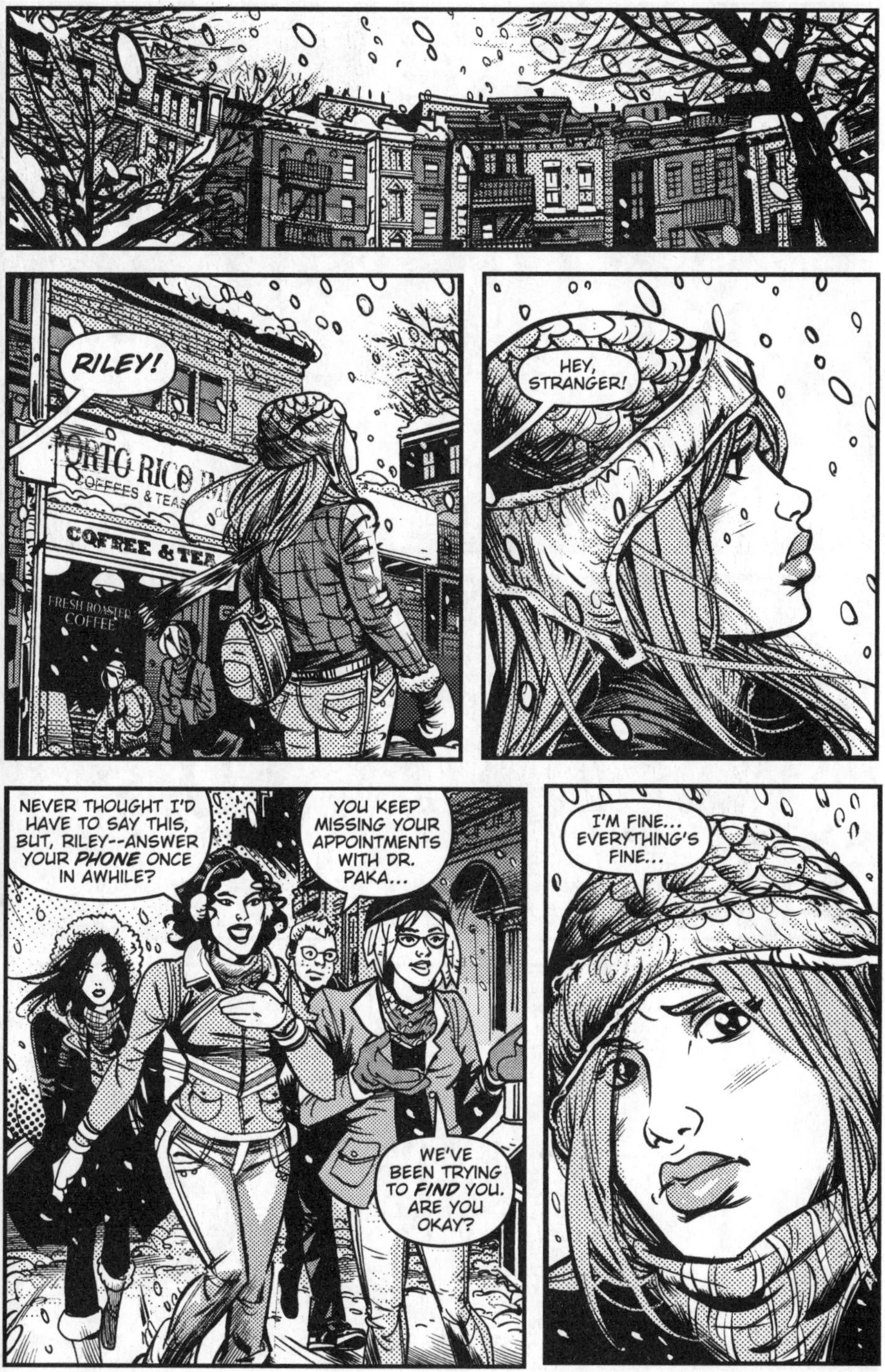
RILEY!
ORTO RICO
COFFEES & TEAS
COFFEE & TEA
FRESH ROASTED
COFFEE
HEY, STRANGER!
NEVER THOUGHT I'D HAVE TO SAY THIS, BUT, RILEY--ANSWER YOUR *PHONE* ONCE IN AWHILE?
YOU KEEP MISSING YOUR APPOINTMENTS WITH DR. PAKA...
WE'VE BEEN TRYING TO *FIND* YOU. ARE YOU OKAY?
I'M FINE... EVERYTHING'S FINE...

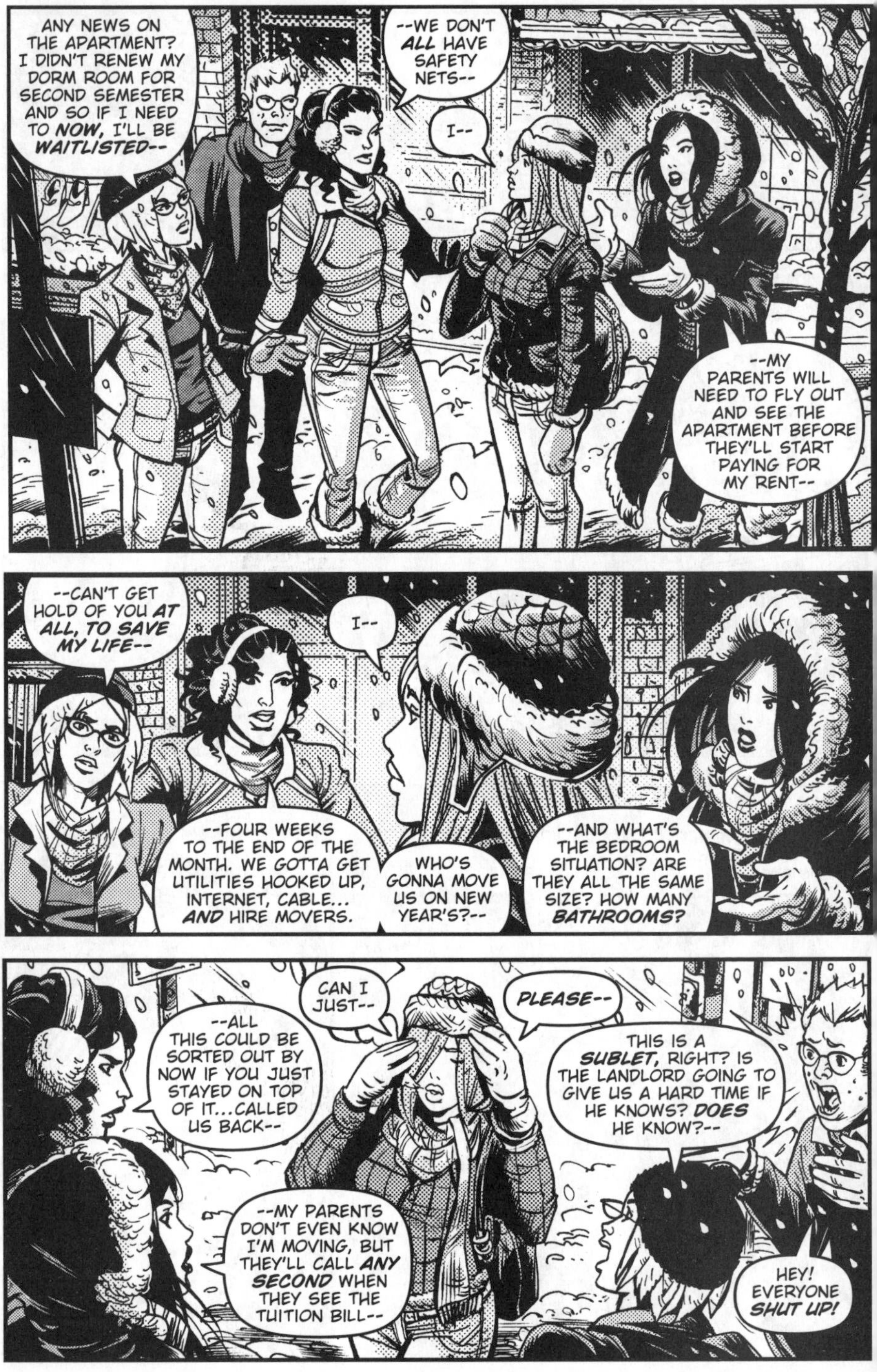
ANY NEWS ON THE APARTMENT? I DIDN'T RENEW MY DORM ROOM FOR SECOND SEMESTER AND SO IF I NEED TO NOW, I'LL BE WAITLISTED--
--WE DON'T ALL HAVE SAFETY NETS--
I--
--MY PARENTS WILL NEED TO FLY OUT AND SEE THE APARTMENT BEFORE THEY'LL START PAYING FOR MY RENT--
--CAN'T GET HOLD OF YOU AT ALL, TO SAVE MY LIFE--
I--
--FOUR WEEKS TO THE END OF THE MONTH. WE GOTTA GET UTILITIES HOOKED UP, INTERNET, CABLE... AND HIRE MOVERS.
WHO'S GONNA MOVE US ON NEW YEAR'S?--
--AND WHAT'S THE BEDROOM SITUATION? ARE THEY ALL THE SAME SIZE? HOW MANY BATHROOMS?
--ALL THIS COULD BE SORTED OUT BY NOW IF YOU JUST STAYED ON TOP OF IT...CALLED US BACK--
CAN I JUST--
PLEASE--
THIS IS A SUBLET, RIGHT? IS THE LANDLORD GOING TO GIVE US A HARD TIME IF HE KNOWS? DOES HE KNOW?--
--MY PARENTS DON'T EVEN KNOW I'M MOVING, BUT THEY'LL CALL ANY SECOND WHEN THEY SEE THE TUITION BILL--
HEY! EVERYONE SHUT UP!

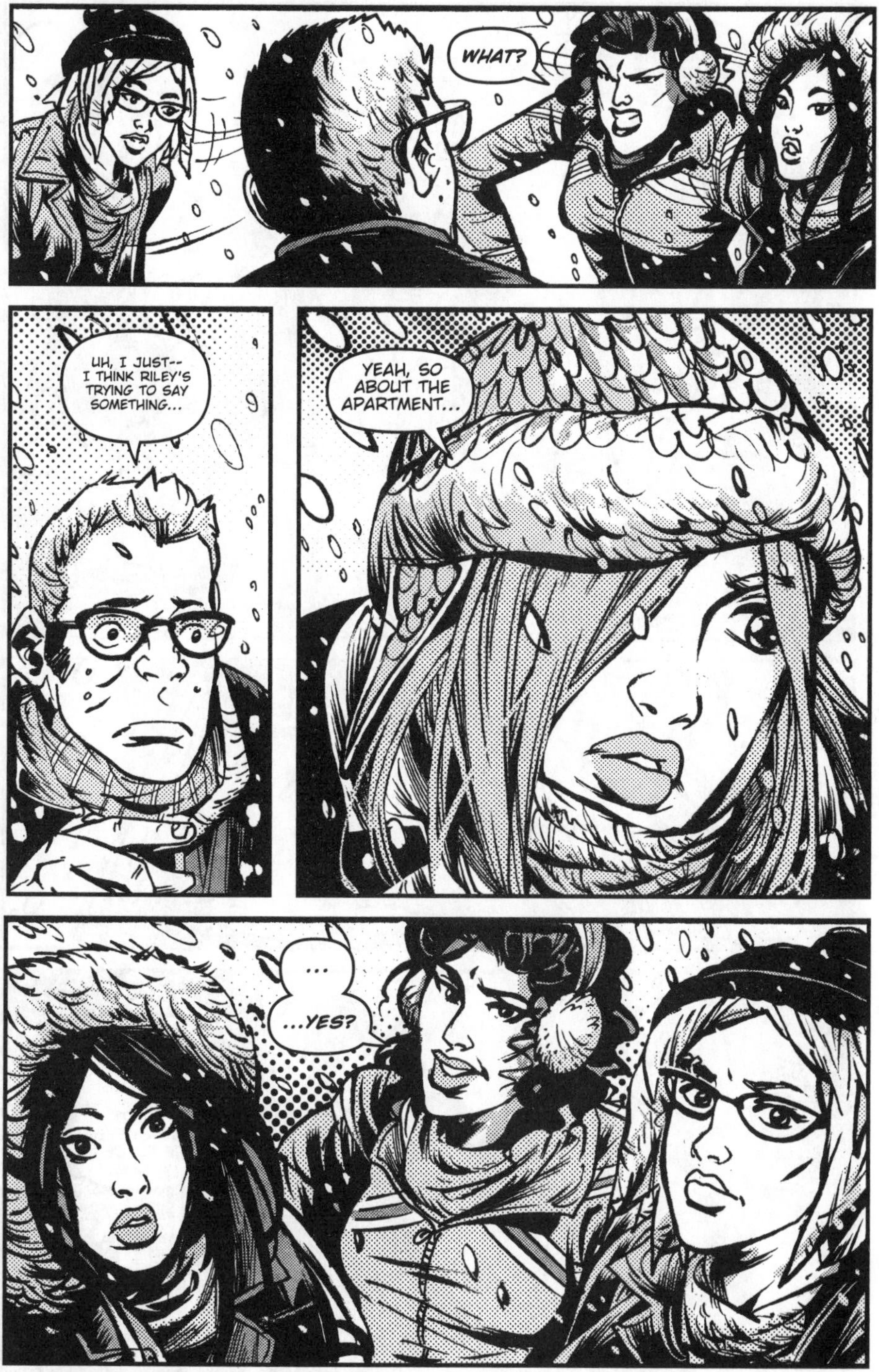
WHAT?
UH, I JUST-- I THINK RILEY'S TRYING TO SAY SOMETHING...
YEAH, SO ABOUT THE APARTMENT...
...
...YES?

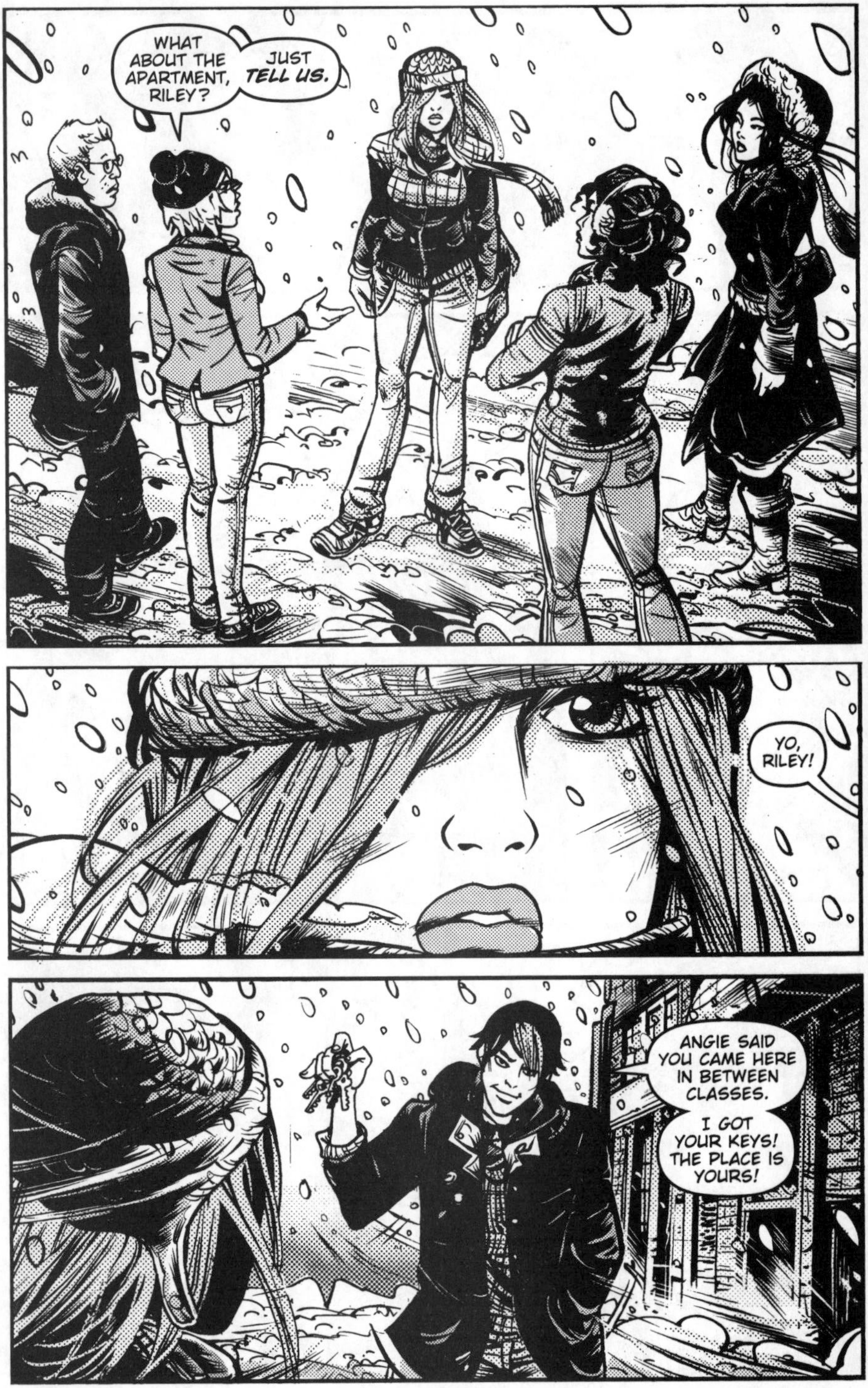
WHAT ABOUT THE APARTMENT, RILEY?
JUST TELL US.
YO, RILEY!
ANGIE SAID YOU CAME HERE IN BETWEEN CLASSES.
I GOT YOUR KEYS! THE PLACE IS YOURS!

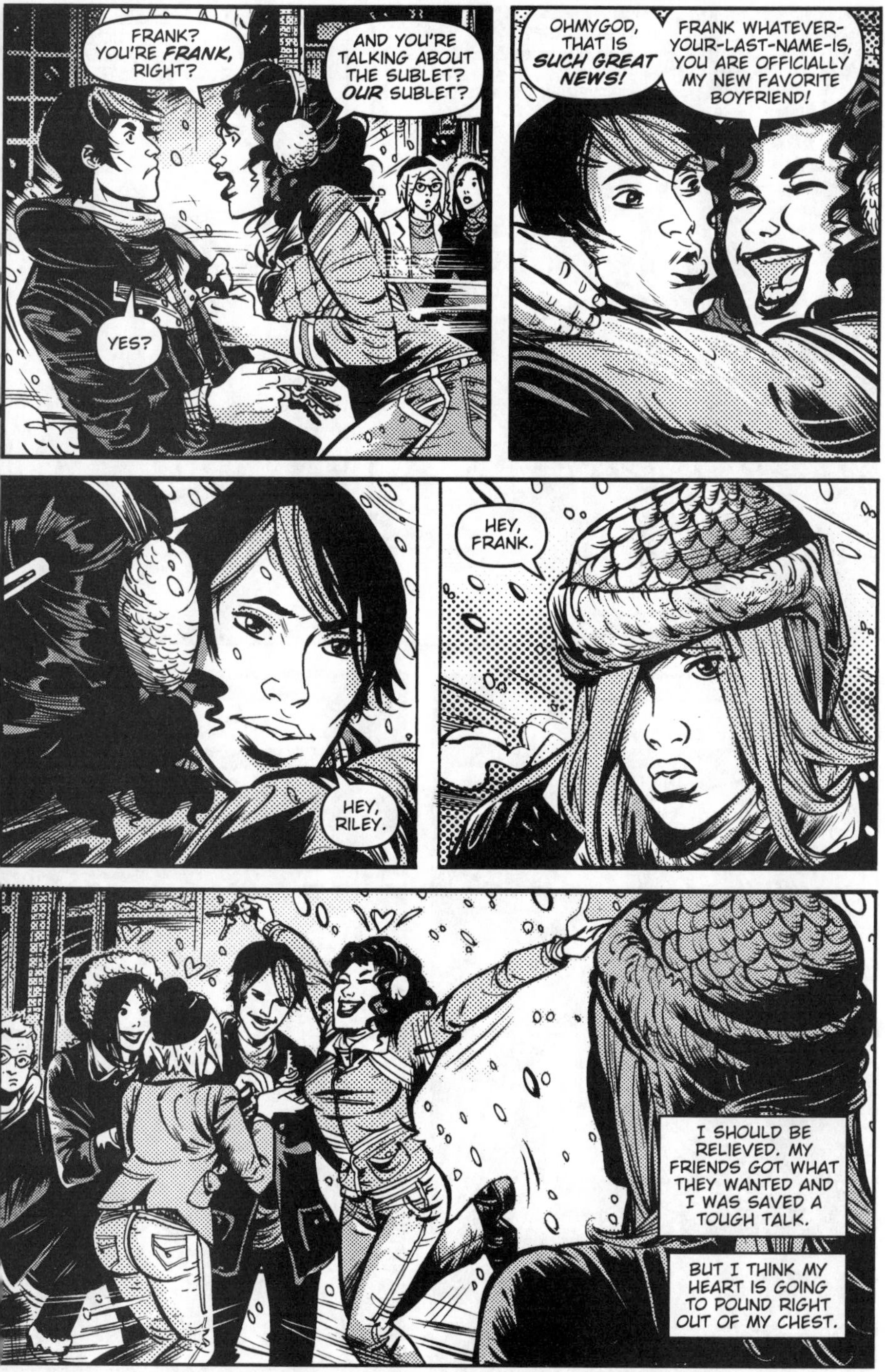

FRANK? YOU'RE FRANK, RIGHT?
AND YOU'RE TALKING ABOUT THE SUBLET? OUR SUBLET?
YES?
OHMYGOD, THAT IS SUCH GREAT NEWS!
FRANK WHATEVER-YOUR-LAST-NAME-IS, YOU ARE OFFICIALLY MY NEW FAVORITE BOYFRIEND!
HEY, RILEY.
HEY, FRANK.
I SHOULD BE RELIEVED. MY FRIENDS GOT WHAT THEY WANTED AND I WAS SAVED A TOUGH TALK.
BUT I THINK MY HEART IS GOING TO POUND RIGHT OUT OF MY CHEST.

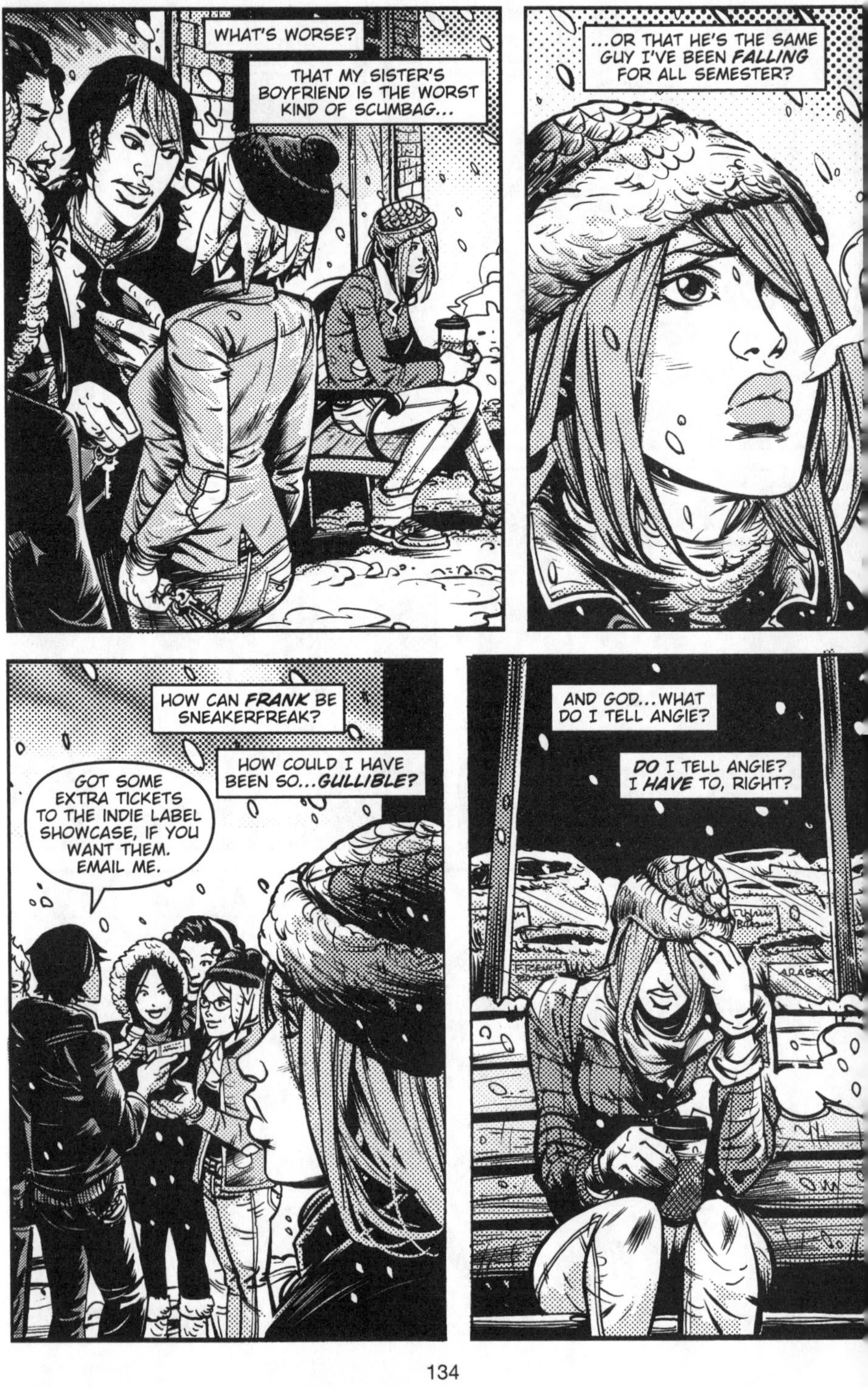
WHAT'S WORSE?
THAT MY SISTER'S BOYFRIEND IS THE WORST KIND OF SCUMBAG...
...OR THAT HE'S THE SAME GUY I'VE BEEN FALLING FOR ALL SEMESTER?
HOW CAN FRANK BE SNEAKERFREAK?
HOW COULD I HAVE BEEN SO...GULLIBLE?
GOT SOME EXTRA TICKETS TO THE INDIE LABEL SHOWCASE, IF YOU WANT THEM. EMAIL ME.
AND GOD...WHAT DO I TELL ANGIE?
DO I TELL ANGIE? I HAVE TO, RIGHT?

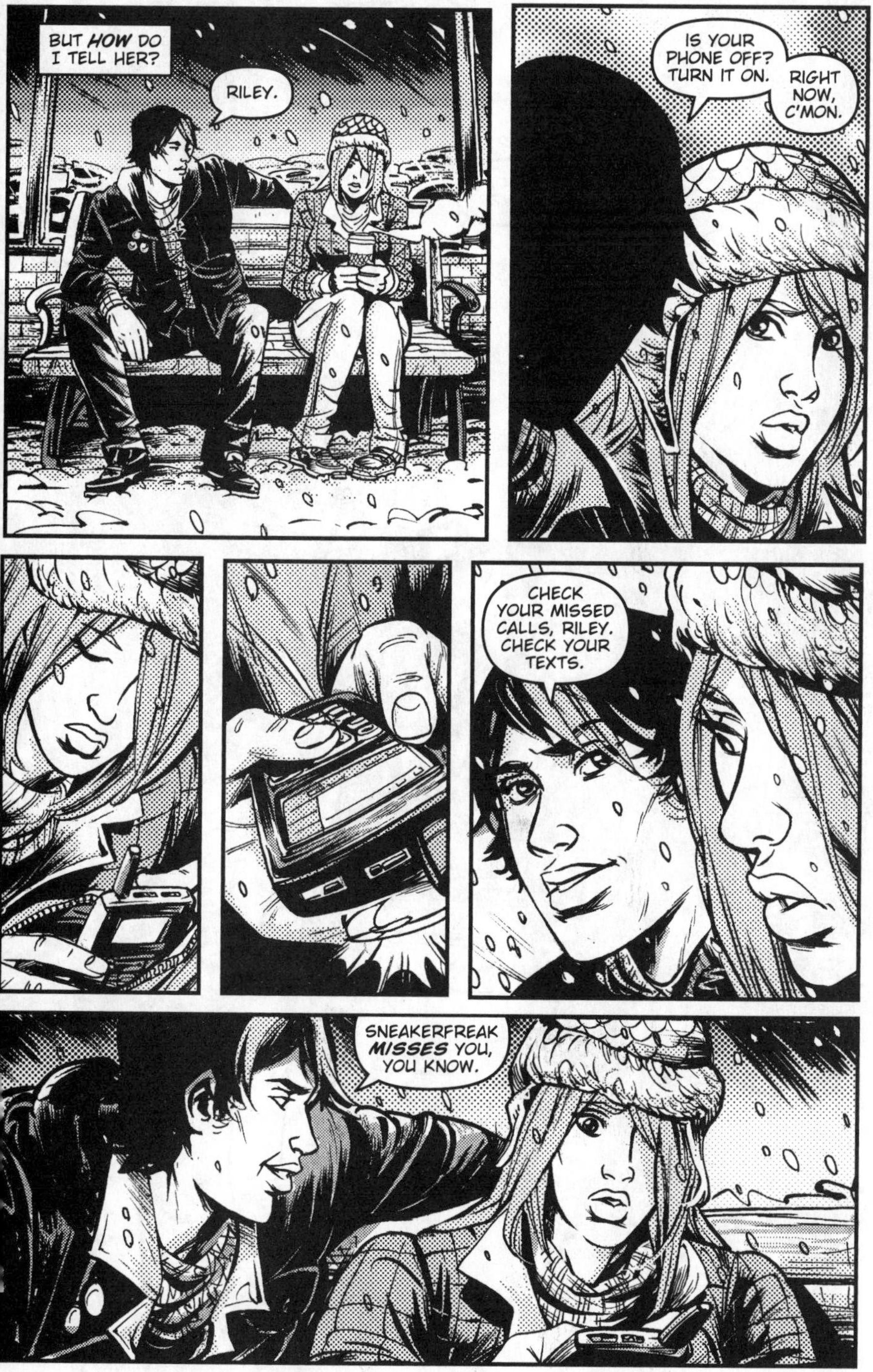
BUT *HOW* DO I TELL HER?
RILEY.
IS YOUR PHONE OFF? TURN IT ON.
RIGHT NOW, C'MON.
CHECK YOUR MISSED CALLS, RILEY. CHECK YOUR TEXTS.
SNEAKERFREAK *MISSES* YOU, YOU KNOW.

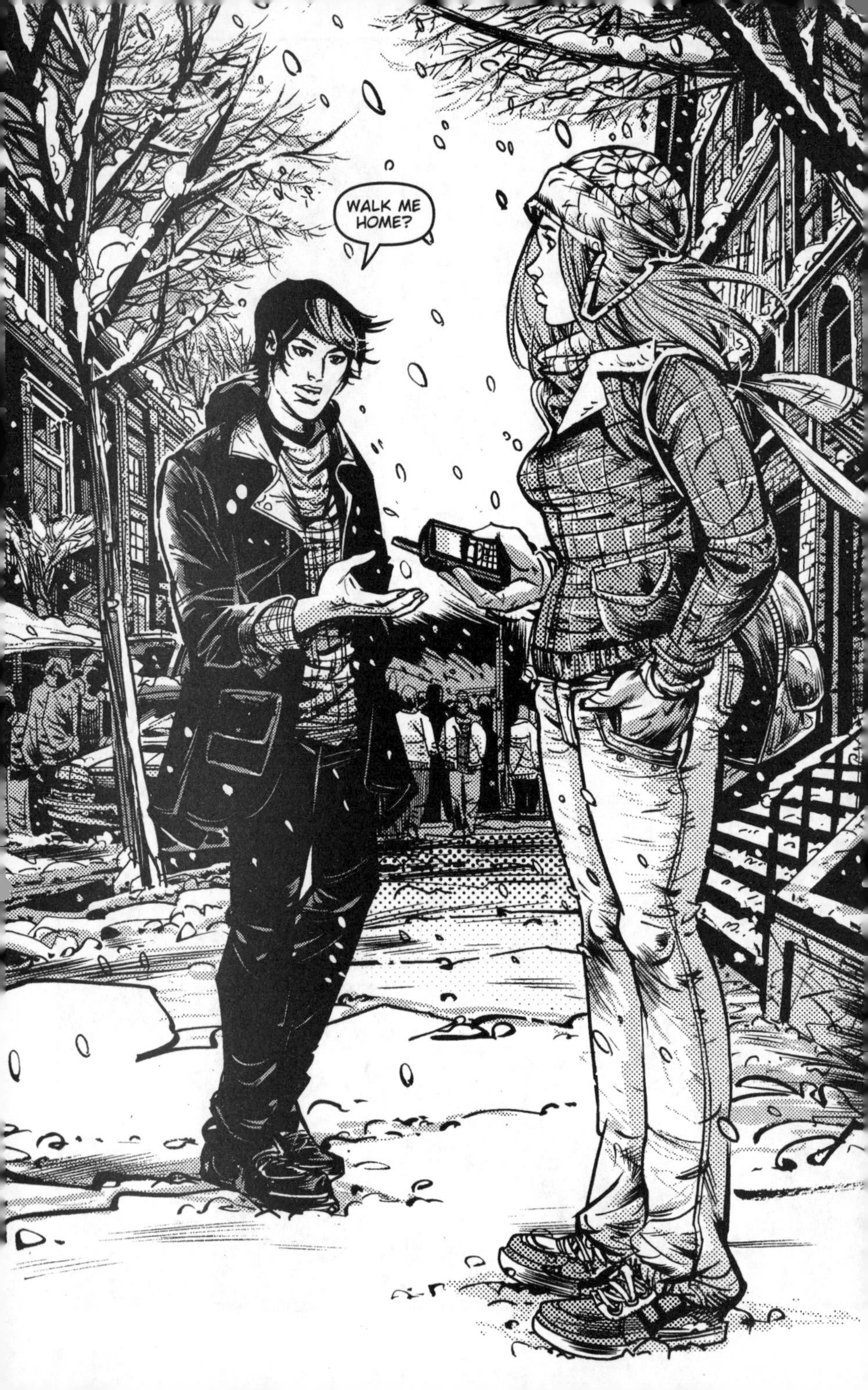
WALK ME HOME?

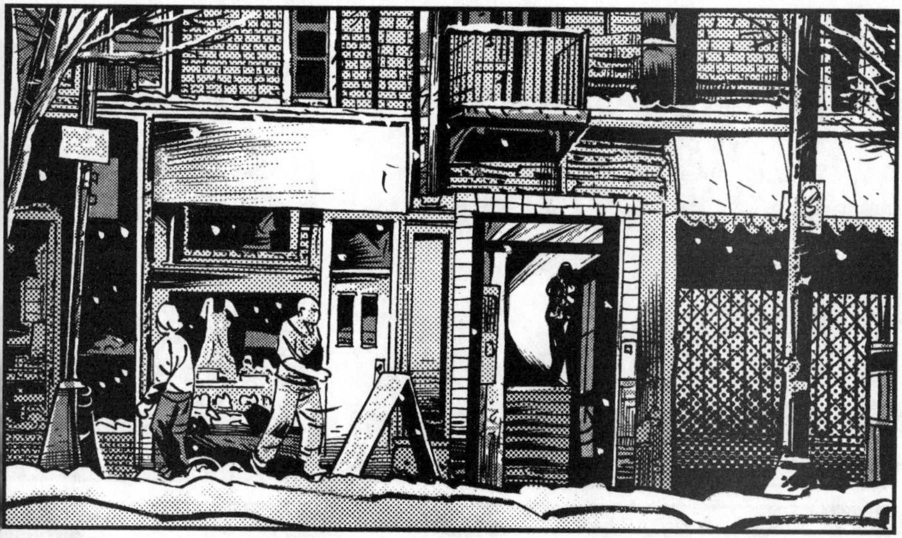

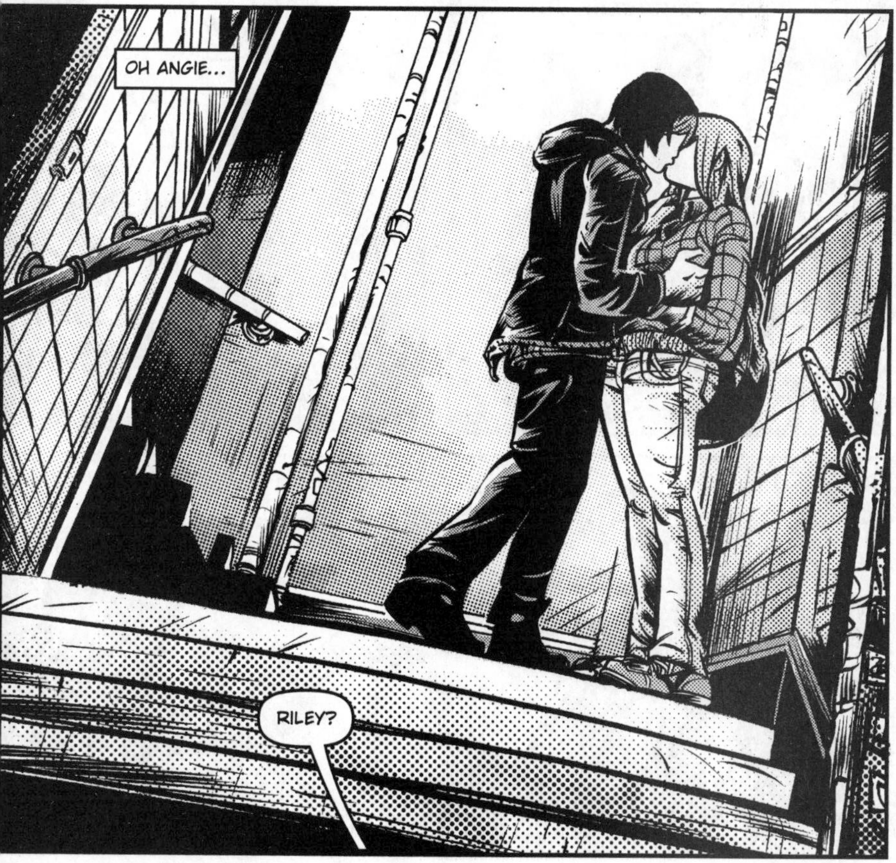
OH ANGIE...
RILEY?

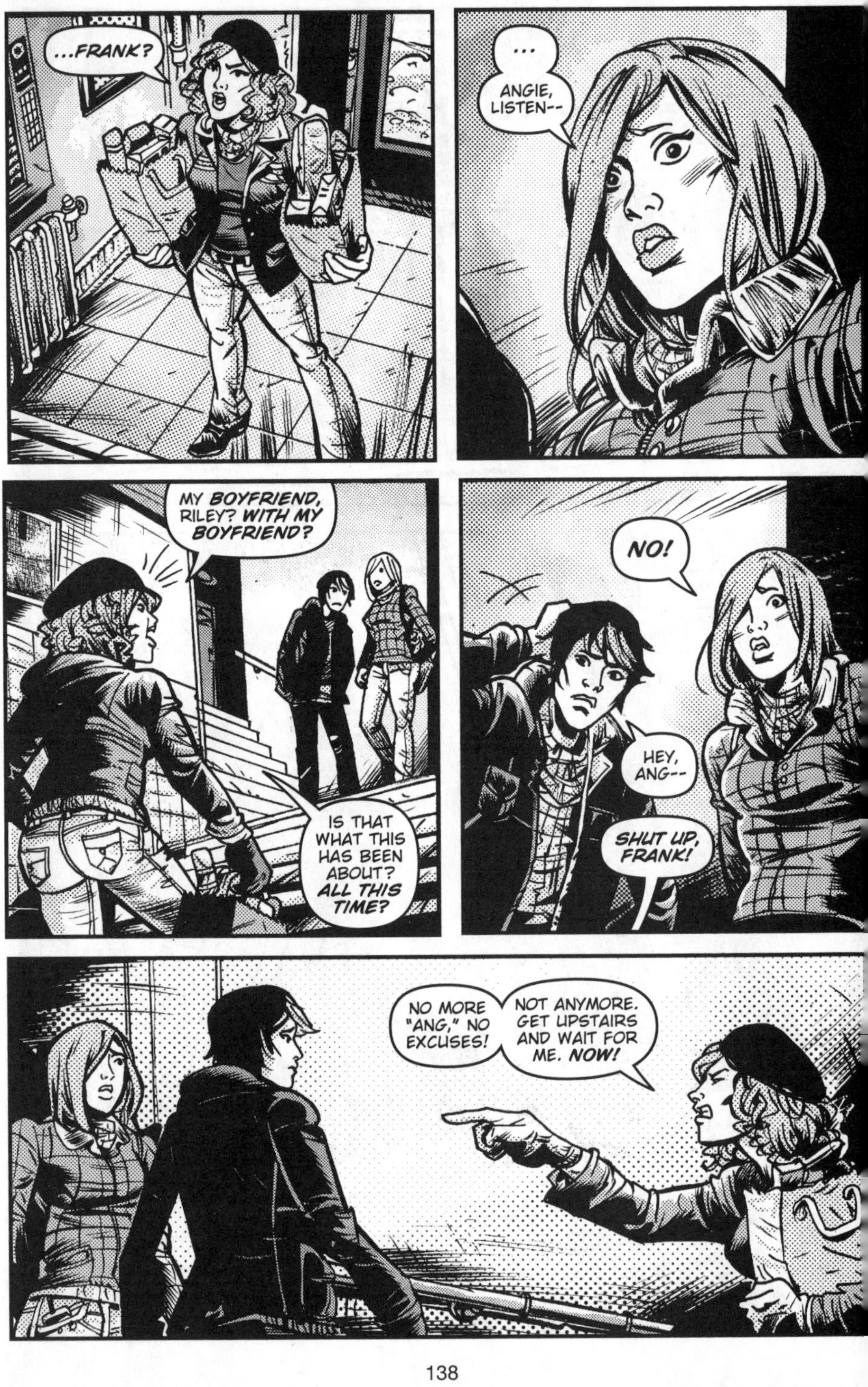
...FRANK?
...
ANGIE, LISTEN--
MY BOYFRIEND, RILEY? WITH MY BOYFRIEND?
IS THAT WHAT THIS HAS BEEN ABOUT? ALL THIS TIME?
NO!
HEY, ANG--
SHUT UP, FRANK!
NO MORE "ANG," NO EXCUSES!
NOT ANYMORE. GET UPSTAIRS AND WAIT FOR ME. NOW!

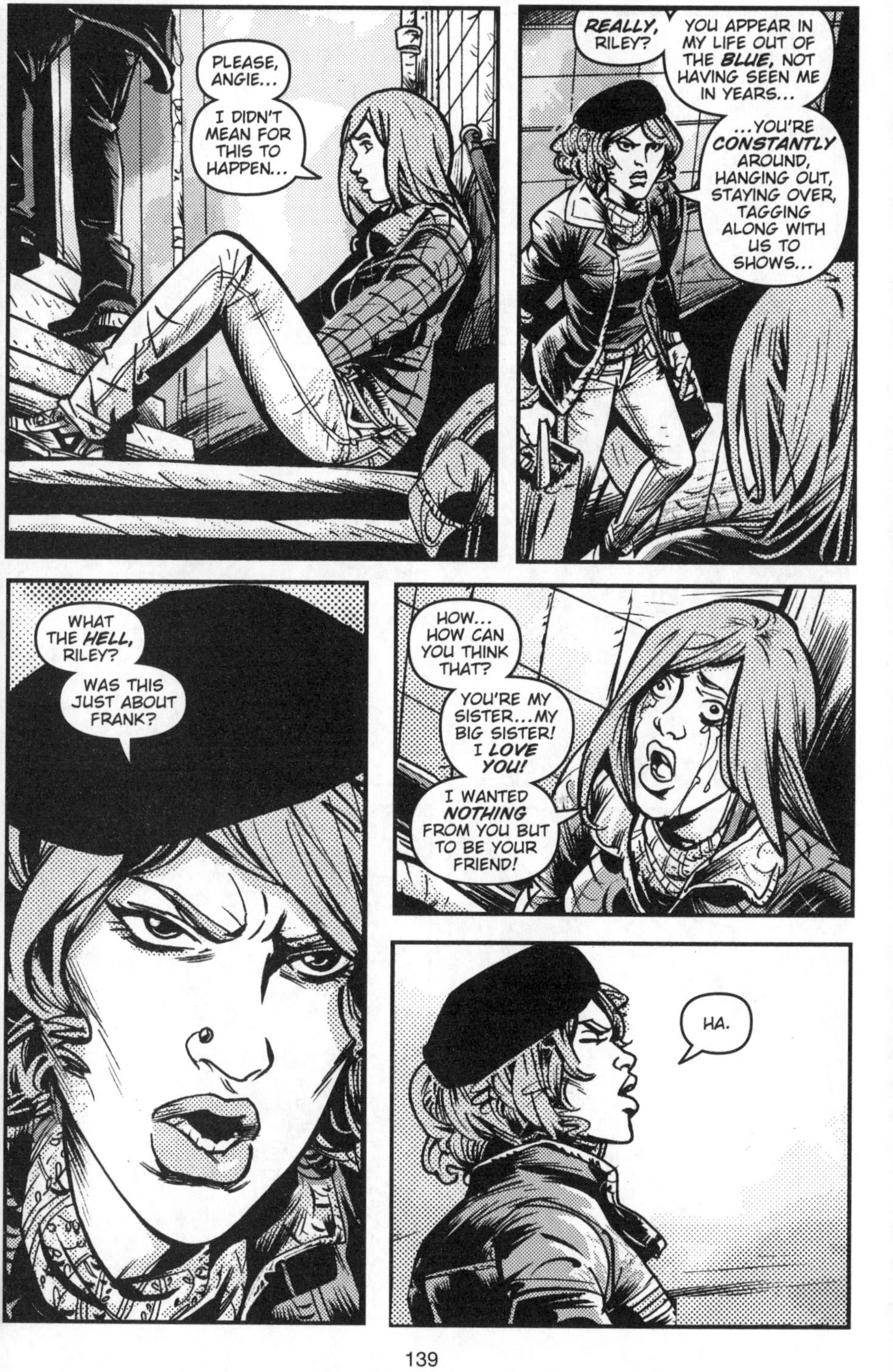
PLEASE, ANGIE...
I DIDN'T MEAN FOR THIS TO HAPPEN...
REALLY, RILEY?
YOU APPEAR IN MY LIFE OUT OF THE BLUE, NOT HAVING SEEN ME IN YEARS...
...YOU'RE CONSTANTLY AROUND, HANGING OUT, STAYING OVER, TAGGING ALONG WITH US TO SHOWS...
WHAT THE HELL, RILEY?
WAS THIS JUST ABOUT FRANK?
HOW... HOW CAN YOU THINK THAT?
YOU'RE MY SISTER...MY BIG SISTER! I LOVE YOU!
I WANTED NOTHING FROM YOU BUT TO BE YOUR FRIEND!
HA.

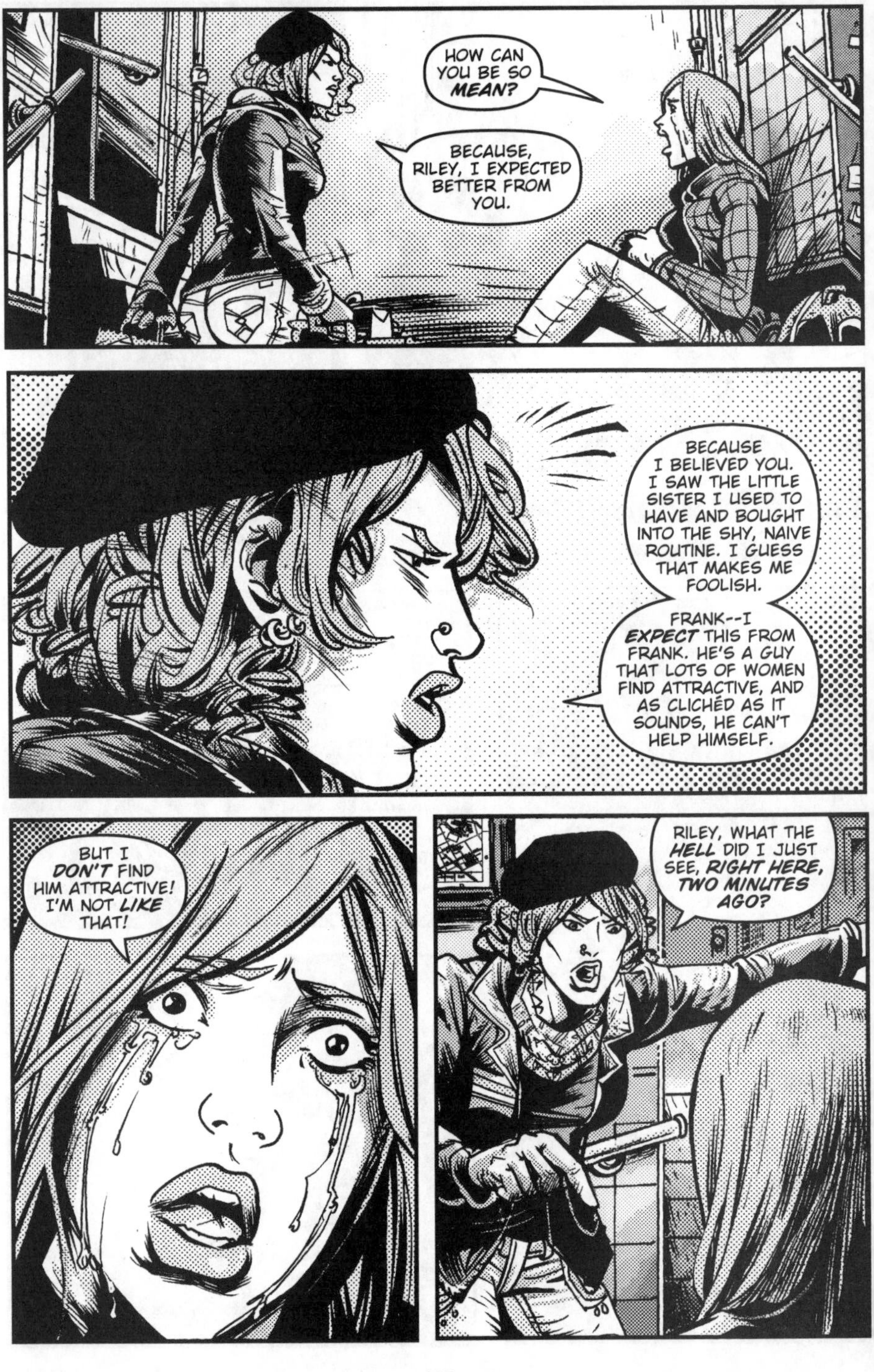
HOW CAN YOU BE SO MEAN?
BECAUSE, RILEY, I EXPECTED BETTER FROM YOU.
BECAUSE I BELIEVED YOU. I SAW THE LITTLE SISTER I USED TO HAVE AND BOUGHT INTO THE SHY, NAIVE ROUTINE. I GUESS THAT MAKES ME FOOLISH.
FRANK--I EXPECT THIS FROM FRANK. HE'S A GUY THAT LOTS OF WOMEN FIND ATTRACTIVE, AND AS CLICHÉD AS IT SOUNDS, HE CAN'T HELP HIMSELF.
BUT I DON'T FIND HIM ATTRACTIVE! I'M NOT LIKE THAT!
RILEY, WHAT THE HELL DID I JUST SEE, RIGHT HERE, TWO MINUTES AGO?

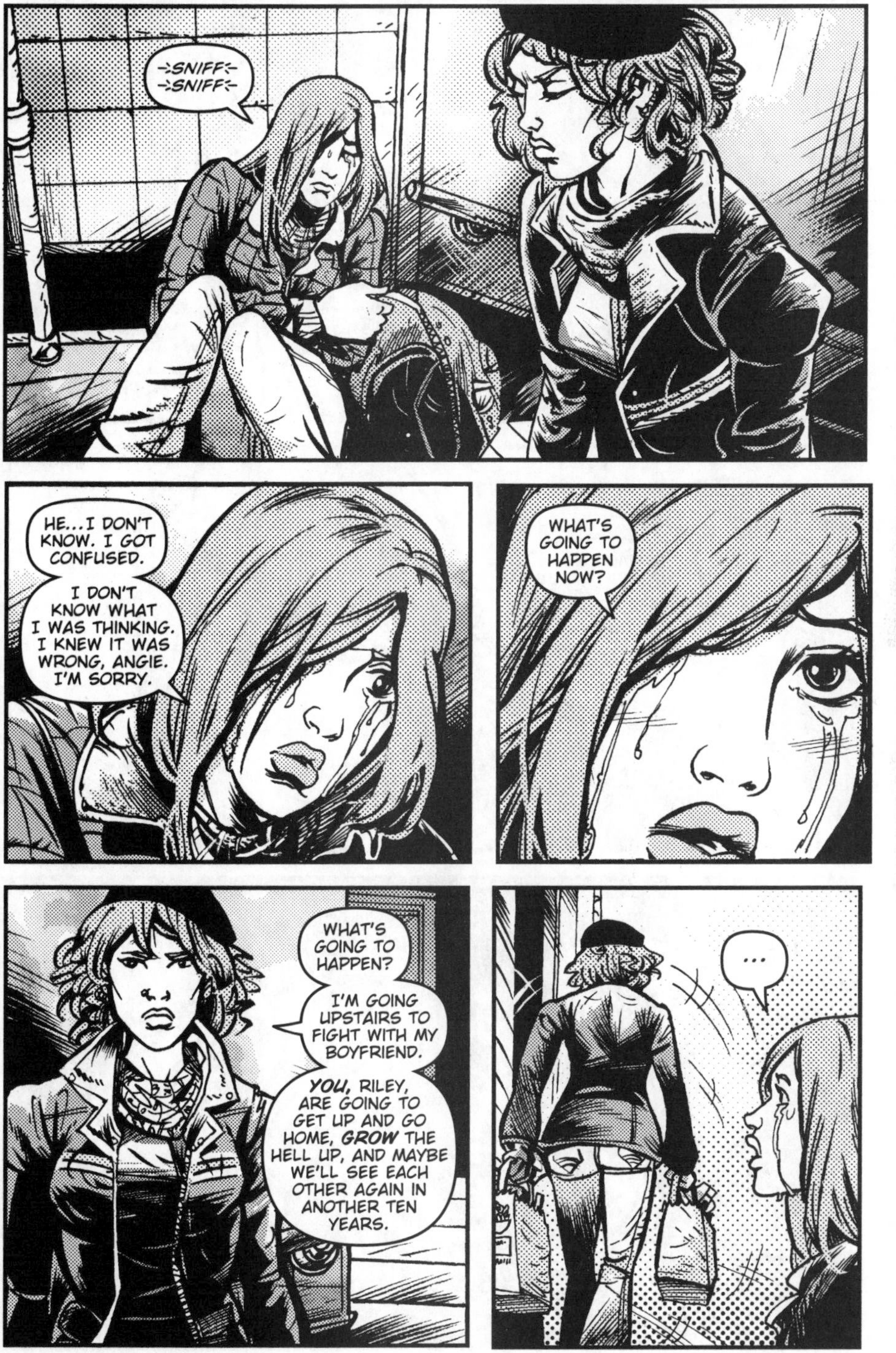

-SNIFF- -SNIFF-
HE...I DON'T KNOW. I GOT CONFUSED.
I DON'T KNOW WHAT I WAS THINKING. I KNEW IT WAS WRONG, ANGIE. I'M SORRY.
WHAT'S GOING TO HAPPEN NOW?
WHAT'S GOING TO HAPPEN?
I'M GOING UPSTAIRS TO FIGHT WITH MY BOYFRIEND.
YOU, RILEY, ARE GOING TO GET UP AND GO HOME, *GROW* THE HELL UP, AND MAYBE WE'LL SEE EACH OTHER AGAIN IN ANOTHER TEN YEARS.
...

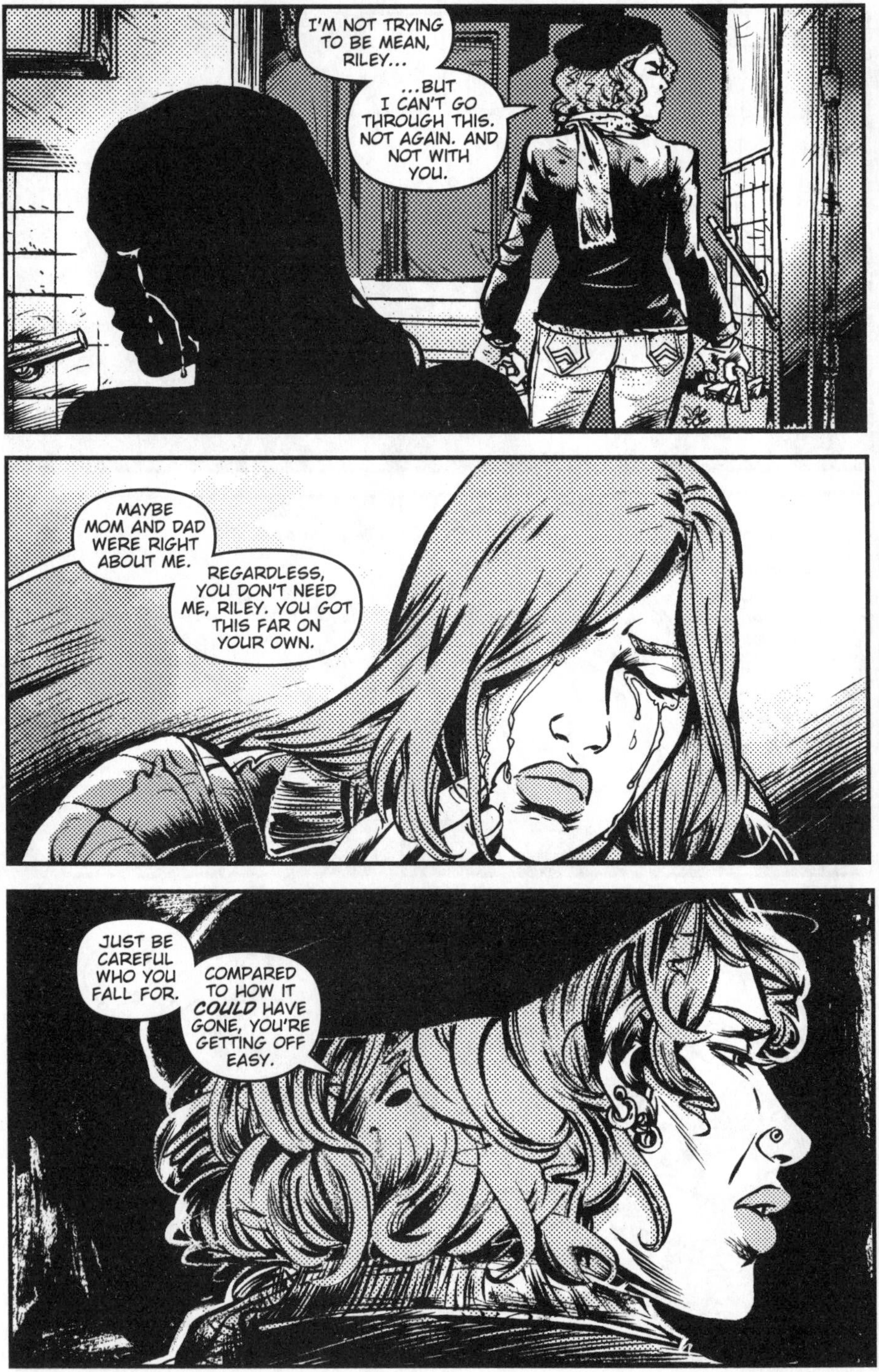
I'M NOT TRYING TO BE MEAN, RILEY...
...BUT I CAN'T GO THROUGH THIS. NOT AGAIN. AND NOT WITH YOU.
MAYBE MOM AND DAD WERE RIGHT ABOUT ME.
REGARDLESS, YOU DON'T NEED ME, RILEY. YOU GOT THIS FAR ON YOUR OWN.
JUST BE CAREFUL WHO YOU FALL FOR.
COMPARED TO HOW IT COULD HAVE GONE, YOU'RE GETTING OFF EASY.

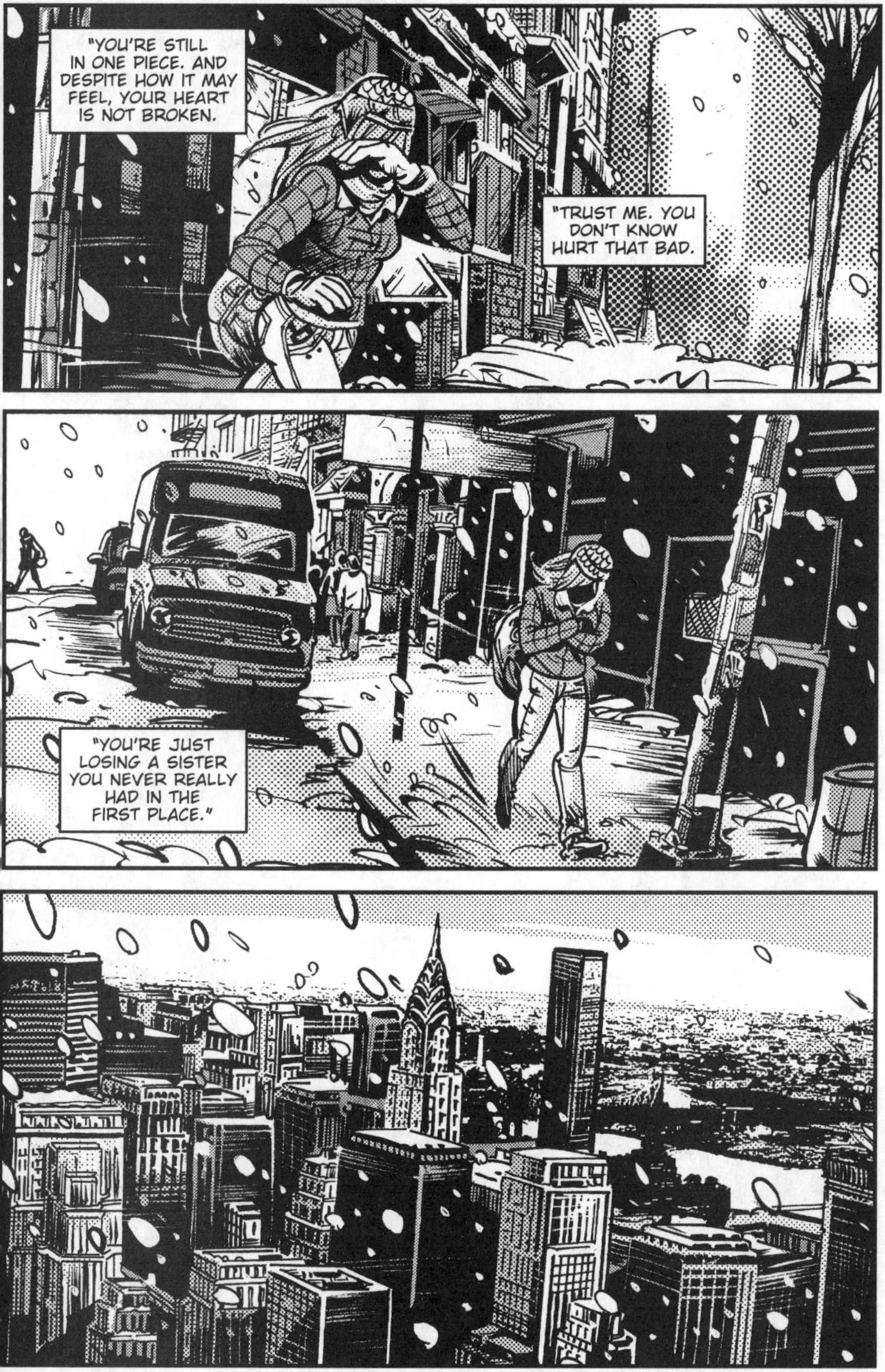
"YOU'RE STILL IN ONE PIECE. AND DESPITE HOW IT MAY FEEL, YOUR HEART IS NOT BROKEN.
"TRUST ME. YOU DON'T KNOW HURT THAT BAD.
"YOU'RE JUST LOSING A SISTER YOU NEVER REALLY HAD IN THE FIRST PLACE."

Epilogue

What Would the Community Think?

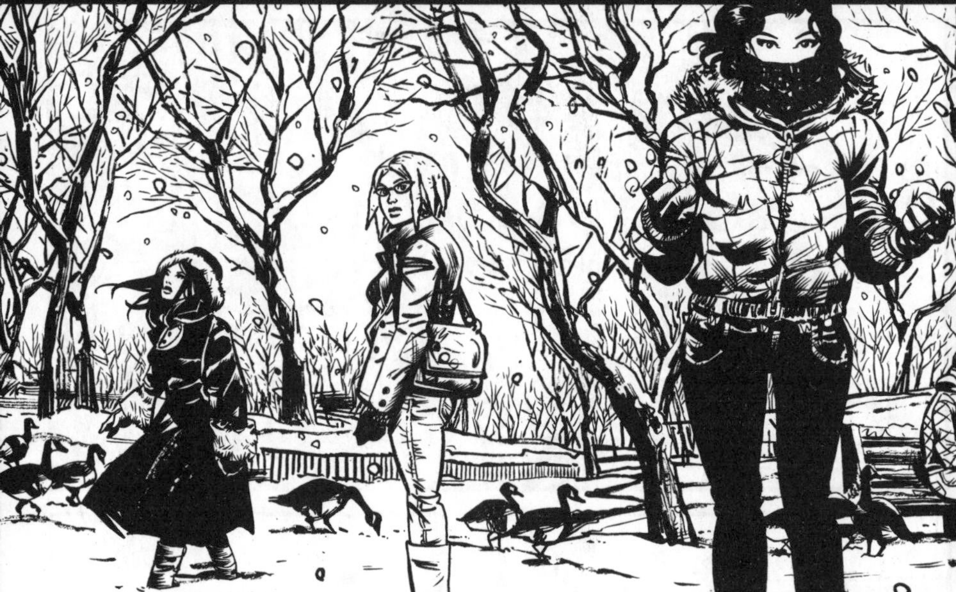

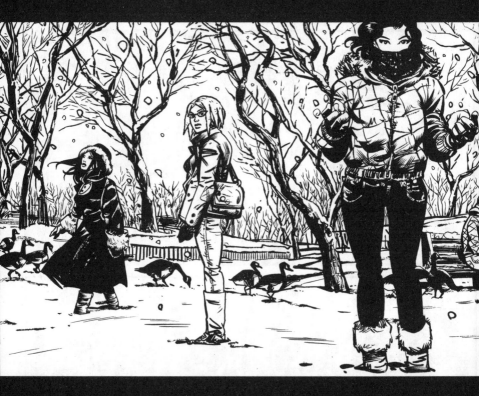

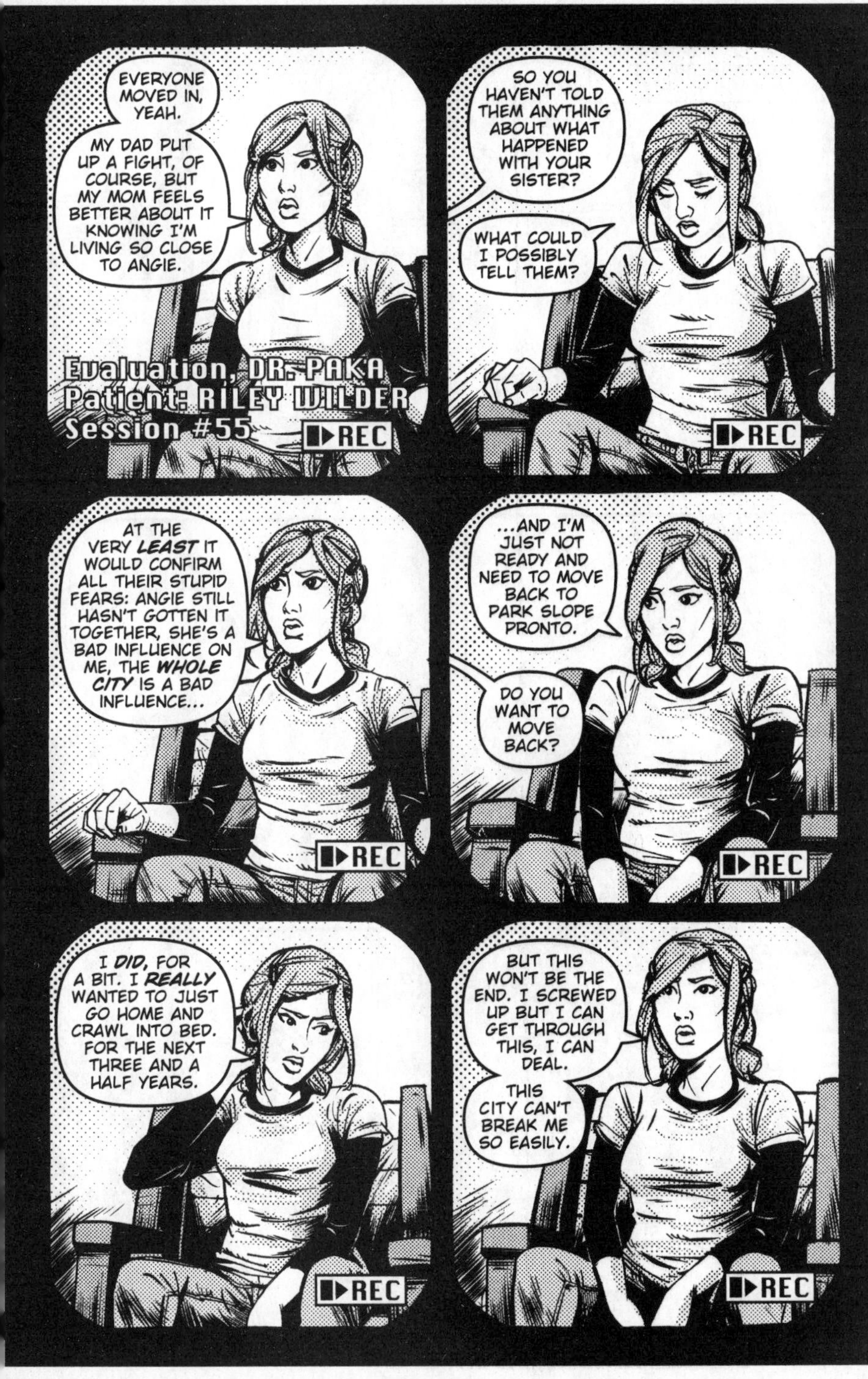
EVERYONE MOVED IN, YEAH.
MY DAD PUT UP A FIGHT, OF COURSE, BUT MY MOM FEELS BETTER ABOUT IT KNOWING I'M LIVING SO CLOSE TO ANGIE.
Evaluation, DR. PAKA
Patient: RILEY WILDER
Session #55
REC
SO YOU HAVEN'T TOLD THEM ANYTHING ABOUT WHAT HAPPENED WITH YOUR SISTER?
WHAT COULD I POSSIBLY TELL THEM?
REC
AT THE VERY LEAST IT WOULD CONFIRM ALL THEIR STUPID FEARS: ANGIE STILL HASN'T GOTTEN IT TOGETHER, SHE'S A BAD INFLUENCE ON ME, THE WHOLE CITY IS A BAD INFLUENCE...
REC
...AND I'M JUST NOT READY AND NEED TO MOVE BACK TO PARK SLOPE PRONTO.
DO YOU WANT TO MOVE BACK?
REC
I DID, FOR A BIT. I REALLY WANTED TO JUST GO HOME AND CRAWL INTO BED. FOR THE NEXT THREE AND A HALF YEARS.
REC
BUT THIS WON'T BE THE END. I SCREWED UP BUT I CAN GET THROUGH THIS, I CAN DEAL.
THIS CITY CAN'T BREAK ME SO EASILY.
REC

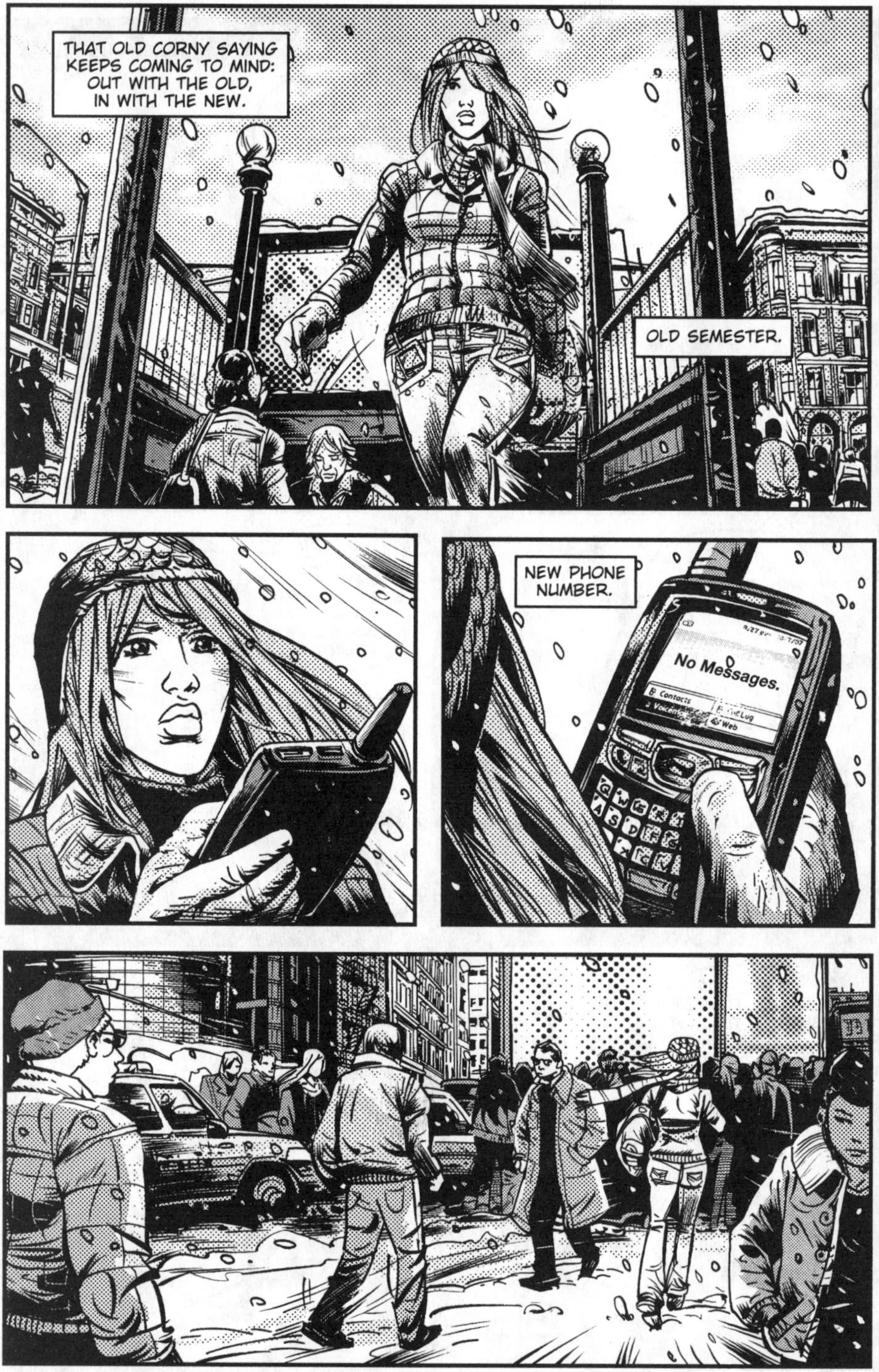
THAT OLD CORNY SAYING KEEPS COMING TO MIND: OUT WITH THE OLD, IN WITH THE NEW.
OLD SEMESTER.
NEW PHONE NUMBER.
No Messages.
Contacts
Web

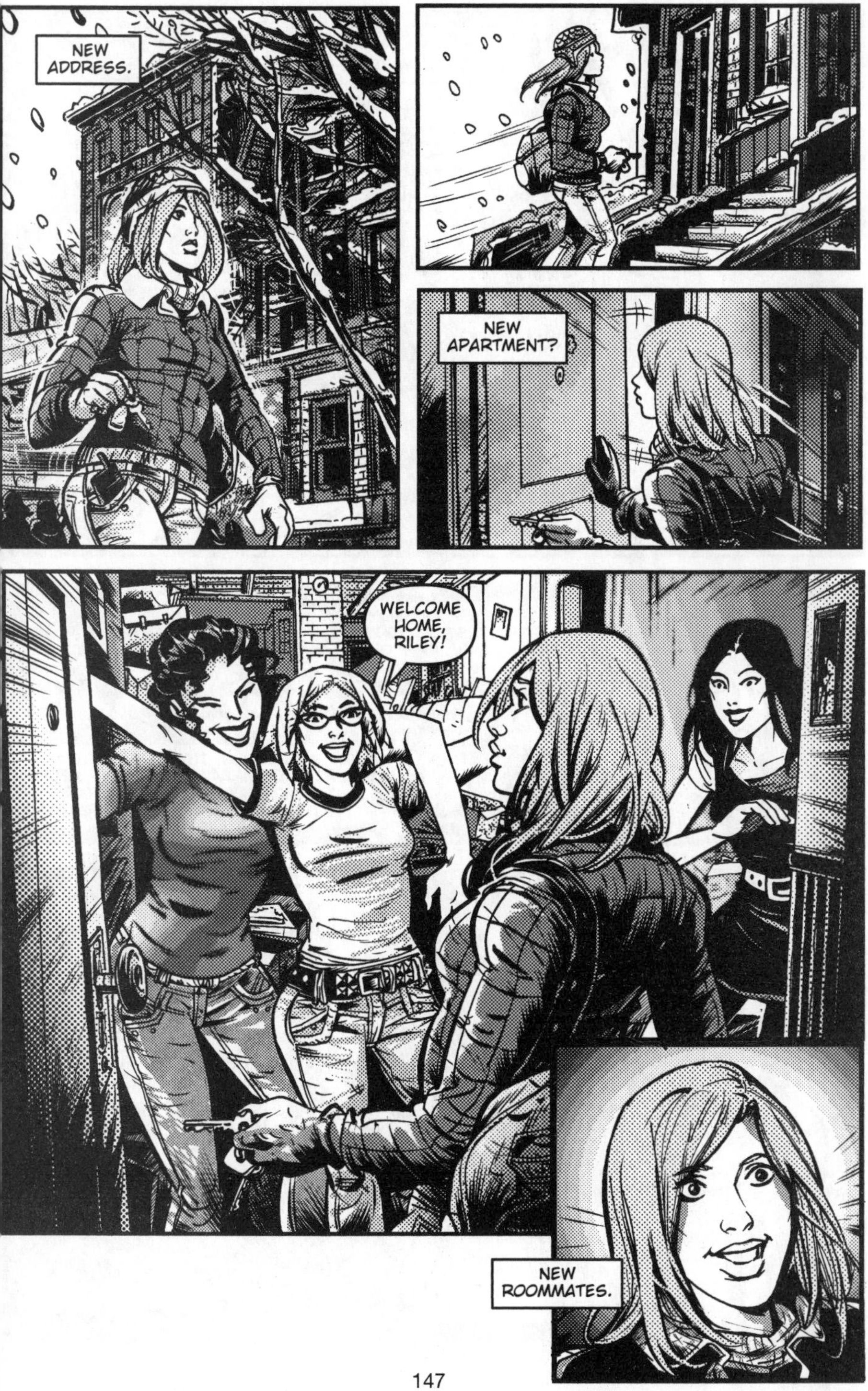
NEW ADDRESS.
NEW APARTMENT?
WELCOME HOME, RILEY!
NEW ROOMMATES.

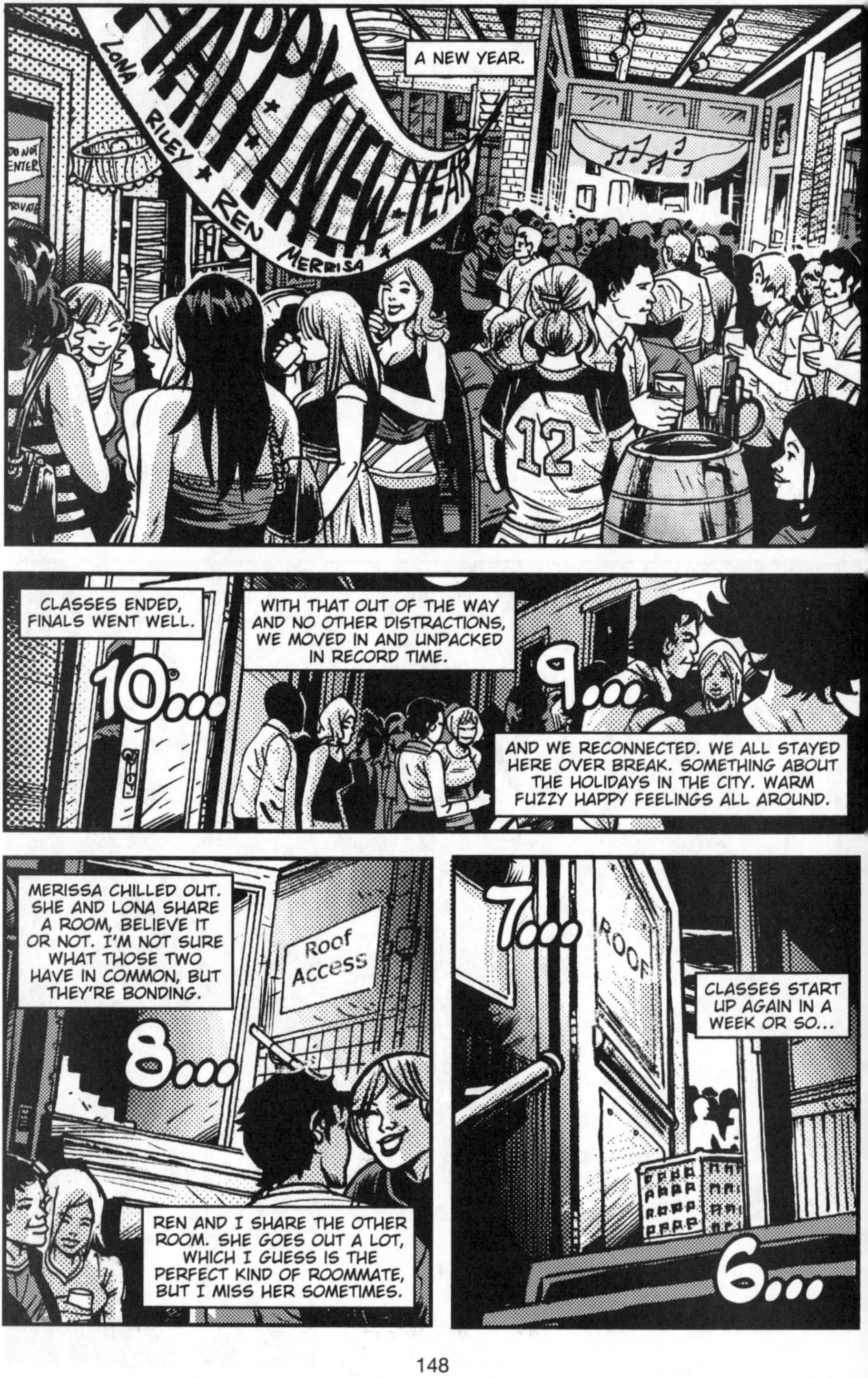
HAPPY NEW YEAR
LONA
RILEY
REN
MERRISA
DO NOT ENTER
PRIVATE
A NEW YEAR.
12
CLASSES ENDED, FINALS WENT WELL.
WITH THAT OUT OF THE WAY AND NO OTHER DISTRACTIONS, WE MOVED IN AND UNPACKED IN RECORD TIME.
10...
9...
AND WE RECONNECTED. WE ALL STAYED HERE OVER BREAK. SOMETHING ABOUT THE HOLIDAYS IN THE CITY. WARM FUZZY HAPPY FEELINGS ALL AROUND.
MERISSA CHILLED OUT. SHE AND LONA SHARE A ROOM, BELIEVE IT OR NOT. I'M NOT SURE WHAT THOSE TWO HAVE IN COMMON, BUT THEY'RE BONDING.
Roof Access
8...
REN AND I SHARE THE OTHER ROOM. SHE GOES OUT A LOT, WHICH I GUESS IS THE PERFECT KIND OF ROOMMATE, BUT I MISS HER SOMETIMES.
7...
ROOF
CLASSES START UP AGAIN IN A WEEK OR SO...
6...

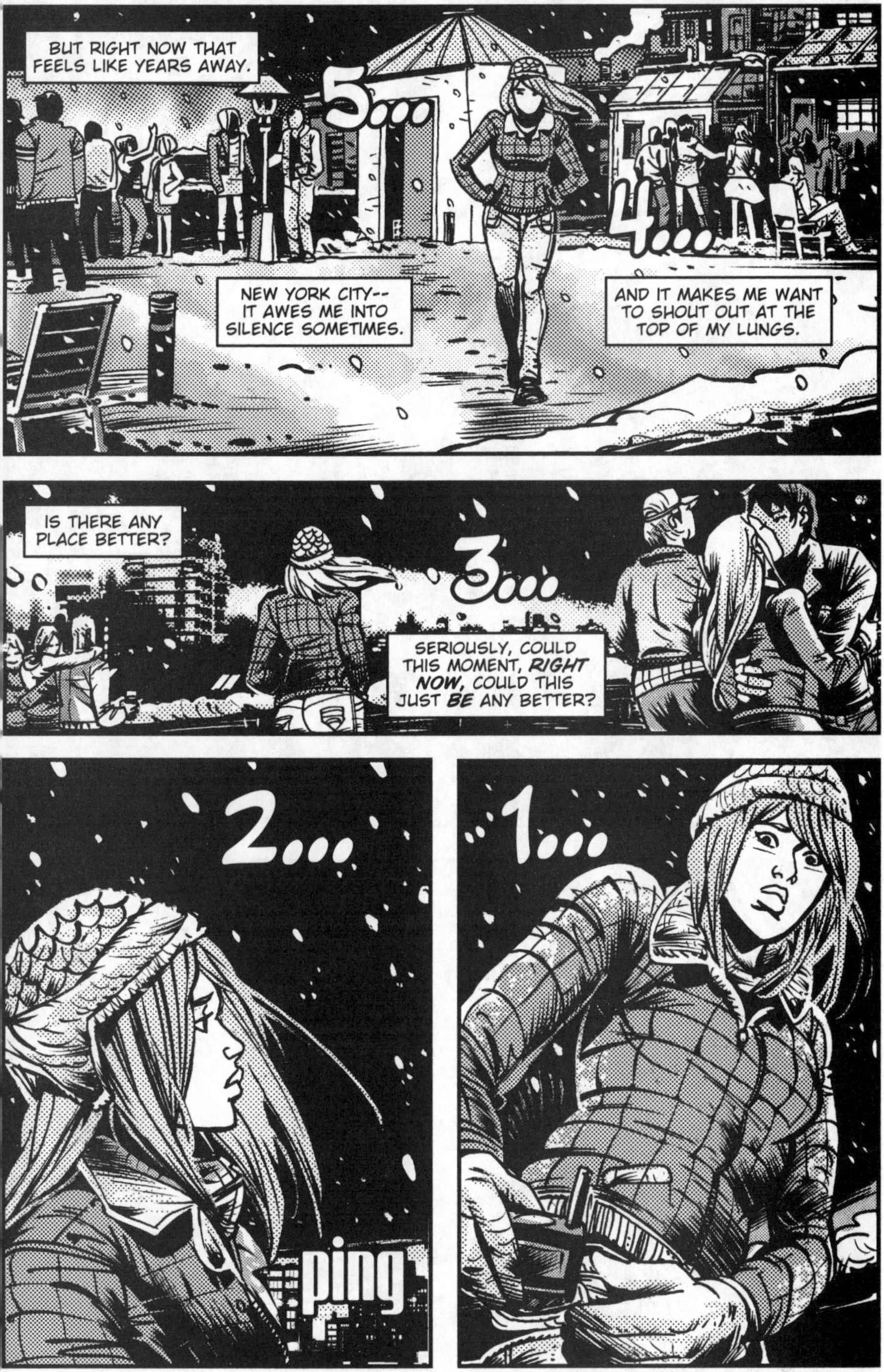
BUT RIGHT NOW THAT FEELS LIKE YEARS AWAY.
5...
4...
NEW YORK CITY-- IT AWES ME INTO SILENCE SOMETIMES.
AND IT MAKES ME WANT TO SHOUT OUT AT THE TOP OF MY LUNGS.
IS THERE ANY PLACE BETTER?
3...
SERIOUSLY, COULD THIS MOMENT, *RIGHT NOW,* COULD THIS JUST *BE* ANY BETTER?
2...
ping
1...

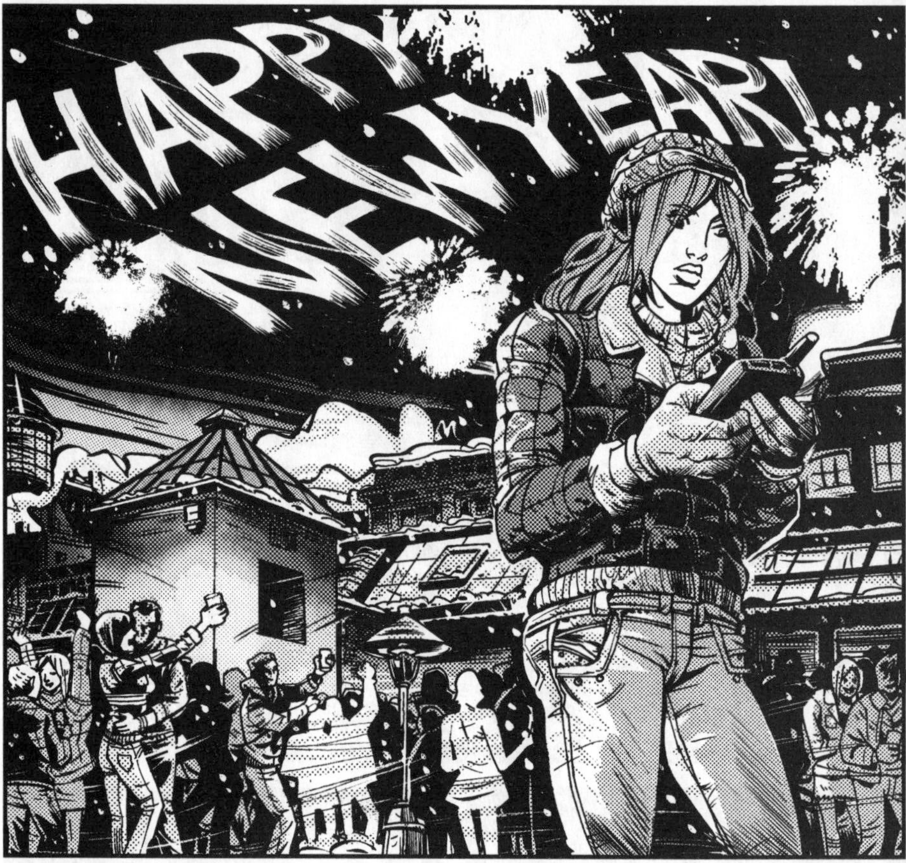
HAPPY NEW YEAR!

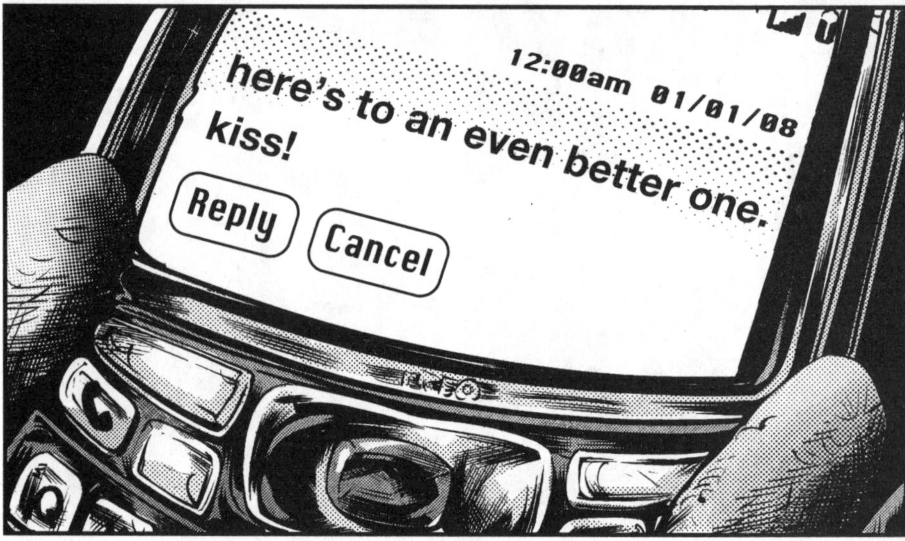
12:00am 01/01/08
here's to an even better one.
kiss!
Reply
Cancel

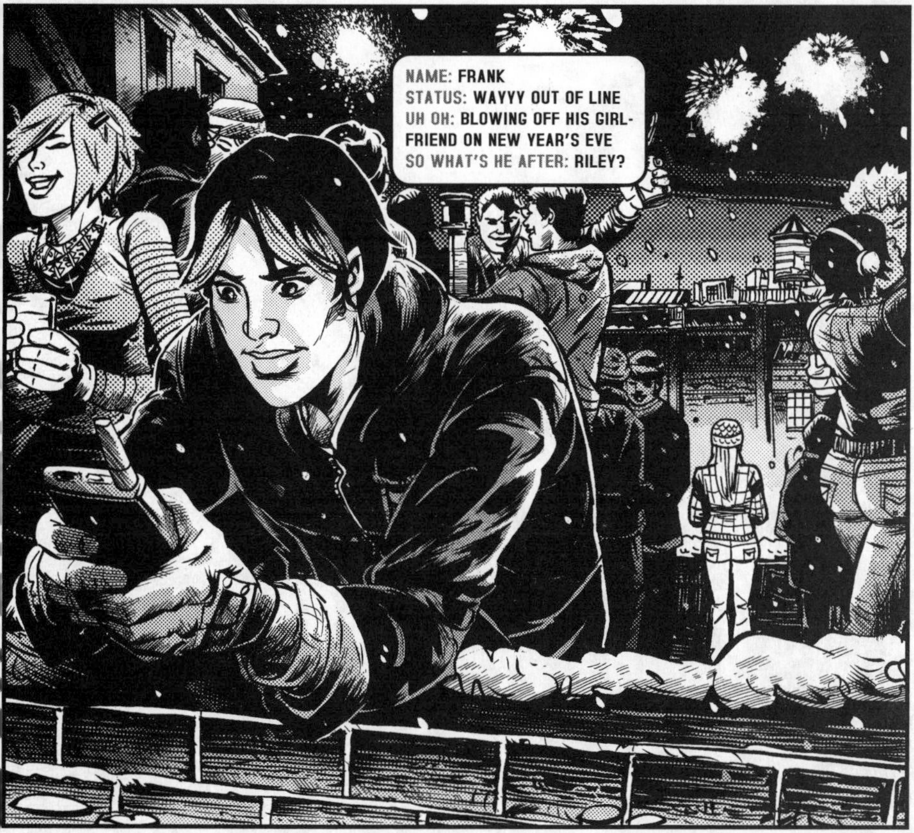
NAME: FRANK
STATUS: WAYYY OUT OF LINE
UH OH: BLOWING OFF HIS GIRL-FRIEND ON NEW YEAR'S EVE
SO WHAT'S HE AFTER: RILEY?

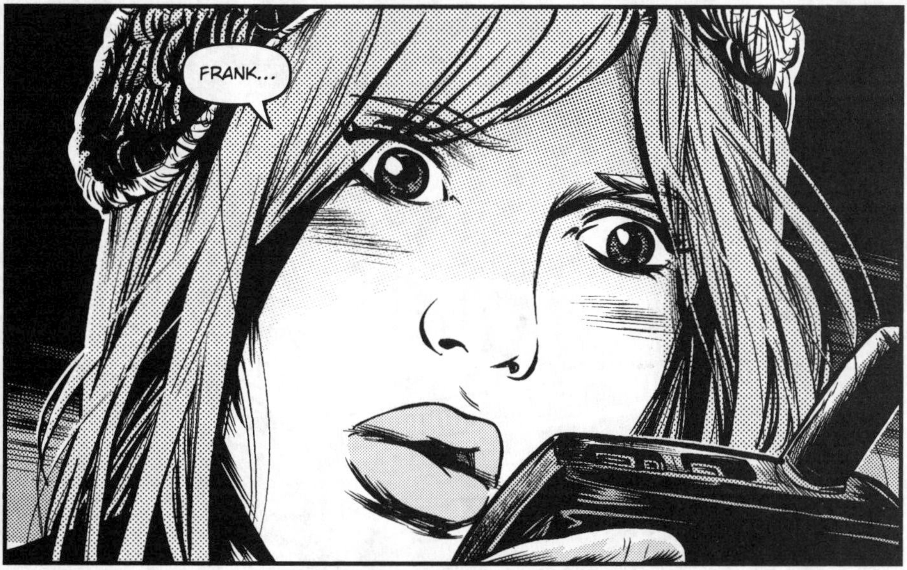
FRANK...

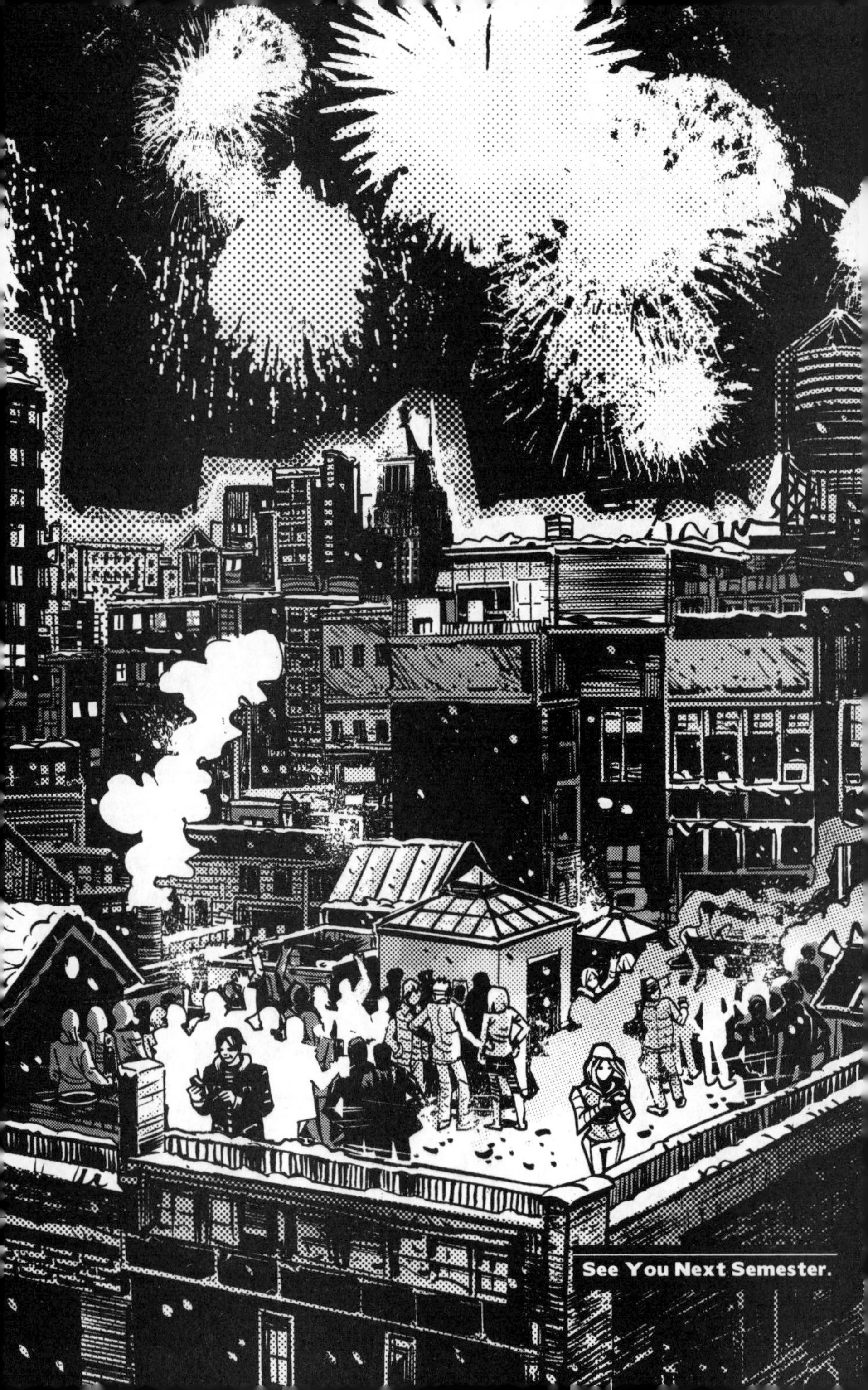
See You Next Semester.

BRIAN WOOD

Brian released his first book in 1997 to considerable critical acclaim and has continued to produce comics and graphic novels at a brisk pace ever since, becoming one of the most important indie creators of the last decade. He has earned multiple Eisner Award nominations, and editions of his work have been published in close to a dozen foreign markets. Standout works include *Demo, Local, DMZ* and *Northlanders.* And just like the characters in *The New York Four*, Brian attended college in New York City where he continues to live with his wife and daughter.

RYAN KELLY

For the past eight years, Ryan has been working as a comic book artist, illustrator, painter and teacher. His work includes the graphic novel *Giant Robot Warriors* as well as the Vertigo series *American Virgin, Books of Faerie, The Vinyl Underground* and the Eisner-nominated series *Lucifer*. Most people know of Ryan's work in the critically acclaimed series *Local* with Brian Wood. You can currently find Ryan in Saint Paul, Minnesota where he lives with his common law wife and his three maniacal little boys. Ryan also has more hats than you.

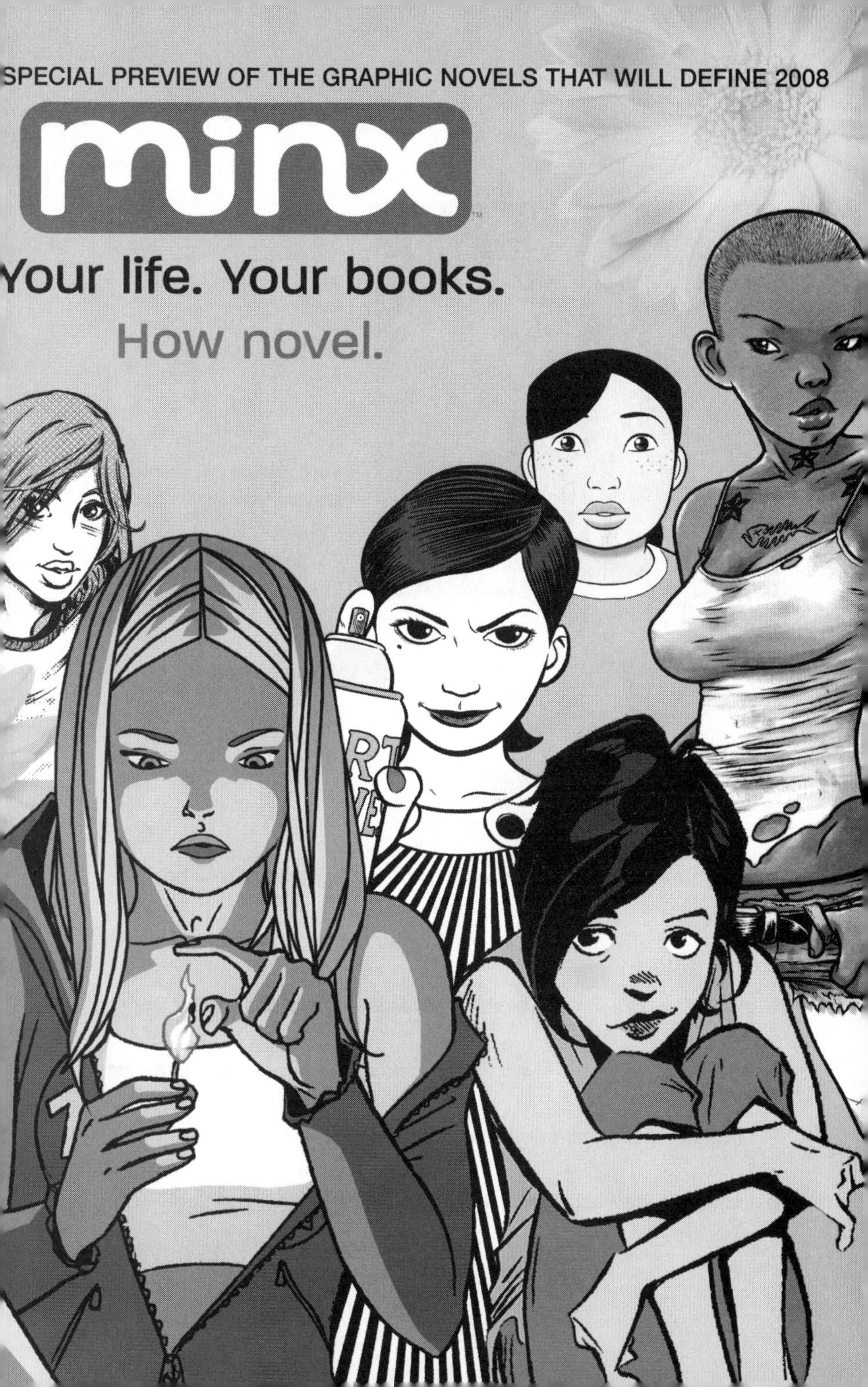
SPECIAL PREVIEW OF THE GRAPHIC NOVELS THAT WILL DEFINE 2008
minx™
Your life. Your books.
How novel.

By the critically acclaimed novelist Rebecca Donner

When Danni and her mom move in with her mom's alcoholic boyfriend,

Danni develops a fierce crush on Haskell, her soon-to-be stepbrother,

who's a hardcore environmentalist. Desperate and confused, Danni

wrestles with what she's willing to sacrifice as she confronts first love,

family secrets and the politics of ecoterrorism – set against the lush

backdrop of the Pacific Northwest.

By REBECCA DONNER & INAKI MIRANDA
AVAILABLE NOW! ∎ Read on.
But please note: The following pages are not sequential.

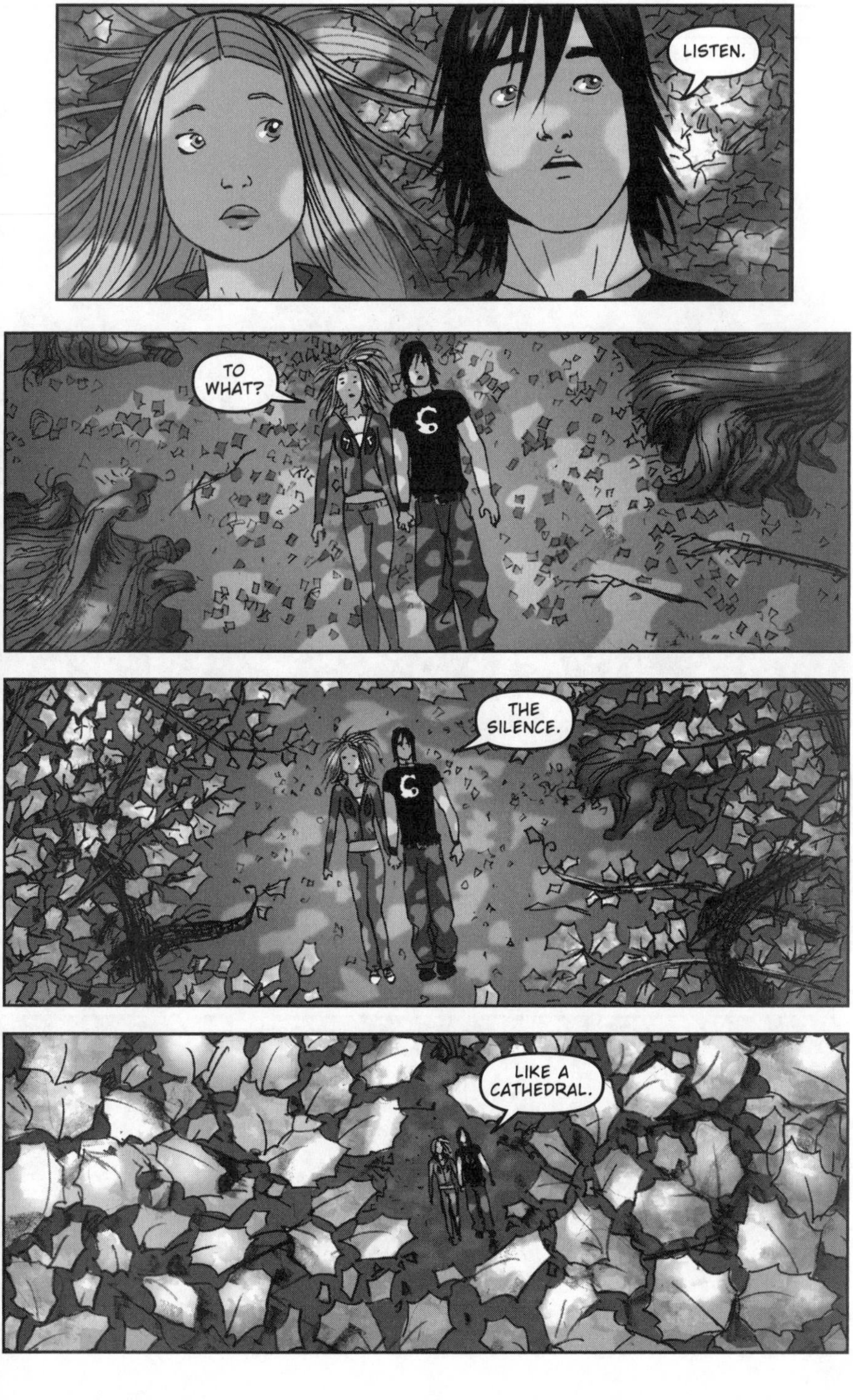
LISTEN.
TO WHAT?
THE SILENCE.
LIKE A CATHEDRAL.

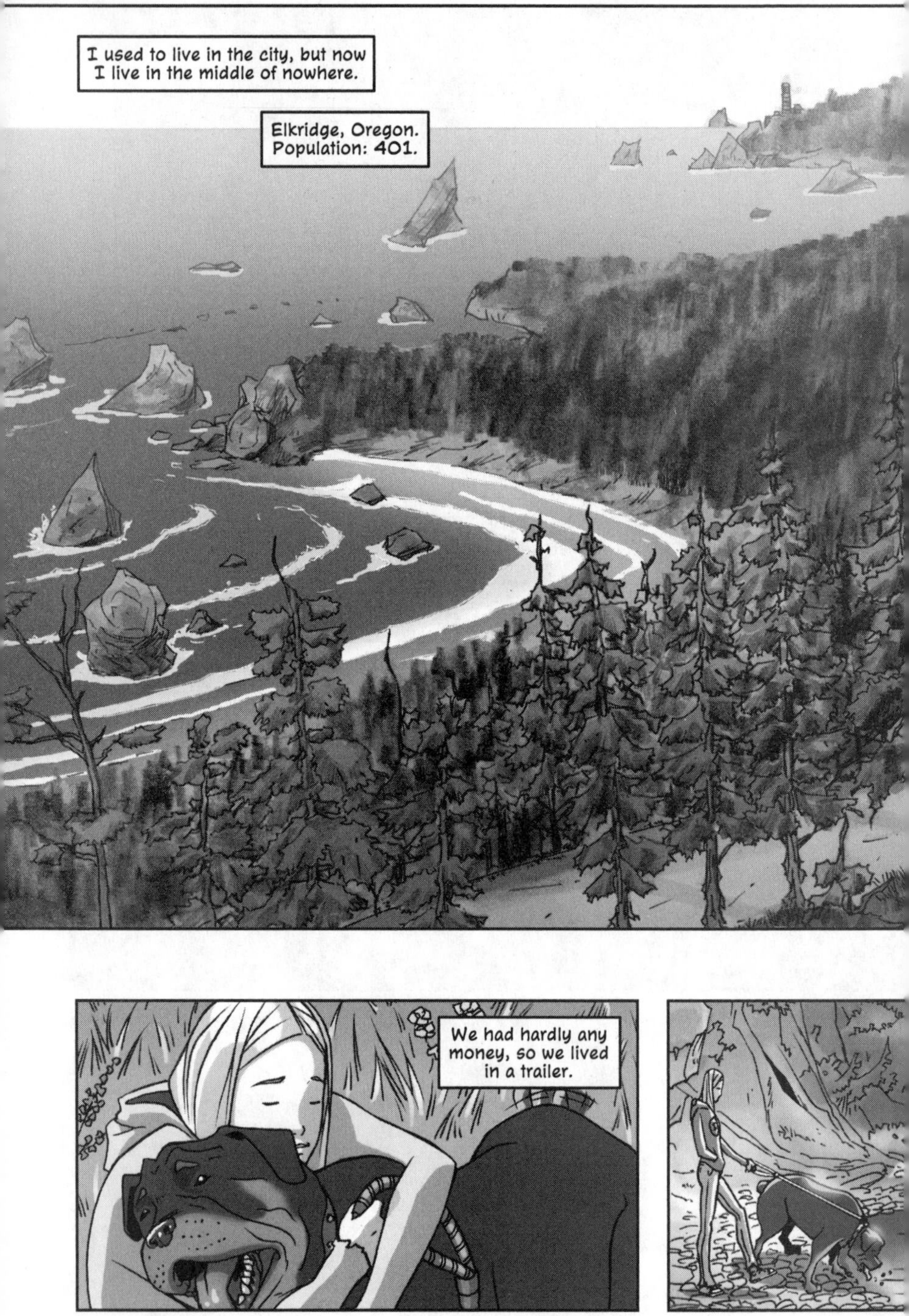
I used to live in the city, but now I live in the middle of nowhere.
Elkridge, Oregon. Population: 401.
We had hardly any money, so we lived in a trailer.

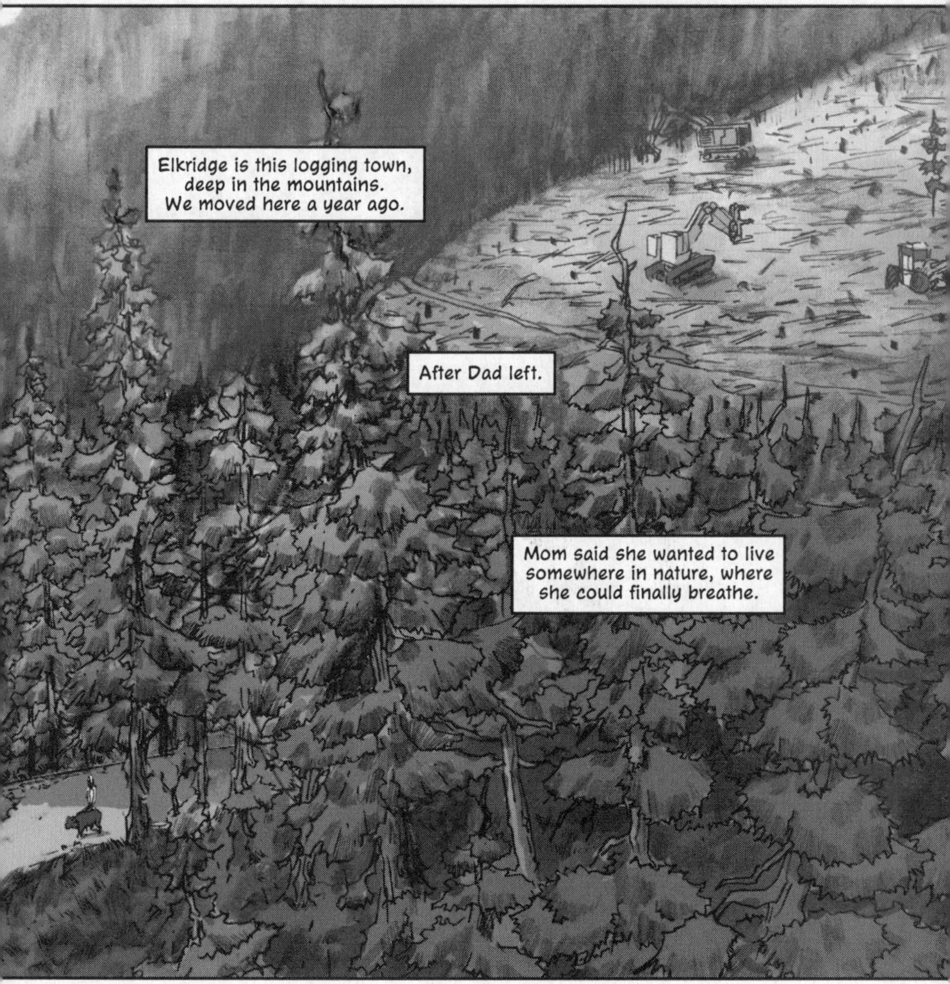
Elkridge is this logging town, deep in the mountains. We moved here a year ago.
After Dad left.
Mom said she wanted to live somewhere in nature, where she could finally breathe.

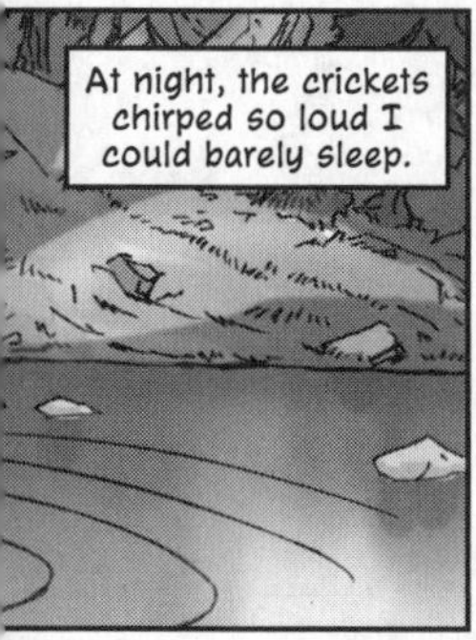
At night, the crickets chirped so loud I could barely sleep.

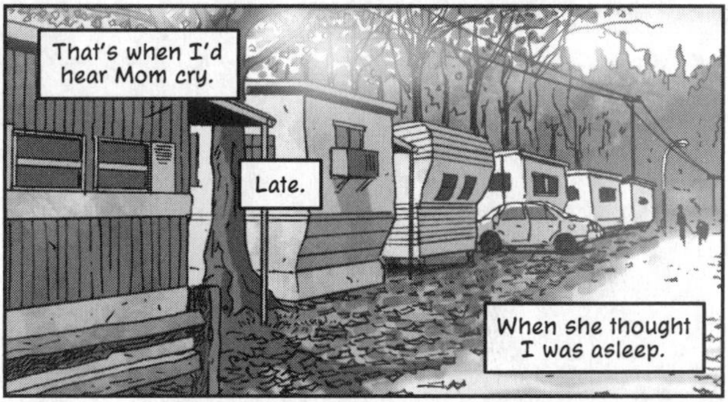
That's when I'd hear Mom cry.
Late.
When she thought I was asleep.

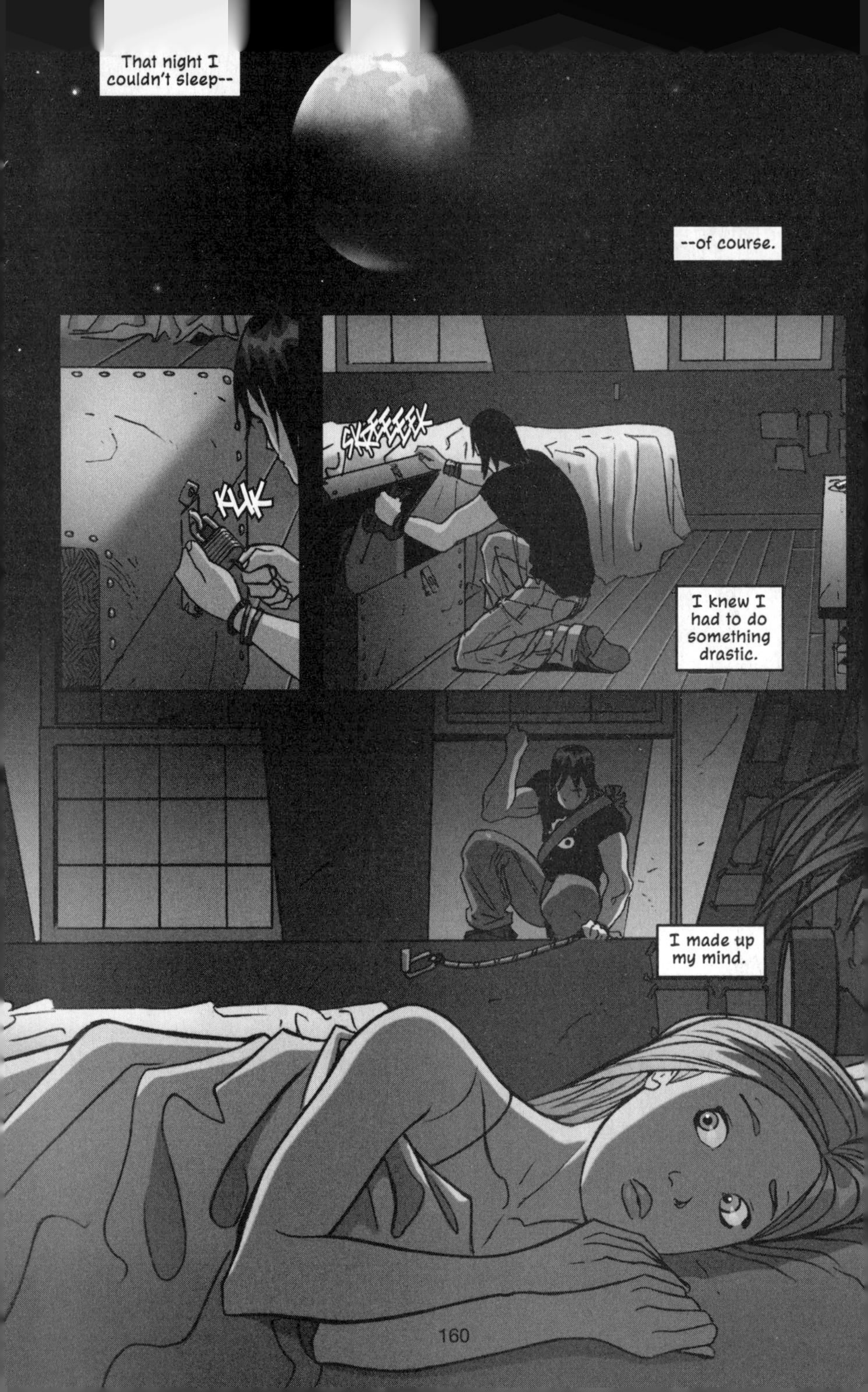
That night I couldn't sleep--
--of course.
KLIK
SKREEEEEK
I knew I had to do something drastic.
I made up my mind.

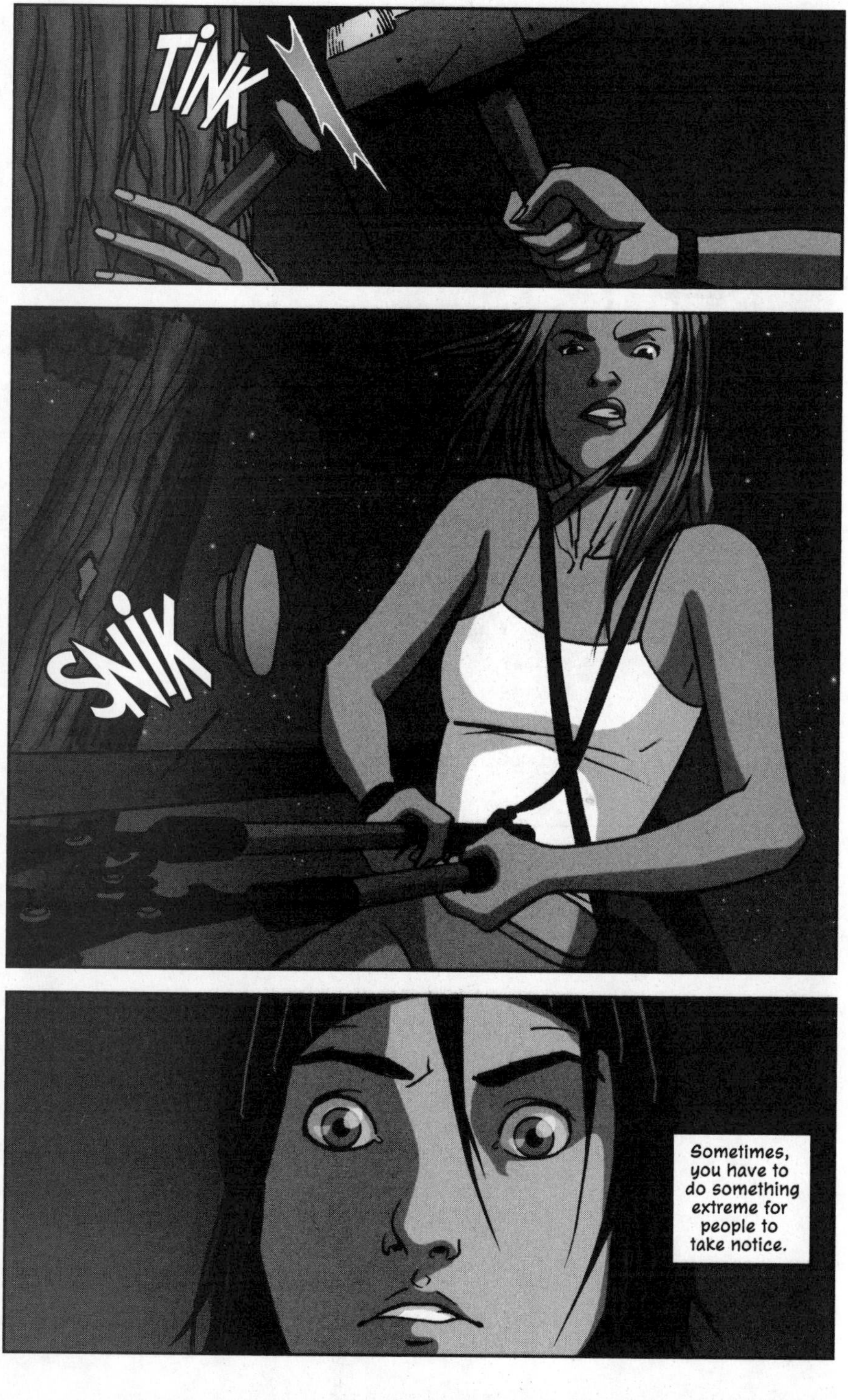
TINK
SNIK
Sometimes, you have to do something extreme for people to take notice.

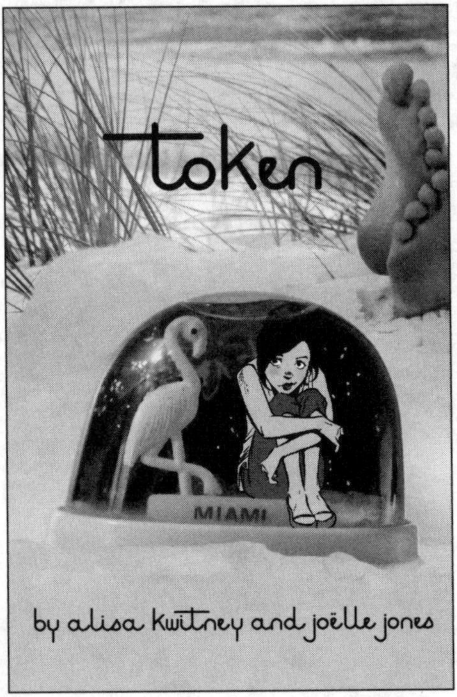
token
MIAMI
by alisa kwitney and joëlle jones

By noted comic book writer and novelist ALISA KWITNEY

Can a Jewish "girl out of time" and a Spanish old soul survive culture clashes and criminal records to find true love in the sun-drenched, sequined miasma that was South Beach in the Big '80s?

By ALISA KWITNEY & JOËLLE JONES

AVAILABLE IN OCTOBER ■ Read on.

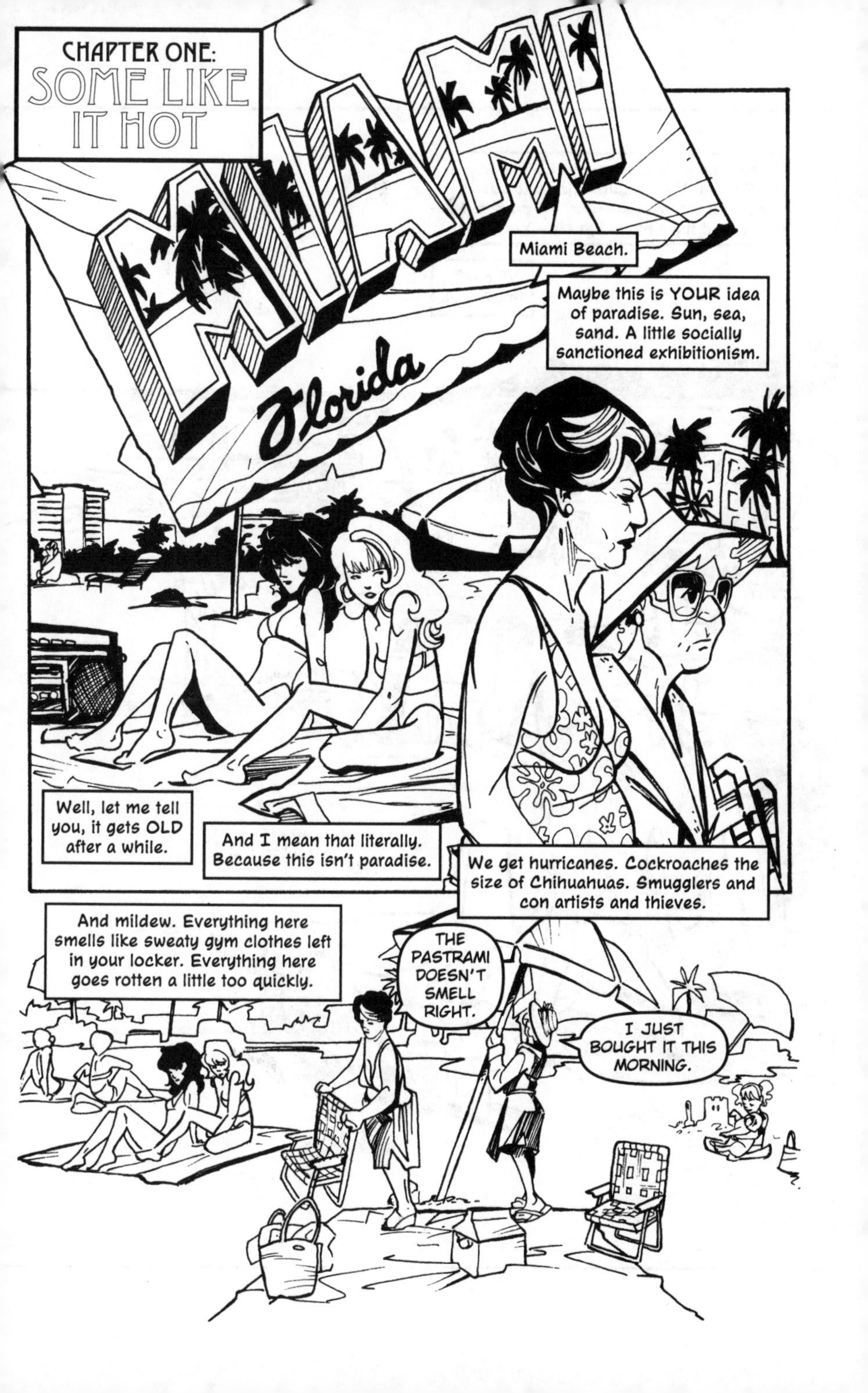
CHAPTER ONE:
SOME LIKE IT HOT
MIAMI
Florida
Miami Beach.
Maybe this is YOUR idea of paradise. Sun, sea, sand. A little socially sanctioned exhibitionism.
Well, let me tell you, it gets OLD after a while.
And I mean that literally. Because this isn't paradise.
We get hurricanes. Cockroaches the size of Chihuahuas. Smugglers and con artists and thieves.
And mildew. Everything here smells like sweaty gym clothes left in your locker. Everything here goes rotten a little too quickly.
THE PASTRAMI DOESN'T SMELL RIGHT.
I JUST BOUGHT IT THIS MORNING.

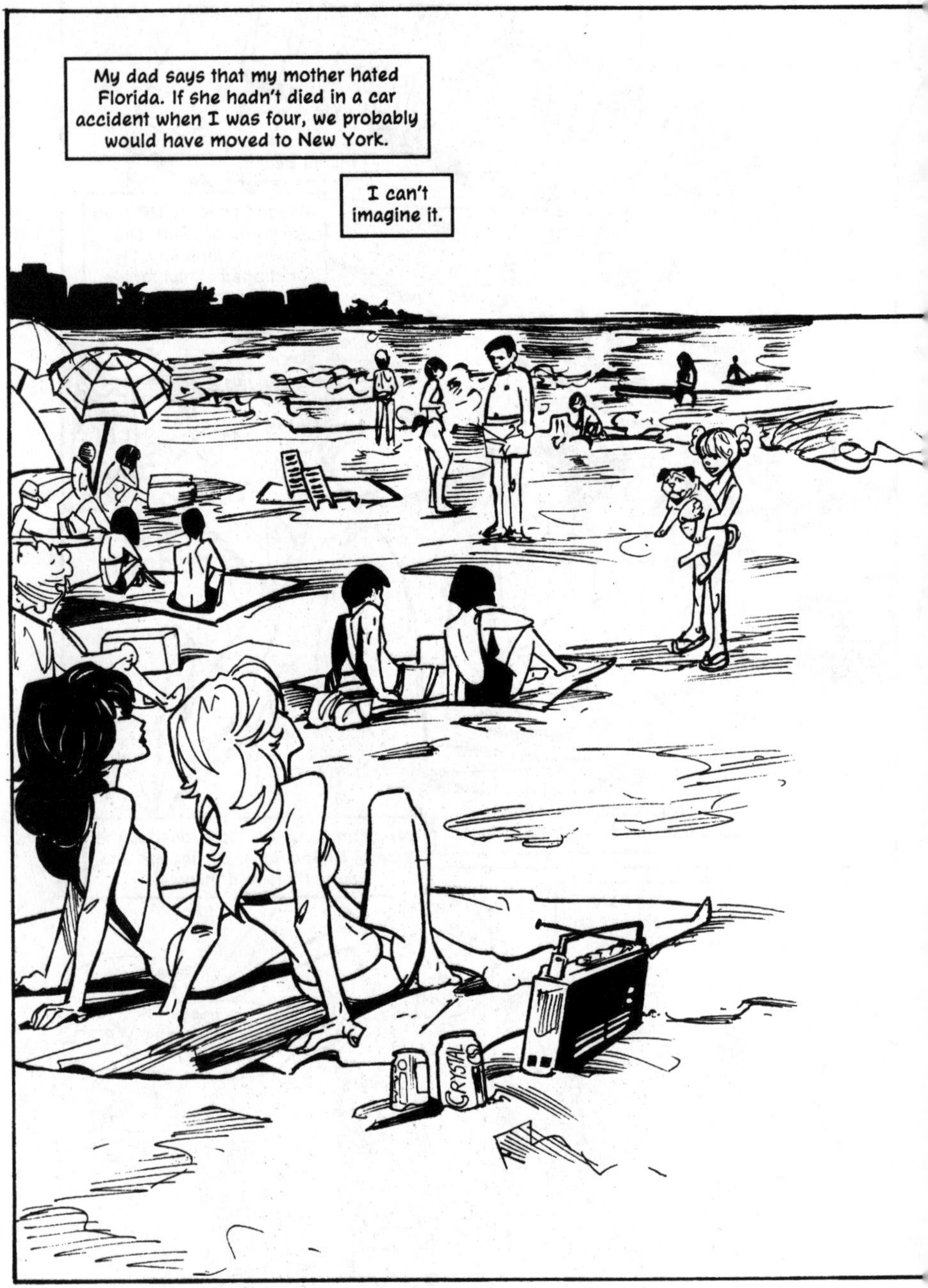
My dad says that my mother hated Florida. If she hadn't died in a car accident when I was four, we probably would have moved to New York.
I can't imagine it.
CRYSTAL

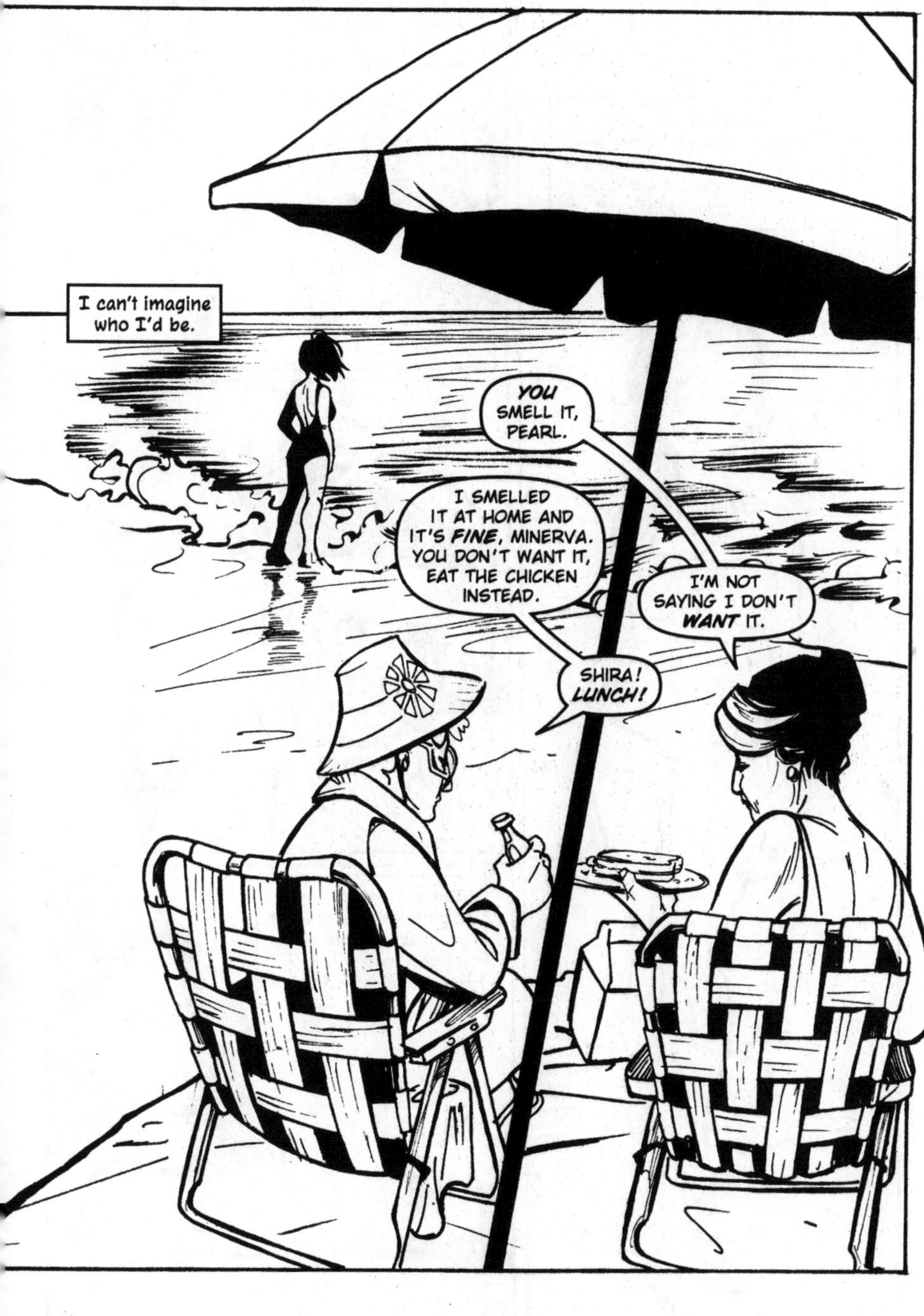

I can't imagine who I'd be.
YOU SMELL IT, PEARL.
I SMELLED IT AT HOME AND IT'S FINE, MINERVA. YOU DON'T WANT IT, EAT THE CHICKEN INSTEAD.
I'M NOT SAYING I DON'T WANT IT.
SHIRA! LUNCH!

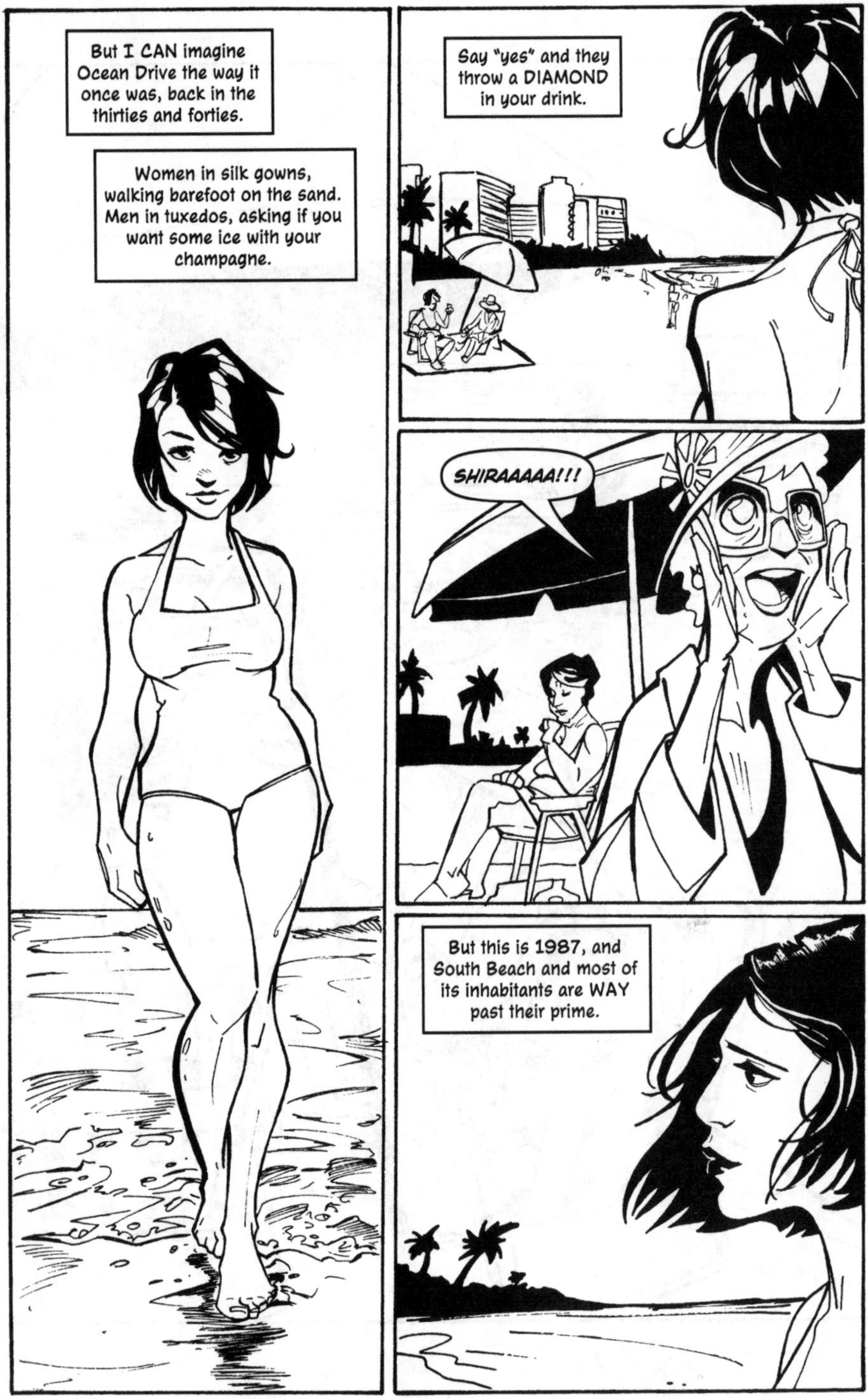
But I CAN imagine Ocean Drive the way it once was, back in the thirties and forties.
Women in silk gowns, walking barefoot on the sand. Men in tuxedos, asking if you want some ice with your champagne.
Say "yes" and they throw a DIAMOND in your drink.
SHIRAAAAA!!!
But this is 1987, and South Beach and most of its inhabitants are WAY past their prime.

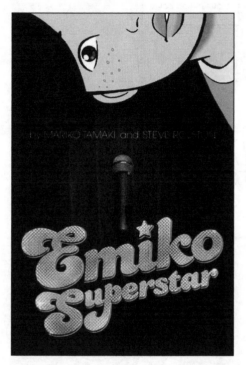

Written by novelist/performance artist MARIKO TAMAKI

A "borrowed" diary, a double life and identity issues fuel a teenager's quest

to find herself before she cracks and commits social suicide.

Watch Emi go from dull suburban babysitter to eclectic urban art star —

compliments of one crazy summer.

By MARIKO TAMAKI & STEVE ROLSTON
AVAILABLE IN SEPTEMBER ∎ Read on.

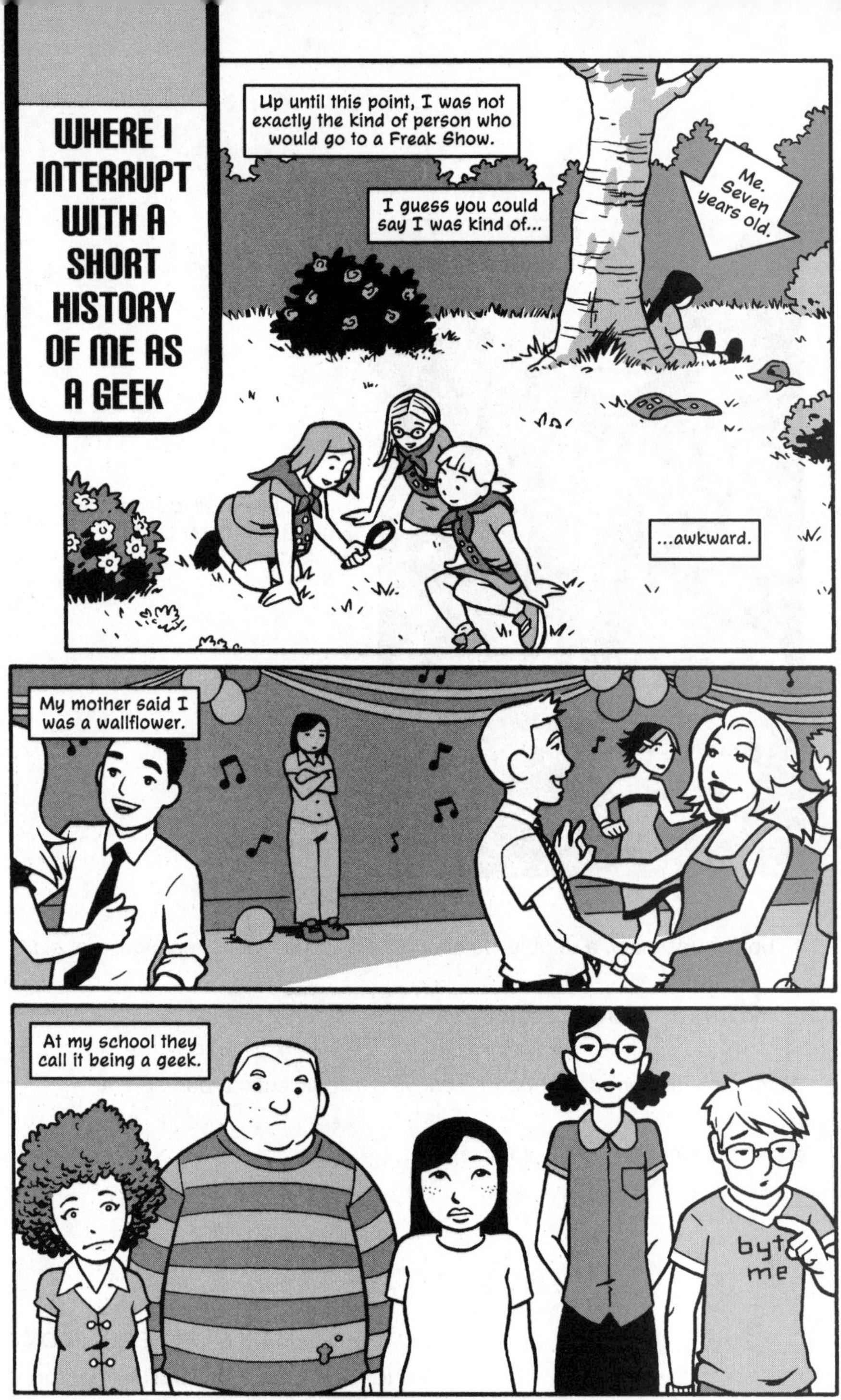
WHERE I INTERRUPT WITH A SHORT HISTORY OF ME AS A GEEK
Up until this point, I was not exactly the kind of person who would go to a Freak Show.
I guess you could say I was kind of...
Me. Seven years old.
...awkward.
My mother said I was a wallflower.
At my school they call it being a geek.
byt me

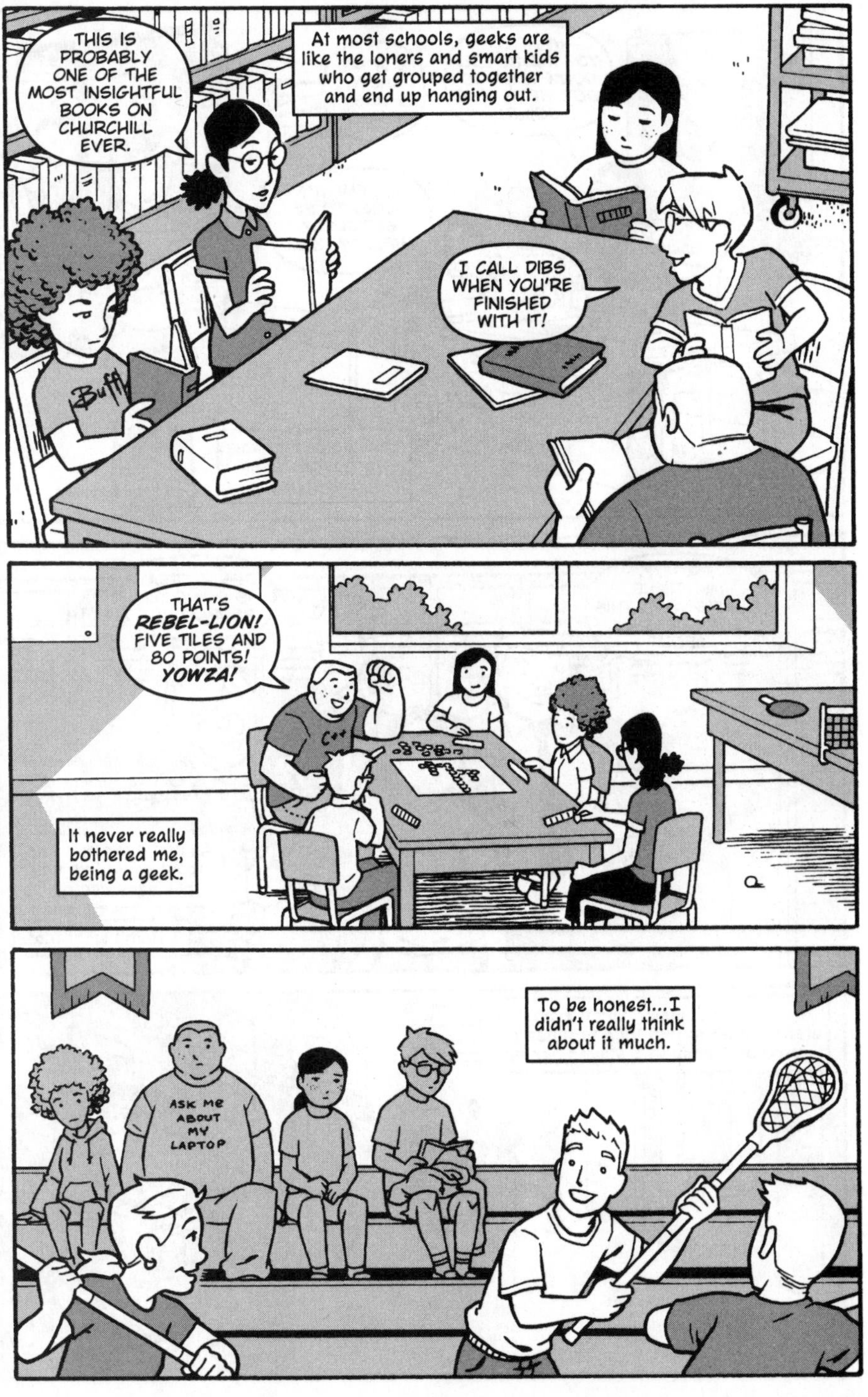
THIS IS PROBABLY ONE OF THE MOST INSIGHTFUL BOOKS ON CHURCHILL EVER.
At most schools, geeks are like the loners and smart kids who get grouped together and end up hanging out.
I CALL DIBS WHEN YOU'RE FINISHED WITH IT!
THAT'S ***REBEL-LION!*** FIVE TILES AND 80 POINTS! ***YOWZA!***
It never really bothered me, being a geek.
ASK ME ABOUT MY LAPTOP
To be honest...I didn't really think about it much.

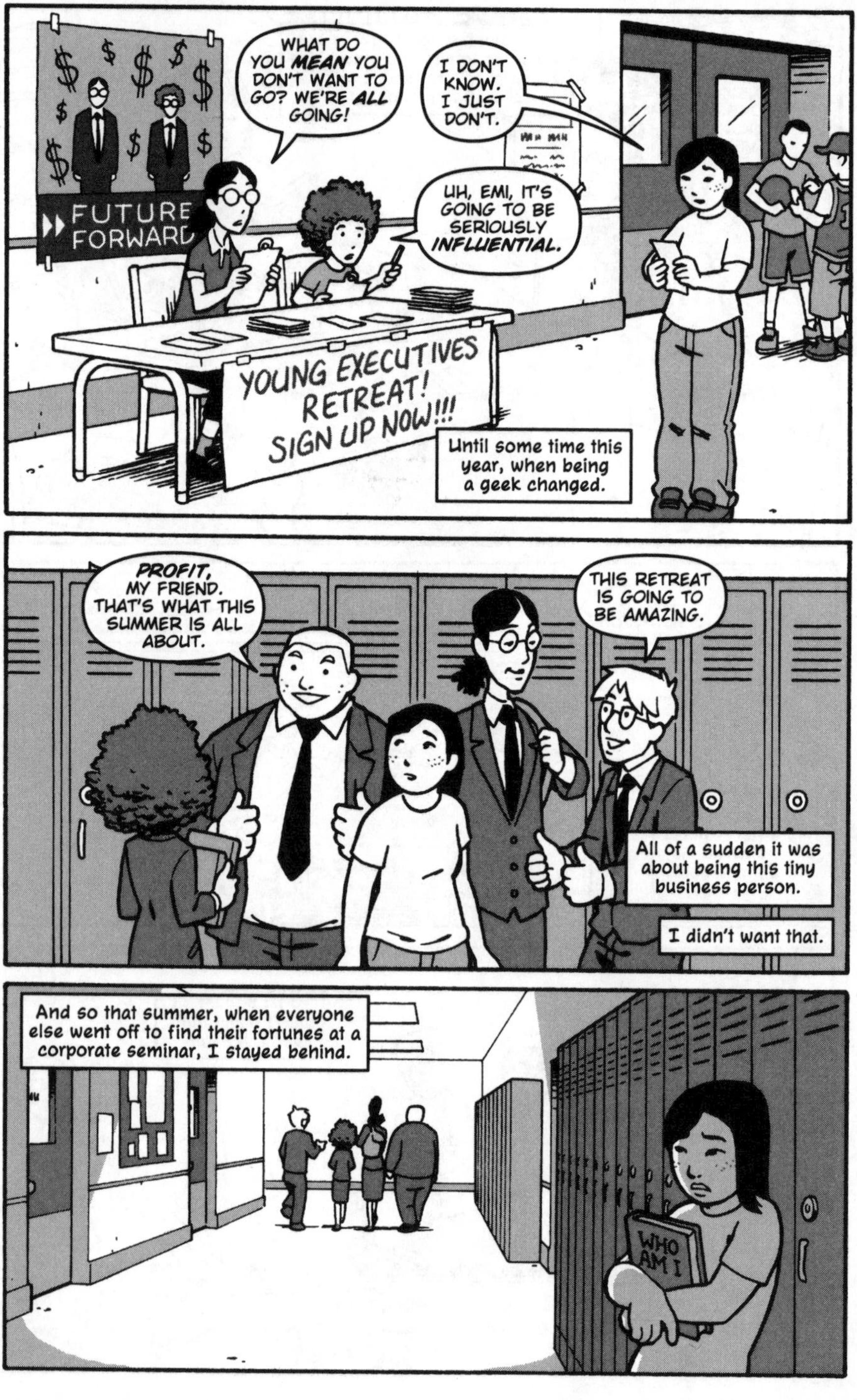

FUTURE FORWARD
WHAT DO YOU MEAN YOU DON'T WANT TO GO? WE'RE ALL GOING!
I DON'T KNOW. I JUST DON'T.
UH, EMI, IT'S GOING TO BE SERIOUSLY INFLUENTIAL.
YOUNG EXECUTIVES RETREAT! SIGN UP NOW!!!
Until some time this year, when being a geek changed.
PROFIT, MY FRIEND. THAT'S WHAT THIS SUMMER IS ALL ABOUT.
THIS RETREAT IS GOING TO BE AMAZING.
All of a sudden it was about being this tiny business person.
I didn't want that.
And so that summer, when everyone else went off to find their fortunes at a corporate seminar, I stayed behind.
WHO AM I

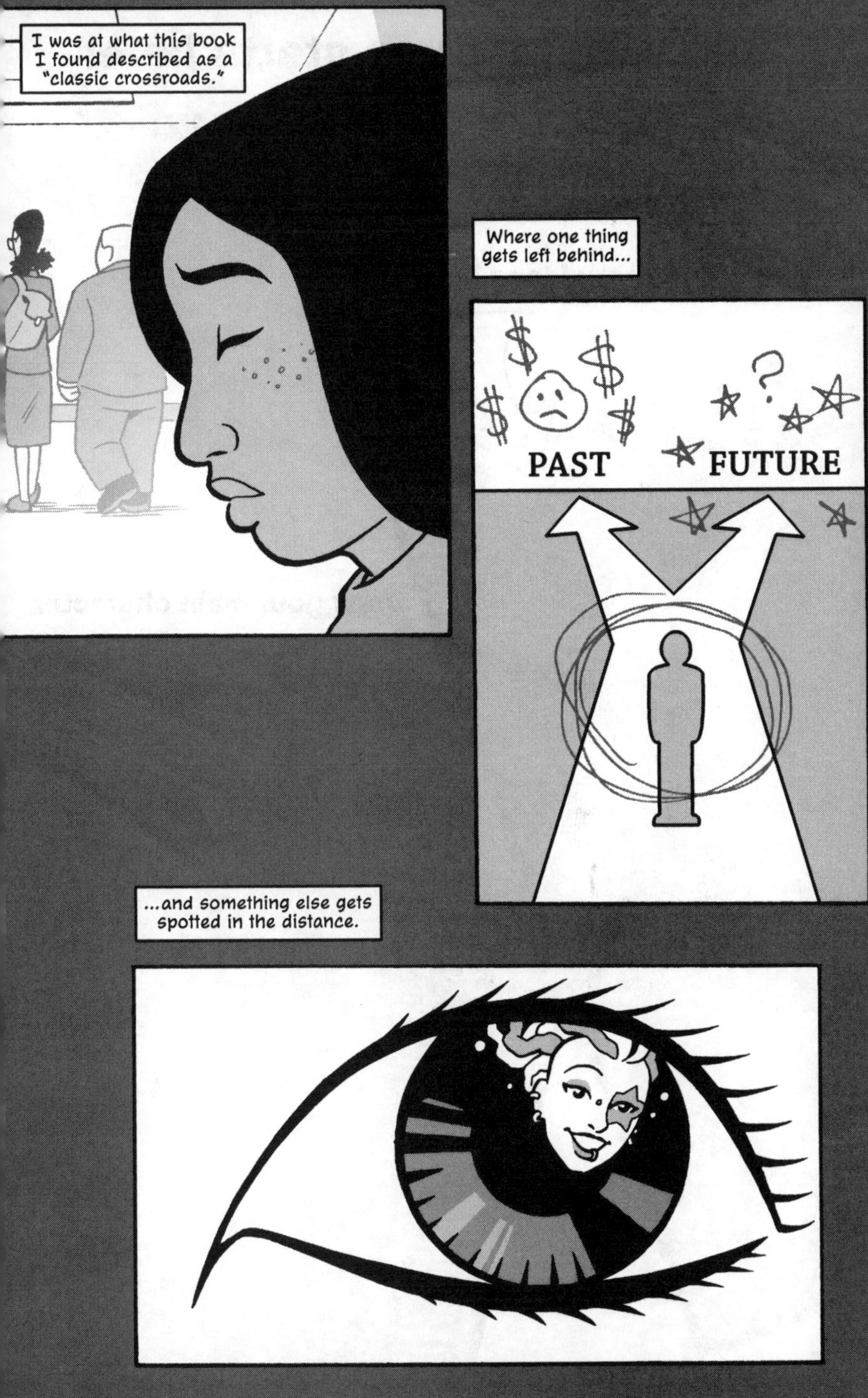
I was at what this book I found described as a "classic crossroads."
Where one thing gets left behind...
PAST
FUTURE
...and something else gets spotted in the distance.

Your life in pictures starts here!

~A DO-IT YOURSELF MINI COMIC~

Write your story ideas here:

Draw your main character sketches here:

Use the following 3 pages to bring it all together.

TITLE: BY:

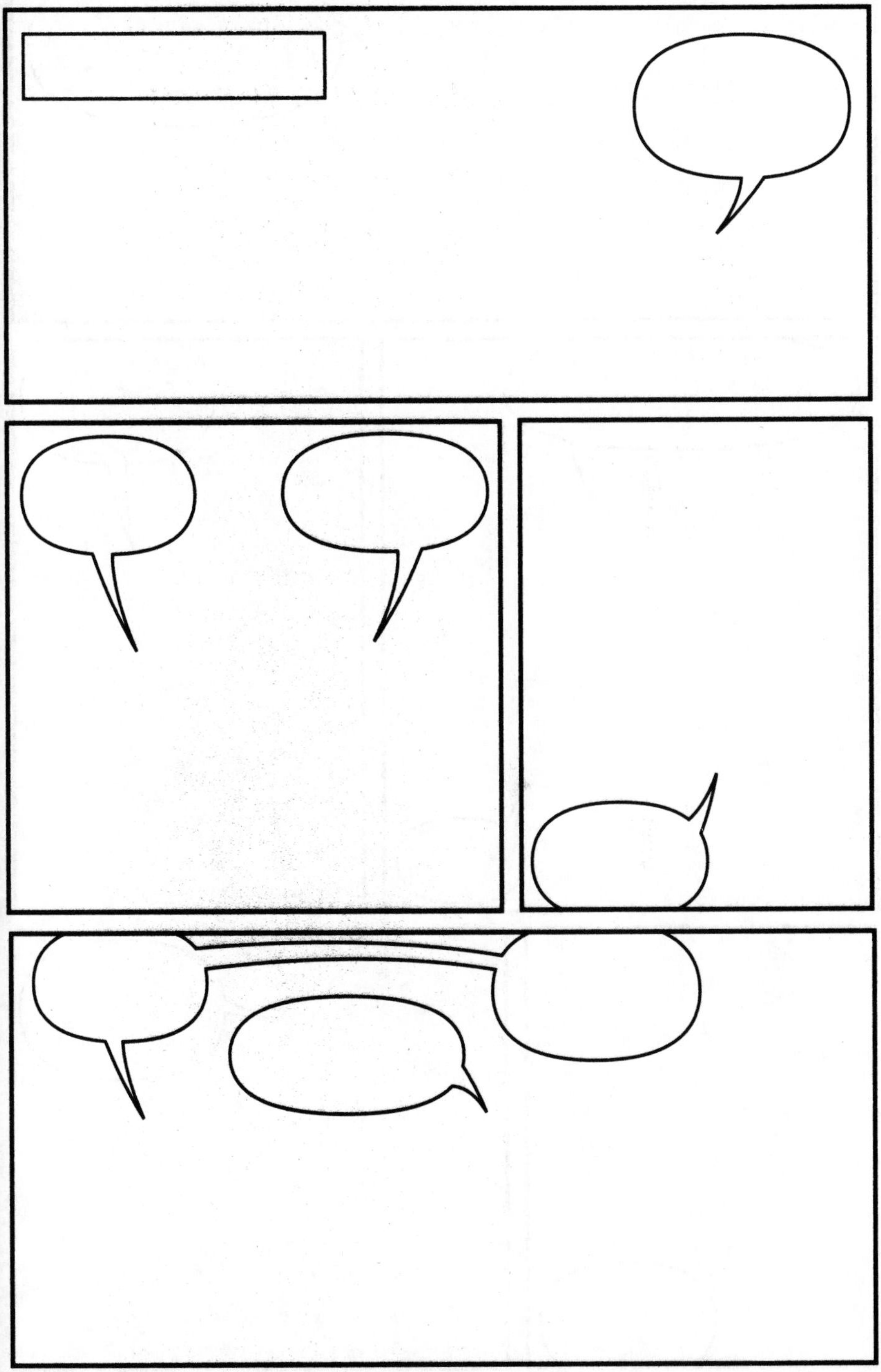

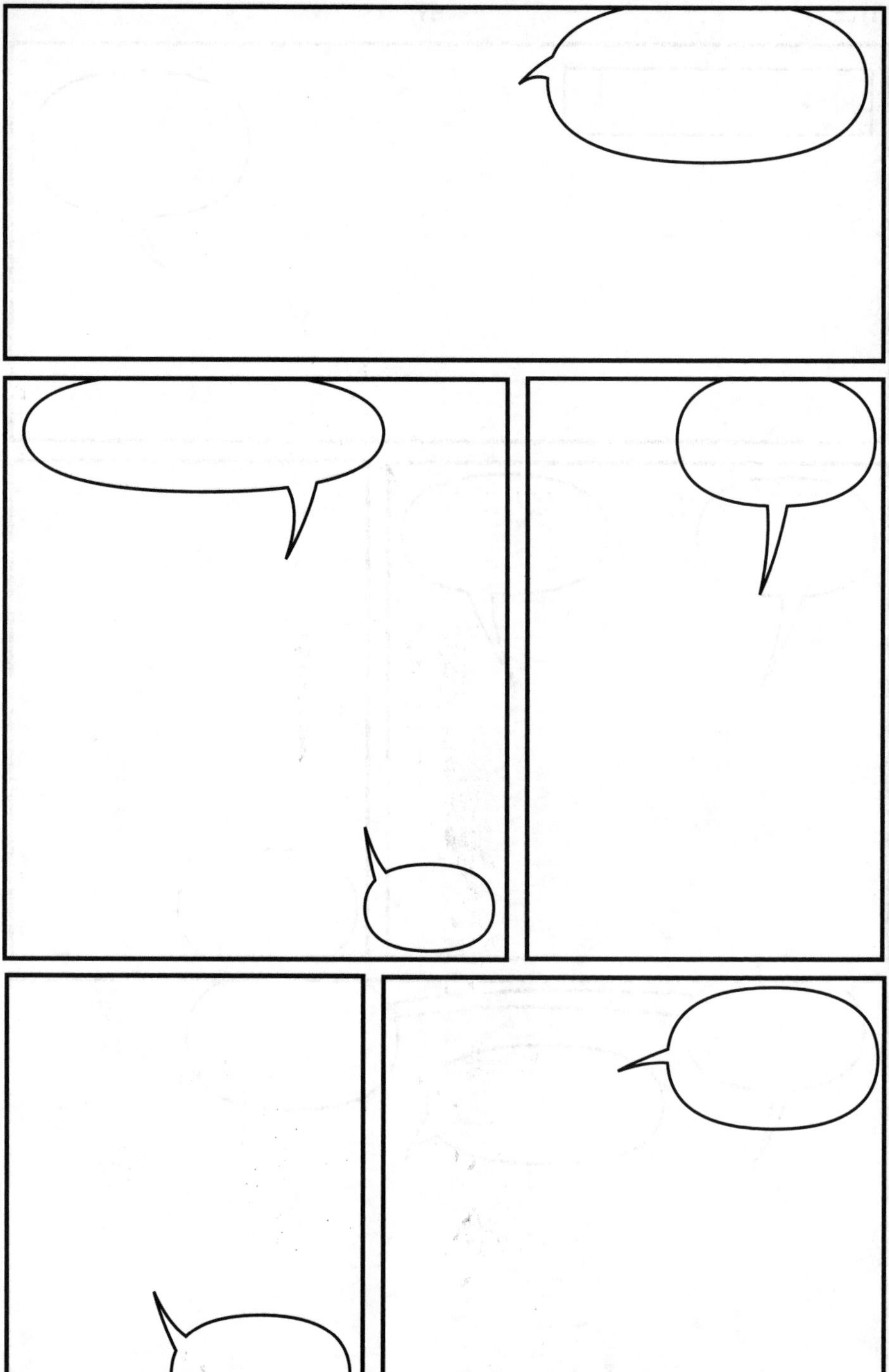

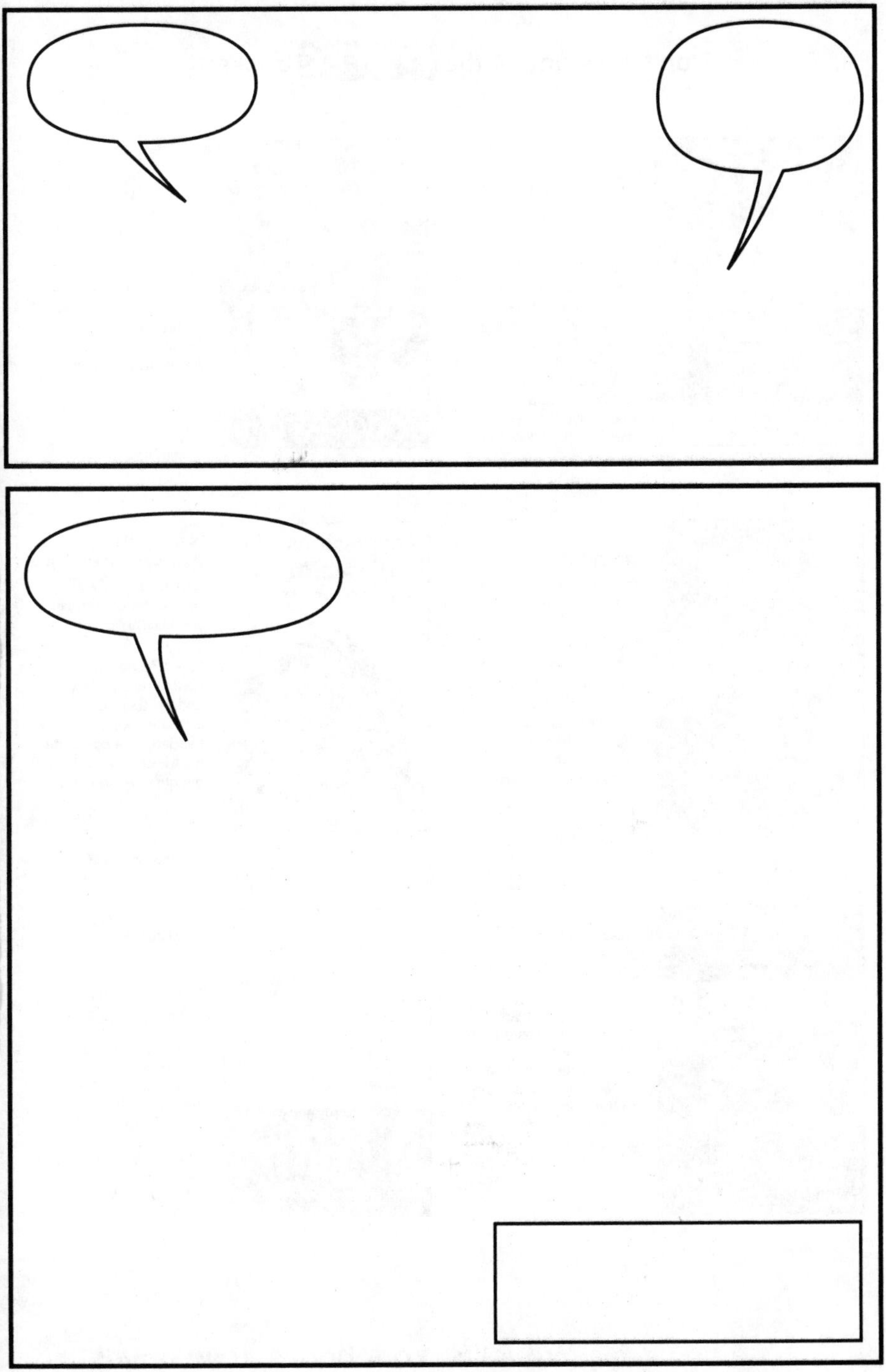

CHECK OUT STORYTELLING TIPS FROM TOP WRITERS AND ARTISTS AT MINXBOOKS.NET

Don't miss any of the minx books:

By the highly acclaimed author of Boy Proof and The Queen of Cool
THE PLAIN JANES
CECIL CASTELLUCCI
and JIM RUGG

THE PLAIN JANES
By Cecil Castellucci
and Jim Rugg

Four girls named Jane are anything but ordinary once they form a secret art gang called P.L.A.I.N. – People Loving Art In Neighborhoods. But can art attacks really save the hell that is high school?

Derek Kirk Kim & Jesse Hamm
Good As Lily

GOOD AS LILY
By Derek Kirk Kim
and Jesse Hamm

What would you do if versions of yourself at 6, 29 and 70 suddenly appear and wreak havoc on your already awkward existence?

Re-Gifters
Mike Carey Sonny Liew Marc Hempel

RE-GIFTERS
By Mike Carey, Sonny Liew
and Marc Hempel

It's love, Korean-American style when a tenacious martial artist falls for a California surfer boy and learns that in romance and recycled gifts, what goes around comes around.

YALSA Winner

confessions of a
blabbermouth
MIKE CAREY LOUISE CAREY AARON ALEXOVICH

CONFESSIONS OF A BLABBERMOUTH
By Mike and Louise Carey
and Aaron Alexovich

When Tasha's mom brings home a creepy boyfriend and his deadpan daughter, a dysfunctional family is headed for a complete meltdown. By the father-daughter writing team.

Included in The New York Public Library's Books for the Teen Age 2008

clubbing

CLUBBING
By Andi Watson
and Josh Howard

A spoiled, rebellious London girl takes on the stuffy English countryside when she solves a murder mystery on the 19th hole of her grandparents' golf course.

kimmie66
AARON ALEXOVICH

KIMMIE66
By Aaron Alexovich

This high-velocity, virtual reality ghost story follows a tech-savvy teenager on a dangerous quest to save her best friend, the world's first all-digital girl.

"Neuromancer for the Hello Kitty crowd."
—Village Voice

Your life. Your books. ***How novel.***

minxbooks.net

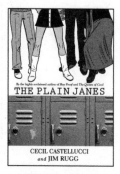

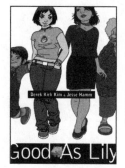

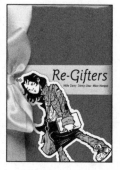

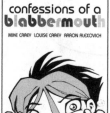

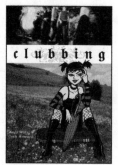

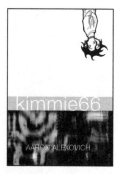